Commonalities in Substance Abuse and Habitual Behavior

Commonalities in Substance Abuse and Habitual Behavior

Edited by
Peter K. Levison
Dean R. Gerstein
Deborah R. Maloff
National Research Council,
National Academy of Sciences

LexingtonBooks
D.C. Heath and Company
Lexington, Massachusetts
Toronto

Library of Congress Cataloging in Publication Data

Main entry under title:
  Commonalities in substance abuse and habitual behavior.

  Includes index.
  1. Substance abuse.   2. Habit.   I. Levison, Peter K.
II. Gerstein, Dean R.   III. Maloff, Deborah R.
RC564.C65   1983   616.86   82-48537
ISBN 0-669-06293-6

Published simultaneously in Canada

Printed in the United States of America

International Standard Book Number: 0-669-06293-6

Library of Congress Catalog Card Number: 82-48537

Committee on Substance Abuse and Habitual Behavior

Louis C. Lasagna, Chair, Department of Pharmacology and Toxicology, University of Rochester School of Medicine and Dentistry

Howard S. Becker, Department of Sociology, Northwestern University

Peter Dews, Department of Psychiatry and Laboratory of Psychobiology, Harvard Medical School

John L. Falk, Department of Psychology, Rutgers University

Daniel X. Freedman, Department of Psychiatry, University of Chicago

Jerome H. Jaffe, University of Connecticut School of Medicine and Veterans Administration Hospital, Newington, Connecticut

Denise B. Kandel, Department of Psychiatry, Columbia University, and New York State Psychiatric Institute, New York

John Kaplan, School of Law, Stanford University

Gardner Lindzey, Center for Advanced Study in the Behavioral Sciences, Palo Alto

Gerald McClearn, College of Human Development, Pennsylvania State University

Charles P. O'Brien, Drug Dependence Treatment Service, Veterans Administration Hospital, Philadelphia

Judith Rodin, Department of Psychology, Yale University

Stanley Schachter, Department of Psychology, Columbia University

Thomas C. Schelling, John F. Kennedy School of Government, Harvard University

Richard L. Solomon, Department of Psychology, University of Pennsylvania

Frank Stanton, New York, New York

Albert M. Stunkard, Department of Psychiatry, University of Pennsylvania Hospital

Richard F. Thompson, Department of Psychology, Stanford University

Peter K. Levison, Study Director

Dean R. Gerstein, Senior Research Associate

Deborah R. Maloff, Research Associate

The project that is the subject of this book was approved by the Governing Board of the National Research Council, whose members are drawn from the councils of the National Academy of Sciences, the National Academy of Engineering, and the Institute of Medicine. The members of the committee responsible for the report were chosen for their special competences and with regard for appropriate balance.

This book has been reviewed by a group other than the authors according to procedures approved by a Report Review Committee consisting of members of the National Academy of Sciences, the National Academy of Engineering, and the Institute of Medicine.

The National Research Council was established by the National Academy of Sciences in 1916 to associate the broad community of science and technology with the academy's purposes of furthering knowledge and of advising the federal government. The council operates in accordance with general policies determined by the academy under the authority of its congressional charter of 1863, which establishes the academy as a private, nonprofit, self-governing membership corporation. The council has become the principal operating agency of both the National Academy of Sciences and the National Academy of Engineering in the conduct of their services to the government, the public, and the scientific and engineering communities. It is administered jointly by both academies and the Institute of Medicine. The National Academy of Engineering and the Institute of Medicine were established in 1964 and 1970, respectively, under the charter of the National Academy of Sciences.

Contents

                Donald J. Weisz and *Richard F. Thompson*   297

Chapter 9   **Commonalities in Substance Abuse:**
                A Genetic Perspective
                Gerald E. McClearn   323

                Index   343

                List of Contributors   357

                About the Editors   359

Preface

Louis Lasagna

Until the 1970s, drug addiction and alcoholism were regarded as superficially analogous but basically unrelated phenomena, and cigarette smoking was not considered an addictive behavior but merely a habit. The current idea of substance abuse—which embraces the excessive use of alcohol, tobacco, many other psychoactive drugs, and even food—suggests the existence of underlying common processes, which are called *commonalities* in this book. This change in viewpoint is related to recent public concern about persistent, harmful patterns of behavior, elicited in part by widespread increases in the recreational use of illegal drugs in the past two decades. It is now accepted that alcoholism occurs in all social classes and is not the special affliction of skid-row outcasts. Cigarette smoking has been identified as threatening to health, yet millions of smokers have been unsuccessful in quitting and openly acknowledge their addiction. The harmful consequences of excessive weight on health are recognized, yet excessive eating and violations of self-restraint programs are endemic.

In this social climate of heightened awareness and worry over substance abuse that often defies self-control, the idea that addiction is a general phenomenon has captured the public's imagination. It has become commonplace for people to describe themselves as "addicted" to a variety of things as disparate as soft drinks, exercise, and watching football on television. Treatment programs modeled after Alcoholics Anonymous now exist for overeaters, compulsive gamblers, and child abusers, among others.

In this context the National Institute on Drug Abuse (NIDA), the branch of the U.S. Department of Health and Human Services that has statutory responsibility for directing research on the causes of excessive use of drugs, wanted an assessment of the scientific evidence indicating that many aspects of excessive substance use, and perhaps other habitual activities, have common biological, psychological, and social roots. In 1976 NIDA requested that the Assembly of Behavioral and Social Sciences (now the Commission on Behavioral and Social Sciences and Education) of the National Research Council establish the Committee on Substance Abuse and Habitual Behavior. Among other tasks, the committee was asked to review and assess the scientific basis for a commonalities approach to research on substance abuse and habitual behavior and to make recommendations to NIDA based on these studies.

A considerable body of scientific knowledge, some parts of it decades old and others quite recent, contributes to a commonalities perspective. Studies of tolerance, withdrawal, and other physical dependence phenomena traditionally have been used to estimate the abuse potential of new drugs. Theoretical constructs to explain addictions on the basis of these processes continue to appear. Since 1960 self-administration by animals of a variety of drugs has shown striking parallels with drug preferences in humans. A growing body of evidence indicates that nicotine is a psychoactive agent that governs the habitual use of tobacco products. The discovery in the 1970s of a chemical receptor in the central nervous system that is specific to opiate drugs and of naturally occurring substances in the body that also bind to these sites raised the hopes of some that a general theory of the biological basis of drug addictions might be found. A wide range of social-science research has shown common group processes and social conditions under which the initiation, persistence, and termination of excessive substance use occur.

Much of this evidence as well as its implications has been reviewed and assessed in the committee's work. In 1977 the committee published an initial report, *Common Processes in Habitual Substance Use*, on general avenues of research on the commonalities theme. Subsequent reports on topics in personal and social control of substance use and alternatives for controlling excessive drinking, cigarette smoking, and marijuana use continued the committee's examination of these questions. [*Issues in Controlled Substance Use* (1980), *Alcohol and Public Policy: Beyond the Shadow of Prohibition* (1981), *Guidelines for Studies on Substance Abuse Treatment* (1981), *Reduced Tar and Nicotine Cigarettes: Smoking Behavior and Health* (1982), and *An Analysis of Marijuana Policy* (1982) are available from the National Academy Press, Washington, D.C.]

In its meetings, working groups, and conferences, the committee as well as outside experts have discussed how best to evaluate a wide range of habitual behaviors with respect to their common properties. For many initially attractive cases, such as compulsive gambling, the scientific evidence was simply insufficient to warrant intensive committee study. These limitations provoked interest in the adequacy of current efforts to collect and evaluate data related to excessive substance use and habitual behaviors.

The committee is grateful to NIDA for its support of the studies that led to this book. The committee is also grateful for the comments of consultants Michael Harner, Roland Griffiths, Alan Marlatt, and James Woods on early drafts of several chapters. Janice Marcus helped to develop an assessment of the literature in the chapter by Donegan, Rodin, O'Brien, and Solomon; and Ira Liebson provided input on clinical parallels to the research described in the chapter by Falk, Dews, and Schuster. Participants in the committee's 1977 Conference on Commonalities, too numerous to mention here, were also helpful in laying the groundwork. This book benefited from constructive review and comment by the Assembly of Behavioral and Social Sciences.

The committee is indebted to its professional staff for their essential role in planning, organizing, and editing this volume—Peter Levison, study director; Dean Gerstein, senior research associate; and Deborah Maloff, research associate. Marie Clark, administrative secretary, and Beverly Blakey, secretary, provided valuable support services.

Summary and
Research Directions

A number of common characteristics, processes, and mechanisms are associated with the habitual use and abuse of substances, including alcohol, tobacco, heroin, other drugs, and food. The search for such commonalities has led to new understanding of these behaviors—their etiology, maintenance, control, and termination. At the same time the distinctions that separate these phenomena should be recognized. This book highlights major commonalities and differences within sociocultural, psychological, and biological frameworks.

Sociocultural Commonalities

The first section of this book examines two distinct sets of sociocultural commonalities. First, Kandel and Maloff discuss sociodemographic commonalities in life-cycle events associated with drugs. Using epidemiological data they note the strong association between youth and the use of drugs, primarily illicit drugs, and the tendency for initial use of a particular class of drugs to occur in a relatively fixed temporal sequence. Further commonalities exist in the social influences that underlie the etiology of drug use, such as peer-group influence, overall societal prevalence, and situational social contexts. Termination of the use of most substances is influenced by demographic status—age, marital status, and employment status. Thus there appear to be several sociodemographic commonalities among illicit substance-use behaviors.

Walker and Lidz, describing the relation of excessive habitual behaviors, including substance abuse, to societal norms and social control systems, locate the commonalities in high-frequency behaviors defined socially as troublesome. They note especially that the normative acceptability or nonacceptability of such behaviors as gambling, drug use, and overeating is ambiguous; the degree of acceptance is heavily influenced by the social context in which the behavior takes place. Similarly, the kind of social control system that is applied to these behaviors reflects their ambiguous nature—both law enforcement agencies and the helping professions have attempted to take primary responsibility for most of the supposed addictive behaviors, leading to conflicting labels of crime and disease. Walker and Lidz conclude that substantial commonalities among these behavior patterns explain the ambiguities in their treatment by society; in particular, those behaviors viewed as troublesome share in common the violation of cultural values of self-control.

Psychological Commonalities

Falk, Dews, and Schuster identify regularities in diverse areas of behavioral research on drug effects that suggest common features in patterns of substance abuse. These areas include drug effects as discriminative and reinforcing stimuli, environmental schedules of reinforcement as sources of behavioral persistence; adjunctive behavior, which is repetitive behavior occurring in excess as a by-product of peculiar but not uncommon environmental conditions. The researchers in this area examine the behavioral consequences of deprivation, pharmacological tolerance and dependence, behavioral bases for the intractability of chronic conditions, and conditioned aversion to substances (ways in which the addictive potential of highly attractive drugs can be modified radically by environmental events). The authors set forth a series of common units and dimensions as theoretical guides for research in environmental and related commonalities, including the reinforcing, discriminative, and temporal properties of drug-taking.

Donegan, Rodin, O'Brien, and Solomon identify six properties common to substance abuse and habitual behavior: (1) the ability of the substance or activity to act as a reinforcer, (2) acquired tolerance (reduced effectiveness of the same dose or exposure), (3) physical dependence and withdrawal, (4) affective contrast—often euphoria followed by dysphoria, (5) the capacity of the substance or activity to act as an effective Pavlovian unconditioned stimulus, and (6) the capacity of states like arousal, stress, or pain to influence use. Reviewing the relevant literature on alcohol, opiates, food, nicotine, and gambling, the authors demonstrate that these six properties are important in the development of many habitual behaviors. However, they note variation in their salience from one substance or behavior to another; that is, the properties differ in the degree to which they influence habitual use. The six properties do not constitute an exhaustive list, the authors note, and "Other factors peculiar to the individual and the circumstances of use interact to determine the overall level of use or how disruptive abstinence will prove to be."

In chapter 5, Lang assesses the possibility that a common personality pattern leads some individuals into the heavy use of recreational drugs. The evidence derives largely from research on the measurement of personality. Lang examines the theoretical and operational specifications necessary to relate observed patterns of substance use to concepts of personality and addictive behavior. He analyzes the problems involved in basing personality profiles on studies of clinical drug-dependent populations. For example, do the test results reflect traits that predispose individuals to heavy substance use, or does heavy substance use itself produce these results? A critical review of representative research on personality factors associated with alcohol, marijuana, and heroin use follows. Lang concludes that no unique personality trait or profile is a necessary or sufficient condition to produce drug or alcohol dependence. But while an addictive personality does not therefore seem to be a viable construct, Lang considers some personality factors, such as impulsiveness and difficulty in delaying gratification, to be possible predisposing factors that in concert with situational and other variables may determine patterns of substance use.

Biological Commonalities

The first three chapters in part III concern the relation of naturally occurring substances and sites in the central nervous system to possible commonalities in the biological bases of addictions and habitual behaviors, from the perspective of certain psychopharmacological agents that have been studied intensively. Simon investigates the role of opiate receptors in opiate addiction. Receptors are sites located on the surface of or inside nerve cells, to which it is believed opiates must bind in order to exert their effects. Simon presents biochemical research evidence for the existence of opiate receptors and their properties. He concludes that while investigators in this area have little doubt that the opiate receptor-endorphin system is important to the development of opiate addiction (endorphins are opiate-like compounds occurring naturally in the body), research efforts in this direction have not been fruitful. Efforts to determine how this system explains chronic morphine effects—in particular, tolerance and dependence—have led largely to negative results.

In the next chapter Bloom reviews neurochemical evidence on the relation between endorphins and drug-addictive behavior. After identifying a set of criteria for establishing a neurochemical basis for abnormal behavior, he applies current knowledge about endorphins to these criteria. Bloom concludes that studies to date have not clarified the role of endorphins in behavior; the hypothesis that there is a particular neurochemical basis for a given pattern of behavior has not been proven. He suggests an alternative hypothesis: abnormal behavior could arise from the unconscious sequences of cell-system interaction that program cognitive strategies for responding to the external or internal environment. These abnormalities could in turn lead to abnormalities in neurotransmitter formation or utilization.

The chapter by Weisz and Thompson explores the hypothesis that endorphins in the brain may mediate general processes of addictive habit formation, if any such exist. They conclude, as do Bloom and Simon, that the evidence is insufficient to assert that endorphins play a central role in the addictive processes of any substance abuse, although some aspects of morphine or heroin addiction clearly are mediated by brain opioids, and some probable link exists between alcohol and food consumption and activity in the brain opioid system. There may be as yet unproven connections between endogenous opiates and substance abuse. For example, the opioid system may be a common link among substances that act to reduce the aversive effects of stress or other stimuli, or endogenous opioids may mediate some environmental factor influencing the likelihood of substance abuse behaviors. Weisz and Thompson conclude by recommending continued research to clarify potential brain opioid involvement in substance abuse.

In the final chapter, McClearn presents a simplified model of gene action through intermediate processes affecting attributes (phenotypes) of the use of substances, such as preference and sensitivity. The central concepts of *pleiotropy*, the effects of a single gene on multiple phenotypic factors, and *polygenic effects*, the influence of multiple genes on a single phenotype, are presented through commentary on two research strategies. The first, breeding experiments with laboratory animals, provides animal models for assessing specific genetic and environmental contributions to commonalities across substances as well as commonalities among processes involved in the use of a single substance. The second strategy employs the methods of quantitative genetics, including studies of twins and families, to isolate the causal contributions of genetic, familial, and general environmental factors to commonalities in substance use and abuse. The author points out the advantages and limitations of each approach and gives examples from the respective literatures.

Research Directions

In its examination of a variety of patterns of excessive substance use and habitual behavior the committee found that certain conceptual and empirical commonalities were useful in organizing the observations that were collected and reviewed. In response to its original charge and for those who might continue this task, the committee has formulated both general advice and specific research directions.

In general, scientific knowledge does not at present provide the basis for a comprehensive theory of excessive, habitual behaviors encompassing the available sociocultural, psychological, and biological evidence. Furthermore, the existing knowledge base does not encourage the committee to recommend a comprehensive program of focused research on commonalities for government or private research planning, although such a program appeared promising at the outset of our work. That we continue to find important differences as well as commonalities among habitual substance use and activity patterns is a factor that persuades us not to recommend heavy investments in a general theoretical approach grounded in commonalities. Compelling and useful regularities do arise, however, when researchers are guided by a coherent scientific frame of reference, as the authors in each case were guided in this book.

The committee believes that the analyses and ideas in this book can stimulate investigators to follow some of the research directions that emerge from a commonalities perspective. Some such research recommendations are defined explicitly in the various chapters, and the committee encourages investigators to draw freely on discussions that parallel their own research interests. The committee has taken explicit research directions from each chapter in the book to provide examples here of how these chapters suggest research on problems related to commonalities.

Sociocultural Commonalities

Kandel and Maloff: The association of drug use with youth and the tendency for users of one drug to use others as well suggest a possible commonality, a broad drug-user subculture, but survey data presented in the chapter reveal the existence of drug-specific peer networks. Research on such networks would clarify the relation between use of a particular drug such as marijuana, participation in the specific drug subculture, and participation in a general drug subculture and would be useful to discover which values, beliefs, and practices are shared across drug-specific networks and which are unique to particular networks. Ethnographic methods are particularly well suited to such detailed analyses.

Because drug-use patterns are known to change over time, it is worthwhile to monitor any changes in the association between age and drug use as young drug users grow older. Following drug users well into adulthood is necessary to disentangle maturational and historical factors, both of which may contribute to the apparent strong relation between youth and drug use. Survey panel studies are appropriate to this objective.

Walker and Lidz: Patterns of substance use and abuse have become redefined over time. This point is often difficult to introduce into contemporary debate because it seems to threaten the legitimacy of current norms, particularly when arguments about redefinition are not based on sound scholarship. Comparative historical analyses of episodes of redefinition of substance-use behaviors, analyses fully specifying and comparing the sociocultural contexts that permit or encourage definitions to change, would be quite valuable. Examples of such episodes include the shifting definitions of heroin use in the early twentieth century and cigarette smoking in the last twenty years. Similarities and differences in such episodes should be clearly and objectively documented.

The often observed conflict between treatment and law enforcement systems for the control of substance abuse may be resolved or constructively channeled by the alternative of organized self-help groups. Prospective research would be valuable in tracing the impact of self-help groups concerned with various habitual behaviors on the two institutional control systems. A sample of areas rich in such groups might be compared with areas more dominated by traditional control systems. The main objective would be to chart the growth and influence of these groups on how substance abuse is viewed, dealt with, and affected by society.

Psychological Commonalities

Falk, Dews, and Schuster: Some drugs appear to be stronger initial reinforcers of behavior than others. The basis and mechanisms of these differences should be sought. Worthy of examination is whether the capacities of small amounts of a drug to maintain large amounts of behavior through environmental arrangements (especially schedules of reinforcement) bear any relation to the differences in initial reinforcing effects.

Further investigation is needed into the features of certain schedules of reinforcement that increase the ability of events to maintain behavior, even events that are not initially reinforcing and may be aversive in other conditions, as in shock-maintained behavior in animals and the abuse of initially nonpreferred drugs in some street drug users.

Donegan, Rodin, O'Brien, and Solomon: In a matrix with substances or activities as the rows and common properties as the columns, the goodness of fit of the identified common properties can be tested. It would be profitable to extend this analysis systematically by adding new substances or common properties to the matrix or by adding to the comparisons quantitative information such as the measured strength of some drug as a reinforcer. Matrix analysis can also be used to explore differences.

Attachment behavior, or imprinting, exhibits common properties with some drug effects (maternal retrieval of offspring experimentally removed from the nest is an example from the class of attachment behaviors). Matrix analysis can be extended to analyze other behaviors drawn from the same general class, observing the goodness of fit. Data parallels to the imprinting results would be compared for common effects.

Lang: Given that personality contributions to heavy substance use are not specific, strategies for future research must be multivariate and take into account the variety of methods of personality assessment, interactions with the social environment, and the need to specify clearly the aspects of substance use or abuse that are of interest.

Many of the personality attributes antecedent to problems with substance use are quite different from those recorded in clinical contexts. This suggests that transitional states from experimental substance use to heavy substance use should be studied to discover how the critical changes occur.

Biological Commonalities

Simon: Isolation and purification of the receptor (or receptors) is necessary to permit understanding of its molecular structure and subunit composition. Antibodies to the receptor could then be made and injected to inactivate them in situ, so the resulting deficits would shed light on their physiological role. The effect of reinserting purified receptors on membrane behavior would be revealing, and purified receptors would make available a variety of techniques to study receptor-ligand interactions, such as fluorescence and electron spin resonance.

Opiate receptors were discovered quite recently, and much work needs to be done before the physiological significance of this system and its possible role in opiate addiction are understood. It may be of considerable interest to continue studies to differentiate types of receptors that may mediate different pharmacological responses to a single agent. Earlier studies of receptor numbers and properties in addicted animals need to be repeated keeping in mind the evidence on multiple types of receptors.

Bloom: Certain cellular and molecular pharmacological evidence shows a relation between endorphins and addictive phenomena. Although logical and experimental specifications for establishing the neurochemical basis of regulatory events underlying behavior can be applied to this relation, at best only correlations between neurochemical observations and a given behavior syndrome have been established. The goal for future research on the role of endorphins should be to establish the experimental evidence needed to show causal relation between a system of neurons operating through secretion of an identifiable transmitter and an abnormal behavioral state.

Weisz and Thompson: Inconclusive evidence links endogenous opioids in the brain with morphine addiction, alcoholism, and obesity. Particularly lacking is evidence indicating that changes in the levels or activities of brain opioids are a result of addictive phenomena. Experiments are needed in which the levels and activities of opioids are monitored prior to, during, and following induction of addictive states. These levels and activities should be determined before and after acute and chronic administration of other drugs of abuse, such as amphetamines and barbiturates.

Only tentative correlations exist between endogenous opioids and behavior and there is no conclusive evidence that such opioids underlie a specific behavior. Further research should be carried out to identify behaviors sensitive to manipulations of the endogenous opioids and to determine specific sites of opioid action in the identified behaviors. Phenomena involving conditioned fear and conditioned anxiety are prime candidates for further research. Brain opioids may play a role in these behaviors; conditioned fear and anxiety may be common to different addictive processes.

McClearn: Established methods of animal research, involving single-gene differences on inbred strains and selectively bred lines, and the human research approach, in which familial and nonfamilial compartments of influence can be identified, have made especially promising contributions to commonalities research.

Other methods not yet brought to bear on commonalities should also be encouraged. The recently developed animal research tool of recombinant inbred strains merits particular scrutiny. Recombinant inbred strains are generated by crossing two inbred strains and repeating the inbreeding from the F2 generation. The pattern of distribution in these new inbred strains of traits for which the original strains differ permits identification of single gene influences and the study of linkage relationships to other genes.

In human research the powerful tool of adoption studies and the special case of twins reared apart could provide highly useful information about commonalities in substance use and abuse.

Part I
Sociocultural Commonalities

1

Commonalities in Drug Use: A Sociological Perspective

Denise B. Kandel and
Deborah R. Maloff

Although drugs like heroin, marijuana, alcohol, and tobacco may differ widely in their biological and chemical action, they share some common characteristics when viewed from a sociological perspective. One of the most striking commonalities revealed by social science research is the strong association between youth and the use of drugs—particularly illicit drugs— in recent history in American society. Use of most drugs begins in early adolescence, peaks around the ages of 18-25, and declines thereafter.

Further, there are commonalities in the social influences and processes that promote initiation, maintenance, and termination of drug use behaviors. For example, association with user groups, overall societal prevalence levels, particular social contexts, conventionality of values and attitudes, and individual familial and work roles may all be important influences upon individuals that determine whether or not drug use will occur.

Epidemiological data on patterns of substance use in the population provide much of the evidence about sociocultural commonalities in substance use. This chapter presents these data and the methods used to collect them. A developmental model of stages of adolescent involvement in drug use and some hypotheses about the common social features of drug use in our society are proposed.

The Epidemiology of Drug Behavior: A Life-Span Perspective

General Population Surveys

Excellent data bases exist on which to assess the extent of use of various drugs in the population and changes in patterns of use. Because drug use often is perceived as a public health hazard, particularly for a large number of young people, and is also frequently thought to be associated with crime, the federal government has initiated and supported systematic data-gathering efforts. To obtain information on the individuals most heavily involved

Work on this manuscript was partially supported by Research Scientist Award DA 00081 from the National Institute on Drug Abuse.

3

in drugs, there has been extensive nationwide monitoring of persons identified by various institutions as having drug-related difficulties (see National Clearinghouse for Drug Abuse Information 1977; Richards 1981). Several ongoing annual data-gathering efforts have been designed to describe the behavior of the population on a regular basis and to provide up-to-date prevalence and incidence data. Data from treatment centers are not integrated with those obtained from general population samples, however.

A number of studies were initiated in the early seventies, in part under the impetus of the National Commission on Marihuana and Drug Abuse (National Commission on Marihuana and Drug Abuse 1972, 1973). Most of our recent knowledge derives from two major continuing nationwide monitoring efforts sponsored by the National Institute on Drug Abuse: Monitoring the Future is based on high school populations. The National Survey is based on general household population samples.

The household surveys of the general population are carried out on an annual or biannual basis by Response Analysis Corporation and the George Washington University. Seven studies have been conducted since 1971; the latest was in winter 1981-82, but published results were not available for the writing of this chapter (Fishburne, Abelson and Cisin 1980; Miller, Cisin, and Harrell 1978). They include not only respondents 18 and over but also additional samples of youths 12-17 years of age, the period in the life cycle when drug use is initiated. Based on structured personal household interviews, these surveys cover the use of a variety of drugs. Some waves of data collection include the use of psychoactive drugs that can be medically prescribed. Samples vary from about 3,000 to over 7,200 respondents (Fishburne, Abelson, and Cisin 1980).

Monitoring the Future is a ground-breaking study that makes use of a sophisticated cohort-sequential design, in which new cohorts of high school seniors are surveyed annually, with subsamples from each senior class followed by mail annually or biannually. The earliest cohort has now been followed since 1975. Initiated by the Survey Research Center of the University of Michigan and directed by Lloyd Johnston and Gerald Bachman, the survey involves annual testings of over 16,000 high school seniors drawn from 130 public and private schools throughout the United States; and longitudinal follow-ups of 2,000-3,000 former students from each class (Johnston 1980; Johnston, Buchman, and O'Malley 1981a). This design makes it possible to disentangle true maturational changes associated with aging from changes due to cohort pecularities or historical circumstances.

Other major sources of epidemiological information include the following:

1. A series of annual surveys of high school students carried out on the total junior high and high school population census in San Mateo County,

California from 1970 to 1977 (Blackford 1977). Survey sizes ranged from 18,000 to 25,000 adolescents.

2. Follow-ups of the Youth in Transition Cohort, a representative sample of tenth grade males in 1966, last interviewed in 1974 at age 23 (N = 1,600), five years after high school graduation (Johnston 1973; O'Malley 1975; Bachman, O'Malley, and Johnston 1978; Johnston, O'Malley, and Eveland 1978).

3. A follow-up of Vietnam veterans discharged in the United States in September 1971, with an oversample of veterans identified with urines positive for opiates, interviewed in 1972 and 1974 (N = 571). In 1974, a matched comparison sample (N = 284) of nonveterans was also included (Robins 1974, 1977, 1978, 1979; Robins, Davis, and Nurco 1974; Robins, Davis, and Wish 1977).

4. A survey of young men 20-30 years old (N = 2,510) drawn from a list sample of all males registered for the draft from Selective Service Boards and interviewed in 1974-75 (O'Donnell et al. 1976; O'Donnell and Clayton 1979, 1982).

5. A national survey of 13,122 junior and senior high school students in grades 7-12 conducted in spring 1974 and resurveyed in 1978 (Rachal et al. 1975, 1976; Harford 1976; Donovan and Jessor 1978; Jessor, Donovan, and Widmer 1980).

6. A two-wave panel survey in 1971-72 of a random sample of 5,600 New York state high school students and their parents (Kandel, Single, and Kessler 1976).

Based on large, representative samples these studies have provided new insights about the epidemiology of drug behavior. They are not without limitations. A major drawback is that household or school samples exclude the individuals most likely to be involved in nonconforming activities, including drug use—the transients, who are without regular addresses, and the school absentees or dropouts. The nature of the biases has been best documented for school samples (Johnston 1973; Kandel 1975a; Annis and Watson 1975; Johnston, O'Malley, and Eveland 1978; Ginsberg and Greenley 1978; Josephson and Rosen; Kandel, Raveis, and Kandel 1982). Since these deviant individuals constitute a small proportion of the general population, their exclusion does not significantly bias the epidemiological estimates reported (see Kandel 1975a; Kandel, Raveis, and Kandel 1982). Nonetheless, their exclusion is likely to cause underrepresentation of the less frequently used drugs and of the heaviest patterns of use. General population surveys are much more useful in learning about general trends and normative drug use patterns than about the extremes of drug behavior.

Because the surveys are based on representative rather than selected or clinical samples, they have led to fundamental revisions in our understanding of extreme forms of drug involvement such as alcoholism or heroin addiction. For example, the modal age of male alcoholics in treatment centers falls between 40 and 49 (Armor, Polich, and Stambol 1978). Surveys of men in the normal population indicate that the most severe drinking problems occur in the early 20s (Cahalan and Room 1974; Celentano and McQueen 1978). Thus the traditional conception of alcoholism as a progressive and irreversible condition does not apply to the general population (Roizen, Cahalan, and Shanks 1978). Similarly, prior to Robins's study of Vietnam veterans and O'Donnell and Clayton's study of young men, knowledge about heroin addicts came mainly from studies of addicts who were treated, arrested, or incarcerated (O'Donnell 1972; Vaillant 1966; Gould et al. 1974; Nurco et al. 1975). The histories of these individuals suggested that the life cycle of heroin addiction was difficult to break and that most addicts tended to relapse, until they either died or "matured out" of addiction in their late 30s (Winick 1962). Robins (1974) and O'Donnell and Clayton (1979), however, reported that addiction was not necessarily a permanent state; young men could give up heroin, even without treatment. The curve of remission rates of formerly addicted Vietnam soldiers eight to twelve months after discharge was the exact mirror image of the curve describing the readdiction rates for addicts released from the Lexington Psychiatric Hospital (Robins, Davis, and Nurco 1974). Furthermore, only one-third of the men addicted during the first discharge year reported being addicted at all during their second or third years after discharge (Robins 1974).

Drugs and Age: A Major Commonality

Patterns of use of various drugs throughout the life cycle illustrate the age-graded nature of drug use (Kandel 1980a). The use of marijuana and other illicit drugs and the use of illegally obtained prescription drugs are most prevalent among individuals 18-25, with sharp declines thereafter. (See O'Donnell at al. 1976.) Although the decline with age is not so sharp, cigarette smoking and drinking also appear to be most prevalent among 18-to 25-year-olds (Fishburne, Abelson, and Cisin 1980).

Age-related trends concerning marijuana are the most striking. Marijuana use among persons younger than 14 is low and increases sharply thereafter; ages 15-17 constitute the period of highest risk for initiation into marijuana use (Miller, Cisin, and Harrell 1978). Alcohol and tobacco are used most intensively in a wider range from 18 to 34. Instances of problem drinking (intoxication) are concentrated more heavily in the early 20s, however (Cahalen and Room 1974). Although use declines after the mid-30s current prevalence of alcohol and tobacco at these ages remains at a fairly high level. For the medically prescribed psychoactive substances, on the other hand, highest rates of use begin at 26, with the age of peak use varying for each of the three major classes of drugs. Whereas the stimulants appear to peak at ages 26-34, sedatives peak after age 50 and the tranquilizers remain at the same levels from age 26 on. Thus medical drug use peaks occur later in life than peaks of illicit drug use (see Kandel 1980a: table 1). One hypothesis to explain the drug use patterns over the life span is that certain uses of illicit drugs in adolescence and young adulthood and the use of psychoactive substances under medical supervision later in the life span may serve similar psychological and social functions for the respective groups of users.

Because the age-related trends are based on yearly cross-sectional studies, they may reflect maturational changes as well as historical differences among cohorts with different drug experiences in adolescence. That is, maturational changes such as the demands of adult work and family roles, may cause people to discontinue their illicit drug use as they grow older. Another likely explanation of differences of use patterns for different age cohorts is the rapid change in prevalence of use over the 1970s: use rates may be lower among older respondents simply because they have had fewer lifetime opportunities for use. Indications are that the decline of use with age may have become *less* substantial in more recent cohorts. No longitudinal studies are yet available that have followed successive cohorts from the teen years through the 30s to establish whether the high rates of marijuana use will persist through the life span. The evidence derived from repeated cross-sectional epidemiological surveys, and now confirmed by one longitudinal study, suggests that the declining use of illegal drugs past the mid-20s presumably reflects, at least in part, a true maturational effect—meaning that it is due to aging, not to social change.

The most direct evidence of a maturational trend is provided by the Youth in Transition male cohort, last interviewed in 1974 at age 23 (Johnston, O'Malley, and Eveland 1978). The number of respondents reporting having used marijuana at least once increased dramatically after high school, from 20 percent in the senior year, to 35 percent a year later, to 62 percent in 1974 at age 24. However, for every drug the percentage of regular users (defined as those who use the drug weekly or more often) was lower in 1974, when respondents were 23 years old, than it had been when respondents were 19-22. The rate for marijuana was lower by one-third, and the decline for the other illicit drugs was even more striking. Similarly, follow-up surveys of heroin users in community settings indicate termination or reduction of heroin use among males in their 20s (Nurco et al. 1975; Robins, Davis, and Wish 1977; Brunswick 1979).

As behaviors generally disapproved by the adult community, illicit drug use can be considered a subcategory of a wide range of disapproved or delinquent behaviors (shoplifting, vandalism, joy riding, and others) that appear to occur predominantly among young people. In some cases the correlation between delinquency and youth is little more than a tautology, for some behaviors are considered delinquent when engaged in by youth but not by adults. Drug use, similarly, includes a category of behaviors that would not be labeled drug abuse if engaged in by adults: drinking. Whether most of these behaviors represent normal adolescent "acting out," engaged in partly because they are traditionally disapproved, is open to question. Nevertheless, it is clear that drug use is largely a youth phenomenon.

We cannot assert that the use of a particular "abused" substance is always associated with youth, however. Opiates, once used quite respectably for medicinal purposes primarily by middle aged, middle class women, became associated with youth only when its reputation changed. One might conclude that it is not the intrinsic appeal of particular chemicals that makes them especially attractive to young people but, rather, the social meanings attached to the drugs in given cultural contexts.

We can speculate on why young people in contemporary American society are more likely than adults or than very young children to use illicit substances. The forbidden aspects of drug use may make it enticing to young people eager to test the limits of allowable behavior or to experiment with unconventional activity. More questioning of authority than adults or children and more willing to take risks, adolescents are prime candidates for ingestion of mind-altering substances. The combination of large blocks of unsupervised leisure time and few familial or work-related responsibilities for young people in our culture makes substance use feasible and may allow the user to feel relatively unconstrained about the need to remain sober.

Drug Behavior in Developmental Perspective

The Developmental Sequences of Drug Use

Another well-established social commonality in our society is that the use of various drugs is interrelated and that users of any type of drug, whether legal or illegal, are much more likely to be users of any other type of drug than nonusers. For example, young people who smoke are also much more likely to have used alcohol or marijuana than nonsmokers. Among the young people 12 to 17 years of age included in the general population survey, the proportion who had ever experimented with marijuana was 81 percent among the current smokers as compared to 24 percent among the nonsmokers (Fishburne, Abelson, and Cisin 1980).

Not only is the use of drugs interrelated at one period in the life cycle, but longitudinal studies have identified important developmental sequences in usage patterns. The legal drugs, alcohol and tobacco, are an integral and crucial part of the sequence. Their use precedes the use of illicit drugs, irrespective of the age at which initiation to illegal drugs takes place (Kandel 1975b, 1980b; Miller 1981).

Current data suggest that at least four distinct developmental stages in adolescent involvement in legal and illegal drugs can be identified: (1) beer or wine, (2) cigarettes or hard liquor, (3) marijuana, and (4) other illicit drugs (Kandel 1975b). However, it is important to keep in mind that arrival at a particular point in the sequence does not indicate that the individual will necessarily progress to other drugs higher up in the sequence. Even though all drug surveys reveal that use of any drug is *statistically* associated with the use of other drugs and that use of different drugs usually follows a predictable sequence, use of one drug does not inevitably lead to use of another.

The developmental process begins with cigarette smoking or alcohol use or both; most of the general population of youth have tried alcohol by the time they are 25. Of the 95 percent of 18-25 year olds in the population who report having tried alcohol (Fishburne, Abelson, and Cisin 1980), most try cigarettes (83 percent of all 18- to 25-year-olds) and, later, marijuana (68 percent). But, although most young people continue to drink, only 43 percent of this age group report being current smokers, and only 35 percent currently use marijuana (report they have used it in the past month) (Fishburne, Abelson, and Cisin 1980). A large number of those who are willing to try drugs discontinue use for one reason or another.

Of those who have tried marijuana, a small percentage (less than half) try other illegal drugs. Slightly more than one-fourth of the 18-25 population report having tried any illegal drug other than marijuana. And of those who try other illegal drugs, only a small percentage report being current users. Less than 0.5 percent of their sample reported using heroin in the last month; 1.2 percent use inhalants; 4.4 percent reported using hallucinogens; and 9.3 percent reported using cocaine (Fishburne, Abelson, and Cisin 1980: 61, 63, 69, 71). These data indicate that only a small percentage of the total youth population proceeds through all four developmental stages of drug use, although most young people pass through the first three stages.

Further evidence of developmental stages is provided by the findings that different social psychological factors predict adolescent initiation into different stages of drug use. Each of four clusters of predictor variables—parental influences, peer influences, adolescent involvement in various behaviors, and adolescent beliefs and values—and single predictors within each cluster assume differential importance for each stage of drug behavior (Kandel, Kessler, and Margulies 1978).

The Implications of Prevalence

Drugs more prevalent in society are used earlier in the sequence; further, they are associated with greater persistence of use over time, higher frequency, and greater amounts of use. As the prevalence of use of a particular drug increases over time, there is an accompanying decrease in age of onset of drug use. Thus the cohorts of high school seniors surveyed in Monitoring the Future report increasingly earlier ages at first experimentation with marijuana including the eighth grade or below (Johnston, Bachman, and O'Malley 1981). And earlier onset of use of any drug is associated with greater involvement in use of all other drugs. Thus the earlier the introduction to legal drugs, the greater the probability that the adolescent will also experiment with illicit drugs. For example, among young adults 18-25 surveyed from the general population in 1979-80, the proportion who had experimented with any illicit drug ranged from 87 percent among those who reported to have first tried alcohol or marijuana at ages 13 or 14, to 47 percent among those who first tried these drugs at ages 15-17, and 5 percent among those who first experimented at age 18 or over (Rittenhouse 1980). The earlier the experimentation with marijuana, the greater the involvement and the greater the likelihood of later involvement with more serious drugs. We are not suggesting that early involvement with marijuana causes later use of other illicit drugs but that common factors leading to early experimentation, along with early marijuana use itself, generally precede heavy involvement in other types of illicit drug use.

The association of prevalence with greater persistence of use, higher frequency, and greater amounts of use, is illustrated by data from studies carried out among urban adolescents in France and in Israel, where striking differences appear in patterns of drug behavior. Two surveys were carried out, in 1977 and 1979, with parallel household structured interviews in each country with samples of 499 youths aged 14-18 in France and 609 in Israel (Kandel, Adler, and Sudit 1981).

While the overall order in the lifetime prevalence of use of drugs is identical in both countries for all drugs, the rates of reported use in France exceed those reported in Israel. These differences are relatively small in the use of beer and wine, are larger with respect to hard liquor and cigarettes, and are highest in the use of illicit drugs (Kandel, Adler, and Sudit 1981). Thus, the proportion having tried hard liquor is 75 percent in France but 52 percent in Israel. The percentage having smoked cigarettes is 82 percent and 44 percent, respectively, and of those having used marijuana is 23 percent and 3 percent.

The relative prevalence of use in each country is associated with important differences in observed patterns of use. In France, where the overall prevalence is highest, also observed are greater persistence of use than in Israel and greater frequency and amounts of use among the users. Among the young people who have ever tried a particular drug, the proportion who report to have used it in the past 30 days is higher in France than in Israel. Similarly, as noted above, in the United States, the ratios of current-to-lifetime marijuana use in individuals 18 and older are higher in the 1979 than in the 1977 general population samples, paralleling the increase in overall lifetime prevalence of use of the substance in more recent cohorts.

Degree of drug involvement is also greater among the users of each drug in France than in Israel. Thus, of adolescents who have ever used alcohol, 23 percent among the French as compared to 7 percent among the Israeli reported using it 40 or more times (Kandel, Alder, and Sudit 1981).

With increased overall prevalence in a culture, group differences in patterns of use become attenuated as the behavior spreads throughout the entire society. Thus the differences in prevalence of use between boys and girls are greater in Israel, where the overall prevalence of use is lower, than in France (Kandel, Adler, and Sudit 1981). Similarly, socioeconomic and sex differences in rates of marijuana use in the United States have tended to diminish or to disappear altogether over the last decade (Kandel 1980a).

Illicit Drug Use and Common Life-Styles

When drug use first came under research scrutiny in the late 1960s, much was made of the deviant status of marijuana and of the countercultural and rebellious meaning that came to be attached to its use. Edward Suchman's (1968) description of marijuana use as reflecting the adoption of a "hang-loose ethic" proved to be very influential. By this term Suchman referred to the disaffection from major institutions that seemed to characterize the users at that time, when a very small proportion of the youth population had ever experimented with marijuana. This situation was very different from the current situation, in which 65 percent of high school seniors throughout the United States report experience with marijuana. Marijuana smoking has become almost a normative behavior among American adolescents.

Yet it is surprising that even today young people who use marijuana hold quite different values and behave differently than nonusers. Despite the fact that over the last decade marijuana use itself has greatly increased in prevalence, the social psychology of marijuana use (including the values, motivations, and behaviors in the users), is very much the same as it was ten years ago (see Jessor and Donovan 1978; Bachman, Johnston, and O'Malley 1981a, 1981b; Kandel 1982). Marijuana users in 1980 show the same patterns of disaffection from major institutions as did users in 1967. There is a continuum of disaffection: the degree of disaffection increases with degree of involvement irrespective of drugs used. These conclusions are based on data from Monitoring the Future, the continuing national surveys of high school seniors and on a follow-up of young adults at ages 24-25. Differences in values and life-styles among young people who use illicit drugs and those who do not are much greater than differences associated with membership in various sociodemographic groups.

The data from Monitoring the Future (Bachman, Johnston, and O'Malley 1981b) are very useful in assessing life-styles, since they are based on current large national representative samples of young people. Bachman and his colleagues divided the high school seniors into five groups according to their lifetime pattern of *illicit* drug use. The drugs include LSD, other psychedelics, cocaine, amphetamines, tranquilizers, methaqualone, barbiturates, heroin or other narcotics. The five groups are defined as those who have never used any illicit drugs; those who have used only marijuana; those who have used "a few pills," that is, at least one of the illicit drugs other than marijuana, but less than three times and not heroin; those who have used "more pills," that is an illicit drug other than marijuana (but no heroin) three times or more; and those who have ever used heroin. Most of the users of these other illicit drugs have also used marijuana, so that this classification is a cumulative one in many respects.

The characteristics of the five groups on several psychological and behavioral dimensions, such as school performance, political and religious attitudes, participation in deviant activities, or traffic accidents, show clear trends (Bachman, Johnston, and O'Malley 1981b). On every single attribute, users of illicit drugs, including those who have used marijuana exclusively, are less conforming than nonusers. In addition, the relation between these attributes and degree of involvement is linear, such that only quantitative differences, distinguish those who use only marijuana from those who have also used "hard" drugs (cocaine, LSD, heroin). For example, on school performance and interest in academic matters, drug users are much more likely than nonusers to be absent from school and to cut classes. Their school performance also is lower. The educational aspirations of marijuana users, however, are very similar to those of nonusers, and other studies (such as Hochman and Brill 1973) suggest that academic performance of marijuana users is no lower than the performance of nonusers.

Users of marijuana and of other illicit drugs have much weaker religious commitment but do not differ greatly from nonusers on political values, except in the importance they attach to law-abiding behavior (Bachman, Johnston, and O'Malley 1981b). This is consistent with the greater participation of users of marijuana and other illicit drugs in delinquent activities. Users are much more likely to have engaged in delinquent acts involving interpersonal aggression, theft, or property destruction.

The users are also much more likely than nonusers to be involved in traffic violations and accidents. Traffic incidents directly attributable to marijuana increase with degree of involvement in illicit drugs other than marijuana and are most frequent among the heroin users. This last finding is related to the fact that the greater the involvement in a range of illicit drugs, the greater the use of marijuana, as measured by frequency of use, amounts used, and duration of "high." Comparable trends were observed in the cohort of former New York State adolescents when reinterviewed in their mid-20s (Kandel 1982).

Common Processes in Learning to Use Drugs

Individuals learn to use substances, both legal and illicit, within social groups that value or approve the substances. Like all learned behaviors, substance use is generally transmitted to novices by teachers. these teachers are often role models or close associates of the novice who present positive images of the substance, as numerous studies have shown (Goode 1970; Gerstein, Judd, and Rovner 1979). Friends, family members, or popular folk heroes may all be teachers of how, when, and where to use substances. In the case of most intoxicating substances, transmission is often from adolescent to adolescent in peer groups. Young people are recruited into an "already existing world" of drug use (Blumer et al. 1976).

The already existing world into which users are initiated may represent the values of society at large (in the case of alcohol), of adolescence (in the case of marijuana), or of particular drug-using subgroups (say, PCP users). Young people may experience any of these social worlds through association with others; the definitions and expectations of the social worlds youngsters experience may determine, in large part, initiation into particular patterns of drug use. Explanations for drug use are to be found, then, not solely in individual motives or factors of availability, but in the particular social reality that confronts the user.

Learning to use substances within social groups may occur by observation and imitation of experienced users. Or the users may actively encourage initiates, promising that certain benefits will follow from use. These benefits may be tied directly to drug effects—euphoria, mainly—or may be related to the approval and positive sanctions of the user group. Belonging to the group may depend upon willingness to use their substances.

The setting in which drug use is transmitted is usually a comfortable and familiar one conducive to associations of pleasure with the new drug. Friends are likely to be taught by friends (and adolescent females likely to be taught by boyfriends) that drug effects are pleasurable and nonthreatening. Experienced users must teach the novice the proper technique for using the drug, how to recognize the presence of drug effects, and finally to perceive these effects as enjoyable (Becker 1963).

While association with drug-using peers is an important determinant of drug use, parental influence is also important, particularly in the initiation into alcohol or tobacco use. First exposures to alcohol use, for example, frequently occur in a family setting. Adolescents who drink are more likely than nondrinking adolescents to have parents who drink (Kandel, Kessler, and Margulies 1978). Nevertheless, peers exert a strong influence on drink-ing patterns as well as on patterns of illicit drug use and cigarette smoking.

The most consistent and reproducible finding in drug research is the strong relation between an individual's drug-related behavior and the con-current drug use of his friends (Alexander and Campbell 1968; Goode 1970; Johnson 1973; Kandel 1973; Burkett and Jensen 1975; Goldstein 1975; Dembo, Schmeidler, and Koval 1976; Kandel et al. 1976; O'Donnell et al. 1976; Brook, Lukoff, and Whiteman 1977, 1980; Kleinman and Lukoff 1978; Orcutt 1978; Smart, Gray, and Bennett 1978; Ellis and Stone 1979; Huba, Wingard, and Bentler 1979, 1980). For no other characteristic except age and sex is the similarity within adolescent friendship pairs as high as it is for marijuana use (Kandel 1978c). Such similarity results not only from socialization, the influence of one friend on the other, but also from a pro-cess of interpersonal selection (associative pairing), in which adolescents with similar values and behaviors seek each other out as friends. Longitudinal data on the formation and dissolution of friendship indicate that selection and socialization contribute about equally to homophily or similarity in values and behaviors (Kandel 1978e).

The group has greater influence at certain points in the process of drug involvement than at others. Friends' behaviors are especially important in predicting marijuana use and relatively less important for predicting drink-ing or the use of illicit drugs other than marijuana (Kandel, Kessler, and Margulies 1978). Available data on sex differences in peer influence indicate that females are more susceptible to peers than are males (Jessor, Jessor, and Finney 1973; Margulies, Kessler, and Kandel 1977). In general, peer behaviors and attitudes that are specifically drug related, the "proximal" social environment, are more influential than the attributes of the "distal" social structure (Jessor and Jessor 1977). Susceptibility to peer influence is related to involvement in peer-related activities (like dating or getting together with friends and to degree of attachment to and reliance on peers rather than parents (Jessor and Jessor 1978; Kandel, Kessler, and Margulies 1978; Brook, Lukoff, and Whiteman 1980).

Rather than indicating the existence of a general drug subculture, studies support the notion of drug-specific social networks of peers, each oriented toward a particular drug. Prior association with users of a particular drug is the strongest predictor of an individual's use of that drug (Jessor and Jessor 1977; Kandel, Kessler, and Margulies 1978). Further evidence is provided by cross-sectional canonical analyses on adolescent users of alcohol, marijuana, tobacco, inhalants, and other illicit drugs. Four different factors emerged in-stead of the single factor that would be produced by a general drug subculture (Huba, Wingard, and Bentler 1979). From a commonalities perspective, use of a variety of drugs does not share a·common foundation of beliefs and values associated with one particular drug subculture.

Of all the investigators who have examined peer influences, only Brook, Lukoff, and Whiteman (1980), after controlling for family and personality characteristics, report mostly negative results. In its design this study differs from others in one important respect: the interval separating contacts with adolescent respondents (three years) is much longer than the usual intervals used (one year or six months). Thus peer influences appear to be immediate and short-lived by comparison with parental influences. Further support for this interpretation derives from Lucas, Grupp, and Schmitt (1975), who found that perceived marijuana use by college students' reference groups in the freshman year weakly predicted marijuana initiation two years later but not four years later. The hypothesis of varying time lags for parental and peer influences should be tested further. The closeness of the parental bond, over and beyond any particular pattern of parental substance use or socialization practices, may reduce the child's involvement in deviant activities, of which drug behavior would be an example (Kandel, Kessler, and Margulies 1978; Brook, Lukoff, and Whiteman 1978; McCord and McCord 1959).

Contextual Factors as Commonalities

Social setting favorable to drug use reinforces and increases individual willingness to use. A striking documentation of contextual effects on drug initiation is provided by Robins's study of Veitnam veterans and nonveterans. In Vietnam during the war drugs of all types were easily available and enforcement of regulations against use were minimal. The Vietnam experience thus hastened the onset of the use of certain drugs and also resulted in the use of marijuana and narcotics by many men who might not have used these drugs otherwise (Robins 1978). Men with attributes indicative of a predisposition to use drugs were even more affected by the drug-facilitating Vietnam environment than men without these characteristics. These findings gain importance from the fact that the change in setting was independent of the actor or of significant others (Robins 1978).

No other drug use study has yet shown such striking contextual effects. Igra and Moos (1977, 1978) developed a comprehensive taxonomy of the social contexts of college dormitories but were unable to document any contextual effects on initiation except when the measure took into account the average extent of drinking in the dormitory. Other contextual characteristics, such as cohesiveness, had no impact. Immediate interpersonal networks may be more important than characteristics of the larger social context. Indeed, Campbell and Alexander (1965) demonstrated in connection with adolescent educational aspirations that contextual effects of schools on aspirations resulted not from the characteristics of the total student body but from those of the adolescent's close friends.

Commonalities and Differences in Termination

General population surveys suggest that use of a number of drugs terminates spontaneously as people approach the mid-20s and 30s. Assuming
that drug users do tend to reduce their drug use as they enter adulthood,
how do we explain this tendency? Further, as already noted, there appear to
be differences among the various substances in their duration throughout
the life span. For example, alcohol use, as noted earlier, both precedes and
outlasts the use of other illicit drugs, while PCP users tend to terminate
PCP use after a year or two (Feldman, Agar, and Beschner 1980). Why are
people less likely to terminate use of some drugs than others?

Alcohol is the most popular drug in society. Numerous customary occasions for use exist, ranging from cocktail parties to formal dinners, to
religious ceremonies, to watching football games on television. Everyone
knows that drinking is acceptable on these particular occasions, and most
drinking is confined to moderate levels in culturally approved situations.
While binge drinking or bouts of intoxication are clearly disapproved in
most cases, drinking as a social ritual is quite compatible with societal standards of proper adult behavior. Thus drinking tends to extend far into the
life span.

The use of most other drugs (with the exception of psychotherapeutic
drugs like Valium) tends to decline more sharply with age for a variety of
reasons. Most drugs have received considerable adverse publicity from the
media. Although personal experience with a drug is likely to be far more
convincing than knowledge available in the media, young people may show
a growing tendency to worry about long-term consequences of drug use as
they leave adolescence. Certainly the publicity about the health effects of
cigarettes seems to have had more impact on adults than on adolescents.
However, negative publicity does have some impact on young people. Recent cohorts of high school seniors express more concern about the potential health hazards of marijuana than earlier cohorts. The recent decline in
proportion of daily marijuana users has been attributed to this increased
concern with health consequences of drug use (Johnston, Bachman, and
O'Malley 1981).

In addition to fear of negative health effects, most adults experience a
reduced opportunity to obtain illicit drugs as they become less involved in
peer social activities and more involved in traditional family- and work-
centered life-styles. Age-mates are the chief sources of supply and information about illicit substances for adolescents. This helps to confine the spread
of illicit substance use beyond adolescence, when peer associations are less
central and access to illicit substances is reduced.

The onset of adulthood marks a major change in life-style. Large
amounts of leisure time typical during adolescence are replaced by involve-

ment with work and family responsibilities. As epidemiological research verifies, labor force participation and marital status are highly correlated with drug use status. Married persons show the lowest rates of use, while the single, the divorced, and those living independently show much higher rates (Henley and Adams 1973; Brown et al. 1974; Robins 1974; O'Donnell et al. 1976; Clayton and Voss 1977; Bachman, O'Malley, and Johnston 1978; Johnston 1980; Kandel 1982). In retrospective reports, being married is one of the most important correlates of abstention from the use of illicit drugs among adults 18 years of age and older in national samples (Cisin, Miller, and Wirtz 1976; Joe and Hudiberg 1978; see also Henley and Adams 1973).

In a prospective follow-up of former high school seniors from Monitoring the Future cohorts at age 19 and 22, Johnston, Bachman, and O'Malley (1980) found no increase in the percentage of daily users among those married as compared to an absolute increase of 2.6 percent in the total sample. Labor force participation is also highly correlated with drug use. The unemployed have the highest rates of use of most drugs, especially alcohol and illicit drugs other than marijuana (Johnston 1974; Robins 1974; Cisin, Miller, and Wirtz 1976; O'Donnell et al. 1976; Brunswick 1979).

No systematic longitudinal analyses have yet been completed that have followed young people through young adulthood to determine whether cessation of use follows or precedes entrance and exit from certain social roles. In the absence of appropriate longitudinal data, the reciprocal relationship between drug use and participation in these various social roles remains to be clarified. We do not know whether or how drug use modifies participation in these social roles, especially the timing of entry into roles and the level and continuity of participation. Does use lead to acceleration or, on the contrary, to postponement of marriage, employment, or childbearing? If there is a postponement, what is its duration? Does drug use lead to a redefinition of social roles? Does the assumption or anticipated assumption of certain roles in work and family cause a decline in use? Are these causal processes the same in different social classes or ethnic groups? Answers to these important questions may begin to emerge in the next several years from longitudinal studies of young adults recently initiated by investigators who are following cohorts of young adults who were first contacted in adolescence (for example, R. Jessor, G. Smith, H. Kaplan, L. Johnston, and D. Kandel). In 1982 R. Clayton and H. Voss began reinterviewing the national sample of young men who were first studied in 1974 at ages 18-29 (see O'Donnell et al. 1976).

Sociocultural Differences among Drugs

Despite commonalities in the use of most drugs—its concentration among young people, transmission in social groups, and relation to such factors as social context, association with users, and adult work and family roles—and despite association of illicit drug use with some common attitudes and values, various drugs differ significantly in their cultural meanings in our society. Alcohol is used by a sizable majority of young people in our society and indeed by a sizable majority of adults. As the most widely used drug, its use is accepted, approved, and perhaps even required in some situations. Everyone knows a good deal about alcohol—its purported effects, how and when to drink—and most people participate at least now and then in drinking rituals. Although there exist a range of drinking styles, with geographic, socioeconomic, and ethnic variations, we might consider learning to drink alcohol as a usual part of adolescent socialization in America. Adolescents are likely to be initiated into drinking by their parents and to be exposed to alcohol before they are exposed to any other drug. More pervasive across age groups than other drugs, its use both precedes and outlasts the use of any other drug.

Because alcohol is an intoxicating substance, cultural recipes require that one must be old enough to "handle it" before being allowed to drink. Becoming a drinker, then, may signify the onset of a new status, or a transition from childhood. Maddox (1962) refers to a process of anticipatory socialization in which adolescents learn to drink from the parental models with the support of age peers. Age peers then exert greater influence in shaping specific drinking behaviors.

Initiation into marijuana use is likely to have a different significance for young people. The recent history of marijuana use, its cultural meaning, and its adherents, suggest a rapidly changing situation. In the early 1970s the drug was a symbol of antiestablishment protest; users committed themselves to an ideology that went far beyond the enjoyment of cannabis as a social ritual. Today, with high use rates, the decline of the hippie movement, and less media attention, marijuana has become an acceptable drug among most adolescents and less of an anathema to adults. But still legally prohibited and largely associated with youth, marijuana may remain symbolic of the *disjuncture* with adulthood. Whereas alcohol is associated with adults, marijuana, insofar as it still has cultural symbolism, is a drug of youth and may symbolize nonconformity with the traditional adult world and acceptance in the youth culture. Knowing how and when to use marijuana, gaining access to the drug, and controlling one's behavior while intoxicated are all part of the marijuana subculture, transmitted largely among adolescents and young adults.

The use of illicit drugs other than marijuana is not nearly as acceptable or prevalent. Although individuals are recruited into the use of such drugs as heroin through association with other drug users, as are new users of marijuana, the use of such drugs as heroin and participation in drug-using groups may be more central to the lives of their users than marijuana use is to marijuana users, in part because of the way society regards these drugs. Marijuana is generally considered to be more benign than heroin or most other illicit drugs, and its increasing prevalence has tended to make people (users, exusers, and nonusers) take it more for granted. Marijuana use poses relatively little threat to most young people and is not nearly as secretive as it once was.

Use of illicit drugs other than marijuana is likely to be a factor of greater import both to users and to the outside world. The perception that it is more dangerous and more daring to try these drugs (than to try marijuana) persists among their users and nonusers alike. But users share a knowledge about drug effects and how to control them that is generally unavailable to the wider public. General societal beliefs about effects of heroin, for example, are sufficient to deter most young people from trying anything so reputedly heinous. Many who would be willing to take the step of smoking marijuana would not be willing to take the more drastic step of involvement with other illicit drugs. Pervasive cultural beliefs and lack of contact with other illicit drugs or their users effectively confines most adolescent drug use to marijuana and alcohol.

Conclusion

A major sociocultural commonality among drugs in our society is their consistent and specific relationship with age. The use of illegal drugs begins in the early teens, peaks in early adulthood, and declines sharply thereafter. The use of cigarettes and alcohol also reaches a peak in early adulthood but does not begin to decline until middle age. By contrast, use of medically prescribed drugs begins in the 20s, when illicit drug use starts to decline, and continues over the life cycle. The decline in the use of illicit drugs in the early 20s parallels the assumption of the social roles of adulthood—employment, marriage, and parenthood. These observations are based on repeated cross-sectional surveys. Longitudinal surveys that follow the same cohorts over time are required to establish with certainty that the decline of involvement in illicit drugs in the late 20s is a true maturational change and not only the result of differing experiences of different cohorts.

Although drug use is primarily concentrated among adolescents and young adults, there is a temporal sequence in the initiation of use of various drugs. The use of alcohol and tobacco, widespread in both the adult and adolescent population, occurs first in the sequence. Young people often learn to use these drugs from their families, with the support of peers who influence particular styles of use. Because use of legal drugs is accepted and approved among adults, onset of use may be considered by young users to signify status transition from childhood.

Use of marijuana, the most widespread illicit drug, usually follows the use of cigarettes and alcohol, the legal drugs. Most adolescents and young adults try marijuana, although many discontinue it. Using marijuana may signify transition into the adolescent youth culture. The strongest predictors of marijuana use are use by friends and values and attitudes favorable to the drug. Contact with other users is crucial to initiation into marijuana use. Contact with other users is also a significant, albeit relatively less significant, factor in the initiation into use of other illicit drugs. Social psychological research indicates that such characteristics as feelings of depression and poor relations with parents are also important. Membership in groups oriented toward the use of a particular drug encourages novices to use. Users at each stage are likely to continue use of drugs of preceding stages as well.

As the adolescent population moves through the stages of use, attrition occurs at each level. Young people do not progress through the complete sequence. They may discontinue use after trying a drug for a number of reasons: dislike of drug effects, lack of continued access to the drug, lack of continued contact with other users, or competing roles, such as employment or marriage.

Although there are differences in the stage at which young people adopt use of different drugs, learning to use a substance is a common social process in which the established user acts as a model for the initiate. Users define drug experiences as pleasurable and transmit cultural expectations to the new users. This transmission almost always occurs within peer groups, although families play a role in introducing legal drugs and in the use of psychoactive drugs to cope with psychological distress.

Reduction of drug use, especially use of illicit drugs, appears to occur as young people experience the growing demands and responsibilities of adulthood. However, these age-related trends are based on cross-sectional data. Longitudinal follow-ups of cohorts in adulthood are needed in order to establish the connection between illicit drug use and participation in social roles. Such studies will disentangle maturational, cohort, and historical factors in the trends observed across the life cycle.

References

Alexander, C.N., Jr., and Campbell, E.Q. 1968. Balance forces and environmental effects: Factors influencing the cohesiveness of adolescent drinking groups. *Soc. Forces* 46:367-374.

Annis, H.M., and Watson, C. 1975. Drug use and school dropouts: A longitudinal study. *Can. Counsel.* 9:155-362.

Armor, D.J.; Polich, J.M.; and Stambol, H.B. 1978. *Alcoholism and Treatment.* New York: Wiley.

Bachman, J.G.; Johnston, L.D.; and O'Malley, P.M. 1981a. Smoking, drinking and drug use among American high school students: Correlates and trends, 1975-1979. *Am. J. Pub. Health* 71:59-69.

Bachman, J.G.; Johnston, L.D.; and O'Malley, P.M. 1981b. *Monitoring the Future: Questionnaire Responses from the Nation's High School Seniors 1980.* Ann Arbor, Mich.: Institute for Social Research, University of Michigan.

Bachman, J.G.; O'Malley, P.M.; and Johnston, J. 1978. *Youth in Transition. Vol. 6. Adolescence to Adulthood—Change and Stability in the Lives of Young Men.* Ann Arbor, Mich.: Institute for Social Research.

Becker, H. 1953. Becoming a marihuana user. *Am. J. Sociol.* 54:235-242.

Blackford, L. 1977. *Summary Report. Surveys of Student Drug Use, San Mateo County, California: Trends in Levels of Use Reported by Junior and Senior High School Students.* San Mateo, Calif.: County Department of Public Health and Welfare, Research Statistics Section.

Blumer, H., et al. 1976. Recruitment into Drug Use. In R. Coombs et al. (eds.), *Socialization in Drug Abuse.* Cambridge, Mass.: Schenkman.

Brook, J.S.; Lukoff, I.F.; and Whiteman, M. 1977. Peer, family, and personality domains as related to adolescents; drug behavior. *Psychol. Rep.* 41:1095-1102.

Brook, J.S.; Lukoff, I.F.; and Whiteman, M. 1978. Family socialization and adolescent personality and their association with adolescent use of marijuana. *J. Gen. Psychol.* 133:261-271.

Brook, J.S.; Lukoff, I.F.; and Whiteman, M. 1980. Initiation into adolescent marijuana use. *J. Gen. Psychol.* 137:133-142.

Brown, J.; Glaser, D.; Waxer, E.; and Geis, G. 1974. Turning off: Cessation of marijuana use after college. *Soc. Probl.* 21:527-538.

Brunswick, A.F. 1979. Black youth and drug use behavior. In G. Beschner and A. Friedman (eds.) *Youth Drug Abuse: Problems, Issues, and Treatment,* pp. 443-492. Lexington, Mass.: Lexington Books, D.C. Heath.

Burkett, S.R., and Jensen, E.G. 1975. Conventional ties, peer influence, and the fear of apprehension: A study of adolescent marijuana use. *Sociol. Quart.* 16:522-533.

Cahalan, D., and Room, R. 1974. *Problem Drinking among American Men.* Monograph 7. New Brunswick, N.J.: Rutgers Center for Alcohol Studies.

Campbell, E.G., and Alexander, C.N. 1965. Structural effects and interpersonal relationships. *Am. J. Sociol.* 71:284-289.

Carr, R. 1978. What marijuana does (and doesn't do). *Human Behavior* (January).

Celentano, D.S., and McQueen, D.V. 1978. Comparison of alcoholism prevalence rates obtained by survey and indirect estimators. *J. Stud. Alcohol* 39:420-434.

Chambers, C. 1971. *Differential Drug Use within the New York State Labor Force.* Mamaroneck, N.Y.: Starch/Hooperating/The Public Pulse.

Cisin, I.H.; Miller, J.D.; and Wirtz, P.W. 1976. *Discontinuing Drug Use.* Washington, D.C.: George Washington University Social Research Group.

Clayton, R.R., and Voss, H.L. 1977. Shaking up: Cohabitation in the 1970s. *J. Marr. Fam.* 39:273-283.

Dembo, R.; Schmeidler, J.; and Koval, M. 1976. Demographic, value, and behavior correlates of marihuana use among middle-class youths. *J. Health Soc. Behav.* 17:176-186.

Donovan, J.E., and Jessor, R. 1978. Adolescent problem drinking—psychosocial correlates in a national sample study. *J. Stud. Alcohol* 39:1506-1524.

Ellis, G.J., and Stone, L.H. 1979. Marihuana use in college—evaluation of a modeling perspective. *Youth Soc.* 10:323-334.

Feldman, H.; Agar, M.; and Beschner, G. 1980. *Angel Dust: An Ethnographic Study of PCP Users.* Lexington, Mass.: Lexington Books, D.C. Heath.

Fine, S., and Kleinman, S. 1979. Rethinking subculture: An interactionist analysis. *Am. J. Sociol.* 85(1):1-20.

Fishburne, P.M.; Abelson, H.I.; and Cisin, I. 1980. *National Survey on Drug Abuse: Main Findings: 1979.* Rockville, Md.: National Institute on Drug Abuse.

Gerstein, D.; Judd, L.; and Rovner, S. 1979. Career dynamics of female heroin addicts. *Am. J. Drug Alcohol Abuse* 6(1):1-23.

Ginsberg, I.J., and Greenley, J.R. 1978. Competing theories of marihuana use: A longitudinal study. *J. Health Soc. Behav.* 19:22-34.

Goldstein, J.W. 1975. Assessing the interpersonal determinants of adolescent drug use. In D.J. Lettieri (ed.), *Predicting Adolescent Drug Abuse: A Review of Issues, Methods, and Correlates*, pp. 45-52. Prepared for the National Institute on Drug Abuse. Washington, D.C.: U.S. Government Printing Office.

Goode, E. 1970. *The Marijuana Smokers.* New York: Basic Books.

Gould, L.; Walker, A.L.; Crane, L.E.; and Lidy, C.W. 1974. *Connections: Notes from the Heroin World.* New Haven, Conn.: Yale University Press.

Harford, T.C. 1976. A national study of adolescent drinking behavior, attitudes, and correlates. Further comments. *J. Stud. Alcohol* 37:1346-1358.

Henley, J.R., and Adams, I.D. 1973. Marihuana use in post collegiate cohorts: Correlates of use, prevalence, patterns, and factors associated with cessation. *Soc. Probl.* 20:514-520.

Huba, G.J.; Wingard, J.A.; and Bentler, P.M. 1979. Beginning adolescent drug use and peer and adult interaction. *J. Consult. Clin. Psychol.* 47:265-276.

Huba, G.J.; Wingard, J.A.; and Bentler, P.M. 1980. Longitudinal analysis of the role of peer support, adult models and peer subcultures in beginning adolescent substances use. *Multivariate Behav. Res.* 15:259-280.

Igra, A., and Moos, R.H. 1977. Drinking among college students: A longitudinal study. Social Ecology Laboratory, Department of Psychiatry, Stanford University, Palo Alto, Calif.

Igra, A., and Moos, R.H. 1979. Alcohol use among college students: Some competing hypotheses. *J. Youth Adolesc.* 8:393-406.

Jessor, R. 1979. Marihuana: A review of recent psychosocial research. In R. Dupont, A. Goldstein, and J. O'Donnell (eds.), *Handbook on Drug Abuse*, pp. 337-354. Rockville, Md.: National Institute on Drug Abuse.

Jessor, R.; Donovan, J.E.; and Widmer, K. 1980. *Adolescent Drinking Behavior. Vol. 2. Psychosocial Factors in Adolescent Alcohol and Drug Use: The 1978 National Sample Study, and the 1974-78 Panel Study.* University of Colorado, Institute of Behavioral Science, Boulder, Colo.

Jessor, R., and Jessor, S.L. 1977. *Problem Behavior and Psychosocial Development—A Longitudinal Study of Youth.* New York: Academic Press.

Jessor, R., and Jessor, S.L. 1978. Theory testing in longitudinal research on marihuana use. In D. Kandel (ed.), *Longitudinal Research on Drug Use: Empirical Findings and Methodological Issues,* pp. 41-71. New York: Hemisphere-Halsted Press.

Jessor, R.; Jessor, S.L.; and Finney, J. 1973. A social psychology of marihuana use: Longitudinal studies of high school and college youth. *J. Pers. Soc. Psychol.* 26:1-15.

Joe, G.W.; and Hudiburg, R.A. 1978. Behavioral correlates of age at first marihuana use. *Int. J. Addict.* 13:627-637.

Johnson, B.D. 1973. *Marijuana Users and Drug Subcultures.* New York: Wiley.

Johnson, B.D., and Uppal, G.S. 1980. Marihuana and youth: A generation gone to pot. In F.R. Scarpitti and S.K. Datesman (eds.), *Drugs and the Youth Culture,* pp. 81-108. Beverly Hills, Calif.: Sage Publications.

Johnston, L. 1973. *Student Drug Use.* Ann Arbor, Mich.: Institute for Social Research.

Johnston, L. 1974. Drug use during and after high school: Results of a national longitudinal study. *Am. J. Pub. Health* 64:29-37.

Johnston, L. 1980. The daily marijuana user. Paper presented at the National Alcohol and Drug Abuse Conference, Washington, D.C., September 18, 1980.

Johnston, L.D.; Bachman, J.G.; and O'Malley, P. 1980. Highlights from Student Drug Use in America, 1975-1980. Ann Arbor, Mich.: Institute for Social Research, and Rockville, Md.: National Institute on Drug Abuse.

Johnston, L.D.: Bachman, J.G.; and O'Malley, P.M. 1981. *Highlights from Student Drug Use in America 1975-1981.* Rockville, Md.: National Institute on Drug Abuse.

Johnston, L.; O'Malley, P.; and Eveland, L. 1978. Drugs and delinquency: A search for causal connections. In D. Kandel (ed.), *Longitudinal Research on Drug Use: Empirical Findings and Methodological Issues,* pp. 137-156. New York: Hemisphere-Halsted Press.

Josephson, E., and Rosen, M. 1978. Panel loss in a high school drug study. In D. Kandel (ed.), *Longitudinal Research on Drug Use: Empirical Findings and Methodological Issues,* pp. 115-133. New York: Hemisphere-Halsted Press.

Kandel, D. 1973. Adolescent marihuana use: Role of parents and peers. *Science* 181:1067-1070.

Kandel, D. 1975a. Reaching the hard-to-reach: Illicit drug use among high school absentees. *Addict. Dis.* 1:465-480.

Kandel, D.B. 1975b. Stages in adolescent involvement in drug use. *Science* 190:912-914.

Kandel, D.B. (ed.) 1978a. *Longitudinal Research on Drug Use: Empirical Findings and Methodological Issues.* New York: Hemisphere-Halsted Press.

Kandel, D.B. 1978b. Convergences in prospective longitudinal surveys of drug use in normal populations. In D. Kandel (ed.), *Longitudinal Research on Drug Use: Empirical Findings and Methodological Issues.* New York: Hemisphere-Halsted Press.

Kandel, D.B. 1978c. Similarity in real life adolescent friendship pairs. *J. Pers. Soc. Psychol.* 36:306-312.

Kandel, D.B. 1978d. Homophily, selection, and socialization in adolescent friendships. *Am. J. Sociol.* 84:427-436.

Kandel, D.B. 1980a. Drug and drinking behavior among youth. In J. Coleman, A. Inkeles, and N. Smelser (eds.), *Annual Review of Sociology,* vol. 6, pp. 235-285. Palo Alto, Calif.: Annual Reviews, Inc.

Kandel, D.B. 1980b. Developmental stages in adolescent drug involvement. in D.J. Lettieri, M. Sayers, and H.W. Pearson (eds.), *Theories on Drug Abuse: Selected Contemporary Perspectives,* pp. 120-127. National Institute on Drug Abuse, Research Monograph Series No. 30. Washington, D.C.: U.S. Government Printing Office.

Kandel, D.B. 1980c. A second look at convergences in longitudinal drug studies: An update. In L. Robins (ed.), *Epidemiology of Drug Abuse.* Geneva: World Health Organization, in press.

Kandel, D.B. 1982. Characteristics of marijuana users in young adulthood. Unpublished paper, Department of Psychiatry, Columbia University.

Kandel, D.B.; Adler, I.; and Sudit, M. 1981. The epidemiology of adolescent drug use in France and Israel. *Am. J. Pub. Health* 71(3):256-265.

Kandel, D.B.; Kessler, R.C.; and Margulies, R.S. 1978. Antecedents of adolescent initiation into stages of drug use: A developmental analysis. *J. Youth Adolesc.* 7:13-40.

Kandel, D.B.; Raveis, V.S.; and Kandel, P.I. 1982. A comparison of former regular students, former school absentees and school dropouts in a follow-up cohort of young adults. Unpublished paper, Columbia University and New York State. Psychiatric Institute, New York, N.Y.

Kandel, D.B.; Single, E.; and Kessler, R.C. 1976. The epidemiology of drug use among New York State high school students: Distribution, trends and change in rates of use. *Am. J. Pub. Health* 66(1):43-53.

Kandel, D.; Treiman, D.; Faust, R.; and Single, E. (1976). Adolescent involvement in illicit drug use: A multiple classification analysis. *Soc. Forces* 55:438-458.

Kleinman, P.H., and Lukoff, I.F. 1978. Ethnic differences in factors related to drug abuse. *J. Health Soc. Behav.* 19:190-199.

Lucas, W.L.; Grupp, S.E.; and Schmitt, R.L. 1975. Predicting who will turn on: A four-year follow-up. *Int. J. Addict.* 10:305-326.

Maddox, G. 1962. Teenage drinking in the U.S. In D. Pittman and C. Snyder (eds.) *Society, Culture, and Drinking Patterns.* New York: Wiley and Sons.

Margulies, R.; Kessler, R.C.; and Kandel, D. 1977. A longitudinal study of onset of drinking among high school students. *Quart. J. Stud. Alcohol* 38:897-912.

Markle, G., and Troyer, R. 1979. Smoke gets in your eyes: Cigarette smoking as deviant behavior. *Soc. Probl.* 26:611-625.

Matza, D. 1964. *Delinquency and Drift.* New York: Wiley and Sons.

McCord, W., and McCord, J. 1959. *Origins of Crime.* New York: Columbia University Press.

Miller, J.D. 1981. *Drug Abuse and the American Adolescent.* National Institute on Drug Abuse Research Monograph Series No. 38. Washington, D.C.: U.S. Government Printing Office.

Miller, J.D.; Cisin, I.; and Harrell, A. 1978. *Highlights from the National Survey on Drug Abuse: 1977.* Washington, D.C.: George Washington University Social Research Group.

National Clearinghouse for Drug Abuse Information. 1977. Resource information on the National Institute on Drug Abuse epidemiological systems and surveys. *Report Series* 37:1-14.

National Commission on Marihuana and Drug Abuse. 1972. *Marihuana: A Signal of Misunderstanding,* Appendix vols. 1, 2. Washington, D.C.: U.S. Government Printing Office.

National Commission on Marihuana and Drug Abuse. 1973. *Drug Use in America: Problem in Perspective.* Washington, D.C.: U.S. Government Printing Office.

Nurco, D.N.; Lerner, M.; Bonito, A.J.; and Balter, M.B. 1975. An approach to the classification of the lifestyles of narcotic abusers. In D.J. Lettieri (ed.), *Predicting Adolescent Drug Abuse: A Review of Issues, Methods, and Correlates.* Washington, D.C.: U.S. Government Printing Office.

O'Donnell, J.A. 1972. Lifetime patterns of narcotic addiction. In M.A. Roff, L.N. Robins, and M. Pollack (eds.), *Life History Research in Psychopathology,* vol. 2, pp. 236-254. Minneapolis: University of Minnesota Press.

O'Donnell, J.A., and Clayton, R. 1982. The stepping-stone hypothesis: A reappraisal. *Chemical Dependencies,* vol. 4. In press.

O'Donnell, J.A., and Clayton, R.R. 1979b. Determinants of early marihuana use. In G.M. Beschner and A.S. Friedman (eds.), *Youth Drug Abuse: Problems, Issues, and Treatment,* pp. 63-110. Lexington, Mass.: Lexington Books, D.C. Heath.

O'Donnell, J.; Voss, H.; Clayton, R.; Slatin, G.; and Room, R. 1976. *Young Men and Drugs—A Nationwide Survey.* Research Monograph 5. Rockville, Md.: National Institute on Drug Abuse.

O'Malley, P.M. 1975. *Correlates and Consequences of Illicit Drug Use.* Unpublished Ph.D. dissertation, University of Michigan, Ann Arbor.

O'Malley, P.M.; Bachman, J.G.; and Johnston, L.D. 1978. Drug use and military plans of high school seniors. *Youth Soc.* 10:65-77.

Orcutt, J. 1978. Normative definitions of intoxicated states: A test of several sociological theories. *Soc. Probl.* 4:385-396.

Rachal, J.V.; Hubbard, R.L.; Williams, J.R.; and Tuchfeld, B.S. 1976. Drinking levels and problem drinking among junior and senior high school students. *J. Stud. Alcohol* 37:1751-1761.

Rachal, J.V.; Williams, J.R.; Brehm, M.L.; Cavanaugh, B.; Moore, R.P.; and Eckerman, W.C. 1975. *Adolescent Drinking Behavior. Attitudes and Correlates.* Rockville, Md.: National Institute on Drug Abuse.

Richards, L.G. 1981. *Demographic Trends and Drug Abuse, 1980-1995.* National Institute on Drug Abuse Research Monograph 35. Washington, D.C.: U.S. Government Printing Office.

Rittenhouse, J.D. 1979. Social psychological aspects of drug abuse. Paper presented at the American Psychological Association Annual Meeting, New York, August.

Rittenhouse, J.D. 1980. Learning drug use: From "legal" substance to marijuana and beyond. Paper presented at the American Psychological Association Annual Convention, Montreal, Canada.

Robins, L.N. 1974. *The Vietnam User Returns.* Final Report. Special Action Office Monograph Series A, No. 2. Washington, D.C.: U.S. Government Printing Office.

Robins, L.N. 1977. Estimating addiction rates and locating target populations: How decomposition into stages helps. In J.D. Rittenhouse (ed.), *The Epidemiology of Heroin and Other Narcotics,* pp. 25-29. NIDA Research Monograph Series 16. Washington, D.C.: U.S. Government Printing Office.

Robins, L.N. 1978. The interaction of setting and predisposition in explaining novel behavior: Drug initiations before, in and after Vietnam. In D. Kandel (ed.), *Longitudinal Research on Drug Use: Empirical Findings and Methodological Issues,* pp. 179-96. New York: Hemisphere-Halsted Press.

Robins, L.N. 1979. Addict careers. In R. Dupont, A. Goldstein, and J. O'Donnell (eds.), *Handbook on Drug Abuse.* Washington, D.C.: National Institute on Drug Abuse.

Robins, L.N.; Davis, D.H.; and Nurco, D.N. 1974. How permanent was Vietnam Drug Addiction? *Am. J. Pub. Health* 64 (Suppl.):38-43.

Robins, L.N.; Davis, D.H.; and Wish, E. 1977. Detecting predictors of rare events: Demographic, family and personal deviance as predictors of stages in the progression toward narcotic addiction. In J.S. Straug, B. Haroutun, and M. Roff (eds.), *The Origins and Course of Psychopathology,* pp. 379-406. New York: Plenum Press.

Roizen, R.; Cahalan, D.; and Shanks, P. 1978. Spontaneous remission among untreated problem drinkers. In D. Kandel (ed.), *Longitudinal Research on Drug Use: Empirical Findings and Methodological Issues,* pp. 197-221. New York: Hemisphere-Halsted Press.

Smart, R.G.; Gray, G.; and Bennett, C. 1978. Predictors of drinking and signs of heavy drinking among high school students. *Int. J. Addict.* 13:1079-1094.

Suchman, E.A. 1968. The "hang-loose" ethic and the spirit of drug use. *J. Health Soc. Behav.* 9:146-155.

Urban, M. 1972. Drugs in industry. In National Commission on Marijuana and Drug Abuse, *Drug Use in America,* vol. 1. Washington, D.C.: U.S. Government Printing Office.

Vaillant, G.E. 1966. A twelve-year follow-up of New York narcotic addicts committed for treatment under the Narcotic Addiction Rehabilitation Act (NARA). *Arch. Gen. Psychiat.* 15:599-609.

Winick, C. 1962. Maturing out of narcotic addiction. *Bull. Narcot.* 14:1-7.

Zucker, R.A. 1979. Developmental aspects of drinking through the young adult years. Chapter 4 in H.T. Blane and M.E. Chafetz (eds.), *Youth, Alcohol and Social Policy.* New York: Plenum Press.

2 Common Features of Troublesome Habitual Behaviors: A Cultural Approach

Andrew L. Walker and
Charles W. Lidz

The current interest in the general behavioral category "substance abuse and habitual behavior" draws on concerns that have been well represented in twentieth-century American social thought. The social sciences, particularly psychology and sociology, have long recognized that some individuals repeatedly engage in types of behavior that are self-destructive or destructive to the individual's essential social relationships (Ross 1907). With America's long cultural interest in sin and vice, it is perfectly natural that irrational destructive behaviors, such as alcoholism or compulsive gambling, would attract the attention of social scientists.

A glance at almost any introductory textbook in psychology, sociology, social work, or counseling will show abundant interest in these phenomena (see, for example, White 1964; Merton and Nisbet 1976) but will also show that analysis of these troubling behaviors has either proceeded in an atomized fashion, considering each category of destructive behavior separately and developing a distinct explanatory scheme for each, or has dealt with them as part of deviant behavior as a whole and not considered their special properties (see Parsons 1951: chap. 7; Merton 1957: chaps. 4, 5). Very little attention has been paid to the common elements of the general behavioral category.

The purpose of this chapter is to examine in historical perspective American society's cultural definitions of "abuse" and the appropriate response to abuse. The intention is to argue that members of the class of behavior patterns referred to as "substance abuse" share a common element of *normative ambiguity,* which contributes to their development, continued performance, and to difficulties in the control of these behaviors by the self and others. Looking at the history of social control efforts in these areas reveals that this class of behaviors has been the historical domain of three distinct mechanisms of social control—religion, laws and medicine, none of which has been successful in finding durable techniques of control.

We wish to thank Howard Becker, John Kaplan, Peter Levison, Louis Lasagna, John Marx, Albert Stunkard, and especially Dean Gerstein for comments and suggestions.

Defining the Class

No clear or obvious consensus exists on what types of behavior are to be considered instances of substance abuse or troublesome habitual behavior. However, two basic definitional criteria seem essential: the behavior must be seen as problem-inducing or undesirable from some clearly identified, socially authoritative perspective, and it must be seen as essentially repetitive. Several behavioral patterns clearly meet these cirteria:

alcoholism and "problem drinking,"

compulsive gambling,

overeating,

cigarette smoking (nicotine addiction), and

drug abuse (or addiction).

Interesting arguments might be adduced for the inclusion of various other behavior patterns—such as child abuse, credit abuse, promiscuity, or television addiction—but the present purpose is to discover the sociocultural meaning of this general class of behavior, not to enumerate all of its components.

The repetitive character of the behaviors under consideration should be underscored. An individual getting drunk need cause little concern unless inebriation is perceived to be a recurring and troublesome activity for the individual in question (Zola 1963). Likewise, an accasional purchase of a lottery ticket is not likely to be confused with compulsive gambling. Only when gambling is repeated and recognized as causing social or financial problems does it become a member of this class of problem behaviors.

From a cultural point of view, the norms against these behaviors probably stem from a cluster of values that define the individualistic strain in Western thought and are deeply rooted in American culture: individualism, freedom, and self-control. These very basic values—along with democracy, achievement and success, equality, progress, and secular rationality—have been consistently identified as "core values" in America by serious analysts of American culture from Tocqueville (1835) through the Lynds (1929), Riesman (1950), Parsons (1959), and Slater (1976). This strong cultural preference for self-reliant, self-controlled individuals is well exemplified in our popular media, where a favorite hero is not necessarily popular or skillful but is always self-directing, self-controlled, and independent (Nelson 1976). Respectability and middle class status are intimately tied to the ability to present oneself as self-directing, "in control of oneself" (Slater 1976).

The common feature of the "abuse" behavior patterns that makes them troublesome in our culture is that they are seen typically to involve a loss of self-control. They are typified as being necessary or pleasurable when done in moderation but destructive when "out of control." Many Americans view a drink, a game of poker, a sumptuous meal, a cigarette, and some drug use as pleasurable but they also assume that no rational person would want the destructive results likely to occur when the activity is repeated immoderately. Presumably no one "in his right mind" would want to get lung cancer, ruin his or her liver, acquire massive debts, or eat to the point of obesity. Thus Amerian culture insists on a tenuous but important line between behavior that is "under control" and that which is "out of control;" the former are acceptable, while the latter are seen as invidious.

Norms: Pattern and Ambiguity

One can readily agree with the argument that each of the behavior patterns listed before is harmful or wrongful, but it is equally undisputable that each is a variant on some behavior practice that is accepted and even encouraged. Specifically, overeating is a variant on eating with enthusiasm; drug abuse and alcoholism are closely related to relaxation and recreation; gambling is a common form of social behavior; and smoking is related to sophistication and relaxation. Stigma results not from the enactment of proscribed activities but, rather, from the overenactment of acceptable activities. As Schur (1980) points out, deviance is generally perceived in "degrees," and in this class of behaviors the problem is that the performer does not restrict the behaviors to an acceptable frequency, location, or intensity.[a] Consequently, although there is probably consensus that the activities, as moral stereotypes, are wrong, the norms governing this consensus are inherently ambiguous; furthermore the judgment that any particular deed is an instance of wrongdoing is complex and depends on the doer's social history. A further complication is that not all Americans wholly agree in their moral rankings of either the stereotyped abuse patterns themselves, or of any specific episode that might be an instance of one of the patterns. For clarification, we need to look more closely at the sources of variation.

Although it is common for people to speak as though norms clearly distinguish between proper and improper behaviors for an entire society,

[a]Unconditional taboos against such "hard" drugs as heroin, PCP, or LSD may seem to violate this "acceptable as long as it doesn't exceed the bounds of propriety" formulation, but we do not think so. The moral meaning of these hard drugs appears to be tied in with the moral meaning of other drugs—such as alcohol and marijuana—that are not unconditionally proscribed. The distinction between legitimate (or acceptable) drug *use* and drug *abuse* is a slippery moral and practical judgment but for the purposes of the present discussion drug abuse may be thought of as any drug use that would invoke serious negative reactions if made wholly public.

the close study of the operation of norms has shown researchers that in practice norms often provide an ambiguous basis for ordinary social practices. Since the 1940s, a series of sociologists and social psychologists have studied the way people conform to or violate norms. While Americans are prone to see the world in moral terms (Lidz and Walker 1980), the relationship between daily behavior and its moral referents is generally indirect. For instance, Sykes and Matza (1957) investigated the way delinquents created moral distance from the implications of their own actions. They found that delinquents removed themselves from apparently clear-cut moral constraints by the use of "techniques of neutralization," which are culturally sanctioned devices of moral logic. Almost all of the delinquents' neutralization techniques reflect norms of moral evasion that are part of American culture in general.

Another aspect of normative ambiguity results from the remarkable cultural pluralism of American society. American culture is not a single monolith of uniform validity to all members of society. Instead, it is an amalgam of subcultures, each having some degree of internal consistency. Although the power of the state is enlisted behind some of these normative systems (the law), there remain a multiplicity of moral perspectives that differ from the law, yet seem equally binding to some members. This cultural pluralism derives from two distinct features of our society: immigration and complexity.

America is a "nation of imigrants" who brought their cultures with them and who sought to follow their particular cultural values in the pattern of their new lives in America (Glazer and Moynihan 1963). Although many of these ethnic subcultures have grown less autonomous, various subcultures remain distinctive to even the most casual observer. Ethnic differences are of considerable pertinence to several of the behavior patterns under consideration. For example, the role of alcohol and the definition of alcoholism differ sharply between the WASP subculture and several immigrant groups (Gusfield 1966; Glassner and Berg 1980; O'Connor 1975). For most of the past century, marijuana was much more freely accepted among blacks and Mexican-Americans than by the rest of the population (Becker 1963).

The second factor behind American cultural pluralism was first defined by Durkhiem, who found that as societies grow larger and more complex, participants in each distinct institutional activity tend to develop and share a distinctive meaning system appropriate to the details of the activity, and societywide consensus exists only at the level of very broad generalities (Durkheim 1933). Thus in an immensely complex society such as modern America, the particular normative commitments of the population vary considerably, depending on age, social class, occupation, education, and so on.

Another aspect of moral ambiguity is the influence of situational variables in the application of norms in the deviance control process. Studies by members of the "interactionist school" (see Rubington and Weinberg 1981) have shown that even where formal norms are clear and agreed upon, their application to any situation involves complex ad hoc decisions that are open to negotiation and interpretation (Kitsuse 1962; Cicourel 1968; Skolnich 1966). These decisions concern when, where, with whom, how often, and "except under what circumstances" the behavior should, may, or should not be performed (Garfinkel 1967; Daniels 1970; Piliaven and Briar 1964). All of these conditions are used by the participants to assess the propriety of behavior in situ, and this assessment appears to be cooperative in its construction. Since a common characteristic of the various abuse behaviors is that they are overenactments of permitted or even encouraged behavior, this line of reasoning suggests that the individual being defined as an abuser is having trouble negotiating a way through the standards of propriety (Hayano 1976). Of course, hundreds of thousands of dollars in gambling debts or wildly irrational behavior resulting from drug intake may present problems that are difficult to explain away, but most instances of the behavior patterns in question are more negotiable.

In emphasizing the normative ambiguity surrounding these behaviors, we have no need or intention of questioning whether they are, in fact, "really" wrong. Our concern here is solely with the implications of ambiguity for the origin, assessment, and control of these behaviors. Normative ambiguity operates not only on abusers but also on those who provide them with necessary services, those who have legitimate personal or occupational concerns for them (such as family, control agents, or policy-makers), and public opinion in general.

Control Ambiguity

Before considering the ramifications of normative ambiguity, we must focus on a second type of ambiguity regarding this class of behaviors: variation in the type of social control applied to them. Since the European Middle Ages, these types of behaviors have almost always been considered troublesome and sometimes have become crimes per se. Periodic attempts at legal control have generally been of short duration and little success. Tobacco was unsuccessfully outlawed in much of seventeenth-century Europe (Szasz 1974); alcohol and some other drugs were outlawed in the United States during some periods of this century (Gusfield 1966; Lindesmith 1963; Musto 1973); and gambling has also been outlawed in America in varying degrees by locality during this century.

Historically, these behaviors were primarily considered sins and thus subject to religious authority, which in most countries meant control by an official church. Church regulation did not concentrate on the acts themselves but on their implications for the person's soul. As sins, these activities were clearly viewed as troublesome, not for society, but for the soul of the performer. So, for instance overeating (gluttony) was a formidable sin but was never punished as a crime. It was wrong because it reflected a failure to control oneself, not because it was a waste of food. Excessive alcohol consumption was considered a personal indulgence which both reflected and caused personal weakness, not a crime because it hurt someone else.

However the eighteenth and nineteenth centuries saw a marked decline in the temporal power of churches, which largely yielded their role as agencies of social control (Erikson 1966). Social control began operating primarily through the helping professions as well as the criminal law. Since then these two control systems have developed an important jurisdictional division: the criminal law has come to focus on the control of deviant *acts*, while the helping professions focus on the control of deviant *individuals*. It may seem tedious to insist on a fundamental distinction between a deviant act and a deviant person, because we normally expect the two to occur together. Culturally, Americans tend to expect that the performers of all deviant acts are personally deviant and to expect deviant people to perform all kinds of deviant acts. Nonetheless, the helping professions organize their knowledge in terms of diagnoses, which involve classes of sick people, whereas the criminal law is organized around types of criminal acts. In principle, for instance, the law recognizes all murder as the same crime, regardless of the type of person who committed the crime. On the other hand, the helping professions may see symptoms of the same disorder (say, inadequate superego formation) in morally trivial acts such as responses to a Rorschach test and morally outrageous acts such as murder; both could indicate the need for the same treatment. In this sense it can be said that the helping professions have picked up some of the functions once performed by churches. They function as mechanisms of social control by acting on the personality, just as the Church once functioned as a mechanism of control by acting on the soul (Lidz and Walker 1977).

While the medieval Catholic Church held a frequently disputed and ambiguous position as to whether the state of one's soul was decided by what God gave the individual (the doctrine of grace) or by what the individual did to please God (the doctrine of works), early Protestant theology was much more clearly committed to the doctrine that the state of one's soul and one's prospects for salvation were a function of Divine Grace. The modern helping professions have adopted a view of mental health that is similar in its main outlines to the Protestant, especially Calvinist, doctrine of grace. From the perspective of the helping professions, the state of one's personality (soul), is determined largely by heredity and environment (grace), not by one's acts (works). Although this modern psychiatric model seems to provide adequate control for disorders such as schizophrenia and anxiety neurosis, it has been much less successful in dealing with abusive habitual behavior. In general, the helping professions have treated self-destructiveness but not gambling, dependency but not drug abuse or alcoholism, hostility and poor self-image but not overeating.

In effect, for the past century or so neither major system of social control has been able to effectively manage the troublesome behaviors in question. Since the wounds these abuses inflict are primarily on the self, it has been difficult (though not impossible) to justify their management by the criminal law. In the case of overeating, we are not aware of *any* effort having been made to define this as illegal; in the other cases, efforts to outlaw them have generally raised the objection that they are "crimes without victims," status crimes not criminal acts.

Efforts aimed at helping those who perform these behaviors have not met with much success either. Psychiatric treatment programs have generally not been able to construct treatment plans based on the Kraepelinian, Freudian, or Neo-Freudian models of psychopathology that have dominated the profession. Instead, treatment programs and associated clinical rationales have been either ad hoc constructions or more recently have been based on theories of social learning and behavior modification—provoking the objection so often heard in the helping professions that behavior modification only treats the symptoms, not the real problem.

While these control ambiguities may seem abstract, they have very concrete ramifications for those who engage in the behaviors and those who seek to control them. These ambiguities provide excuses, confusions, objections, obfuscations, and justifications that neutralize the legitimacy and hence blunt the effect of efforts to remedy the behaviors. Agents of control from both the legal and medical systems are often faced with persuasive attempts to exploit the confusion about which standards and remedies are appropriate. The possibilities of moral sleight-of-hand are exemplified in the following conversations, recorded by the authors in the course of ethnographic research on heroin use and control (Gould et al. 1974):

DeJean (the Prosecutor) and I (the researcher) were talking and waiting for Nelson (a defense attorney) to finish talking with a client, when another defendant came up to us.

Defendant:	Excuse me, you're the Prosecutor, aren't you?
Prosecutor:	Yeah.
Defendant:	Can't you and me settle this thing without him? (Pointing to the Public Defender on the other side of the Court)
Prosecutor:	What's on your mind?
Defendant:	Well, I mean, you're not going to send me away, are you?
Prosecutor:	Why shouldn't I? You were dealing, weren't you?

Defendant: Yeah, man, but I had a big habit to support. Where else
                  was I going to get $75 a day? Besides, what good is it gonna
                  do to send me away? I need treatment.
                                              (Lidz and Walker 1977:311)

In this conversation, an addict is using the rhetoric of treatment to undermine the legitimacy of punishment. But in the treatment center, an addict
can use the rhetoric of control to undermine the legitimacy of therapueutic
treatment demands:

Clinician: What's your name?
Applicant: LeRoy Jones.
Clinician: How old are you?
Applicant: Twenty-three.
Clinician: What are you looking for?
Applicant: I don't know. What programs you got?
Clinician: What do you mean? I just described them to you.
Applicant: I mean, I don't need any of them programs. What I
                  need is to kick my habit.
2nd Clinician: You mean to detoxify?
Applicant: Yeah.
2nd Clinician: Detox is not a program. We don't even consider it
                  treatment. We can arrange for you to get detoxed, we
                  have a detox program, but that would only be to get
                  you ready for treatment.
Applicant: But I don't need no treatment. I can take stuff or
                  leave it. I went six years without getting no habit. I
                  don't got no mental problem or nothing, so I don't
                  see why I need a program.
                                              (Gould et al. 1974:157-158)

This may strike some readers as inconsequential talk, but therapeutic and
legal mechanisms of control cannot adequately function without the legitima-
tion that such arguments deny. Both systems count on the deviant's cooperation in his or her own processing (Sykes 1958). The clinician must be able to
count on at least minimal patient participation in treatment. Without the
cooperation of the defendants and their lawyers in plea bargaining, no prosecutor could manage his or her case load. Perhaps equally important, the
sense of questionable legitimacy created by this control ambiguity under-
mines the morale of control agents, who find this sort of work demoralizing
and look for innovative alternatives (Gould et al. 1974).

In short, while the practical difference between actor and act may be
slight, a stark difference exists between the criminal law and the helping
professions. For the most part, the criminal law requires the behaviors it
punishes to be voluntary and the individuals to be in control of their
behavior. Actions not meeting these tests, such as unintentional acts or acts

by persons deemed deficient in the capacity for self-control such as (children or the mentally handicapped) are not punishable by the criminal law. In contrast, the helping professions generally insist on treating personality disorders. Voluntary acts that happen to get the performer in trouble are not their concern; instead, they are concerned only with behavior that reflects essential flaws in the makeup of the psyche.

Substance abuse and other troublesome habitual behaviors fall between these two positions. As individual acts, they are certainly voluntary. One does not ordinarily eat, smoke, drink, use drugs, or gamble without some conscious, voluntary participation in the activity. Unlike the schizophrenic, whose hallucinations seem to appear regardless of a desire for them, or even the insomniac, who simply cannot voluntarily go to sleep, these behaviors all involve voluntary actions that the individual can, at least for a while, stop. Yet there is something compelling about these behaviors, at least for some people, that makes it hard for the individual to control them indefinitely. This compulsiveness seriously undercuts the legitimacy of a punishing response, since the performer can claim, as did the addict just quoted, that the punishment will not prevent further deviance because the behavior is out of his control.

Another feature common to most abusive behaviors that is a source of problems for their legal control is the victimless nature of the activities. In deciding whether wrong has been done, Americans tend to give considerable weight to harm that has been done to others by the activity (Schur 1965). In the behavior patterns in question, it is somewhat difficult for others to establish their claim that they were harmed as a direct result of wrongdoing by the alleged deviant (Hirshberg 1980). This is not to say that credible claims of victimization are impossible to make, but their acceptance seems to require demonstration of a well-established history of serious impropriety. Without this evidence, and given the normative ambiguity of the behaviors, negotiations between the performer and those who might sanction him or her concerning the propriety of the behavior often dissolve into discussions of "good taste" without actually articulating an agreed-upon evaluation. Hence while the behavior in question may raise profound doubts in the minds of both the performer and others, the situational factors of any instance of enactment often provide sufficient opportunities to make excuses so as to preclude a binding and agreed-upon moral judgment.

The Self-Help Alternative

Partly in response to the difficulties in application of medical and legal controls to these behavior patterns, a new type of control mechanism has emerged in the years since World War II that at least partially overcomes some of the problems. This control mechanism is the self-help group (Caplan and Killea 1976). Typically, these are voluntary associations with a membership consisting entirely of people who have or have had a specific personal or social problem (Gartner and Reissman 1977). They typically have the twin goals of (1) mutual support and encouragement for overcoming their problem in the proper manner and (2) finding and helping others with the same problem (Katz and Bender 1976). Some of the better known groups that deal with the behaviors we have been discussing are Alcoholics Anonymous, Synanon, Narcotics Anonymous, Gamblers Anonymous, Overeaters Anonymous, and TOPS.

Most of these groups are derivative of the Alcoholics Anonymous model (Bassin 1977). That model in turn seems to derive from the temperance movement of the last century, based on mass meetings at which forbearance from drunkenness was pledged in the fashion of traditional revival meetings with their focus on repentance and salvation from sin (Blumberg 1977).

The self-image promoted in these groups is that the members, either because of their past experience with the troublesome behavior or because of basic underlying difficulties, are fundamentally different from other people in that they are especially susceptible to the problem that is the group's focus. The identification of self with the problem is fundamental, hence (for instance) the self-introduction of all members of AA as "My name is _____ and I'm an alcoholic." Backsliding is the most feared form of deviance, and group members are expected to help one another on a daily basis by continuous encouragement in the battle against their habit (Blumberg 1977).

Whatever the problems with self-help groups, they have certain advantages over both the criminal law and the helping professions as mechanisms of control. The biggest advantage derives from members being taught that they are not responsible for their status, but they are responsible for their actions—which neatly finesses several of the ambiguities discussed earlier. While the member's unsought status as an alcoholic, heroin addict, or other abuser is acknowledged and responsibility for past wrongdoings thus mitigated, the individual thereby acquires a special responsibility to refrain from the behavior in the future. The member's obligation to refrain is enhanced, rather than mitigated, by the doctrine of special status. Moreover, because of the acknowledgment of extraordinary difficulty in refraining from the troublesome behavior, members in good standing have a basis to claim greater moral courage than the average person. By refraining in the face of extraordinary temptation, the member can achieve enhanced moral status because of his or her deviant nature.

A second advantage of self-help groups is that they provide members with a new primary-group affiliation. Substance abuse and destructive habitual behaviors often occur with the intimate support and involvement of others, and so gamblers or addicts who decide to quit or even overeaters who decide to go on a diet may find themselves cut out of participation in activities essential to their respective primary support groups (Hunter and Kilstrom 1979). An advantage of self-help groups as a mechanism of control is that they provide a new support system, which helps minimize the degree to which loneliness supplements other pressures to return to the troublesome behavior.

A final interesting feature of self-help groups that have recently emerged is that they are structurally similar to each other. Strong congruences are present in the relationships between group members, the role of higher status members, the format of meetings, the enforcement of rules, and so on, although markedly different motives and ideologies have given birth to the various groups. Some were organized initially as religious efforts, while others have always been thoroughly secular; some have been formed as extensions of the traditional helping professions, while others are profit-making organizations. Despite these and other differences, all of these groups have developed essentially the same structural approach to the problem of control and identity transformation (Marx and Lidz 1981).

Etiology

Given the normative and control ambiguities common to the various forms of substance abuse and habitual behavior, it is worthwhile to look at the extent to which they may contribute to a commom etiology (origin and course of development) of the behavior. Since all of the behavior patterns in question imply not just the occurrence of an act but, rather, a repetitious pattern of behavior, and since each individual act might well be acceptable or tolerable if it were not repeated inappropriately, etiology must be viewed as a process rather than an event. This process begins with the first enactment of prescribed or acceptable behavior by a "normal" person and ends with a chronic enactment of proscribed behavior by a person with a soiled identity. This transition from acceptable to unacceptable performances is well illustrated by alcohol abuse. Clearly the occasional consumption of alcoholic beverages is culturally defined as pleasurable and an experience that many adults will voluntarily seek. Consuming alcohol is an integral element in many adult occupational, recreational, and even religious situations, so learning how to drink is an extremely common aspect of socialization in America today (Strauss 1976; Barnes 1981). Likewise, gambling begins with behaviors indistinguishable from recreation: children matching pennies, "gentlemen's bets" with no money involved, setting a price for the winner of a competition, playing poker with chips instead of "real money," and speculating in the stock market (Zola 1963).

Even for those categories of abusive behavior where the proscription appears to be unconditional, such as the absolute taboo against using heroin, covert ambiguities may inhabit the larger moral schema in which the particular proscription is embedded. In contemporary America, for instance, the moral status of heroin is part of a larger moral schema that also includes marijuana, barbiturates, amphetamines, and various other "street drugs" (Lidz and Walker 1980: chap. 2). The partial or conditional acceptance achieved by those other drugs in the last several decades may have undermined the authority of the heroin taboo. Research conducted by the authors (Gould et al. 1974; Lidz and Walker 1980) suggests that ambiguity in the moral status of heroin may have been increased during the heroin crisis (ca. 1971) by too broad attacks on all "drug abuse" by socialization and social control agencies. By not differentiating between heroin and other street drugs these agencies were able to use the moral abhorrence of heroin to heighten the condemnation of marijuana and other street drugs, but the backlash was that as the other illicit drugs gained acceptance, consensus on the heroin taboo waned.

The proscriptions against abusive patterns of behavior such as compulsive gambling and overeating are perfectly clear when an advanced, fully developed pattern is encountered, but at earlier stages in the adoption of the behavior its performance is likely to be met with acceptance and reciprocity. If later instances of the same type of behavior are to be judged deviant (by either the performer or associates), a reversal or reinterpretation of the initial definition must be accomplished. But as time passes and the behavior gradually becomes part of the customary routine of the participants' lives, its reinterpretation as deviant behavior becomes increasingly difficult (Lesieur 1979). Moreover, while the negative ramifications of the behavior may be apparent to an outside observer, it may be difficult for the participants to take a detached view of activities that had their origins in approval and reciprocity. The ambiguity of the definition of these behavior patterns is such that an individual or even a group may become quite committed to one of them before being exposed to a negative evaluation.

Several other common elements in the etiology of abusive behavior patterns also derive from normative ambiguity. Each form of behavior requires participation in a support or delivery system that is often commercialized (Zola 1963; Kaplan 1979). The activities are not spontaneous outbursts of isolated individuals but, rather, are inextricably embedded in a supporting web of continuing personal and impersonal social relations. These support systems are not necessarily clandestine, subterranean networks; indeed they may be as legitimate as a fraternal organization, country club, workplace, or corner drugstore (although in drug abuse and gambling, subterranean support systems may be involved as well) (Kaplan 1979). When a person assumes a role in one of these networks, it may not be seen as a cause for alarm. In fact, given that the performer generally serves as a customer (broadly construed) in these systems, his participation is generally warmly encouraged by other participants who have a "stake" in the operation of the system. Any sense that the participants in the support system are not doing the individual a favor will also be at least partly neutralized by the moral ambiguity of the behavior. So, for instance, the parents who overfeed a child can excuse it as "So? She likes to eat," or "Maybe he has a hormone imbalance," or "She's not fat, she's just chubby." Given the core legitimacy of the activity in question (having a snack, taking a cigarette break with coworkers, or accepting the offer of some diet pills from a relative), observable performance of the activity does not connote deviance. Indeed, most of the coperformers in these initial stages will stay within the limits of propriety and never have their behavior labeled troublesome. It is only in retrospect, after an abuser's behavior has been morally redefined, that the support system becomes morally questionable.

A final characteristic of the process of becoming involved in these behavior patterns is that performance of the activity comes to be ritualized and of considerable importance to the solidarity of primary groups. In their most benign form, most of these activities are defined as forms of relaxation and occasions for enjoyable sociability. The performance of these activities (in their benign form) is usually defined as "taking a break" from a pattern of instrumental activities. So for the individual who is experimenting with the activity, the performance is likely to be associated with strong feelings of group identification (Langer 1976; Zola 1963; Zimmerman 1977). In the early stages of the development of the pattern of overenactment, the individual may intensify performances as a means of acquiring prestige in the primary group. At later stages, efforts at reducing (or eliminating) performance of the behavior may very well be complicated by a fear of loss of status.

Conclusion

We have tried here to illustrate several common features in substance abuse and troublesome habitual behavior by decoding the cultural context in which they are defined in contemporary America. We believe that the normative or moral ambiguities that attach to these forms of deviance have consequences for (1) the effectiveness with which our traditional systems of social control respond to these problems, (2) the mechanisms of social control that have recently emerged in response to them, and (3) the etiological sequences that lead to them.

Superficially it may appear that the only thing these behaviors share is that they are often loosely referred to as "addicting." Actually, this usage marks a particular place in our culture: patterns of behavior that are troublesome because they violate important values embodied in self-control. However, abuse behaviors have been ambiguously defined and evaluated in American society. We have discussed this ambiguous definition under the two rubrics of moral and control ambiguity. We have suggested that these ambiguities are closely related to the persistence of these behaviors. Because of them, neither the criminal law nor the traditional helping professions have been markedly successful with abuse behaviors, but there is reason to believe that self-help groups may well produce a new institutional system of social control for them, more effective and perhaps more durable than other contemporary approaches to social control. The acceptability of collective self-help as a principal form of control for all or most patterns of substance abuse and troublesome habitual behaviors remains to be seen.

References

Anderson, Stephen C. 1980. Self-esteem of Abusive Parents: The Impact of Clinical Intervention Services. Ph.D. dissertation, University of Texas at Austin.

Barnes, Grace. 1981. Drinking among adolescents: A subcultural phenomenon or a model of adult behaviors. *Adolescence* 16(61):211-219.

Bassin, Alexander. 1977. The miracle of the TC: From birth to post-partum insanity to full recovery. Paper presented at the Second World Conference on Therapeutic Communities, Montreal, Canada.

Becker, Howard. 1963. *Outsiders.* New York: Free Press.

Blumberg, Leonard. 1977. The ideology of a therapeutic social movement: Alcoholics Anonymous. J. Stud. *Alcohol* 3(11):2122-2143.

Bybee, R.W. (ed.) 1979. Violence toward youth in families. *J. Soc. Issues* 35(2):1-173.

Caplan, G., and Killen, M. 1976. *Support Systems and Mutual Help: Multidisciplinary Explorations.* New York: Grune and Stratton.

Cicourel, Aaron. 1968. *The Social Organization of Juvenile Justice.* New York: Wiley.

Daniels, Arlene. 1970. Normal mental illness and understandable excuses: The philosophy of combat psychiatry. Am. Behav. Scient. 14(2):167-184.

Durkheim, Emile. 1933. *The Division of Labor in Society.* Glencoe, Ill.: The Free Press.

Erikson, Kai. 1966. *Wayward Puritans.* New York: Wiley.

Garfinkel, Harold. 1967. *Studies in Ethnomethodology.* Englewood Cliffs, N.J.: Prentice-Hall.

Gartner, Alan, and Reissman, Frank. 1977. *Help in the Human Services.* San Francisco: Jossey-Bass.

Glassner, Barry, and Berg, Bruce. 1980. How Jews avoid alcohol problems. Am. Soc. Rev. 450(4):647-663.

Glazer, Nathan, and Moynihan, D. Patrick. 1963. *Beyond the Melting Pot.* Cambridge, Mass.: MIT Press and Harvard University Press.

Gould, Leroy; Walker, Andrew; Crane, Lansing; and Lidz, Charles. 1974. *Connections: Notes from the Heroin World.* New Haven, Conn.: Yale University Press.

Gusfield, Joseph. 1963. *Symbolic Crusade: Status Politics and the American Temperance Movement.* Urbana, Ill.: University of Illinois Press.

Hayano, David. 1976. The professional poker player: Career identification and the problem of respectability. *Soc. Prob.* 24 (5):556-564.

Hirshberg, Beth. 1980. Who speaks for the child and what are his rights? *Law Human Behav.* 4 (3):217-236.

Hunter, R.S. and Kilstrom, N. 1979. Breaking the cycle in abusive families. *Amer. J. Psychiatry* 136 (October):1320-1322.

Kaplan, H.R. 1979. Convergence of work, sport, and gambling in America. *Ann. Am. Acad. Pol. Soc. Sci.* 445 (September):24-38.

Katz, A.H., and Bender, E. (eds.) 1976. *The Strength in Us: Self-help Groups in the Modern World.* New York: New Viewpoints.

Kitsuse, John. 1962. Societal reaction to deviant behavior. *Soc. Prob.* 9 (3):247-256.

Langer, John. 1976. Drug entrepreneurs and dealing subculture. *Soc. Prob.* 9 (3):310.

Lesieur, H. 1979. Compulsive gamblers' spiral of options and involvement. *Psychiatry* 42(February):79-87.

Lidz, Charles, and Walker, Andrew. 1977. Therapeutic control of heroin: Dedifferentiating legal and psychiatric controls. *Sociol. Inquiry* 97 (3, 4):294-321.

Lidz, Charles, and Walker, Andrew. 1980. *Heroin, Deviance and Morality.* Beverly Hills, Calif.: Sage Publications.

Lindesmith, Alfred. 1965. *The Addict and the Law.* Bloomington: University of Indiana Press.

Lynd, Robert, and Lynd, Helen. 1929. *Middletown.* New York: Harcourt and Brace.

Merton, Robert. 1957. *Social Theory and Social Structure,* rev. ed. Glencoe, Ill.: The Free Press.

Musto, David. 1973. *The American Disease: Origins of Narcotic Control.* New Haven, Conn.: Yale University Press.

Nelson, John. 1976. *Your God Is Alive and Well in Popular Culture.* New York: Westminster.

O'Connor, Joyce. 1975. Social and cultural factors influencing drinking behavior. *Irish J. Med. Sci.* (June suppl.):65-71.

Parsons, Talcott. 1951. *The Social System.* Glencoe, Ill.: The Free Press.

Parsons, Talcott. 1959. "Voting" and the equilibrium of the American political system. In E. Burdick and A. Brodbeck (eds.), *American Voting Behavior.* New York: The Free Press.

Piliavin, Irving, and Briar, Scott. 1964. Police encounters with juveniles. *Am. J. Sociol.* 70 (September):206-214.

Riesman, David, with Nathan Glazer and Reuel Denney. 1950. *The Lonely Crowd: A Study of the Changing American Character.* New Haven, Conn.: Yale University Press.

Ross, Edward. 1907. *Sin and Society.* New York: Harper & Row.

Rubington, Earl, and Weinberg, Martin (eds.) 1981. *Deviance: The Interactionist Approach,* 4th ed. New York: Macmillan.

Schur, Edwin. 1965. *Crimes without Victims.* Englewood Cliffs, N.J.: Prentice-Hall.

Schur, Edwin. 1980. *Interpreting Deviance.* New York: Harper & Row.

Skolnick, Jerome. 1966. *Justice without Trial.* New York: Wiley.

Slater, Phillip. 1976. *The Pursuit of Loneliness: American Culture at the Breaking Point,* rev. ed. Boston: Beacon Press.

Strauss, Robert. 1976. Alcoholism and Problem drinking. In R. Merton and R. Nisbet (eds.), *Contemporary Social Problems,* 4th ed. New York: Harcourt Brace Jovanovich.

Sykes, Gresham. 1958. *Society of Captives.* Princeton, N.J.: Princeton University Press.

Sykes, Gresham, and Matza, David. 1957. Techniques of neutralization: A theory of delinquency. *Am. Sociol. Rev.* 22 (December):664-670.

Szasz, Thomas. 1974. *Ceremonial Chemistry: The Ritual Persecution of Drugs, Addicts, and Pushers.* Garden City, N.Y.: Doubleday.

Tocqueville, Alexis de. 1835. *Democracy in America.* 1954 edition published by Vintage Books, New York.

White, Robert. 1964. *The Abnormal Personality,* 3rd ed. New York: Ronald Press.

Zimmerman, Don. 1977. You can't help but get stoned: Notes on the social organization of marijuana smoking. *Soc. Probl.* 25 (2):198.

Zola, Irving. 1963. Observations on gambling in a lower-class setting. *Soc. Probl.* 10 (4):353-361.

Part II
Psychological Commonalities

3 Commonalities in the Environmental Control of Behavior

John L. Falk, Peter B. Dews,
and *Charles R. Schuster*

Environmental arrangements to generate persistent behavior and guide its development along lines that are either advantageous and productive or maladaptive have extraordinary and rather unexpected power. The phenomena and situations that demonstrate this power may seem, at times, a little removed from the personal management and clinical problems. But several areas of investigation, although primarily using animals, bear crucially upon the human problems of substance abuse and habitual behavior. The continuity between animal and human biology and biopsychology has been hard-won intellectual ground. Historically, discontinuities between animal and human behavior were emphasized in order to judge activities as lowly (animal) or advanced and worthy (human). While antisocial or self-destructive activities were regarded as eruptions from man's dark, atavistic origins, such behavior is more a characteristic of human beings than of animals. It usually requires special circumstances of confinement and manipulation in laboratories, circuses, zoos, or even well-intentioned households to drive animals mad (Keehn 1979). But if animals are subjected to special histories or controlled regimens, unusual or excessive behavior can indeed be generated. Perhaps such results demonstrate the origins of extravagant, disruptive, or just plain persistent behavior in humans.

In the early 1960s it was with considerable interest that investigators discovered that animals implanted with intravenous catheters injected themselves repeatedly with drugs having abuse liability in humans (Johanson 1978). Furthermore, they failed to inject certain drugs that humans do not abuse or that they report as unpleasant (such as the major tranquilizer phenothiazines). Pressing a lever activated a syringe pump containing a drug solution. The patterns of drug intake and the toxicities produced by the different classes of abused drugs were similar to those observed in human drug abusers. For example, when continuous access to psychomotor stimulants was allowed, animals often administered these agents to themselves in cyclic patterns leading to central nervous system toxicity, including convulsions, often leading to death.

It is commonly presumed that drugs are abused because of their property of producing a pleasant or euphoric state, particularly in persons lacking other sources of satisfaction. This view locates the reason for abuse primarily in the structure of the drug molecule interacting with a susceptible individual. But the structure of the agent self-administered, while important, is not the only factor producing persistent, excessive intake. Indeed in the human situation it may be only a minor sustaining factor. Neither the quality of the substance used nor the particular psychological makeup of the user is as critical as the way in which the *consequences* of drug-taking relate to circumstances governing its availability and to the regimens controlling the entire range of commodities and services important for the person.

In general, the schedule of environmental circumstances that determines when, in what portion, and according to what behavioral requirements a crucial commodity (food, money, social interaction) is to be provided has the power to generate great behavioral persistence. A good deal of such persistent behavior is adaptive. But some of it can be counterproductive and even inimical to the health of the individual. Furthermore, it is not only the present texture of the environmental rules and constraints that governs behavior. For example, the kind of prior behavioral experience an individual has had with a powerful environmental event such as electric shock will determine what sort of effect drugs produce when such events are encountered in the drugged condition (Barrett 1977). Thus a subject's history of response to the event will determine the direction such an event exerts on behavior when a drug is introduced. Perhaps it is a truism that drugs affect individuals differently. One person might become agitated and anxious when administered amphetamine, while another might experience a burst of creative work. Experiments with animals have the definite potential of sorting out the source of such behavioral differences since both the past history and current commerce with important commodities and events can be made explicit.

In view of the ubiquity with which a host of drug classes can maintain chronic abuse in laboratory animals, clearly something rather basic and biologic about drugs explains how they promote behavior to obtain them. There is no need to appeal to some special psychopathological condition to explain continued abuse. Perhaps it is the rather widespread incidence of *controlled* drug-taking, gambling, and eating that needs to be explained rather than the loss of control. In any event, there is considerable concordance in how animals and humans classify drugs with respect to their self-injection liability (Griffiths and Balster 1979; Johanson and Balster 1978). But drugs have a variety of stimulus functions beyond those that might induce abuse. By asking the right kinds of questions about the behavior of animals we can see how they sort these additional stimulus functions into classes, much as we might ask humans to give verbal reports about what the drug effects "feel like." Here again, animals classify drugs rather as people do when asked about their subjective effects.

Literally multitudes of people have experienced the effects of alcohol and other drugs, and yet the number of occasional or controlled users appear to outweigh the number of abusers by far. Furthermore, abuse is often a result of the entire situation in which a substance is taken, rather than solely a function of an insidious, cumulative, pharmacological effect. The rapid disappearance of heroin abuse in the majority of addicted Vietnam veterans returning home is a case in point (Robins, David, and Nurco 1974). It seems that simple exposure to and experience with a drug with potent abuse liability is not a sufficient condition for learning or maintaining a problematic habit.

How does it happen, then, that commodities and activities admittedly possessing some initial degree of appeal on a biological basis can become so greatly enhanced in value that sometimes the abuser's life appears to continue completely in their service? The power of environmental constraints to entrain persistent behavior is one factor. Goods and events important to the individual that are provided only intermittently after a particular behavior occurs come to command long sequences of such behavior. This persistence is, of course, usually quite adaptive. But there are curious side-effects to intermittent provisioning. The periodic nature of intermittent rewards can in itself enhance the strength of the reward. This relation is somewhat similar to Adam Smith's idea of value, in which labor is the true measure of commodity value: "The real price of everything . . . is the toil and trouble of acquiring it" (Smith 1976:133). But there is more to the enhancement of rewards than simply the work involved in attaining them intermittently. The intermittent schedule itself somehow produces this effect. Two rather striking examples of this will be described later at some length. In one, animals work to produce electric shocks known to be aversive under most circumstances. They do this for long periods of time as a function of how the shocks are introduced and the manner in which they interact with ongoing behavior (Morse and Kelleher 1970). The second reward-enhancing phenomenon is the capacity of an intermittent reward schedule to greatly strengthen ancillary behavior. For example, an intermittent food-delivery schedule can produce strong, adjunctive biting and attack behavior, or massive fluid intake, without such behavior being directly rewarded and strengthened by the food delivery. These activities occur as curious but powerful and persistent side-effects of the intermittent availability of food and other commodities (Falk 1971, 1977).

It is fair to ask whether these reward-enhancing effects of constraints in commodity availability are simply contrived laboratory situations having little application to real-life situations. By way of a brief answer, it is worth pointing out that while both nature and society usually provide rewards for us, these are available (alas) *intermittently* rather than continuously. Food must be foraged, territory defended, and mates attained under limited-resource situations fraught with difficulties. Therefore, the exaggeration of normally occurring behavior can result from fairly usual interactions with our environment.

From this brief introduction to schedule effects the reader may be able to discern where our discussion is to lead. The intermittent scheduling of commodities and activities having biological and social importance can give rise to a number of reward-enhancing phenomena that can capture behavior to yield extraordinary persistence. Without such scheduling, many of the abusive and habitual behaviors we view as problematic might remain at manageable, noninjurious levels. But a drug such as heroin usually is available only by hustling. And hustling is often a long sequence of complex behavior that is rewarded only intermittently. The sources of reward are likewise complex. Obviously, the immediately rewarding commodity being hustled is the heroin itself. But in light of the poor quality of street heroin (its considerable dilution and adulteration), with the attenuated degree of physical dependence it actually produces, there must be additional sources of reward sustaining the hustling. Indeed, in some circles considerable social prestige is inherent in attaining a "big habit" and in aspiring to be a "righteous junkie" (Sutter 1966). The schedule of availability and the hustling it often sustains can produce a prospect so desirable that the merely "hopeful junkie" (an individual with no discernible heroin dependence) will beg admission to a methadone maintenance program if only to be identified as one who "leads the life."

The findings reported here have some bearing on the question of whether commonalities exist among the factors producing abuse and excessive kinds of behavior. They have bearing on the question of whether there are, for example, common determinants of alcoholism and excessive gambling, with individual choice of one or the other behavioral excess more a matter of fortuitous social exposure to the particular substance or activity than of rigidly determined, individual conditions. Stated another way, perhaps there are reasons to believe that from relatively few constellations of generating factors many kinds of habitual and excessive behavior can flow. If such commonalities do exist it would simplify both the search for determinants (as research in one problem area would have implications for other areas) and therapeutic generality (as procedures for alleviating one sort of excess might have application to a host of behavior problems). The hope of attaining leverage in both basic research and therapeutic application motivates us to search for the common determinants of a set of vexing behavioral problems.

Stimulus Properties of Drugs

Drugs as Discriminative Stimuli

For many years pscyhotropic drugs have been characterized and classified by their subjective effects. For example, morphine and related narcotic analgesics produce a unique spectrum of subjective effects that can be reliably distinguished from other psychoactive drugs by experienced narcotics users. Even within the analgesic class, mixed agonists and antagonists (like cyclazocine) can be discriminated readily from morphine by experienced users (Haertzen 1970). Until recently, measures of drug-induced changes in subjective states were possible only with humans, because only humans can say how a drug makes them "feel." In the past two decades, however, behavioral methods have allowed animals to discriminate between various centrally acting drugs. What makes this research so exciting is the striking concordance between the classification of drugs by humans based upon subjective effects and that by animals, who categorize drugs on the basis of their discriminative stimulus properties. This led researchers to the working assumption that the component of drug action responsible for the discrimination between various classes of psychotropic drugs by animals is analogous to the component of action responsible for the differences in the subjective effects of these drugs in humans. There are practical and ethical advantages to using animals for certain types of psychotropic drug research. Perhaps of greater importance is that the use of animals allows control over the subject's past history (including prior drug experiences), which may markedly alter the behavioral response to drugs (McKearney and Barrett 1978). The development and refinement of methods that allow the use of animals for investigation of the subjective effects of drugs are therefore of extreme importance. For this reason we will describe methods developed for this purpose and present some representative findings.

In most experiments in behavioral pharmacology, animals are trained to engage in some standard performance through operant conditioning. Behavior is brought under control by allowing behavior to produce certain stimuli. Such stimulus events are called *reinforcers* when it can be demonstrated that they increase the frequency of the acts that produce them. For example, the provision of a food portion to a deprived animal increases (reinforces) the performance of a simple act such as pressing a lever when some presses are followed by food presentation. Likewise, the termination of noxious electric shock as a consequence of pressing a lever can reinforce the act of lever-pressing. Stimulus cues often are used to signal when a specific act such as lever-pressing might be followed by the reinforcing event. Stimuli uniquely associated with the potential availability of the reinforcer are called *discriminative stimuli*. The onset of a light or tone is often used as a discriminative stimulus to inform the animal that a specific bit of behavior, such as lever-pressing, may now be reinforced. In the well-trained animal (under the appropriate motivated conditions) the discriminative behavior (lever-pressing) can be evoked with great reliability and precision by turning on the discriminative stimulus. After this type of stimulus control is established, it is possible to alter systematically the discriminative stimulus (a tone's loudness or pitch, for example) and determine how this changes the frequency of occurrence of lever-pressing. To the extent that the altered discriminative stimulus continues to control the behavior, the animal is said to *generalize* from the training discriminative stimulus to the test stimulus. In more common terms, the animal is indicating how similar the two stimuli are.

The same procedure has been used to establish drugs as discriminative stimuli. Considering drugs as stimuli seems to stretch the usual definition of stimulus events since stimuli are generally conceived as operating through receptors of one of the classical sensory systems. When used in a purely functional sense, the term *drug stimulus* does not depend upon an understanding of the sensory systems involved. In the present context the stimulus event is defined as the administration of a drug by an appropriate route into the body. Lack of knowledge about the anatomical location or neurochemical mediating system in no way alters the functional relation between the drug stimulus and behavior. Lack of information about the manner in which stimulus energy is transduced into neural events is not peculiar to drug stimuli as shown by the interest in the stimulus properties of Xrays, for which the receptors and transduction mechanisms are also largely unknown (Garcia et al. 1964).

A number of problems are unique to using drugs as discriminative stimuli. For example, onset and termination of drug stimuli are only imprecisely under the control of the experimenter. Further, most drugs are long-acting, which prevents the rapid change of stimulus conditions. (For a more complete discussion of some problems peculiar to drugs as discriminative stimuli, see Schuster and Balster 1977.) Nevertheless, behavior can be brought under the discriminative control of drugs. Several examples may demonstrate the generality of these findings. In recent experiments, Holtzman and his colleagues have used a discrete-trial avoidance-escape procedure in which animals (rats and monkeys) prevent the onset of or terminate an electric shock by pressing one of two levers (Schaefer and Holtzman 1977, 1978; Shannon and Holtzman 1977). Which of the two levers was to be effective on any particular day depended upon whether the animal had been injected with a drug (morphine or cyclazocine) or a control solution (saline placebo). That is, the informative discriminative stimulus for the animal was the presence or absence of a particular drug in the body, rather than a light or tone. After a criterion performance for discrimination between a drug and placebo was reached, drug *test sessions* were periodically conducted. In a test session a dose of a drug differing from the drug used during training sessions was administered to determine whether it would generalize to the training drug or to the placebo. During any particular training session, only one of the two choice levers was effective in preventing shock. Thus the reinforcement—the shock or warning-stimulus—terminated, itself could serve as a potent cue as to which lever was correct on any day of training. To deal with this problem on test days, depression of either lever satisfied the avoidance-escape requirement. Thus, on test days which lever was effective in shock avoidance-escape could not function as a cue to signal the animal which lever to press. Only the drug served as a discriminative stimulus to guide the choice of which to press.

In one study using rats, after about 8-10 weeks of training, most animals pressed almost exclusively on the correct lever on training days when injected with either morphine or saline. Subsequently a variety of psychotropic drugs was investigated to determine which produced morphine-like discriminative effects (a rat would press on the morphine-appropriate choice lever when given a morphinelike test drug.) Chlorpromazine, d-amphetamine, ketamine, mescaline, pentobarbital, physostigmine, and scopolomine all failed to exert morphinelike discriminative stimulus control. In contrast, other opiates (methadone, for one) did exert morphinelike discriminative stimulus control.

Studies in which monkeys were trained to discriminate between cyclazocine and placebo were comparable to the one with rats. Monkeys can discriminate readily between cyclazocine and placebo. Studies in humans show that cyclazocine produces subjective effects distinctly different from morphine. In the monkey, morphine did not substitute for cyclazocine as a discriminative stimulus, indicating that, as in humans, cyclazocine and morphine produce distinctive stimulus effects. Furthermore, monkeys trained to discriminate cyclazocine did generalize to drugs such as nalorphine, levallorphan, and ketocyclazocine, all of which produce a common set of dysphoric subjective reactions in humans.

This series of experiments by Holtzman and his colleagues has demonstrated convincingly that generalization tests in animals can be used to classify drugs in the opiate class as well as those with mixed opiate agonist-antagonist activity. Further, the classification derived from the animal experiments is in striking agreement with that based upon the subjective effects of these drugs in humans.

Methods for studying the discriminative stimulus properties of hallucinogenic drugs have held forth the possibility of the development of an animal model of drug-induced hallucinations. Hallucinations are a prominent feature of schizophrenia as well as variety of drug-induced toxic psychoses. The investigation of such phenomena are clearly limited in human research both for ethical and practical reasons. Thus methods offering ways of studying such processes in animals are of considerable interest. Using procedures similar to those described in the Holtzman experiments, Winter (1974) showed that rats can be brought under the discriminative stimulus control of mescaline, a hallucinogenic drug. Furthermore, he showed that drugs such as 2,3,4 trimethoxyphenethylamine and 3,4 dimethoxyphenethylamine, which produces mescalinelike effects in humans also produce mescalinelike discriminative stimulus control in rats. As with opiates, there is a marked concordance between hallucinogenic drugs classified on the basis of their subjective effects in humans and their discriminative stimulus effects in animals.

Techniques for the study of drug stimulus control have several practical applications. First, for psychotropic drugs they may be a useful means of categorization. If a laboratory had several groups of rats, each trained using a different class of drug as a discriminative stimulus, it would be easy to determine whether a new chemical substance produced stimulus effects similar to those exerted by any of the drug classes. An alternative to using groups of animals would be to train individual animals to respond differentially depending on whether they had been pretreated with an opiate, sedative, hypnotic, stimulant, or hallucinogenic drug. Although this may sound overly elaborate, the technology for producing such sophisticated, discriminating animals is available (Donald Overton, personal communication).

These procedures for drug evaluation and categorizing may prove even more useful in clarifying certain conceptual issues. For example, it is a common assumption that drugs are abused because of the nature of the subjective effects they produce. By investigating both the discriminative effects and the self-administration of drugs (where the drug itself serves as the reinforcing stimulus) it may be possible to determine the interrelation of these two stimulus functions. This might be done by neurochemical or behavioral manipulations to investigate whether both functions are affected comparably.

A final issue relating drug discrimination to the problems of drug abuse has to do with the fact that discriminative stimuli often acquire *conditioned reinforcing* effects by being closely associated in time with the delivery of a reinforcer. In human drug-taking contexts, considerable peer group social reinforcement often accompanies the person's commerce with a drug. In this way it is possible that drugs that do not readily function as reinforcers may come to serve first as discriminative stimuli and through this role become reinforcers. This association may account for some of the unusual and idiosyncratic drugs sometimes self-administered by humans.

Drugs as Reinforcing Stimuli

In addition to serving as discriminative stimuli, some psychotropic drugs can function as reinforcing stimuli in animals and humans. As stated previously, a reinforcer is any stimulus that increases the frequency of behavior that produces it. For example, a rhesus monkey can learn to press a lever if this behavior produces the administration of certain drugs. Lever-pressing is an act whose frequency can be increased if it produces a reinforcing drug. Experiments of this type are commonly spoken of as drug self-administration experiments. Interest in demonstrating that drugs can serve as reinforcers stems mainly from the need for an animal model of human drug abuse. Such an animal model is used currently in three ways: (1) as a means of predicting a new drug's abuse potential, (2) to assess pharmacologic and environmental factors that can diminish drug-taking behavior and therefore might have therapeutic application, and (3) as a tool for investigating the basic biobehavioral mechanisms underlying drug-seeking behavior. The relevance of data derived from animal studies of drug self-administration to the human problems of drug abuse rests upon the validity of two assumptions: (1) drugs that are reinforcers for animals serve the same function in humans, and (2) behavioral and physiologic problems resulting from the self-administration of a drug are comparable in animals and humans. Over the past two decades animal studies have given strong support to the validity of these two assumptions. Since this literature has been reviewed extensively (Schuster and Thompson 1969; Schuster and Johanson 1974; Goldberg 1976; Johanson and Balster 1978), only some of the major findings will be summarized and implications for the area of substance abuse indicated.

One of the most striking findings in this area of research is the concordance between the types of drugs that serve as reinforcers in animals and those commonly abused by man. A review (Johanson and Balster 1978) of studies in which rhesus monkeys were used listed a variety of drugs serving as reinforcers: narcotic agonists (such as heroin, morphine, methadone, codeine), mixed agonist-antagonists (buprenorphine, nalbuphine, propiram), psychomotor stimulants (cocaine, amphetamines), and central nervous system depressants (alcohol, barbiturates). On the other hand, narcotic antagonists (nalorphine, naloxone), major tranquilizers (chlorpromazine, haloperidol), cholinergic agonists and antagonists (arecoline, physostigmine, scopolamine), as well as hallucinogens (LSD, mescaline, $\triangle$-9-THC) were not self-administered by the monkey. With the exception of the hallucinogens, these findings in the rhesus monkey generally predict the abuse potential of these classes of drugs in humans. Although less work has been done, similar results have been obtained in drug self-administration studies using other species of mammals—mice, rats, cats, dogs, squirrel monkeys, baboons, and chimpanzees. The assumption that the same drugs can serve as reinforcers in animals and humans appears generally valid. This biological generality questions the assumption that drug self-administration in humans necessarily indicates psychopathology (Schuster, Renault, and Blaine 1979). It would thus seem reasonable to use animal drug self-administration studies to screen new drugs for their abuse potential.

The second use of an animal model for drug abuse has to do with investigations of variables affecting the animals' drug-seeking behavior. An illustration of this type of investigation is provided by Bonese and colleagues who demonstrated that monkeys can be immunized against the reinforcing actions of heroin (Bonese et al. 1974). In this study, monkeys were first trained to press a lever for intravenous heroin reinforcement. Subsequently, the animals were given immunizing injections of an antigen made by chemically combining bovine serum albumen with morphine (Wainer et al. 1973). This antigen caused the formation of antibodies that would bind heroin when it was introduced into the animal's blood. Since the heroin was bound in the blood, it could not gain access to the brain to exert its reinforcing effects. Under these circumstances the rate of level pressing declined to near zero. This study illustrates that an animal model of drug dependence can be used to evaluate a particular intervention with potential therapeutic application.

A second illustration of this use of an animal model has to do with the effects of food deprivation on drug-seeking behavior. Food deprivation increases the alcohol consumption of both mice and rats (as found in Meisch and Thompson 1973, for example). More recently, however, Carroll et al. (1979) have reported that food deprivation increases the self-administration of a variety of drugs when the drugs are self-administered either orally or intravenously. It is important that this manipulation affects the intake of a wide variety of drugs, because it rules out explanations based upon caloric factors (alcohol) or changes in drug distribution and metabolism. This fascinating finding is particularly relevant to the issue of commonalities between various types of substance abuse. When it can be shown that the same manipulations have common effects on behavior maintained by different classes of reinforcers (food and several kinds of drugs), it suggests a heretofore unrecognized relation.

The third use of an animal model of drug abuse is based on the fact that the use of animals allows manipulations that would be impossible for ethical or practical reasons in humans. Investigating the basic biobehavioral mechanisms underlying drug dependence, often entails surgical interventions, neurochemical measures, and behavioral manipulations that could not be carried out using human beings. Such procedures would be necessary to determine the role of a particular neurotransmitter in the reinforcing effects of a drug, say, or to discover how the environment might affect a drug's capacity to serve as a reinforcer. One study illustrating this use of an animal model is concerned with accounting for some perplexing clinical observations. Discontinuing the chronic morphine treatment of a dependent person precipitates withdrawal signs and symptoms that begin a few hours after the last dose of morphine, reach a peak in 24-48 hours and gradually subside over the next few days. After long abstinence from morphine, postdependent humans report that certain components of the abstinence syn-drome recur (Wikler 1965). Wikler suggested that abstinence signs become classically conditioned to specific environmental features. This could result because withdrawal has occurred previously under particular environmental discriminative stimulus conditions. Hence, when the stimulus conditions recur, even though the person has remained drug-free for a long time, they could trigger the recurrence of the morphine withdrawal syndrome. Wikler hypothesized that the conditioned abstinence changes could motivate relapses to drug-taking. Goldberg and Schuster (1967, 1970) and Goldberg, Woods, and Schuster (1969) demonstrated, using rhesus monkeys physically depen-dent upon morphine, that environmental stimuli associated with nalorphine-induced abstinence can become conditioned stimuli, capable of eliciting a variety of component responses of the abstinence syndrome. These condi-tioned responses included emesis, salivation, and increased heart rate as well as disruption of food-maintained behavior. These conditioned changes were remarkably resistant to extinction. Further, they could be elicited in full strength after one to four months of complete morphine abstinence. Finally, conditioned stimuli associated with nalorphine-induced abstinence produced large increases in the rate of morphine self-administration by rhesus monkeys. More recently, conditioned opiate withdrawal signs have been ex-perimentally demonstrated in human beings (O'Brien 1975; O'Brien et al. 1977). These studies strongly support theories relating conditioned abstinence phenomena to the problem of relapse to drug use.

Animal drug self-administration procedures, then, can generate a valid and reliable animal model of human drug dependence. Further, this model can be used in a variety of ways to study the biobehavioral basis of drug dependence.

Investigating the abuse potential of drugs in humans and in animals generally has been accomplished by two rather different approaches. Animal studies employ drug self-administration procedures, whereas in human ex-periments a test drug is administered by the experimenter and its subjective effects are compared to those produced by known drugs of abuse (like heroin, amphetamine, or barbiturates). In the human experiment, certain subjective effects have been labeled "euphoria"; these changes are believed to be especially predictive of a drug's abuse potential. In recent years investigators have combined these two approaches by conducting experiments in which humans are allowed to self-administer drugs and subjective effects are measured concurrently. This combination permits a direct examination of the concordance between subjective changes produced by a drug and its actual self-administration under a variety of environmental conditions. In addition, it allows investigation of the relation between subject variable (personality in-ventory items, type and extent of psychopathology, prior drug use) and drug self-administration along with its subjective effects.

The setting for most of this research has been the hospital ward. In 1965 Mello and Mendelson published the first of a series of studies involving free-choice ethanol administration by alcoholics in a controlled ward environment. This early work has been summarized by Mello (1972). Subsequently, research has been reported on the self-administration of marijuana (Miles et al. 1974; Angle and Parwatikar 1973), sedatives (Griffiths, Bigelow, and Liebson 1976b; Pickens et al. 1977) and nicotine (Mello and Mendelson 1971; Griffiths, Bigelow, and Liebson 1976a).

In contrast, some studies have allowed experimental subjects to self-administer psychotropic drugs in the laboratory but return to their normal environment after drug ingestion. Using this approach, codeine, methadone, and pentazocine have been studied in heroin addicts (Schuster 1975). More recently, Johanson and her colleagues have investigated the self-administer of d-amphetamine (Johanson and Uhlenhuth 1978, 1980a, 1981a), diazepam (Johanson and Uhlenhuth 1980b), fenfluramine (Johanson and Uhlenhuth 1981b), and diethylpropion (Johanson and Uhlenhuth 1978). The results of these studies are of interest since they demonstrate that the subjective effects produced by a drug do not necessarily predict whether the drug actually will be self-administered. It remains for further research to determine the conditions under which subjective effects are the basis of the reinforcing effects of the drug.

Schedules Imposed by the Environment as a Source of Behavioral Persistence

Substance Abuse and Excessive Behavior: The Puzzle of Their Persistence

An outstanding feature of substance abuse and excessive behavior is the apparent irrationality of these activities. The activities seem to produce more harm than benefit for the individual. How could creatures have evolved such powerful, wasteful, and even self-destructive propensities? Not only are the activities apparently irrational, but also an apparent disparity exists between the immediate consequences of the behavior and its strength. The rush of an intravenous injection is transient, and with street-quality heroin, rarely dramatic. Yet, the drug somehow can support day-long hustling and determine a whole subculture. Is it the momentary thrill of wagering that sustains the habitual "loser" gambler, or the transient taste of food that leads to the bulemic person's eating binges, with their consequent abdominal pain and vomiting? The traditional account given for apparently small satisfactions maintaining large amounts of self-destructive activity has been to assume that some powerful motivation must exist. Faced with the discrepancy between the harmful effects of a dedication to heroin and the strength of the habit, it was assumed that heroin must be producing a state of ecstasy in the vulnerable victim of such intensity that it compels the continuation of the habit. Similarly, powerful subconscious mechanisms are posited for overeating and for gambling. No independent evidence exists for these various motivations; they are intended merely to explain the phenomena for which they were invented. Their tautological nature prevents them from being of either practical or heuristic value.

Another characteristic of excessive behavior is that, although it can be extremely strong, consistent in pattern, and can persist for years and years (as in the smoker who consumes 50 cigarettes a day for decades), it can, nevertheless, go away completely. Many heavy smokers have quit altogether and so have many heavy drinkers. Such drastic changes in a habit have been regarded as exceptional and difficult to achieve. That is because such changes are most likely to occur when there are substantial and at least temporarily immutable changes in key features of the environment. They are very difficult to achieve under ordinary circumstances. The large experiment performed incidentally by the Vietnam War is particularly valuable in this respect. Large numbers of men with substantial usage of heroin while in the army in Vietnam when heroin was cheap and easy to come by were repatriated and discharged into the entirely different environment of civilian United States. The number continuing heroin use back in the states fell to a small fraction of its level in Vietnam (Robins, David, and Nurco 1974). Evidently environmental factors can be more important than enduring personality characteristics in determining whether an individual will abuse an agent. Undoubtedly individuals differ in susceptibility, but there is nothing like a dichotomy between abusers and nonabusers. The great majority of people will either abuse or not, depending on circumstances.

An extraordinary variety of substances are abused: substances that tend to put you to sleep like alcohol and barbiturates; substances that tend to keep you awake like cocaine and amphetamines; substances that do neither in particular, like nicotine. Food and drink are abused by being taken in too large quantities. Indeed, the problem becomes one of identifying substances that are not abused, and when we find one, such as chlorpromazine, we study it to see what special properties it has that prevent it from being abused. It strains credibility to believe that all substances abused have a unique, common biological property or even a few specific properties that lead them to be abused. It seems more likely that the genesis of abuse is something other than a specific effect of the agent. Our attention is drawn to features other than those inherent in the specific drug effects themselves, or in the smells and tastes of foods, or in the thrill of gambling. It appears, then, that the mechanisms generating excessive behavior are not predominantly derived from either the compelling nature of an agent or the peculiar pliancy of the victim but, rather, from the interactions among the individual, the agent, and the environment context.

Over the last thirty years investigations have been conducted on determinants of behavioral activities of a variety of laboratory animals, from mice to monkeys. The studies have uncovered features of behavioral activities that have interesting similarities to the characteristics of abusive and excessive activities just described. Perhaps the same processes being studied in the laboratory are at work in maintaining excessive behavior in society. Recognizing the similarities is one thing, but proving an identity of mechanism is, not surprisingly, hard to achieve. The purpose of this section and the next is to describe enough of the discoveries on how persistent and excessive behavior is instituted in the laboratory for the reader to see the similarities between these and the human social and clinical problems we see in substance abuse. Although little has been proven about the genesis of the latter as yet, we hope to convince the reader of the conceptual advantage of the new formulations and the lines along which they could guide research for further elucidations.

On the Generation of Persistence

When an animal is deprived of food for a time and is placed in a chamber in which a small portion of food is delivered whenever a simple activity occurs, for example, when a lever is pressed, it is not surprising that the acvitity starts to occur repeatedly, a relation called *reinforcement*, described earlier. However, rather unexpected patterns of presses result when lever-presses are only intermittently reinforced by food delivery. In general, lever-pressing is much more stable and persistent when it is reinforced intermittently. The particular pattern of behavioral persistence is a function of the rules governing when a lever-press (or other simple activity) will deliver a food portion (Ferster and Skinner 1957). These rules or conditions for the intermittent delivery of reinforcing stimuli (food in the examples so far) are referred to as "schedules of reinforcement." If the reader will bear with us for a moment, we will describe a few of these schedules of reinforcement and the resulting patterns of persistence they produce. Unusual and long-maintained persistence is, after all, one of the hallmarks of excessive behavior and hence claims our interest.

One simple kind of intermittency is to present a reinforcing stimulus when a particular behavior, such as a lever-press, has occurred x times. Such a schedule is called a fixed-ratio schedule, or FRx schedule. With a range of values of x, repeated exposure to FRx produces very rapid rates of pressing, as high rates as have been achieved by any schedule. A monkey under FR50 with a suitable level may register rates of two or three or more per second, so that the fifty presses are made in 15 seconds or even less. Now it is obvious that the higher the rate, the sooner the reinforcing stimuli will occur. Curiously, it is hard to prove that it is this feature of the schedule that is responsible for the high rates. Indeed, with higher values of x, the subject is more likely to pause after the reinforcement, although the pause is in no way required by the schedule. The pause increases the time between reinforcements, yet the subject does pause, then presses at a high rate, which calls into question the assumption that the high rate occurs because interreinforcement time is minimized. Thus, even with this simple schedule, patterns of pressing emerge that would not have been predicted solely from consideration of the schedule requirement. The patterns of lever-pressing in time engendered by schedules characteristically show features that are not directly demanded by the requirement. This is one aspect of schedule-controlled behavior that makes its study so fascinating.

Another simple schedule uses time to determine when a particular behavior will be followed by a reinforcing stimulus, for example, the first lever-press after x seconds have elapsed. Such a schedule is called a fixed-interval schedule or FI x-second schedule. Over a very wide range of values of x, from 50 or 60 up to many thousands, a characteristic pattern of lever-pressing in time emerges after repeated exposures. At the beinning of the x-second interval there is little or no pressing, then pressing starts and increases in frequency until a substantial rate is achieved, which is sustained until the x seconds have elapsed and the reinforcing stimulus has occurred, whereupon the whole cycle starts again. The schedule produces persistent behavior, though the pattern is even more different from what is specifically required by the schedule (a single press after x seconds) than is the pattern under FRx.

A final simple schedule that will be mentioned briefly here substitutes the constant value x of FIx by an interval that varies from cycle to cycle. Such a schedule is called variable-interval schedule, or VI x-second schedule, where x seconds is now the average time that must elapse. With suitable values of x and suitable variability of x, VI x seconds produces a relatively constant rate, a steady, persistent repetition of the recorded behavior; again *persistent* behavior.

These schedules, other simple schedules, and much more complex concatenations of schedule arrangements can maintain persistent behavior in subjects stably for months on end. At this point it is perhaps clear that *the persistence of behavior patterns engendered by schedules of reinforcement is more a function of the rules governing the conditions under which a reinforcing stimulus will be delivered than of the amount of inherent, reinforcing property of the commodity itself.* The persistence of behavior, while often directed toward biologically relevant commodities and activities, is nevertheless curious because the persistence is much greater than might be expected considering the often lean consequences that sustain schedule performance. Not only do small food or drug portions engender remarkable persistence, but stimuli having no obvious utility or discernable hedonic consequences also can sustain persistent behavior leading to their delivery.

Persistent and excessive behavior usually is not just a matter of the repetition of a simple, unitary act but typically involves long chains of complex behavior that lead to consequenes often considered trivial or even negative. In fact, a usual defining characteristic of excessive behavior is that a disproportion exists between the amount of complex, directed behavior and the small or even nonutilitarian reward value of its consequences, not to mention the often overtly self-destructive results.

The objective study of persistent and excessive behavior is not limited to the counting of simple units such as lever-pressing. Simple schedules, such as the ratio and interval schedules just described, can be used as components to build more complex schedules. For example, behavior can be maintained under schedules in which a reinforcing stimulus is delivered only after the completion of several simple-schedule components. These complex schedules (called *second-order schedules*) usually present a brief stimulus (such as a flash of light or a tone) when the subject completes each of the simple, component schedules. The brief stimulus also is presented when the reinforcing stimulus is presented, so that it has become associated with reward delivery. Second-order schedules are of interest because long chains of behavior frequently are involved in problematic and persistent behavior such as substance abuse and gambling. There is reason to believe that stimuli that have been associated with drug-taking, or drug-withdrawal, for example, come to elicit drug self-administration or the abstinence syndrome, respectively. The power of stimuli associated with drug-taking to maintain persistent drug-directed behavior that finally leads to delivery of the drug illustrates how schedules of environmental events are intimately involved in sustaining substance abuse. In an experiment by Goldberg, Kelleher, and Morse (1975) on rhesus monkeys, a red light appeared for 2 seconds each time 10 lever-presses were completed (FR10) during one-hour sessions. The first FR10 completed after one hour had elapsed resulted in the red light and an opportunity for the subject to extend its arm through an opening in the cage and receive an intramuscular injection of cocaine by a technician. In other words, reinforcement with cocaine was programmed on an FIx schedule of 60 minutes; the FIx differs from the simpler FIx schedules previously described in that an FR10 response requirement replaced the single lever-press of the earlier example. Schedules like this composed of smaller schedule requirements instead of single responses are called "second order." In the present example, the ten lever-presses that turned on the red light each displayed the typical FRx pattern described before. Also, the frequency of the FRxs increased toward the end of the hour. This increase in turn is a typical FI*x* schedule pattern, only in this complex case a behavioral unit is a complete FR*x* instead of a simple lever-press. Thus, the entire complex, second-order schedule performance was maintained throughout the hour only by the repeated delivery of a brief, environmental stimulus (red light) upon the completion of each behavioral unit. These red-light stimuli, in turn, had attained the power to sustain persistent, behavioral units throughout the hour by becoming associated with drug delivery at the end of the daily sessions. Complex schedules such as this reveal how environmental events acquire the power to sustain the persistent behavior necessary for the development and maintenance of drug taking and all its preceding activities and rituals.

The Normal Sources of Inappropriately Persistent Behavior: Incorporating Past Experience

Perhaps the most puzzling aspect of many kinds of excessive behavior is how harmful consequences of the activities can have so little deterrent power. Why does a person persist in gambling or drinking too much in the face of the mounting problems often produced by these activities? Is it due to a peculiarly human streak of masochism? Or is it due to a personality trait that makes some people, but only some people, susceptible to loss of control? Perhaps neither of these supposed factors is mainly to blame. The thesis presented here is that current circumstances and past history work through perfectly normal factors influencing drug-related conduct. Especially important are the factors relating to the scheduling of consequences for behavioral activities. The thesis would be strengthened greatly, however, if it could be shown that animals self-inflict biologically useless and even noxious stimuli repeatedly and persistently by reason of past scheduling and current circumstances. As a matter of fact, it is possible to do that. An understanding of how this comes about is best developed by a more or less chronological narrative. Some liberties have been taken with exact chronology in favor of a logical development, but all experiments mentioned have really been performed.

Two lines of research converged to make the culminating series of experiments conceptually possible. In the late 1930s, a new approach to experimental "anxiety" was proposed. It was argued that the most important aspect of anxiety was the suppression of normal behavioral activities. A series of experiments was devised. Rats pressed a lever under a FI 4-minute schedule of food delivery for one hour each day. After considerable exposure to this schedule, when consistent daily behavior had been obtained, an additional aspect was added to the situation. In the middle of the session a tone was sounded for 5 minutes and at the end of the tone an electric shock was delivered to the feet of the animal through the grid on which it stood. After a number of presentations of tone concluded by shock, the rat all but ceased pressing during the tone period, only to resume when the shock had been delivered. Normal pressing for food, then, was suppressed during the tone.

Some years later, investigators found that if a rat were to receive an electric shock at regular intervals, but each press of a lever would postpone the delivery of the next shock by some period, for example, 20 or 30 seconds, then the rat would press the lever at a rate such that shocks were received only infrequently. What happens when a tone concluded by an electric shock is superimposed on responding maintained by this postponing schedule? Surprisingly, the lever-pressing rate went up instead of down during the tone period. In further experiments, the delivery of shock was discontinued except for the shock at the end of the tone. Under this condition, pressing ceased *except* during the tone (Sidman et al. 1957). That is, it occurred only during a distinctive stimulus that preceded a shock. Presses were entirely without effect on the occurrences of shock or anything else.

Let us now consider an independent line of experiments. During the 1950s, it had been shown that the effects of a drug were greatly influenced by the rate of the recorded behavior on which the drug effect was superimposed, and the rate was, of course, dependent on the schedule of reinforcement. The particular patterns of pressing produced by different schedules are differentially sensitive to the effects of drugs. As described previously, FI schedules give rise to a smoothly increasing rate of pressing throughout each cycle. The question arose whether various drugs altering this cyclic waxing and waning of pressing rate would have the same effect if superimposed on an identical but reversed pattern of pressing in time. Such a pattern would show a maximum rate of pressing at the beginning of each cycle and a slowdown to essentially no pressing at the end of each cycle. To try to produce such a pattern, a squirrel monkey was trained under a VI schedule for food. Recall that such a schedule characteristically engenders a steady, sustained pressing rate. On this sustained pressing was superimposed the additional feature that at the end of 10 minutes, for a 1-minute period, every press was followed by a noxious electric shock to the tail. The investigators anticipated that pressing would start in each cycle at the usual rate under VI and then slow down and cease as the time approached when a press would produce a shock. Nothing of the kind happened. On the contrary, the frequency of pressing during the 10-minute period actually started to *accelerate*, so that the monkey pressed faster and faster as the time approached when a press would produce a shock. Monkeys were pressing several times faster just before a press produced a shock than at any time under the earlier program when there were no shocks at all. As soon as the first shock was delivered, however, pressing immediately ceased until the end of the 1-minute period during which each press would be shocked. Then pressing began again at the usual VI rate. Deliveries of food were then discontinued. The animals continued to press during each 10-minute period, but there started to be a pause at the beginning and then an acceleration of pressing through the rest of the period (typical of behavior usually seen under FI schedules) until a shock was delivered. They then stopped pressing for the rest of the 1-minute period when additional shocks would have been given, only to start again and increase the rate through the next 10-minute period. Thus, we have an animal pressing repeatedly, showing a definite pattern of rates, when the only consequence of pressing was the occasional delivery of a severe electric shock. That the electric shock had not been magically transformed into a different type of stimulus, a positive stimulus, is shown by the shock being as effective as ever in suppressing lever-pressing during the 1-minute period following the initial shock.

The phenomenon of animals continuing to press when the only consequence is a severe electric shock is not transient. One of the monkeys in the original experiment was exposed to some 170 sessions over a period approaching a year, pressing an average of over 4,000 times per session, or a total of some 700,000 presses, maintained only by 1,900 shocks of 12.6 milliamperes. Shock-producing presses were reduced when shock was reduced in intensity and disappeared when shock was removed, only to return when shock was reinstated at the original intensity.

Two points deserve emphasis. One is that these monkeys had never pressed a lever to postpone a shock. It is not, therefore, possible to attribute the maintenance of pressing by shocks to spurious shock-postponement behavior as there was no history of postponement. Second, in the later phases of these experiments the monkeys were fully fed, so that responding could not have been maintained by food deprivation.

Shock-consequence patterns of lever-pressing have been generated by quite different scheduling procedures as well.

1. On a shock postponement-maintained lever-pressing schedule, if press-produced shock is added, and then the postponement part of the schedule is removed, the result is continued pressing maintained only by the presses occasionally producing a shock.
2. Start with a response that a monkey makes spontaneously when shock is delivered. A squirrel monkey in a restraining chair with a chain attached to its collar vigorously pulls the chain when a shock is given to the tail; the chain-pulling may be called a spontaneous response to the shock in that it has not been trained or otherwise regularly related to the experimental conditions; however, this response occurs regularly to shock. Next, chain-pulling is made to *produce* the shock on an FI schedule. Initially, an inevitable shock is delivered if one is not self-

administered within 1 minute of the end of the fixed interval, but this provision can later be removed so that shocks are delivered only as a result of pulling. Again, patterns typical of FI schedules emerge (Morse et al. 1967). It is important to note that in these naive monkeys chain-pulling had never resulted in either shock-postponement or food delivery. These findings have been confirmed repeatedly by several investigators with other schedules and other species (see Byrd 1969; McKearney 1968; Malagodi et al. 1978). So animals will indeed self-inflict noxious stimuli repeatedly, solely as a consequence of how they are introduced to these stimuli and the current schedule of stimulus availability.

What can addicts tell us about their habit? If you ask the addict, gambler, or overeater why he does it you can get a variety of answers. But why should people be able to intuit causes of their behavior? We do not expect causal discernment with respect to cancer or TB, though given a chance, many victims will relate a breast cancer to trauma, or TB to foul air; we give such intuited reasons little credence. Why then are we so furious with alcoholics for not telling us truly why they go on drinking? If pushed, they will give us reasons. It is easiest to get "satisfactory" reasons if you put words into people's mouths. For example, it has been suggested that individuals start taking and continue taking heroin because each does causes a state of euphoria. Euphoria is that hypothetical state of transient ecstasy of such intensity as to account rationally for the individual taking the drug despite the pain and trouble it causes. The postulation of euphoria came from the insistence for some rational account of abuse in familiar terms. In terms of a hedonic equation, drug abuse costs so much that there must be pleasure commensurate to overcome the deterrents and to maintain abuse. This supposed pleasure was postulated to account for drug abuse. Persistent shock self-administration in animals removes the necessity for postulating a hedonic component to overcome clearly noxious consequences. The shocks themselves were demonstrably aversive to these animals during the experimental session: When allowed access to another lever that turned off the shock self-administration schedule for 1-minute periods under an FI 3-minute schedule, monkeys worked on this lever to repeatedly turn off the schedule of self-administration of shock that was programmed on the other lever. Nevertheless, they simultaneously worked on the lever that delivered shocks under a VI 3-minute schedule (Barrett and Spealman 1978).

Other evidence questions the hedonic explanation of excessive behavior. For example, it is well known that animals will press a lever that produces electrical stimulation of various brain sites. But if a temporal pattern of these self-stimulations is played back into the electrode of the very animal that had produced the pattern, the animal will now press a lever to *escape* from the stimulation (Steiner et al. 1969). What is reinforcing on one occasion or within one context is not necessarily so given even slightly different circumstances. Perhaps even more germane to our present concerns is evidence that drug doses that are self-administered by animals will also be avoided by the same animals when different conditions are arranged. For example, rats were allowed to self-administer d-amphetamine intravenously. They were then exposed to a conditioned aversion-learning arrangement. In this procedure they were allowed to drink a saccharin solution and then switched over to intravenous self-administration of apomorphine, rather than d-amphetamine, during their usual self-administration session, which followed saccharin drinking. It had been shown in previous experiments that apomorphine maintains intravenous self-administration behavior in the rat. When the rats were allowed to drink saccharin solution the next day, however, their intake was attenuated, demonstrating that the self-administered apomorphine produced some conditioned aversion (Wise et al. 1976). The paradox then is: How can a self-administered drug be both a reinforcing stimulus and an aversive stimulus for the same animal at the same time? The same unsettling dualities revealed by the shock self-administration and the brain self-stimulation research must now be extended to drug self-administration.

It is becoming clear that the events that sustain behavior because they function as reinforcing stimuli are far more complex than was apparent only a few years ago. Research on shock self-administration demonstrates unequivocally that noxious stimuli can come to take on some of the properties of traditional reinforcing stimuli with appropriate sequences of experience. Of course, many commodities and activities require no special sequencing of experience to function as reinforcing stimuli; but they too contain aversive components that are demonstrable (compare with Wise et al. 1976; Spealman 1979). An experiment by Spealman (1979) is particularly illuminating in this regard. By pressing a lever, squirrel monkeys self-administered intravenous doses of cocaine under a VI 3-minute schedule of reinforcement. At the same time, animals could press a second lever that was programmed on an FI 3-minute schedule to terminate the schedule of cocaine availability for 1-minute periods. Typical schedule-controlled pressing was maintained simultaneously by the VI schedule of cocaine self-injections and by the FI schedule of termination of the cocaine schedule. This unexpected duality in the motivational aspect of cocaine is all the more impressive when it is known that monkeys consistently chose intravenous cocaine in preference to food in a continuous choice situation, even after several days of reduced food intake (Aigner and Balster 1978). Nevertheless, some part of substance abuse and other persistent and seemingly self-destructive acts may, like shock, require a degree of special experiential sequencing in order to function as more and more powerful reinforcers important within the individual's entire style of life. We need to know how the noxious components become overwhelmed so that they no longer attenuate the person's commerce with negative substances and activities. Further, we need to know how the potential aversive aspects of these powerful reinforcement situations can be made manifest to yield therapeutic effects. For example, in Spealman's (1979) experiment, the availability of a suitable, alternative behavior resulted in periods of abstinence from cocaine, a result that could point the way toward effective techniques in the self-management of drug-taking.

Adjunctive Behavior

At the beginning of the 1960s studies on schedule-induced, or adjunctive, behavior were initiated. It is perhaps more accurate to say that the first study just happened. Normal laboratory rats were exposed daily for about three hours to a feeding schedule during which they earned the major portion of their ration by pressing a lever in special, individual chambers (Falk 1961). A small (45-milligram) food pellet was delivered for a lever-press at variable times averaging one pellet per minute. Technically, this is called a "variable-interval 1-minute schedule (VI 1 minute)." This schedule permits an animal to press freely on a lever at any time, but a lever-press is reinforced by the delivery of a food pellet only intermittently (from a few seconds to 2 minutes since the last press was reinforced). A lever-press then pays off intermittently and no cue informs the animal exactly when a pellet will be delivered for a press. The animals were maintained at about 80 percent of their normal, adult, free-feeding body weights. This regime produced a moderate lever-pressing rate throughout each daily session.

Water was always available to the animals, during the experimental session as well as in their home cages. Consequently, water deprivation never occurred. Yet this schedule of food delivery resulted in an extreme intake of water during each session. When animals are constrained with respect to the availability of their food supply, and their daily feeding opportunities are dispersed in time by permitting each small food pellet only after a certain interval of time has elapsed since the provision of the previous pellet, then a marked, concomitant high water intake occurs. There is no physiological reason for this excessive drinking. It is well known that many animal species often drink near and during meal times. But the drinking produced by various schedules of constrained food delivery rate is quite massive. When a food pellet was earned on the variable-interval 1-minute schedule, it was consumed rapidly and then about 0.5 milliliter water was drunk, usually prior to the resumption of further lever-pressing. This post-pellet water consumption resulted in over 90 milliliters being drunk during each session, which was almost one-half of the animals' body weight. By comparison, the 24-hour daily water intake of these rats prior to the start of the experiment when food was not rationed was about 27 ml. The exaggerated water ingestion is all the more impressive and curious in that the usual effect of food limitation in the rat is a *decrease* in water intake. Consequently, this food-schedule-induced over-drinking (polydipsia) occurred in contrast to the typical, physiological effect. Another way of measuring the excessive aspect of this polydipsic phenomenon is to give control sessions during which animals receive the same total number of food pellets all at once as a single feeding (Falk 1967). Under these conditions, animals drank about one-tenth the amount of water in 3.5 hours as they did when pellets were spread out over time by the variable-interval 1-minute schedule.

Neither traditional physiological and nutritional, nor behavioral considerations were able to give an account of the generation of this persistent polydipsia, which lasts month after month as long as the intermittent feeding conditions remain in effect (Falk 1969). A powerful behavioral phenomenon such as schedule-induced polydipsia is unlikely to be the only excessive behavior generated by schedule conditions as ubiquitous as intermittently delivered food.

Under quite similar food intermittency schedule-induced aggression or attack can occur. For example, a pigeon earning small portions of food intermittently in an experimental chamber that also contains a semirestrained pigeon shows a pattern of directed attack against it shortly after the delivery of each of the food portions (Azrin, Hutchinson, and Hake 1966). Again, as in the case of schedule-induced polydipsia, the attack level is quite excessive as measured against nonintermittent food conditions (either no food available, or the ration given as a single large portion). This aggressive behavior can take many forms. For example, squirrel monkeys will repeatedly bite a rubber hose after the intermittent delivery of each small food portion (Hutchinson et al. 1968).

It should be noted that these excessive behaviors are not reflexive; they are not automatically evoked responses to the delivery of food. Animals will perform considerable work to obtain short opportunities to drink or to attack in conjunction with these intermittent food-delivery schedules. That is, if the water or the restrained pigeon is not freely available in the situation, the animals will work repeatedly in order to attain excessive access to them (Cherek, Thompson, and Heistad 1973; Falk 1966).

Behaviors other than polydipsia and aggression also can become excessive under food intermittency conditions. Hyperactivity in animals (Levitsky and Collier 1968) and human beings (Fallon et al. 1979), consumption of nonfood materials (pica) (Villarreal 1967), escape responses (Azrin 1961), and of particular interest in the present context, drug intake (Gilbert 1978), have all been investigated.

What, precisely, are the conditions necessary to induce exaggerated behavioral adjuncts? The most important is that a well-motivated organism receive small portions of an important commodity distributed over time. If these portions are either too close together or too far apart in time, then the adjunctive behavior will not occur excessively. There is, then, an effective range of average delivery times between portions that produces excessive behavior, and longer or shorter values are less effective (Falk 1969). The schedule rules governing the delivery of a portion are much less important to the generation of excessive adjunctive behavior than the time between these deliveries. Thus, fixed or variable times between deliveries, or the type and number of behavioral acts required for delivery, while modulating adjunctive behavior somewhat, are not critical determining factors. Indeed, organisms show the behavioral excesses in the absence of any specific behavioral requirements for portion delivery.

Motivational exigency also determines the degree of behavioral excess. Within limits the greater the decrease in body weight (produced by the total amount of food allowed), the greater the adjunctive excess in polydipsia, aggression or escape (Falk 1981). But even when animals essentially are allowed to determine their own daily feeding patterns, with the only constraint being a 1-minute spacing between successive pellets, polydipsia is evident even though almost normal body weight is maintained (Petersen and Lyon 1978). The major factor, then, given a modicum of motivation, appears to be the degree of portion spacing of a valued commodity.

The generation of excessive adjunctive behaviors as a function of intermittent schedules of reinforcement occurs not only in the rat, pigeon, and squirrel monkey, but in the mouse, rhesus monkey, gerbil, chimpanzee, and human as well. Other species will undoubtedly be added to this list as research continues. Although most of the work in this area has utilized food deprivation and the spaced delivery of small food portions, the intermittent delivery of other commodities also generates adjunctive excesses. Schedule-induced activity in rats has been produced by intermittent access to water; conversely, overdrinking has been produced by scheduling running-wheel access. In humans, hyperactivity, polydipsia, and smoking have been induced by the scheduled presentation of monetary rewards, game playing, or problem-solving (Clarke et al. 1977; Fallon, Allen, and Butler 1979; Muller, Crow, and Cheney 1979; Wallace et al. 1975; Wallace and Singer 1976). Thus adjunctive behavior reveals a considerable degree of generality both in the kinds of commodities or behavior sequences whose intermittency constitutes a generator condition and in the variety of resulting adjunctive activities.

The controlled, intermittent access to important or critical commodities and activities induces persistent and excessive adjunctive behavior. These exaggerated activities are interesting from both theoretical and practical perspectives in that they are *not* generated by the contingent provision of reinforcers for engaging in the activities as is the case with traditional contingent reinforcement of a particular behavior. These excessive varieties of behavior do not seem to be in the service of bodily homeostatic, regulatory mechanisms. The behavior develops quickly when the organism is exposed to the conditions that produce it and remains stable as long as the environmental conditions generating it remain in effect. The behavioral excesses occur, then, as adjuncts to a schedule governing the availability of some *other* class of reinforcing events.

Now it is of some interest to establish whether this excessive behavior bears any relation to those excesses in humans classed as substance abuse or habitually exaggerated activities. For such a case even to be plausible, at least three points should be established. First, there must be evidence that adjunctive behavioral excesses occur in humans under appropriate generating conditions. This has been confirmed. Second, the generating conditions should be rather nonspecific in terms of the particular characteristics of the intermittently available commodity. It should be sufficient that the commodity or activity be motivationally important and scheduled within a certain effective range of intermittence values. Again, available evidence confirms the generality of this relation: several kinds of scheduled events have been demonstrated to induce various sorts of excessive behavior. Third, generator schedules should be able to institute and maintain drug abuse in animals under conditions that otherwise would not lead to excessive drug-taking. Unless the relation holds for animals, the human homology would be a difficult argument to sustain. Again, several drug classes are chronically accepted in excess under appropriate schedule-induction conditions. These include oral indulgence of barbiturates, narcotic analgesics, amphetamines, chlordiazepoxide, and ethanol (see review by Gilbert 1978).

Food-schedule-induced increases in *intravenous* drug self-administration in animals have been demonstrated for heroin, methadone, cannabis, and nicotine (Oei, Singer, and Jeffreys 1980; Smith and Lang 1980; Takahashi and Singer 1980). For example, ethanol was drunk excessively by a group of rats exposed continuously to an intermittent feeding schedule (Falk, Samson, and Winger 1972). The ethanol solution was preferred to water and some other solutions and the chronically excessive intake resulted in severe physical dependence on ethanol. Comparable animals maintained under similar nutritional conditions but not fed on an intermittent schedule did not drink as much alcohol as the scheduled animals, nor did they show evidence of physical dependence (Falk and Samson 1975).

Alcohol and other drugs are reinforcing agents to animals and humans. But under many circumstances, particularly when taken orally, they are weak reinforcers. What some schedules can do is to exaggerate their reinforcing properties, thereby increasing their intakes. Now both nature and society seldom provide an even flow of the commodities important to survival and maintenance of an accustomed style of life. Life in many ways is a set of complex intermittent schedules. The adjunctive behavior that could be induced by such natural schedules would depend upon what behavior alternatives were available to the individual. The adjunctive behavior displayed is to some extent a function of the opportunities present in the environment. For animals the presence of a fluid to drink allows excessive drinking to occur. Hyperactivity will occur if a running wheel is made available. In humans the alternative opportunities provided by the environment are probably critical in determining what behavioral excesses occur. Excessive drug-taking, violence, exercise, or even scientific and literary endeavor will be functions of what particular environments supply. But even with creative or productive alternatives to drug-taking available, there is no assurance that an individual will take advantage of such opportunities. A past history enabling a person to utilize a potential opportunity may be critical. It is more probable that those persons lacking complex behavioral repertoires will turn to more readily available, easily consumed adjuncts such as drug-taking. A society must take care to provide alternative behavioral repertoires that help its members creatively and productively. If commodity access is limited, as it often is, in such a way that adjunctive behavior occurs persistently, then it is desirable that this excessive behavior at least be reactive and productive. Whether adjunctive behavior will be personally destructive, like gambling, drug-taking, or excessive television watching or, on the other hand, involve creative and single-minded persistent efforts will be a function both of the environmental opportunities and the behavioral repertoires built into the person by a particular history.

Compulsive, seemingly irrational, and downright self-destructive behavior is, on the face of it, one of the most baffling aspects of substance abuse and excessive behavior. In the very texture of the environmental rules (schedules) governing commodity availability lies one of the powerful generators of behavioral persistence. When these factors are combined with stimuli that are strong reinforcers, the conditions for the initial capture of the stream of behavior are present. These processes can be augmented by becoming associated with both internal and environmental discriminative stimuli. Further, experiential sequencing can alter behavior toward noxious stimuli so that the subject, rather than escaping or avoiding them, will come to satisfy schedule conditions that actually deliver them repeatedly. Finally, the induction of excessive, adjunctive behavior by rather simple schedule conditions demonstrates how commodity constraint in one realm can result in habitual and overindulgent behavior in a seemingly unrelated domain. It should be emphasized that these are all normal processes demonstrable in normal, unselected subjects. In none of these cases are bizarre, extreme manipulations or conditions imposed. The commerce with life's commodities that is arranged in most of the research described is similar to that probably encountered by most subjects attempting to exploit an ecological niche in competition with other species and their own neighbors, or in just working for a living. From normal sources extreme results can flow.

The Behavioral Consequences of Deprivation

The abuse of substances as well as extreme religious cult and political activist behavior often are thought of as determined rather directly by deprival states. The suffering proceeding from inadequate access to the commodities of this world, which is, in turn, a consequence of deprivation of civil rights and economic opportunities, is viewed by many as the underlying cause of excessively maladaptive and antisocial behavior. By this "deprivation hypothesis" much extreme behavior is assumed to occur because of a chronic disequilibrium between what individuals need and what they can attain. So pervasive is the deprivation hypothesis that when chronic maladjustment exists a prior deprival state frequently is assumed to be the cause.

Chronically short and uncertain supply of life's necessities may facilitate unwanted behavior, but the case is by no means clear. Necessity can be the mother of invention, so that at least some extreme new behavior is productive. To this must be added the warning that when we consider chronically excessive behavior even the most dispassionate observer is faced with moral and ethical evaluations of such behavior. The term "abuse" implies either illicit or unconventional behavior with, at the very least, negative social or medical consequences if not complete moral and physical deterioration. The term "habitual" implies a sort of self-indulgent or situational enslavement. We are short on terms for activities that are extravagant or unconventional but on hindsight prove to be rather benign or to possess some social or personal utility. Leaving aside such moral-ethical issues for the moment, it is worthwhile to determine if deprivation facilitates behavior and how any such facilitation might be characterized.

Compensatory Response to Privation

A large body of classic research in physiology has shown that when an organism is subjected to conditions that threaten the balance of its internal environment it mobilizes a number of adjustive mechanisms to maintain or restore a state of equilibrium. For example, when the body is exposed to the cold, heat is conserved by peripheral vasoconstriction and core temperature maintained by an increased utilization of energy stores. Curt Richter extended the work of Claude Bernard and Walter Cannon by showing that behavioral adjustments also contribute to the maintenance of constancy in the internal environment (Richter 1942-43). He showed, for example, that bodily imbalances produced by endocrine damage or nutritional deficits often were corrected when animals were given the opportunity to compensate by selectively ingesting from a range of dietary components. The adrenalectomized rat losing large amounts of sodium in the urine will soon die, but it will survive it given the opportunity to drink 3 percent sodium chloride solution, a fluid almost totally rejected by a normal rat. This kind of deficit-induced compensatory behavior has been studied intensively and a wide range of deficits have been shown to give rise to behavior that is appropriate in correcting the deficiency.

Not only adjustive behavior can be produced by deficits, but behavior apparently unrelated to any direct, corrective function also may increase. The deficit-induced facilitation of behaviors unrelated to the correction of the deficit is of interest for several reasons. A particular deficit can produce ancillary behavior that is troublesome: it might be personally maladaptive or antisocial. A history of deprivation, if not a current deficit, often is thought to be the source of presently inappropriate behavior. Such conceptions are common in developmental and psychoanalytic theories. Finally, deprivation may increase unrelated behavior that is ultimately advantageous to the individual. It may not serve to alleviate an immediate deficit, nor can it remedy a history of imbalance or injustices. But given the right opportunities, increased behavior can bring the organism into contact with unexpected sources of reward.

The main body of experimental work on the effects of deprivation deals with food deficits. It is by no means certain that the results of food intake limitation are at all representative of the outcomes produced by other states of deprivation. But as a first approximation of what we might expect from the study of such states, an examination of the general behavioral effects produced by food-limitation regimens may prove worthwhile.

Semistarvation in Human Beings

During the latter part of World War II, the physiological and behavioral effects of chronic semistarvation were investigated in a group of 32 conscientious objector volunteers (Keys et al. 1950). A 12-week control period preceded 24 weeks of semistarvation, followed by 12 weeks of restricted rehabilitation during which subjects received somewhat increased rations allowing them to gain weight slowly. Some subjects were studied for 8 more weeks of unrestricted rehabilitation. About one-half of the subjects were seen at 8- and 12-month follow-up sessions. During the semistarvation phase, subjects lost a mean of 24 percent body weight.

In the semistarvation studies, subjects did not report that hunger decreased over time. They remained preoccupied with food and eating in a variety of ways. Surprisingly, men began to dawdle over meals for almost two hours, although they became irritated if the serving was slow. Cookbooks, menus, and food prices became of major concern. Gum-chewing and smoking increased greatly, as did water intake. "Souping" was prominent: soup was drunk, and hot water was then repeatedly added to the solid part, heavily salted, and drunk before the solids were eaten. Tea and coffee ingestion increased so much that it became necessary to limit their intake to 9 cups per day. Gum had to be similarly restricted. One subject even chewed up to 40 packages per day. Significantly, individuals who previously had not used tea, coffee, or cigarettes became habitual users.

During starvation, depression and irritability increased and grooming deteriorated. Subjects became "increasingly quiet, somber, apathetic, and slow in motion" (Keys 1952). Social behavior decreased with more and more time being spent alone. Kitchen utensils and small appliances were acquired on shopping trips, but also ill-afforded purchases were made: collections of old books, knickknacks, and other admittedly useless articles. "Many of the men began to collect and to hoard any items at hand, and some of the men were disturbed that they could not resist acquiring useless 'junk' " (Keys 1952).

Many of the changes continued during the 12-week, controlled-rehabilitation period of refeeding. Appetites were insatiable and food concerns remained of paramount importance. Heavy use of tea and coffee continued, as did "souping." During rehabilitation, depression and irritability often did not improve with refeeding. Only toward the end of rehabilitation did sociability, humor, and enthusiasm reappear. Sex drive and fantasy, which had all but disappeared during semistarvation, began to reappear. The deteriorated table manners and extreme avoidance of any wasting of food persisted. Even after 20 weeks of rehabilitation, food was still a vital concern of almost one-half of the subjects.

Many behavioral features of semistarvation and rehabilitation bear similarities to the behavior often characteristic of heavy drug use and dependence. The ritualization of consumption of a commodity in short supply, particularly, responses that increased the consummatory aspects of interaction with the substance were apparent. When food was not available, redirected responses occurred (chewing, smoking, drinking) that employed response mechanisms similar to those used in eating. Such behavior recalls the behavior of "needle freaks" and vein "jacking" practices of some heroin users. The deteriorated social behavior characteristic of semistarvation also has its parallel in drug abuse contexts. While part of the socially unproductive or criminal behavior of drug abusers can be attributed to the lack of legally sanctioned ways for obtaining drugs, part may also be due to the user's economy of scarcity affording only meager and uncertain supplies. The semipermanence of the behavioral changes wrought by food limitation also demonstrates the resistance of the changed interests and distant social behavior to simple physiological rehabilitation.

It is interesting that some of the concerns about food and its ritualized handling characteristic of the semistarvation subjects are seen also in anorexia nervosa patients. Food is dawdled over, and there is a general preoccupation with it. Recipes, cooking for others, gourmet cooking, and food advertisements claim considerable attention. Food is dreamed about. Meal duration is long; food is cut into tiny pieces with extreme amounts of chewing. When self-control of food intake does break down, eating often occurs in binges (A.J. Stunkard, personal communication).

Ancillary Responses to Dietary Manipulations in Animals

The ingestive and other behaviors of animals in response to the experimental induction of specific hungers or the adulteration of a diet with a poison reveal additional features of how deficits determine widespread changes in behavior. Animals learn to reject foods that are nutritionally deficient or contain a poison substance. New dietary alternatives become preferred. When no alternative food choice is made available, behavior in the presence of the deficient or adulterated diet is instructive. Considerable spillage of food from the cup occurs, which is also common when normal rats are offered unpalatable diets. Redirected feeding behavior is observed, with an increased chewing on wood and wire parts of the caging. After being poisoned in conjunction with a particular food, animals return to eating a familiar, safe food; if they have been ingesting a nutritionally deficient diet and are then given a food choice, the new diet is preferred to the old, inadequate one.

Thus, the animal's response to nutritional deficit or poisonous adulteration is a redirection of consummatory behavior. Without an alternative source of food, the rejection of a suboptimal diet is accompanied by increases in behavior that are directed at the food but are nonconsummatory (spillage). Other behavioral increases would be classified by ethologists as "redirected activities" (wood gnawing). Pica (the eating of a nonnutritive substance) was produced in rats in conditioned-aversion experiments when animals were presented with the fluid (saccharin solution) they had been conditioned to reject (Mitchell et al. 1977). When a dietary alternative is made available after a history of component deficiency or adverse adulteration of the original food, the alternative food begins to be eaten not so much as a neophilic response but, rather, by default, since the first diet is actively rejected (Rozin and Kalat 1971).

Facilitation of Drug-Taking by Food Deprivation

Food deprivation is a powerful determinant of oral and intravenous drug intake (Carroll, France, and Meisch 1979; Carroll and Meisch 1980). Rats allowed unlimited food drank less etonitazene (a potent morphinelike drug) than when maintained on a food-deprivation regimen. This decrease began about one week after the start of unlimited food access. A decrease in the daily food ration increased subsequent etonitazene intake. These effects were not due to any general change in activity occasioned by food limitation because presses on a control lever (which did not deliver a drug solution) were few and did not vary with the food regime. Further work showed that the increased etonitazene intake was not due to some nonspecific increase in liquid intake. Oral intake of etonitazene was doubled under food-limitation conditions when rats were given 24-hour access to etonitazene in their home cages. In rats maintained at 75 percent of their free-feeding weights, feeding them their daily ration one hour before, or during a one-hour etonitazene-availability session only slightly decreased drug intake compared with the large decrease observed during unlimited feeding. This suggests that the effects of meal recency or gastrointestinal absorption effects.

The second time rats drinking etonitazene were food deprived, drug intake increases occurred much more rapidly. An increasing trend in etonitazene and cocaine intake over successive impositions of food deprivation also occurred with the intravenous self-administration route. Because the number of self-infusions did not increase on intervening food-satiated days, it would appear that the development of tolerance cannot explain the increase. Food deprivation also increased the oral intake of phencyclidine solution in rhesus monkeys. Similarly, the intravenous self-administration of nicotine (Lang et al. 1977; Smith and Lang 1980), d-amphetamine (Takahashi, Singer, and Dei 1978), and heroine (Oei et al. 1980) was greatly enhanced by food deprivation.

Deprivation and Reactivity

A number of classic studies on the relation between deprivation and general activity appeared to indicate that, within limits, as deprivation increased, so did activity. It was assumed that deprivation increased the state of need for the commodity withheld and that the resulting drive state had an energizing function on the level of general activity. The increases in activity in some species were assumed to be the direct consequence of the physiological changes produced by deprivation. This assumption was called into question by the work of Campbell and Sheffield. They interpreted their studies as showing that deprivation sensitized the organism to respond to environmental changes, particularly those predicting availability of the rationed commodity. When the environment was held constant, the ambulatory activity of deprived rats increased very little. Deprivation, then, would facilitate responsiveness to relevant environmental cues, rather than producing an unlearned, general activation of spontaneous behavior.

The studies using food deprivation were confirmed under water-deprivation conditions, although the effects were generally less dramatic (Campbell 1964). Both food- and water-deprivation conditions in rats increased response rates on a lever that turned on a dim light in contrast to a lever that produced no such stimulus change (Tapp 1961). Thus the conclusion holds under at least two kinds of deprivation and two kinds of stimulus change that deprivation enhances the rat's reactivity to environmental stimulation.

The deprivation-produced increase in reactivity can result in serious negative consequences given the proper configuration of environmental opportunities and constraints. For example, rats allowed a daily one-hour feeding period, and with continuous access to a running wheel, showed progressive increases in running and decreases in body weight, ending in death for all animals. Control animals on the same feeding schedule but without access to running wheels maintained a greater food intake and constant body weight (Routtenberg and Kuznesof 1967). This voluntary self-starvation has been confirmed by other investigators and results from the increased activity and decreased food intake produced by the combination of the schedule of food availability with a continuous opportunity for running. The combination is lethal and it is important to note that it is not the inevitable result of the deprivation condition itself; the control animals maintain themselves quite satisfactorily.

Deprivation and Invention

Deficit-facilitated acquisition of a spontaneous solution to a complex environment problem may be illustrated by a study of tool-using in the Northern blue jay. Jones and Kamil (1973) noted that a jay raised in their laboratory learned somehow to tear pieces off from sheets of newspaper kept under its cage, form the pieces with its beak, and use such fashioned tools to rake in food pellets that were out of reach. The behavior was acquired when the bird had been deprived of food. Other jays raised in the laboratory acquired similar tool-using behavior when deprived of food in the presence of food pellets that were out of reach.

Conclusions

While the examples of deficit facilitation of behaviors are quite diverse, perhaps a few tentative generalizations may be drawn that apply to the initiation and persistence of substance use and other new behaviors. The imposition of an environmental deficit condition can be regarded as a constraint placed upon a class of behavior. Thus, a food-limitation regimen constrains feeding behavior in terms of both its temporal and quantitative aspects. Constraints in food availability have been shown in formal experiment and in informal observation to facilitate behavior. The least complicated to categorize are those in which acts are relevant to correcting a deficit. The acts typically increase in patterns that minimize the effect of the imposed constraint. Such behavior solves the problem of food deficit by making the acquisition of additional food more probable, by conserving body heat, and perhaps by changing one's relations within a social group.

Another set of acts are deficit-related but not clearly corrective. This is behavior usually classed as general activity. As noted previously, it can increase with deprivation and is thought to reflect an increased responsiveness to constraint-regimen cues (food-relevant discriminative stimuli). It could be described as orienting behavior. Its extreme manifestation in the animal self-starvation experiments results in behavior that is anything but corrective.

A third kind of behavior also involves responses to the constrained commodity. It might be expected that when a portion of the commodity becomes available, the deprivation regimen would ensure a high rate of consummatory behavior making short shrift of the portion. This does not always occur. Under some circumstances, a paced manipulation of the commodity and its context appears. A clear example of this is the protracted meal-eating time of the semistarved human subjects and in anorexia nervosa. This amounted to rather solitary food ceremonials in the semistarved subjects, with a paced and reverent savoring of the ration. Levity in those involved in food service was deeply resented by subjects. Recipe and menu collection and discussion were prominent activities. Unhurried appreciation and prolongation is actually common behavior with regard to rare or valued commodities and activities such as fine food and wines, theatrical performances, nature walks, and sexual engagements. The ceremonial aspect of the consummatory activities often pervades the entire context: preparations, ancillary features of the setting, and savored reminiscences of the event by pictures, souvenirs, or a shared cigarette. Drug-taking ceremonials have been reported to partake of this same aesthetic. Perhaps it is most common in the weekend drug "chipper."

But it is the commodity-deficit facilitation of unrelated behavior, bearing an indirect or occult relation to the constraint imposed, that is perhaps of prime interest. In the semistarvation experiments, the constraint of two meager daily meals resulted in excessive gum chewing, smoking, tea and coffee drinking, "souping," and so on. Significantly, some of these subjects had never before smoked or drunk tea or coffee. Had these studies been done two or three decades later, it is interesting to speculate what substance use might have been learned. While some of this facilitated behavior is similar to the redirected activities (pica, chewing) of the deficient-diet-maintained animal, or rats faced with consuming the substance to which a conditioned aversion had been trained, other behavior would seem to have a more complex relation to the deficit condition. The purchasing of various useless, ill-afforded articles is one example. However, lest it appear that only redirected consummatory movements and useless, intrusive behavior are facilitated, it should be recalled that food deprivation and the presence of out-of-reach food pellets occasioned the acquisition of untrained tool-using behavior in the majority of the blue jays tested.

Imposition of a constraint on feeding increases the consumption of various pharmacologically active substances by animals and humans. Animals increase their consumption of ethanol, phencyclidine, and etonitazene. They engage in pica. Human beings consume tea, coffee, gum, cigarettes and previously nonpreferred foods. Further, feeding constraints greatly increase the intravenous self-administration of etonitazene, cocaine, d-amphetamine, nicotine, and heroin in animals.

An important feature of behavioral facilitation effects of deprivation is that, in some instances, they produce persistent changes in behavior. For example, the rather slow reversibility of the behavior effects of semistarvation on humans was discussed. In the drug self-administration studies in animals, repeated exposure to food deprivation led to a more rapid increase in drug intake on subsequent occasions. Finally, the inventive acquisition of tool-using by the laboratory-raised blue jays when simply deprived of food produced a new, complex skill that could then be used on subsequent occasions to adjust to a food constraint.

Behavioral Consequences of Drug Abstinence

Tolerance and Dependence

Drugs in the opiate, sedative-hypnotic, and minor tranquilizer classes produce both tolerance and physical dependence. The term "tolerance" means that following repeated administration, the drug dosage administered must be increased in order to achieve the effect originally produced by the drug. The degree of tolerance developed depends upon the drug and the dosage regimen as well as a host of other pharmacologic and environmental variables

(Krasnegor 1978). Tolerance does not necessarily develop equally to all actions of a drug. For example, marked tolerance to the respiratory depressant effect of morphine is observed, but little tolerance develops to its effect on the gastrointestinal tract. One of the most insidious aspects of drug abuse is the seemingly inexorable tendency for addicts to increase their drug consumption over time. This has both social and economic consequences as well as exposing the individual to doses of drugs that may produce irreversible bodily harm. It is commonly presumed that this increased intake over time is caused by the development of tolerance to the reinforcing actions of the drug. That is, as tolerance develops, more drug must be ingested to satiate the addict's need for the drug. It is fascinating that there is little experimental data relevant to this assumption and that which does exist does not support (Schuster 1978). Laboratory studies have been conducted in which naive monkeys were allowed to self-administer morphine intravenously. When allowed access to fairly high doses of morphine (1.0 milligrams/kilogram (weight of one subject)/injection) intake showed a gradual increase over a 4- to 6-week period and remained stable thereafter (Schuster 1970). It is impossible to determine in this type of experiment whether the increased intake is a function of tolerance to the reinforcing actions of the drug or to the general depressant actions that prevents the animal from self-injecting higher doses of morphine initially. Tolerance to the depressant actions of morphine has been demonstrated repeatedly. That this latter may be the case is suggested by the observation that when lower doses of morphine are self-injected (say, 0.025 milligrams/kilogram/injection), the animals do not show a gradual increase but, rather, reach asymptotic intake in only a few days (Woods and Schuster 1968). Research that discriminates between these two alternatives is clearly necessary for us to conclude that tolerance develops to reinforcing actions of drugs. Many but not all drugs that produce tolerance produce physical dependence as well. Physical dependence is a condition resulting from the chronic administration of a drug that is revealed by the occurrence of a spectrum of physiologic and behavioral changes when the drug administration is stopped or when an antagonist drug is administered. The spectrum varies with the drug producing the dependence. Further, the physiologic changes characteristic of the withdrawal syndrome are reserved when the drug producing physical dependence is administered. Thus the physical dependence liability of a drug at present can be demonstrated only by removal of the drug.

Both cross-tolerance and cross-dependence exist between certain drugs. As a matter of fact this is one of the ways in which classes of drugs are defined. Thus the "opiate" class of drugs is in part defined by the existence of cross-tolerance and cross-dependence between the drugs constituting the group. For example, animals tolerant to heroin are tolerant to methadone. Further, methadone substitutes for heroin withdrawal syndrome.

Physical Dependence: Relevance to Drug-Taking

It is a common assumption that drugs that produce physical dependence initially may be taken for their positive reinforcing effects, but that their continued use is maintained because they allow escape from, or avoidance of, the aversive properties of the withdrawal syndrome. Several lines of evidence question this assumption. Wikler (1965) has pointed out there is no reason why experienced addicts could not gradually withdraw themselves from the drug in a relatively painless manner. It is difficult to see, therefore, why an addict would continue to take drugs simply to avoid or escape from the distress of withdrawal.

A controlled laboratory study has shown that treatment with methadone at a dose level that prevented withdrawal diminished but did not completely suppress opiate-seeking behavior in humans (Jones and Prada 1975). In a study allowing dogs to self-administer morphine in unlimited quantities, noncontingent methadone infusions produced only a transitory decrease in the taking of morphine (Jones and Prada 1977). Thus heroin and morphine have reinforcing effects even in subjects whose physical need for the drug has already been satisfied by methadone administration.

Other lines of evidence also question the role of physical dependence in generating drug-seeking behavior. Khazan, Weeks, and Schroeder (1967) obtained electroencephalographic (EEG) and electromyographic (EMG) recordings from rats surgically prepared with chronic indwelling intravenous catheters. First, the animals were made physically dependent upon morphine by programmed infusions of the drug. Subsequently they were required to lever-press 10 times to receive a morphine injection (fixed-ratio-10 schedule of reinforcement). Under these conditions, the rats showed a characteristic pattern of lever-pressing. Every two to three hours, the animals began lever-pressing and rapidly completed the FR10 requirement. The relevant portion of this study concerns whether any changes indicative of withdrawal could be found in the EEG or EMG recordings at the time a rat began lever-pressing for drug. To do this, these investigators compared the EEG and EMG recordings immediately preceding lever-pressing behavior for morphine with recordings obtained when the rats were deprived of drug to produce withdrawal. These physiological measures did not show any changes indicative of withdrawal in the period immediately preceding the initiation of lever-pressing for morphine. Thus in terms of EMG and EEG measures, there was no indication that animals began lever-pressing for morphine because of the onset of withdrawal. Woods and Schuster (1968) demonstrated that rhesus monkeys will work for very low doses of intravenous morphine. These doses were so small and intermittent that physical dependence did not develop. Such evidence seriously questions the assumption that opiate-seeking behavior is generated primarily by the aversive properties of withdrawal.

Both alcohol-dependent monkeys and humans show periods of voluntary abstinence despite the consequent intense withdrawal symptoms, including even convulsions (Mello and Mendelson 1970; Woods, Ikomi, and Winger 1971). It would appear, therefore, that even intense withdrawal symptoms do not automatically generate drug-seeking behavior.

Another aspect to the withdrawal syndrome must be noted. Namely, this syndrome may be a performance maintained by unsuspect sources of reinforcement. For example, when a heroin addict is arrested and brought to a prison hospital, the dosage of opiate drug that is prescribed by the physician depends upon the intensity of the withdrawal symptoms displayed. Since higher doses of opiates are more desirable, the addict may display more intense signs and symptoms. Observations of patients in heroin detoxification wards as well suggest that the duration of withdrawal is influenced by environmental factors. When certain privileges are conditional upon being drug-free, the number of days patients request drug during detoxification is shortened. It would appear that withdrawal may be markedly modified by environmental factors. Such environmental factors may be of particular importance when physical dependence is low. This is certainly the case in the United States today for most heroin addicts since the drug available is so expensive and of such low quality.

The experimental data do not support the conception that drugs that produce physical dependence are taken simply to avoid or escape from the aversive properties of the withdrawal syndrome. This does not mean, however, that the reinforcing efficacy of such drugs is not increased when the subject is undergoing withdrawal. Thompson and Schuster (1964) studied changes in morphine-reinforced behavior under conditions of withdrawal induced by 24 hours of drug deprivation or by the administration of nalorphine (a morphine antagonist). Monkeys worked on a chained fixed-interval fixed-ratio schedule for intravenously administered morphine. The schedule was in effect for a single morphine injection every sixth hour of the day. This schedule was selected because, with other reinforcers, fixed-interval lever-pressing rate proved to be a sensitive measure of deprivation conditions. Under withdrawal conditions induced by 24 hours of deprivation from morphine, the animals' lever-pressing rate in the fixed interval rose markedly above that observed under the baseline deprivation condition of 6 hours. A comparable increase was obtained when these animals were pretreated with the morphine antagonist nalorphine, again demonstrating that withdrawal can amplify drug-seeking behavior. Physical dependence, then, is not necessary for a drug to function as a reinforcer, but once dependence is established, it can increase the intensity of drug-seeking behavior.

Deprivation of morphine in dependent animals not only increases rate of responding for the drug but also causes a disruption in stimulus control over drug-seeking behavior. Schuster and Woods (1968) examined the effects of deprivation in rhesus monkeys allowed to self-inject morphine for a one-hour period (signaled by the illumination of a red light) every sixth hour of the day. After several months on this schedule, animals were obtaining a sufficient amount of morphine to be physically dependent. Lever-pressing for morphine rarely occurred in the absence of the red light signaling morphine availability. However, when extinction procedures were introduced (either by substituting saline for morphine or by having presses during the red light produce no consequences), pressing rates in the presence of the red light increased markedly. Further, and more important in this context, pressing in the absence of the red light showed an increase from near zero levels to over 1,000 presses per day for the first few days. This disruption of the normal stimulus control in drug-seeking behavior correlated with the onset and gradual diminution of the withdrawal syndrome.

At the same time that withdrawal produces an increase in drug-seeking behavior, other aspects of the behavioral repertoire are disrupted. In the study by Thompson and Schuster (1964), both food-reinforced and electric-shock-avoidance behaviors showed a progressive disruption as withdrawal signs increased in intensity. Thus it would appear that withdrawal from morphine channels behavior into drug-seeking and disrupts behavior maintained by other reinforcers.

Comparable studies with drugs that do not produce physical dependence show quite different results. Deprivation from cocaine, for example, a drug that does not produce physical dependence, does not disrupt stimulus control for cocaine-seeking behavior. Further, behavior maintained by other reinforcers was not disrupted during this period of cocaine deprivation (C.E. Johanson, personal communication). These observations suggest that deprivation may cause a breakdown in normal stimulus control of behavior only with drugs that produce physical dependence. Clearly, more research should be conducted in this area since the implications of this hypothesis for understanding some of the antisocial acts associated with heroin addiction may be related to this phenomenon.

It is of interest to note that studies with behavior maintained by water or food reinforcement do not show a breakdown in discriminative stimulus control as a function of deprivation. Comparable studies using drugs and food as the reinforcers are needed to determine whether drugs producing physical dependence are unique in this regard.

The evidence involving either tolerance or physical dependence processes in habitual drug-taking is not presently strong. For example, Cappell and LeBlanc (1979) conclude that "it remains a strong hypothesis if not an act of faith that physical dependence plays a central role in the maintenance of the self-administration of alcohol and psychoactive drugs. However, opiates represent the only drug class for which evidence for this hypothesis is at all strong."

Conditioned Aversion

In 1955 Garcia and colleagues reported that rats given a saccharin solution to drink and subsequently exposed to gamma radiation developed an aversion to saccharin (Garcia, Kimeldorf, and Koelling 1955). This report was followed by a variety of studies demonstrating that numerous drugs (Gamzu 1977), rotation-induced sickness (Braveman 1977), and radiation exposure, can produce an aversion to foods and fluids. Further, the phenomenon has been demonstrated in many animal species, including humans. In the period since Garcia's original report, conditioned gustatory aversion has been one of the most intensely studied phenomena in biopsychology. Learning theorists have had a particular interest in this research since some of the conditions under which gustatory aversion can be obtained appear to violate the traditional laws of learning. Generally, learning theorists have interpreted this phenomenon as an instance of classical conditioning. As originally shown by Pavlov, certain reflex responses can be brought under the control of new stimuli through temporal association with the reflex. Thus, for example, Pavlov demonstrated in dogs that the salivary response elicited by food could be brought under the control of an auditory stimulus by temporally pairing the two stimuli. The food in the paradigm was called an unconditioned stimulus (UCS) and the salivation elicited by food, the unconditioned response. The tone that acquired the ability to elicit salivation was termed the conditioned stimulus (CS) and the salivation it elicited the conditioned response. Conditioned gustatory aversion has been interpreted as an instance of such classical conditioning in which the taste and smell of the food or fluid functions as the conditioned stimulus and the drug, physical rotation, or radiation as the unconditioned stimulus that produces responses incompatible with eating or drinking (gastrointestinal disturbances mainly). The smell or taste of the food or fluid thus comes to evoke responses incompatible with ingestion. Several findings, however, suggest that this phenomenon may have some unique characteristics making it difficult to interpret within the usual classical conditioning framework.

It is one of the fundamental principles of learning that the acquisition of a conditioned response is most rapid when the CS-UCS interval is in the range of 0.5 seconds. However, numerous studies have shown that conditioned gustatory aversions can occur with a single pairing of the CS and UCS even when their presentation is separated by hours (Garcia and Hankins 1977).

A second way in which the conditioned gustatory aversion studies appear to deviate from the general principles of classical conditioning concerns the nature of the stimulus event to be used as the conditioned stimulus. It was generally assumed that any stimulus in a moderate range of intensities that does not itself produce a strong reflex response can serve as a conditioned stimulus. Although rarely explicitly stated, it was assumed that all stimuli were equal in their ability to function as conditioned stimuli. Experiments conducted by Garcia and his colleagues have shown convincingly that in rats certain stimuli can be used as conditioned stimuli more readily than others. One of the early studies (Garcia and Koelling 1966) compared taste and olfactory cues from a drinking solution with noise and bright lights as the conditioned stimuli and electric shock or treatment with lithium chloride (at a toxic dose level) as the unconditioned stimuli. Specifically, one group of rats was allowed to drink a flavored solution and this was followed for half of this group by the injection of lithium chloride and for the other half by the delivery of painful electric shock. A second group of rats was allowed to drink "bright-noisy" water and this experience was followed by either electric foot shock or treatment with lithium chloride. The results demonstrated that rats given the foot shock learned to avoid bright-noisy water, but animals given the flavored solution followed by shock continued to drink this solution. Thus, it would appear that the exteroceptive cues (light and sound of the water) readily acquired conditioned stimulus control over the rats' behavior whereas the taste and smell of the drinking solution did not. This could be attributable to simple differences in discriminability of the two types of stimuli were it not for the fact that these findings were reversed in the second group of rats receiving lithium chloride as the unconditioned stimulus. In this group the animals given the solution with a distinctive taste and odor learned to avoid this solution whereas the animals given the bright-noisy solution did not. This experiment, as well as a host of others, has led Garcia and Hankins (1977) to conclude that, under all variations, the same curious inequalities persisted. Apparently rats could neither learn that the taste of food and drink was paired with the pain of shock nor learn that the auditory-visual signal was paired with illness. Although species may differ in the nature of the stimuli showing such inequalities, generally taste cues and subsequent illness are most readily associated. This has important implications for therapists using conditioned aversion in the treatment of behavioral problems. In the treatment of alcoholics, many therapists have used the taste of alcohol as the conditioned stimulus followed by drug-induced nausea as the unconditioned stimulus. Under these conditions, strong conditioned aversion was readily produced (Lemere and Veogtlin 1950). When electric shock was substituted for the drug-induced nausea as the unconditioned stimulus, no aversion to alcohol was obtained (MacCulloch et al. 1966). When these same therapists used electric shock to produce aversion to pictures of homosexual activities, however, they were successful. It would thus appear that with conditioned aversion not all stimuli are equally able to serve as conditioned stimuli and that certain CS-UCS types are more readily conditionable than others in both animals and humans.

A third factor suggesting the uniqueness of the conditioned aversion phenomenon concerns the issue of novelty of both the conditioned and unconditioned stimuli. A number of experiments have demonstrated that novel foods and fluids will become conditioned stimuli more readily than familiar ones. This fact makes intuitive sense since animals tend to eat a variety of substances and there must be a mechanism for determining which will be associated with any subsequent illness. By necessity, a poisoned food is likely to be a novel one or else the animal would probably already be dead. It would therefore make sense, for example, that rats would associate radiation sickness with novel food rather than familiar food if they have ingested both types prior to being ill. An experiment by Revusky and Bedarf (1967) has confirmed this hypothesis by demonstrating that rats radiated after ingesting both a novel food and a bland, familiar one avoided the novel food subsequently but not the familiar one. Similar results have been obtained by Kalat and Rozin (1970).

Preexposure to stimuli to be used as unconditioned stimuli markedly curtails their effectiveness in the conditioned taste aversion procedure. Bravemen (1977) reviewed a series of experiments demonstrating that preexposure to a drug limits its functioning as an unconditioned stimulus in a conditioned aversion procedure. He cites studies demonstrating that exposure to one drug may prevent another drug from acting as an unconditioned stimulus. Most striking, however, are the findings that preexposure to nonpharmacological manipulations such as forced rotation in a wheel also prevents certain drugs from functioning as unconditioned stimuli. Bravemen maintains that the common factor among these manipulations is that of stress, with consequent activation of the pituitary and adrenal glands. This hypothesis is supported by data showing that drugs that block the activation of the adrenal gland by ACTH attenuate lithium-chloride induced aversions to milk (Hennessy et al. 1976). Further, the administration of various ACTH analogues as well as other drugs known to stimulate ACTH production prolong already established conditioned aversions (Rigter and Popping 1976).

What are the implications of the conditioned aversion phenomenon for the problems of drug abuse? Many of the same drugs that can be used to produce conditioned aversions are as well self-administered by the same species of animals at similar dosage levels. (See discussion of the experiments of Wise, Yokel, and DeWit (1976) in the earlier section, Environmental Schedules as Sources of Behavioral Persistence.) This indicates that the ability to function as an aversive event or as a positive reinforcer is not an inherent property of the drug alone but depends upon the relation of the presentation of the event to ongoing behavior. The conditioned taste aversion phenomenon may explain aversions to certain types of alcoholic beverages shown by people. As stated previously, taste and olfactory cues readily become conditioned stimuli when they are followed by aversive events, particularly those involving gastrointestinal disturbances. Thus if a novel alcoholic beverage was followed within hours by illness, it is not unlikely that conditioned aversion to this beverage would occur. What is surprising is not that such conditioned aversion can occur in man, but rather that it is not a more common phenomenon, since the ingestion of alcohol and other drugs by neophytes is often followed by sickness (heroin producing emesis, for example). The key to this may lie partly in the fact that conditioned aversion occurs most readily to taste cues. Thus novel alcoholic beverages might be expected to become conditioned stimuli more readily than the stimuli associated with taking a tasteless pill or an injection. The phenomenon or preexposure may as well contribute to the relative infrequency of conditioned aversion phenomenon in man. It would appear that tolerance to the aversive properties of many drugs develops much more readily than to their positive reinforcing effects. Thus if people for social reasons were to repeat drug experiences, the possibility of developing aversion to stimuli associated with the drug would be low. Further, the fact that preexposure to one drug may confer tolerance to the aversive properties of other drugs enhances this mechanism's generality.

Long-Term Consequences of Behavior Patterns

Among the kinds of persistent behavior that are inappropriate or excessive and that can result in various, direct, toxic consequences is long-term administration of high doses of methamphetamine, which can produce lasting alterations in brain chemistry (Fischman and Schuster 1975; Wagner et al. 1980). But it is possible for persistent behavior to yield indirect effects that also can be considered toxic in that they impair flexibility and adaptation. The existence of a long-term behavior pattern in itself can produce behavioral consequences that may be characterized in a number of ways.

   Whatever the reinforcing stimuli might be that maintain a chronic behavior, the performance itself provides discriminative stimuli for continuance of the pattern. Such discriminative stimuli also may become conditioned reinforcers since they lead to reinforcing stimuli and become associated with them. A chronic pattern of behavior, rich in discriminative and conditioned reinforcing stimuli, may be resistant to change. Even in the face of altered consequences for the behavior, the pattern may persist. This rigidity, or loss of plasticity, has been characterized by claiming that long-term habits become functionally autonomous and no longer require even occasional reinforcing stimuli for their maintenance. Whether complete functional autonomy of a habit ever really develops, or whether an occasional reinforcer maintains the persistence, is a question that remains unsettled. But whatever the case, there has been no lack of examples of nonadaptive persistence in human behavior. Formal demonstrations and an analysis of how this can come about were provided by a series of experiments (Weiner 1970). Subjects were required to press a lever for points exchangeable for money. When they had experienced pressing on a fixed-ratio 40-second schedule of reinforcement for a number of sessions, transferring them to a fixed-interval 10-second schedule of reinforcement, which in addition cost them points for lever-pressing, failed to produce a decreased rate of pressing, and cost the subjects part of their potential earnings. The inappropriate and nonadaptive persistence of a high pressing rate under the "fixed-interval cost" schedule was produced by the subjects having had a history of reinforcement during high-rate pressing occasioned by the fixed-ratio schedule. The same inappropriate high rate was produced in other subjects even though they had experienced several extinction sessions (no reinforcements for pressing) for fixed-ratio pressing prior to being transferred to the fixed-interval cost schedule. However, Weiner found in further work that if subjects had had a history of being reinforced on a schedule that required a low rate of pressing, a later history of fixed-ratio reinforcement did not produce the nonadaptive high rate on the fixed-interval cost schedule. In this case, even a remote history of being reinforced for a low pressing rate was sufficient to allow adjustment to the fixed-interval cost schedule. Even when subjects were exposed to a history of fixed-ratio reinforcement and then retained the inappropriate high rate when transferred to the fixed-interval cost schedule (as in the first experiment), they could be redeemed to low-rate pressing on this schedule if they now received several sessions of being reinforced for low-rate pressing. In other words, even subjects pressing at an inappropriately high rate owing to a fixed-ratio history could be "cured" by receiving reinforcement for a time *only* for low-rate pressing. This experience provided them with the critical behavior repertoire that allowed pressing at the appropriate rate to occur when the fixed-interval cost schedule was reintroduced.

This series of experiments illustrates how a current or previous pattern of behavior can operate to curtail the acquisition of a new, adjustive pattern. Behavioral history can produce a kind of fatefulness, so that as one persists with old, partially workable repertoires, new and more productive ones remain unacquired. But thankfully the introduction of a strong schedule that forces an innovative repertoire upon one by reinforcing *only* the appropriate behavior pattern provides a history that later permits adaptive adjustment to a new circumstance.

While it is possible to characterize the results of the Weiner (1970) experiments in terms of a lack of adaptive flexibility, the behavioral implications of establishing prior patterns often cannot be typified in such evaluative terms. Instituting a long-term behavior pattern can produce a profound change on other concurrent or subsequent behavior, but the change need not be described as an impairment in adaptive flexibility. Of special interest for our present considerations are recent studies that have demonstrated that major determinants of how a drug dose affects behavior can be a function of (1) other scheduled behavior elicited at other times within that context and (2) experience with prior schedules.

Let us briefly illustrate these effects. If animals are reinforced with food delivery for lever-pressing but also receive an occasional electric shock for a press, the result is a decrease in pressing rate relative to a no-shock condition. The decreased rate of behavior, in this case lever-pressing, produced by following some instances of it with shock, defines the shock as a punisher of that behavior under the conditions of the experiment. Behavior that has been suppressed by being punished generally is not increased by amphetamine, even though this drug is typically quite effective in increasing low rates of behavior (Geller and Seifter 1960). However, there are contextual conditons under which d-amphetamine produces marked *increases* in behavior which has been suppressed by punishment. Lever-pressing in squirrel monkeys maintained by a fixed-interval 10-minute schedule of food delivery was suppressed (punished) by presenting a shock after every thirtieth lever-press (McKearney and Barrett 1975). During alternate 10-minute periods in the session, one of two discriminative stimuli was presented that indicated that either lever-pressing would have no effect (extinction) or that it would postpone the delivery of electric shock. In sessions where the extinction component was in effect, d-amphetamine produced the typical decrease in punished behavior. When the shock-postponement schedule was in effect during the alternate 10-minute periods, d-amphetamine produced marked increases in punished behavior. (Increases in shock-postponement lever-pressing also occurred.) The direction of the effect that d-amphetamine had on punished behavior, then, depended upon the context in which the punished behavior occurred. In related experiments, amphetamine and methamphetamine increased punished lever-pressing when the alternate periods of the schedule were shock self-administration, rather than shock postponement, components (McKearney 1979).

A study by Barrett (1977) demonstrated that prior experience with a shock-postponement schedule led to increases in punished lever-pressing under d-amphetamine; monkeys without this past history showed the usual lack of increase in punished behavior under d-amphetamine. When these latter monkeys were given shock-postponement experience and transferred back to the punished lever-pressing schedule again, they now responded to d-amphetamine with an increase in punished behavior.

Recall that in the human semistarvation studies many of the behavioral changes produced by chronic undernutrition persisted during the rehabilitative period of refeeding. In particular, food-related activities appeared to undergo quite long-lasting, perhaps permanent, changes.

Contemporary, contextual behavior patterns, as well as a history of prior patterns, can alter the very direction in which a drug changes punished behavior. These studies, together with Weiner's work on nonadaptive persistence and inflexibility proceeding from experience with a prior schedule, indicate how an individual's alternative repertoires, as well as prior adjustments within a situation, can radically alter reactions to environmental demands and to drugs. The human semistarvation studies produced a set of complex behavioral changes, some of which improved only slowly with rehabilitation, while others may have remained permanently. Analyses such as these build important bridges to disciplinary specialties traditionally concerned with the effects of an individual's entire life situation and past experiences on present behavioral reactions and adjustments.

Commonalities in Substance Abuse and Habitual Behavior

The identification of some of the common factors that determine the disparate kinds of behavior involved in the untoward intake of various substances and in exaggerated and intrusive routines could help to direct investigations so that if common processes do in fact underlie different abuses and excesses they would stand revealed. Furthermore, theory concerning the substrates of commonality might flower from such research or might even now give it a fruitful direction. Hence some attempt to set forth units and dimensions of measurement is overdue. And perhaps it is not premature to adopt a few theoretical guides, if only to energize those of us with structural presumptions.

Stimulus Commonalities

Given the varied substances and activities that can engage behavior excessively, it is probably not fruitful to search for either a common chemical structure or pathologic defect to explain these excesses. A common thread does run through these activities in one sense: When a person cannot engage in his or her preferred form of behavioral excess, another excess may be substituted. This can manifest in many ways. Individuals identified as overusers of a substance may not specialize in just that one substance. Polydrug abuse has become increasingly common. It entails simultaneous abuse of agents from more than one pharmacological class in some persons and also considerable flexibility in the choice of which drug currently dominates. Such selection is often more a matter of convenience and availability than of pharmacologic action. When heroin becomes unavailable, alcohol becomes a frequent substitute. A history of self-administering one agent can increase the probability that another perhaps borderline reinforcing agent will now be abused. For example, research with monkeys has shown that animals reluctant to self-inject ethanol solutions in significant amounts will do so after a history of self-injecting a stimulant. Likewise, experience in self-injecting phencyclidine makes delta-9-THC a far more effective reinforcer for monkeys. The extent to which abused substances and excessive activities are mutually substitutable is at present uncertain. Just as alcoholism sometimes replaces heroin abuse, in some persons a new-found and all-consuming religious conviction appears to substitute for heroin.

The commonality of drugs that function as reinforcing stimuli for animals (particularly monkeys) and humans is impressive. There are few exceptions to the concordance between drugs that act as powerful reinforcers for animals and those having abuse liability for humans. Further, agents not self-injected by animals are seldom abused by humans.

The commodities and habitual activities that engage behavior chronically and excessively may possess several common properties. Drugs, foods, gambling, and aggressive episodes all have *prompt effects on the person or upon their immediate environment*. The preferred drugs of abuse are typically those with a rapid onset of effect. Gamblers prefer fast "action," that is, a high rate of play with an immediacy of consequence for each wager. Even state lotteries have come to appreciate the prompt-effect factor by instituting an "instant lottery" in which the purchaser rubs off a number and is informed forthwith of the result. The attack behavior in spouse or child abuse produces a rapid environmental change, as does the act of exposure engaged in by the sexual flasher.

Not only do these commodities and activities have prompt effects, but also they are *brief in duration of action*. As a rule, drugs having a short duration of action are preferred by the abuser to long-acting agents. Likewise, the effect of each unit of attack of gambling and flashing behavior seems brief, although the prodromes and longer term consequences may be quite protracted.

A third common characteristic is somewhat more abstract than either promptness or brevity of action. This is saliency. Abusive episodes of drug- or food-taking attacks or gambling produce a sharp and immediate break in life's routines, even though the situations occasioning these episodes for a person may be relatively invarient and the episodes themselves highly ritualized. This aspect of *ritualized saliency*, as is the case with rapidity and brevity of action, does not in itself elicit excessive behavior. After all, we often take care to introduce salient and ritualized features into life's routines without these becoming problematic. An afternoon handball session, a before dinner drink, accelerating from a particular stop light, or a weekly football wager are all rapid and brief in action, as well as having ritualized salience, but statistically they usually do not produce excessive behavior. However, they all typify the kinds of activities with abuse liability.

Even in the case of heroin, the number of addicts is probably low when compared to the number of persons exposed.

Recall for a moment the studies in which animals self-administered electric shocks known to be aversive. Shocks that can be proven noxious to the same animals under slightly altered circumstances nevertheless sustain self-administration under intermittent, recurrent schedules. Again, upon delivery the shocks are prompt and brief in action and possess a ritualized saliency under those schedule conditions yielding stable self-administration. Electric shock is, of course, an interesting test case of the three common stimulus properties suggested as being important in the excessive engagement of behavior. It is not positively hedonic nor has its self-administration been claimed to possess any immediate, remote, or phylogenic history of adaptive value.

Drugs and other substances have discriminable properties that can come to direct behavior. Animals and humans can "tell the difference" not only between a particular drug state and not being drugged but also between two drugs or between two dose levels of the same drug. Drug stimuli are behaviorally discriminable stimuli that can come to direct behavior as can a sweet taste, an appealing perfume, or the martial music of one's country. Note that some of these stimuli probably come to direct behavior mainly through their intrinsic properties (sweets, cocaine), others because their intrinsic properties become associated with other sources of reinforcement (perfumes), and still others because of the social context in which they have occurred (flags, music). Research indicates that individually housed monkeys given continuous and unlimited intravenous access to stimulants such as cocaine or d-amphetamine self-inject them excessively as if such agents possessed irresistible intrinsic properties. But with less-ready access to them, or given other drug classes (such as opioids), self-injection is not so extreme. As indicated previously, agents such as ethanol or delta-9-THC may require a history of self-injection of other drugs before they are reliably self-administered. Drugs and other substances such as foods, then, are discriminable stimuli that have complex common properties. They can function almost as an irresistable sweet under special conditions, with little tendency to become cloying with repeated exposure. Alternatively, they may function as haunting perfumes to which one returns repeatedly given the appropriate circumstances. Or they may be like a flag or favorite haunt, deriving their reinforcing properties mainly by becoming associated with powerful social reinforcers. While some substances may be more like sweets than flags, most fall between these extremes. But more important, substances can be moved back and forth along this continuum by their association with social and schedule factors. This malleability constitutes their most important property. The frequent use of heroin by young American soldiers serving in Vietnam, where availability and peer acceptance of the drug were high and competing reinforcers were few, contrasts with the rapid abandonment of usage upon return to the United States, where social acceptance and ready availability are less and other reinforcers could compete effectively. *Malleability of the reinforcing function by schedule arrangements and consequences*, then, is a fourth common property of the commodities and activities that engage behavior excessively and intrusively. This fourth property leads naturally into a second class of commonalities.

Environmental Commonalities

Environmental constraints on the availability of various crucial reinforcers can lead to increases in behavior in a variety of ways. Deprivation, particularly food deprivation, increases general activity by increasing reactivity to relevant environmental discriminative stimuli. Deprivation also seems to produce ritualized consumption of the rationed commodity as evidenced by food and drug ceremonials when these commodities are in short supply. Imposition of a constraint on feeding increases the oral consumption of various substances by animals and humans. Animals increase oral intake of ethanol, phencyclidine, and etonitazene and the self-injection of various drugs. They engage in pica. Humans consume large amounts of tea, coffee, gum, and cigarettes. The effect of food deprivation on the intake of other pharmacologically active substances by humans has not been studied.

When deprivation of an important commodity or activity is combined with a schedule of availability requiring the fulfillment of certain conditions, then considerable behavioral persistence can result. The power of schedules of intermittent reinforcement to generate persistence is common across a wide variety of reinforcing stimuli. This kind of persistence, then, has as its origin the particular schedule of reinforcement in force, rather than the nature of the particular reinforcing stimuli employed. Indeed, remarkable persistence of behavior is sustained by many sorts of small and momentary reinforcing consequences.

Some schedules of reinforcement constitute a second kind of environmental commonality in that they can underlie the generation of a variety of excessive sorts of behavior: Schedule-induced or adjunctive behavior occurs as an excessive-behavior side-effect to many schedules of reinforcement commonly in use. Such behavioral excesses include drug overindulgence and repetitive attacks. Both schedule-maintained and schedule-induced behavior demonstrate the common environmental sources of many kinds of intense and persistent behavioral excesses.

Schedules of reinforcement can function to alter stimuli thought to act primarily as positive or negative reinforcing events. The role of schedules in modulating reinforcing stimuli is important to understand in relation to the environmental sources of substance abuse and habitual behavior and their alleviation. Schedules can, by means of ritualized salience, transform a noxious, aversive stimulus into one whose delivery supports the performance of the schedule. Further, schedule-induced behavior reveals that schedules have the power to enhance greatly the reinforcing efficacy of various ancillary commodities and activities so that they engage behavior excessively.

To summarize, the imposition of deprivation constraints and of schedules are general conditions giving rise to a host of remarkable behavioral increases. Obviously behavior might well be expected to become directed toward the attainment of the constrained commodity, but it is interesting that so much behavioral persistence can be sustained by so little positive reinforcement. In second-order schedules, for example, performance can be sustained for hours by an episode of drug delivery at the end of the day's session. What is surprising, however, is the occurrence other behavioral increases produced by deprivation and by schedules. These increases are seemingly unrelated to the deprivation imposed or the commodities made available by the schedule. For example, food deprivation yields dramatic increases in oral and intravenous drug-taking. Further, schedule arrangements can bring about alternations in the reinforcing function of an aversive stimulus such as shock transforming it into a positive sustainer of behavior. Similar arrangements (schedule-induction) can endow many ordinary commodities and activities with rather extraordinary reinforcing power so that fluids, drugs, attacks and other activities exhibit a severity and persistence of overindulgence analogous to compulsive and addictive behavior.

Commonalities in Agent-Host-Environment Interactions

Substance abuse and excessive behavior may now be described as a set of general interactions (commonalities) among an agent (a drug or valued commodity), a host (the individual), and the environment (the physical, economic, and social setting). The substitutability of one drug for another or some activity for a drug, often characteristic of the excessive user, can be viewed as en environmentally determined phenomenon. The phenomenon of substitutability is not just a function of what commodity is available or its price, nor the development of tolerance, nor specific ennui with an endless search for novel "kicks." Rather, the schedule of availability is perhaps the underlying common determinant. Schedules of reinforcement directly produce behavioral persistence; indirectly they can induce excessive adjunctive behavior. Searching out these generating schedules in the lives of individuals is a task having significance for both theory and therapeutic application. From this point of view, "hustling up" a drug may be of greater importance than what specific agent presently is hustled. Further, the social sharing of the drug-using experience is substitutable across agents. The social reinforcers involved in drug-using are of considerable importance and range from "Bowery bottle clubs" to the mutual timing of drugs within a using clique to "get off" together at a public event such as a concert.

The fact of animal and human cross-species commonality with respect to drugs producing addiction liability indicates that the initial reinforcing property of a substance is not capricious. Agents do differ in their initial engagement of behavior, but agent quality is not crucial for the production of persistent and excessive engagement. This is a function of reinforcement schedules and other generating conditions. The pharmacological actions of a substance are of undoubted importance in the initiation of use and the variety of environmental conditions under which this use occurs. A substance with strong intrinsic reinforcing properties does not require much in the way of a special history of exposure sequencing to engage behavior as does an event such as electric shock presentation. Neither does it require special environmental lacks and deprivations. Substances such as these are of greatest social concern since they progress most easily toward abuse. But no matter how intrinsically seductive a reinforcing agent may be, persistent and excessive use requires current or historical environmental enhancing factors.

In the search for commonalities among substances of abuse and kinds of excessive behavior, it seems improbable that a class of agents producing a particular sort of physiologic or neurochemical effect precipitating overindulgence can be delineated. Abuse and behavioral excess are not simply functions of exposure to a strongly reinforcing stimulus. Suggested mechanisms such as ritualized salience and other mechanisms of reinforcer malleability loom larger in the consideration of chronic, exaggerated behavior than do ready reinforcers such as the prompt effects of brief duration. Attempts at specifying a personality typology of persons prone to excess have not met with any signal success. Neither harsh nor permissive environments in themselves can mandate untoward excesses. But agents, individuals, and environments can all contribute to a dynamic interaction resulting in persistent, excessive behavior.

If an individual's situation in life is such that massive amounts of persistent work are required to earn daily bread, or to maintain social position, then the excessive work generated, while perhaps undesirable, cannot be considered pathological. While the environmental situation may be harsh, demanding, or unstable, behavioral persistence with regard to it would be judged a sensible response. Excessive behavior, whether we consider it in any instance to be a sensible strategy, a charismatic style, or a pathologic distortion, can be analyzed in terms of the set of conditions that produce it. What conditions are necessary and sufficient for instituting and maintaining strong and persistent behavior? If some features of the provoking conditions seem curious or the behavioral output appears irrational and even self-destructive, then so much the better for the characterization of "excess" and "abuse." A good place to start might be by sustaining the behavior (whatever act or complex performance might be chosen) by the provision of a powerful reinforcing stimulus contingent upon the individual engaging in that behavior. A strong reinforcer might be a drug dose or a bit of social approval. Small, even subtle or trivial, amounts of such reinforcing stimuli can sustain behavior quite powerfully. For building abuse, it is best if the reinforcer can be consumed and appreciated readily. Reinforcing stimuli that can be enjoyed by exerting little or no skill will be most widely successful. For example, a book, painting, or computer all require some skill in order to function as reinforcing stimuli, while commodities such as psychoactive drugs require little beyond minimal initiation to be consumed and appreciated.

In order to generate persistence, one might want to provide the readily appreciated reinforcer under some schedule of intermittent reinforcement. To gain maximal control over behavioral output, it is best that the subject have no competing reinforcing stimuli available in the situation. An environment providing few alternatives in the way of reinforcing opportunities satisfies this condition. Even with alternatives present, if the subject has had little chance to develop the skills to take advantage of them, the very absence of such reinforcing repertoires makes abuse of the immediate and readily appreciated reinforcer more probable. Once a person has become used to depending upon local, immediate reinforcers, a fateful, behavioral trajectory can curtail more varied and adaptive repertoires. If the individual comes not to care about acquiring skills, working, or establishing enduring social relations, the result can be behaviorally toxic. The toxicity is not so much due to what is done but, rather, to the consequences of not meeting responsibilities or developing potential.

Schedules of commodity availability, then, have a good deal to do with abuse. An intermittently reinforced schedule of persistent hustling may be required for attaining adequate drug supplies. Sparse schedules of reinforcement with respect to life's other crucial commodities and activities can induce a wide range of adjunctive behavioral excesses. Both these direct and indirect schedule effects serve to enhance the reinforcing efficacy of the commodities capturing the initial stream of behavior. The lack of alternative environmental opportunities and an adequate range of repertoires further constricts behavior to some abusive or excessive channel, enhancing its importance and output by default. Such constrictions come about by economic and educational privations and, once instituted, have long-term consequences characterized by nonadaptive inflexibilities to life's circumstances. Privations themselves reveal a remarkable commonality of effects. Food deprivation yields increased oral ingestion and self-injection of several classes of drugs in animals. It, as well as the deprivation of other commodities besides food, synergizes a variety of excessive, schedule-induced activities. Both these commonalities occur in several species.

For its maintenance excessive behavior often receives a good deal of social reinforcement from the invidiual's immediate friends and associates. The reinforcing engagement with a group afforded by the local, social acceptance of excesses not condoned by society at large should not be underestimated. It can have a stabilizing, simplifying effect on an otherwise aimless or anxious existence.

Directives for Research

1. There is now a considerable body of research on drug-seeking behavior in animals and humans that has clarified which drugs are self-administered habitually. The results of this work correlate rather well with the abuse liability of such drugs in human beings. Furthermore, subjective ratings by volunteers of the desirability of the effects produced by various drugs agree with this picture. We need to know now whether certain subjective effects are crucially involved in actually producing habitual drug-seeking. Is there indeed a constellation of subjective effects that are helpful in explaining and predicting the abuse of various kinds of drugs? The technology for obtaining answers to these questions is now available within animal, as well as human, research inquiries.

2. The ubiquity of habitual drug self-administration uncovered in the past decade of work has been remarkable. A variety of animal species will overindulge in a wide range of drugs. In order to clarify the rather general mechanisms of positive reinforcement in such persistent drug-taking, we need to study carefully a number of negative cases in which drugs (chlorpromazine, nalorphine) are *not* self-administered by choice and hence have no apparent abuse liability in animals or humans. What is it that may be unique about such drugs that make them negative cases? These drugs need to be characterized both behaviorally and neurochemically.

3. Many individuals at all levels of society grow up in proximity to others abusing drugs and may even be initiated into drug-taking at some time during their development, yet remain aloof from drugs. Despite a social background and initial exposure similar to habitual drug users, they are negative cases. They fail to progress to sustained abuse. We need studies of these people to determine why such apparent candidates for abuse are resistant. Are crucial aspects of their situation during development contributing to a later resistance? Is there something unique about their current situation that is important in deflecting them from drug-taking and maintaining them on such a course?

4. From an evaluative perspective, habitual drug abuse involves some behavior sequences that are too strong and persistent (drug-hustling, drug-taking) and others that are often too weak and easily disrupted (legitimate occupational concerns). Basic research is needed on how to strengthen weak behavior, particularly when the rewards for such behavior are often long delayed. The techniques of how to sustain and encourage delicate but ultimately adjustive behavior require development. Equally important, is the need for a technology of interference with strong and excessive behavior, particularly when it competes with adjustive behavior. Attempts to attenuate unwanted behavior can result in objectionable side-effects: aggressive reactions, escape, undue tyrannical controls. While considerable laboratory lore has accumulated on how to strengthen weak behavior and attenuate unwanted behavior, practical and ethical concerns need to be worked out in actual therapeutic contexts. Immediate positive reinforcement (rewards) for desired behavior cannot always be applied. The ultimate negative consequences of unwanted and self-destructive behavior are often long-delayed. Both laboratory research and work within practical, social contexts with human beings needs to be carried forward on the techniques of strengthening and attenuating complex sequences of behavior. Such modification would enable us to redirect the abuser toward more socially appropriate and individually productive modes of behaving.

5. Some drugs appear to be stronger initial reinforcers of behavior than others. Reliable measures of these differences are needed. Often a great deal of behavior will be engaged in for the delivery of a rather small amount of a drug. What environmental conditions determine great behavioral persistence for small drug rewards? That is, what environmental factors enhance the reward value of drugs? Do drugs differ in their sensitivity to such factors? Often the entire context in which drug-seeking and drug-taking occurs seems to support these activities as a life-style by providing a matrix of social and conditioned reinforcement. These contextual factors are suspected of being of prime importance in maintaining drug-taking. We need both laboratory and clinical studies of how these factors may be sustaining drug relapse or conditioned abstinence and how they operate to displace alternative adjustive behavior.

6. While the possible neurochemical and subjective experience bases underlying drug reinforcement effects have been considered, a satisfactory explanation framed in terms of a neurochemistry of pleasure seems unlikely. Evidence has been presented from a number of studies showing that animals will work to self-administer noxious electric shocks persistently if these are introduced under rather simple, scheduled conditions. What is it about certain schedules of drug availability that enhances the attractiveness of a variety of drugs? Like electric shock, many drugs lead to noxious consequences. In the case of drugs, the negative aspects may be delayed (ultimate

medical or socially punishing consequences, for example), but sometimes they are not. Animals will self-administer cocaine to the point of convulsions and then resume once again. All of these are stimuli that possess noxious and negative effects that nevertheless can sustain persistent behavior leading to their delivery. The behavior does not appear, then, to be sustained by carefree, hedonistic sources. The analysis of such situations may well illuminate one of the central problems of drug dependence: Why is abuse stably maintained in the face of various, strong negative consequences?

7. Excessive and persistent overindulgence also can occur as a side-effect (adjunct) to a schedule of limited availability of an important commodity. We need to know how general adjunctive behavior effects are and whether the environmental sources of adjunctive behavior contribute to an explanation of human drug abuse and other excessive behavior (such as aggression). Animal research indicates that severe and chronic adjunctive behavior (drug overindulgence, hyperactivity, aggression) results from a schedule of intermittent food availability. Scant work has been done on scheduling commodities other than food to determine if they are equally powerful in generating excessive behavior. What is it about the intermittent delivery of limited rations that induces extravagant and abusive behavior? Adjunctive behavior research needs to be applied to drugs using a greater variety of commodity-limitations as inducing events. An inadequate rate of social as well as "hard" commodity rewards may underlie drug abuse and other compulsive behavior. Study of these phenomena may aid us in constructing a useful and explicit general theory of the sources of excessive behavior.

8. We need to know whether drug reinforcers are similar to other rewarding agents or if they possess unique properties. For example, recent research has shown that food deprivation can increase the intake of several kinds of drugs both orally and intravenously. It is not known whether this enhancement is unique to drugs or is characteristic of a wider range of rewarding events. Nor is it known whether the deprivation of important commodities other than food (social rewards, monetary gain) can lead to increased drug-taking. Research should try to clarify whether environmental variables have common properties for enhancing or suppressing behavior when applied across various types of reinforcing events. Schedules of reward limitation often generate surprisingly strong and excessive behavioral adjuncts and the general conditions producing such phenomena need to be clarified. It is no longer adequate or even useful to say simply that social or nutritional deprivation as a general condition can lead to excessive, abusive behavior. We need to know explicitly the quantitative details of how this comes about so that therapeutic strategies of intervention can be designed.

9. Two of the most striking phenomena that occur with repeated administration of many drugs are the induction of tolerance and physical dependence. While the induction of physical dependence cannot explain the initial attraction to a drug nor its reinforcing efficacy in the early stages, nevertheless physical dependence in its manifestation during withdrawal may enhance the control over behavior exerted by a drug. The withdrawal of a drug like morphine that has been sustaining physical dependence leads to disruption in the discriminative stimulus control of behavior as well as interference with other adjustive behavioral repertoires. The breakdown of these functions occasioned by withdrawal needs to be compared to their functioning under conditions where important commodities other than drugs are withdrawn (for example, food) in order to determine if drugs with dependence liability are unique disrupters of behavior in these regards. If indeed they are, then we can begin to specify how physical dependence on drugs might differ from other need states in its behavioral implications. A gradual increase in the amount of a drug self-administered daily sometimes is observed both in humans and animals. This increase often has been assumed to reflect the development of tolerance to the reinforcing effects of the drug. Current evidence does not suggest, however, that the acquisition of tolerance can explain either the increase in drug intake or a continuance of drug-seeking. Tolerance to the reinforcing effect of drugs is not an evident feature of the drug self-administration research with animals. We need research on the question of whether tolerance acquisition in itself leads to inexorable increases in intake. For example, the increases sometimes observed may be only permissive as tolerance to the depressing or disruptive aspects of a drug develops. In the case of both tolerance and physical dependence, then, it is by no means clear at present whether these pharmacological processes are at all major contributors to either the maintenance or augmentation of drug-taking. These issues need to be addressed by critical experiments.

10. Some agents, such as cocaine, easily can be established as reinforcers under a broad variety of environmental conditions in the laboratory and are known to be widely abused by humans. Nevertheless, it is possible to show that under some conditions these drugs have aversive effects and are avoided (Spealman 1979). Investigation of the conditions under which such seductive drugs can have their aversive properties predominate would have important implications for prevention and treatment.

11. Several ingestional disorders in humans appear similar to behavioral excesses induced in animals. Bulemia, anorexia nervosa, and psychogenic polydipsia are human disorders that recently have attracted a good deal of interest. A detailed animal model of psychogenic polydipsia notwithstanding, there is no assurance that because the topographies of the behavior are similar an identity of the underlying process in animals and humans exists.

As in the case of substance abuse, the question of whether there are privations and reward intermittencies that induce similar kinds of excessive behavior in humans, as in animals, remains largely a task for future research. The current studies with humans are encouraging, but the intriguing possibility of an identity of mechanism remains to be investigated both by controlled laboratory experiments and by the analysis of the natural history of these disorders.

References

Aigner, T.G., and Balster, R.L. 1978. Choice behavior in rhesus monkeys: Cocaine versus food. *Science* 201:534-535.

Angle, H.V., and Parwatikar, S. 1973. Methadone self-prescripted by heroin addicts in an inpatient detoxification program. *Psychol. Rec.* 23:209-214.

Azrin, N.H. 1961. Time-out from positive reinforcement. *Science* 133: 382-383.

Azrin, N.H., Hutchinson, R.R., and Hake, D.F. 1966. Extinction-induced aggression. *J. Exp. Anal. Behav.* 9:191-204.

Barrett, J.E. 1977. Behavioral history as a determinant of the effects of d-amphetamine on punished behavior. *Science* 198:67-69.

Barrett, J.E. 1978. Behavior simultaneously maintained by both presentation and termination of noxious stimuli. *J. Exp. Anal. Behav.* 29:375-383.

Bonese, K.R., Wainer, B.H., Fitch, F.W., Rothberg, R.M., and Schuster, C.R. 1974. Changes in heroin self-administration by rhesus monkey after morphine immunisation. *Nature* (London) 252:708-710.

Braveman, N.S. 1977. What studies on preexposure to pharmacological agents tell us about the nature of aversion-inducing treatment. In T.M. Barker, M.R. Best, and M. Domjan (eds.), *Learning Mechanisms in Food Selection*, pp. 511-532. Houston: Baylor University Press.

Byrd, L.D. 1969. Responding in the cat maintained under response-independent electric shock and response-produced electric shock. *J. Exp. Anal. Behav.* 12:1-10.

Campbell, B.A. 1964. Theory and research on the effects of water deprivation on random activity in the rat. In M.J. Wayner (ed.), *Thirst*, pp. 317-334. New York: Pergamon Press.

Cappell, H., and LeBlanc, A.E. 1979. Tolerance to, and physical dependence on, ethanol: Why do we study them? *Drug Alcohol Dependence* 4:15-31.

Carroll, M.E., France, C.P., and Meisch, R.A. 1979. Food deprivation increases oral and intravenous drug intake in rats. *Science* 205:319-321.

Carroll, M.E., and Meisch, R.A. 1980. Oral phencyclidine (PCP) self-administration in rhesus monkeys: effects of feeding conditions. *J. Pharm. Exper. Ther.* 214:339-346.

Cherek, D.R. Thompson, T., and Heistad, G.T. 1973. Responding maintained by the opportunity to attack during an interval food reinforcement schedule. *J. Exp. Anal. Behav.* 19:113-123.

Clark, J., Gannon, M., Hughes, I., Keogh, C., Singer, G., and Wallace, M. 1977. Adjunctive behavior in humans in a group gambling situation. *Physiol. Behav.* 18:159-161.

Falk, J.L. 1961. Production of polydipsia in normal rats by an intermittent food schedule. *Science* 133:195-196.

Falk, J.L. 1966. The motivational properties of schedule-induced polydipsia. *J. Exp. Anal. Behav.* 9:19-25.

Falk, J.L. 1967. Control of schedule-induced polydipsia: type, size, and spacing of meals. *J. Exp. Anal. Behav.* 10:199-206.

Falk, J.L. 1969. Conditions producing psychogenic polydipsia in animals. *Ann. N.Y. Acad. Sci.* 157:569-593.

Falk, J.L. 1971. The nature and determinants of adjunctive behavior. *Physiol. Behav.* 6:577-588.

Falk, J.L. 1977. The origin and functions of adjunctive behavior. *Animal Learn. Behav.* 5:325-335.

Falk, J.L. 1981. The environmental generation of excessive behavior. In S.J. Mulé (ed.), *Behavior in Excess: An Examination of the Volitional Disorders.* New York: Free Press.

Falk, J.L., and Samson, H.H. 1975. Schedule-induced physical dependence on ethanol. *Pharmacol. Revs.* 27:449-464.

Falk, J.L., Samson, H.H., and Winger, G. 1972. Behavioral maintenance of high concentrations of blood ethanol and physical dependence in the rat. *Science* 177:811-813.

Fallon, J.H., Jr., Allen, J.D., and Butler, J.A. 1979. Assessment of adjunctive behaviors in humans using a stringent control procedure. *Physiol. Behav.* 22:1089-1092.

Ferster, C.B., and Skinner, B.F. 1957. *Schedules of Reinforcement.* New York: Appleton-Century-Crofts.

Fischman, M.W., and Schuster, C.R. 1975. Behavioral, biochemical and morphological effects of methamphetamine in the rhesus monkey. In B. Weiss and V. Laties (eds.), *Behavioral Toxicology*, pp. 375-394. New York: Plenum Press.

Gamzu, E. 1977. The multifaceted nature of taste-aversion-inducing agents: Is there a single common factor? In T.M. Barker, M.R. Best, and M. Domjan (eds.), *Learning Mechanisms in Food Selection*, pp. 477-510. Houston: Baylor University Press.

Garcia, J., Buchwald, N.A., Feder, B.H., Koelling, R.A., and Tedrow, L.F. 1964. Ionizing radiation as a perceptual and aversive stimulus. In T.J. Haley and R.S. Snider (eds.), *Response on the Nervous System to Ionizing Radiation*, pp. 673-686. New York: Little, Brown.

Garcia, J., and Koelling, R.A. 1966. Relation of cue to consequence in avoidance learning. *Psychonomic Sci.* 4:123-124.

Garcia, J., Kimeldorf, D.J., and Koelling, R.A. 1955. A conditioned aversion towards saccharin resulting from exposure to gamma radiation. *Science* 122:157-159.

Garzia, J., and Hankins, W.G. 1977. On the origin of food aversion paradigms. In T.M. Barker, M.R. Best, and M. Domjan (eds.), *Learning Mechanisms in Food Selection*, pp. 3-32. Houston: Baylor University Press.

Geller, I., and Seifter, J. 1960. The effects of meprobamate, barbiturates, d-amphetamine, and promazine on experimentally induced conflict in the rat. *Psychopharmacologia* 1:482-492.

Gilbert, R.M. 1978. Schedule-induced self-administration of drugs. In D.E. Blackman and D.J. Sanger (eds.), *Contemporary Research in Behavioral Pharmacology*, pp. 289-323. New York: Plenum Press.

Goldberg, S.R. 1976. The behavior analysis of drug addiction. In S.D. Glick and J. Goldfarb (eds.), *Behavioral Pharmacology*, pp. 283-316. St. Louis: C.V. Mosby.

Goldberg, S.R., Kelleher, R.T., and Morse, W.H. 1975. Second-order schedules of drug injection. *Fed. Proc.* 34:1771-1776.

Goldberg, S.R., and Schuster, C.R. 1967. Conditioned suppression by a stimulus associated with nalorphine in morphine dependent monkeys. *J. Exp. Anal. Behav.* 10:235-242.

Goldberg, S.R., and Schuster, C.R. 1970. Conditioned nalorphine-induced abstinence changes: persistence in post-dependent monkeys. *J. Exp. Anal. Behav.* 14:33-46.

Goldberg, S.R., Woods, J.H., and Schuster, C.R. 1969. Morphine: conditioned increases in self-administration in rhesus monkeys. *Science* 166: 1306-1307.

Griffiths, R.R., and Balster, R.L. 1979. Opioids: similarity between evaluations of subjective effects and animal self-administration results. *Clin. Pharmac. Ther.* 25:611-617.

Griffiths, R.R., Bigelow, G., and Liebson, I. 1976a. Facilitation of human tobacco self-administration by ethanol: a behavioral analysis. *J. Exp. Anal. Behav.* 25:279-292.

Griffiths, R.R., Bigelow, G., and Liebson, I. 1976b. Human sedative self-administration: effects of interingestion interval and dose. *J. Pharm. Exp. Ther.* 197:488-494.

Haertzen, C.A. 1970. Subjective effects of narcotic antagonists cyclazocine and nalorphine on the addiction research center inventory (ARCI). *Psychopharmacologia* 18:366-377.

Hennessy, J.W., Smotherman, W.R., and Levine, S. 1976. Conditioned taste aversion and the pituitary-adrenal system. *Behav. Biol.* 16:413-424.

Hutchinson, R.R., Azrin, N.H., and Hunt, G.M. 1968. Attack produced by intermittent reinforcement of a concurrent operant response. *J. Exp. Anal. Behav.* 11:489-495.

Johanson, C.E. 1978. Drugs as reinforcers. In D.E. Blackman, and D.J. Sanger (eds.), *Contemporary Research in Behavioral Pharmacology*, pp. 325-390. New York: Plenum Press.

Johanson, C.E., and Balster, R.L. 1978. A summary of the results of a drug self-administration study using substitution procedures in rhesus monkeys. *Bull. Narc.* 30:43-54.

Johanson, C.E., and Uhlenhuth, E.H. 1978. Drug self-administration in humans. In N. Krasnegor (ed.), *Self-Administration of Abused Substances: Methods for Study*, pp. 68-85. National Institute on Drug Abuse Research Monograph 20, DHEW Publication No. (ADM) 78-727. Washington, D.C.: Government Printing Office.

Johanson, C.E., and Uhlenhuth, E.H. 1980a. Drug preference and mood in humans: d-amphetamine. *Psychopharmacology* 71:275-279.

Johanson, C.E., and Uhlenhuth, E.H. 1980b. Drug preference and mood in humans: diazepam. *Psychopharmacology* 71:269-273.

Johanson, C.E., and Uhlenhuth, E.H. 1981a. Drug preference and mood in humans: repeated administration of d-amphetamine. *Pharmacol. Biochem. Behav.* 14.

Johanson, C.E., and Uhlenhuth, E.H. 1981b. Drug preferences in humans. *Fed. Proc.*, in press.

Jones, B.E., and Prada, J.A. 1975. Drug-seeking behavior during methadone maintenance. *Psychopharmacologia* 41:7-40.

Jones, B.E., and Prada, J.A. 1977. Effects of methadone and morphine maintenance on drug-seeking behavior in the dog. *Psychopharmacologia* 54:109-112.

Jones, T.B., and Kamil, A.C. 1973. Tool-making and tool-using in the Northern blue jay. *Science* 180:1076-1078.

Kalat, J.W., and Rozin, P. 1970. "Salience": a factor which can override temporal contiguity in taste-aversion learning. *J. Comp. Physiol. Psychol.* 71:192-197.

Keehn, J.D. (ed.) 1979. *Origins of Madness: Psychopathology in Animal Life*. New York: Pergamon Press.

Keys, A. 1952. Experimental induction of psychoneuroses by starvation. In *The Biology of Mental Health and Disease*. New York: Hoeber.

Keys, A., Brozek, J., Henschel, A., Mickelsen, O., and Taylor, H.L. 1950. *The Biology of Human Starvation*. Minneapolis: University of Minnesota Press.

Khazan, N., Weeks, J.R., and Schroeder, L.A. 1967. Electroencephalo-graphic, electromyographic and behavioral correlates during a cycle of self-maintained morphine addiction in the rat. *J. Pharmacol. Exp. Ther.* 155:521-531.

Krasnegor, N.A. (ed.) *Behavioral Tolerance: Research and Treatment Implications.* National Institute on Drug Abuse Research Monograph 18. Washington, D.C.: U.S. Government Printing Office, 1978.

Lang, W.J., Latiff, A.A., McQueen, A., and Singer, G. 1977. Self-administration of nicotine with and without a food delivery schedule. *Pharmacol. Biochem. Behav.* 7:65-70.

Lemere, G., and Voegthin, W.L. 1950. An evaluation of the aversion treatment of alcoholism. *Quart. J. Stud. Alc.* 11:199-204.

Levitsky, D., and Collier, G. 1968. Schedule-induced wheel running. *Physiol. Behav.* 3:571-573.

MacCulloch, M.J., Feldman, M.P., Orford, J.F., and MacCulloch, M.T. 1966. Anticipatory avoidance in the treatment of alcoholism: a record of therapeutic failure. *Behav. Res. Ther.* 4:187-196.

Malagodi, E.F., Gardner, M.L., and Palermo, G. 1978. Responding maintained under fixed-interval and fixed-time schedules of electric shock presentation. *J. Exp. Anal. Behav.* 30:271-279.

McKearney, J.W. 1968. Maintenance of responding under a fixed-interval schedule of electric shock-presentation. *Science* 160:1249-1251.

McKearney, J.W., and Barrett, J.E. 1975. Punished behavior: increases in responding after d-amphetamine. *Psychopharmacologia* 41:23-26.

McKearney, J.W. 1979. Interrelations among prior experience and current conditions in the determination of behavior and the effects of drugs. In T. Thompson and P.B. Dews (eds.), *Advances in Behavioral Pharmacology*, vol. 2, pp. 39-64. New York: Academic Press.

McKearney, J.W., and Barrett, J.E. Schedule-controlled behavior and the effects of drugs. In D.E. Blackman and D.J. Sanger (eds.), *Contemporary Research in Behavioral Pharmacology*, pp. 1-68. New York: Plenum Press.

Meisch, R.A., and Thompson, T. 1973. Ethanol as a reinforcer: effects of fixed-ratio size and food deprivation. *Psychopharmacologia* 28:171-183.

Mello, N. 1972. Behavioral studies of alcoholism. In B. Kissin and H. Begleiter (eds.), *The Biology of Alcoholism*, vol. 2, pp. 219-291. New York: Plenum Press.

Mello, N.K., and Mendelson, J.H. 1965. Operant analysis of drinking patterns of chronic alcoholics. *Nature* 206:43-46.

Mello, N.K., and Mendelson, J.H. 1970. Experimentally-induced intoxication in alcoholics: a comparison between programmed and spontaneous drinking. *J. Pharmacol. Exp. Ther.* 173:101-116.

Mello, N.K., and Mendelson, J.H. 1971. Drinking patterns during work contingent and noncontingent alcohol acquisition. In N.K. Mello and J.H. Mendelson (eds.), *Recent Advances in Studies of Alcoholism*, pp. 647-686. Washington, D.C.: U.S. Government Printing Office.

Mendelson, J.H., Rossi, A.M., and Meyer, R.F. (eds.) 1974. *The Use of Marihuana: A Psychological and Physiological Inquiry*. New York: Plenum Press.

Miles, C.G., Congreave, G., Gibbins, R., Marshman, J., Devenyi, P., and Hicks, R. 1974. An experimental study of the effects of daily cannabis smoking on behavior patterns. *Acta Pharmacol. Toxicol.* 34:1-44.

Mitchell, D., Winter, W., and Morisaki, C.M. 1977. Conditioned taste aversions accompanied by geophagia: evidence for the occurrence of "psychological" factors in the etiology of pica. *Psychosomat. Med.* 39:402-412.

Morse, W.H., and Kelleher, R.T. 1970. Schedules as fundamental determinants of behavior. In W.N. Schoenfeld (ed.) *The Theory of Reinforcement Schedules*, pp. 139-185. Englewood Cliffs, N.J.: Prentice-Hall.

Morse, W.H., Mead, R.N., and Kelleher, R.T. 1967. Modulation of elicited behavior by a fixed-interval schedule of electric shock presentation. *Science* 157:215-217.

Muller, P.G., Crow, R.E., and Cheney, C.D. 1979. Schedule-induced locomotor activity in humans. *J. Exp. Anal. Behav.* 31:83-90.

O'Brien, C. 1975. Experimental analysis of conditioning factors in human narcotic addiction. *Pharmacol. Rev.* 27:533-543.

O'Brien, C.P., Testa, T.J., Brady, J.P., and Wells, B. 1977. Conditioned narcotic withdrawal in humans. *Science* 195:1000-1002.

Oei, T.P.S., Singer, G., and Jefferys, D. 1980. The interaction of a fixed time food delivery schedule and body weight on self-administration of narcotic analgesics. *Psychopharmacology* 67:171-176.

Peterson, M.R., and Lyson, D.O. 1978. Schedule-induced polydipsia in rats living in an operant environment. *J. Exp. Anal. Behav.* 29:493-503.

Pickens, R., Cunningham, M.R., Heston, L.L., Eckert, E., and Gustafson, L.K. 1977. Dose preference during pentobarbital self-administration by humans. *J. Pharmacol. Exp. Ther.* 203:310-318.

Revusky, S., and Bedarf, E.W. 1967. Association of illness with ingestion of novel foods. *Science* 155:219-220.

Richter, C.P. 1942-43. Total self regulatory functions in animals and human beings. *Harvey Lect. Ser.* 38:63-103.

Rigter, H., and Popping, A. 1976. Hormonal influences on the extinction of conditioned taste aversions. *Psychopharmacologia* 46:255-261.

Robins, L.M., David, D.H., and Nurco, D.W. 1974. How permanent was Vietnam drug addiction? *Am. J. Pub. Health* 64:38-43.

Routtenberg, A., and Kuznesof, A. 1967. Self-starvation of rats living in activity wheels on a restricted feeding schedule. *J. Comp. Physiol. Psychol.* 64:414-421.

Rozin, P., and Kalat, J.W. 1971. Specific hungers and poison avoidance as adaptive specializations of learning. *Psychol. Rev.* 78:459-486.

Schaefer, G.J., and Holtzman, S.G. 1977. Discriminative effects of morphine in the squirrel monkey. *J. Pharmacol. Exp. Ther.* 201:67-75.

Schaefer, G.J., and Holtzman, S.G. 1978. Discriminative effects of cyclazocine in the squirrel monkey. *J. Pharmacol. Exp. Ther.* 205:291-301.

Schuster, C.R. 1970. Psychological approaches to opiate dependence and self-administration by laboratory animals. *Fed. Proc.* 29, no. 1 (January- February):2-5.

Schuster, C.R. 1975. Drugs as reinforcers in monkey and man. *Pharmacol. Rev.* 27:343-356.

Schuster, C.R. 1978. *Theoretical Basis of Behavioral Tolerance: Implications of the Phenomenon for Problems of Drug Abuse.* National Institute on Drug Abuse Research Monograph 18, pp. 4-17.

Schuster, C.R., and Balster, R.L. 1977. The discriminative stimulus properties of drugs. In T. Thompson and P.B. Dews (eds.), *Advances in Behavioral Pharmacology*, vol. 1, pp. 86-138. New York: Academic Press.

Schuster, C.R., and Johanson, C.E. 1974. The use of animals for the study of drug abuse. In R.J. Gibbons, Y. Israel, H. Kalant, R.E. Papham, W. Schmidt, and R.G. Smart (eds.), *Research Advances in Alcohol and Drug Problems*, vol. 1. New York: Wiley.

Schuster, C.R., Renault, P.F., and Blaine, J. 1979. An analysis of the relationship of psychopathology to non-medical drug use. In R.W. Pickens and L.L. Heston (eds.), *Psychiatric Factors in Drug Abuse*, pp. 1-19. New York: Grune and Stratton.

Schuster, C.R., and Thompson, T.I. 1969. Self administration of and behavioral dependence on drugs. *Ann. Rev. Pharmac.* 9:483-502.

Schuster, C.R., and Woods, J.H. 1968. The conditioned reinforcing effects of stimuli associated with morphine reinforcement. *Intern. J. Addict.* 3:223-230.

Shannon, H.E., and Holtzman, S.G. 1977. Further evaluation of the discriminative effects of morphine in the rat. *J. Pharmacol. Exp. Ther.* 201:55-66.

Sidman, M., Herrnstein, R.J., and Conrad, D.G. 1957. Maintenance of avoidance behavior by unavoidable shocks. *J. Compar. Physiol. Psychol.* 50:553-557.

Smith, A. 1974 (orig. 1776). *The Wealth of Nations.* Harmondsworth, England: Penguin Books.

Smith, L.A., and Lang, W.J. 1980. Changes occurring in self administration of nicotine by rats over a 28-day period. *Pharmacol. Biochem. Behav.* 13:215-220.

Spealman, R.D. 1979. Behavior maintained by termination of a schedule of self-administered cocaine. *Science* 204:1231-1233.

Steiner, S.S., Beer, B., and Shaffer, M.M. 1969. Escape from self-produced rates of brain stimulation. *Science* 163:90-91.

Sutter, A.G. 1966. The world of the righteous dope fiend. *Issues Criminol.* 2:177-222.

Takahashi, R.N., and Singer, G. 1980. Effects of body weight levels on cannabis self-injection. *Pharmacol. Biochem. Behav.* 13:877-881.

Takahashi, R.N., Singer, G., and Oei, T.P.S. 1978. Schedule induced self-injection of d-amphetamine by naive animals. *Pharmacol. Biochem. Behav.* 9:857-861.

Tapp, J.T. 1969. Activity, reactivity, and the behavior-directing properties of stimuli. In J.T. Tapp (ed.), *Reinforcement and Behavior*, pp. 146-177. New York: Academic Press.

Thompson, T., and Schuster, C.R. 1964. Morphine self-administration food-reinforced and avoidance behaviors in rhesus monkeys. *Psychopharmacologia* 5:87-94.

Villarreal, J. 1967. Schedule-induced pica. Paper read at Eastern Psychological Association, Boston, April.

Wagner, G.C., Ricaurte, G.A., Seiden, L.S., Schuster, C.R., Miller, R.J., and Westley, J. 1980. Long-lasting depletions of striatal dopamine and loss of dopamine uptake sites following repeated administration of methamphetamine. *Brain Res.* 181:151-160.

Wainer, B., Fitch, F.W., Rothberg, R.M., and Schuster, C.R. 1973. In vitro morphine antogaonism by antibodies. *Nature* (London) 241:537-538.

Wallace, M., and Singer, G. 1976. Adjunctive behavior and smoking induced by a maze solving schedule in humans. *Physiol. Behav.* 17:849-852.

Wallace, M., Singer, G., Wagner, M.J., and Cook, P. 1975. Adjunctive behavior in humans during game playing. *Physiol. Behav.* 14:651-654.

Weiner, H. 1970. Human behavioral persistence. *Psychol. Rec.* 20:445-456.

Wickler, A. 1965. Conditioning factors in opiate addiction and relapse. In D.M. Wilner and G.G. Kassebaum (eds.), *Narcotics*. New York: McGraw-Hill.

Winter, J.C. 1974. Hallucinogens as discriminative stimuli. *Fed. Proc.* 33:1825-1832.

Wise, R.A., Yokel, R.A., and DeWit, H. 1976. Both positive reinforcement and conditioned aversion from amphetamine and from apomorphine in rats. *Science* 191:1273-1275.

Woods, J.H., Ikomi, and Winger, G.D. 1971. The reinforcing property of alcohol. In M.H. Roach and W.M. McIssac (eds.), *Biological Aspects of Alcohol*, pp. 371-388. Austin: University of Texas Press.

Woods, J.H., and Schuster, C.R. 1968. Reinforcement properties of morphine, cocaine and SPA as a function of unit dose. *Intern. J. Addict.* 3:231-237.

4

A Learning-Theory Approach to Commonalities

Nelson H. Donegan,
Judith Rodin,
Charles P. O'Brien, and
Richard L. Solomon

The goal of this chapter is to identify common properties of substances and activities of abuse. The focus is upon alcohol, opiates, nicotine, food, and gambling (collectively referred to as substances). We begin with this list because its entries are of current concern to society—it is common knowledge that repeated experience with these substances can lead to such extensive use that the individual or society judges the pattern of use to be undesirable. These substances have the capacity to gain considerable control over individuals' behavior, and reducing such control can be very difficult. Here we will be concerned with how these substances gain control but not with the criteria for determining what level of use is excessive, that is, when use turns into abuse. Identifying variables that influence the ability of substances to gain control over behavior should be a step toward developing more successful methods of modifying patterns of use that are considered problematic or even toward preventing their becoming problematic.

Habitual substance use is a complex, multiply determined phenomenon; the variables governing and defining use and abuse range from biochemical to sociocultural. In constructing a list of candidate common properties, we have selected several that have been or could plausibly be used to explain how experience with these substances can result in habitual use and why such behavior can be difficult to modify. These properties are as follows:

1. Ability of the substance to act as an instrumental reinforcer.
2. Acquired tolerance. Repeated use can result in reduced effectiveness of the substance.
3. Development of psychological and physiological dependence with repeated use. Repeated use produces withdrawal effects that motivate further use.
4. Affective contrast. The substance tends to produce an initial affective state (euphoria) which is then followed by an opposing state (dysphoria).
5. Ability of the substance to act as an effective Pavlovian unconditioned stimulus.

6. Ability of various states (general arousal, stress, pain) to influence substance use.

As can be seen from the list, the level of analysis chosen here is primarily behavioral. The approach to understanding the development of habitual use of substances draws upon theories of instrumental and Pavlovian conditioning. Consistent with this strategy is the speculation that an understanding of how the substances of interest gain control over behavior does not require accounts unique to each substance but, rather, that factors important in influencing the level of use of one substance will share common roles in influencing the use of other substances. In fact, it is likely that these factors play a significant role in the development and maintenance of many habitual behaviors (a point addressed below in detail).

In the first section of the chapter representative reports are presented on each of the five substances with regard to each of the six common properties. A 5×6 matrix is constructed, with substances as rows and properties as columns. The matrix is built column by column: for each property reports relevant to each of the five substances are summarized. The reports are not to be considered an exhaustive review of the literature but, rather, the findings that best comment on the point under consideration. Instead of covering all the instances of commonalities, we present cases that are representative and instructive. It remains for future analysis to determine on the basis of all extant data how broad or circumscribed the view of commonalities needs to be. We do not comment on differences although there surely must be many, based on the different pharmacological properties of these various substances for example. This too remains a task for future research.

Common Properties

Reinforcement

To say that a substance is used at a level considered to be excessive by the standards of the individual or society and that reducing the level of use is difficult is one way of saying that the substance has gained considerable control over the individual's behavior. In the language of behavior theory, the substance acts as a powerful reinforcer: behaviors instrumental in obtaining the substance become more frequent, vigorous, or persistent. The control a reinforcer exerts over an individual's behavior depends upon the conditions under which the substance is available (the contingencies or schedules of reinforcement and the number and kinds of reinforcers to which the individual has access) as well as the intrinsic properties of the reinforcer (both quantitative and qualitative). See chapter 3 for an in-depth analysis of schedule effects.

One way of evaluating the reinforcing potential of a susbtance is to allow subjects to administer the substance to themselves by engaging in simple instrumental behavior, say pressing a lever to receive fixed amounts of a drug. Understandably, almost all of the systematic research on the reinforcing properties of drugs has been carried out on animal subjects.

Alcohol. Deneau, Yanagita, and Seevers (1969) assessed the reinforcing potential of ethanol by arranging for rhesus monkeys to have continuous access to discrete amounts of ethanol, which could be self-administered by intravenous infusion. Under such conditions, subjects would self-administer ethanol at doses of 200 mg/kg (milligrams per kilogram of their body weight), their responding being limited to daylight hours. The greatest intake occurred at the start of each day. Interestingly, subjects occasionally abstained from ethanol for several days in spite of the severe abstinence syndromes that resulted. However, termination of ethanol self-administration was not observed when ethanol was only available on a limited schedule, say for a three-hour period out of every twenty-four hours (Winger and Woods 1973). Within these limited periods, subjects showed initial bursts of responding, which trailed off to infrequent bursts. When the amount of ethanol delivered at each infusion was varied, the frequency of self-administration increased as the dose per injection increased from 5 to 75 mg/kg, but increasing the dose level from 75 to 500 mg/kg did not result in increased administration (Woods, Ikomi, and Winger 1971).

When rats (Meisch and Thompson 1971, 1974) or rhesus monkeys (Meisch, Henningfield, and Thompson 1975) were given access to ethanol solutions, responding to gain access to the solution increased and then decreased as the concentration of the solution was increased, with peak responding occurring at 4-8 percent (volume/volume) concentrations. Total intake, on the other hand, increased monotonically with solution concentration.

Opiates. Deneau, Yanagita, and Seevers (1969) evaluated the reinforcing potential of morphine by requiring rhesus monkeys with indwelling catheters to press a level for discrete amounts of the opiate. With morphine continuously available, subjects increased their daily intake up to the sixth and seventh week of the experiment (asymptotic daily dosage ran between 50 and 100 mg/kg; individual infusions were set at 0.5 mg/kg). None of the subjects voluntarily discontinued self-administration. When intake of morphine was interrupted due to equipment failure, subjects showed "typical and severe abstinence syndromes during which they pressed the lever almost continuously in attempts to obtain morphine injections" (p. 37). Schuster and Villareal (1968) and Woods and Schuster (1971) showed the reinforcing properties of opiates to be a function of dose level, noting that subjects self-administered the opiate at low dosage levels at which withdrawal symptoms do not develop. That is, observable withdrawal symptoms are not a necessary condition for morphine to exhibit reinforcing properties.

Nicotine. Rats can learn to self-inject nicotine (Clark 1969; Hanson, Ivester, and Morton 1977; Lang, Latiff, McQueen, and Singer 1977; Pradhan and Bowling 1971), as can monkeys (Deneau and Inoki 1967; Yanagita 1973, 1976). Hanson, Ivester, and Morton (1979) reported that for drug-naive rats, 30-60 mg/kg intravenous injections of nicotine produced maximal rates of self-administration. Interestingly, rats pretreated with nicotine and subsequently allowed to self-administer nicotine showed levels of responding higher than those of rats pretreated with saline solution. Hanson et al. also observed that doses greater than 100 mg/kg, which resulted in convulsions following each injection, were self-administered at rates significantly higher than for controls receiving saline solution.

Food. The reinforcing potential of food is amply documented in the voluminous literature on instrumental conditioning (for example Kimble 1961, Mackintosh 1974, and the *Journal of the Experimental Analysis of Behavior*, *Journal of Experimental Psychology*, and *Journal of Comparative and Physiological Psychology*). In general, the ability of response-contingent food presentation to gain control over behavior is an increasing function of the food's palatability, quantity, and the extent of the individual's hunger (Konorski 1967).

Gambling. The success of lottery systems, on-track and off-track betting on horse races, and casinos attests to the fact that many individuals find various types of gambling attractive. With regard to systematic, controlled evaluations of the kinds of gambles individuals prefer, most research has been directed at the development and evaluation of expected-utility theory, a formalized normative model of rational choice (Raiffa 1968; Tversky and Kahneman 1974). Laboratory experiments typically involve contrived gambles for small stakes and a large number of repetitions of very similiar problems. Unfortunately, these very aspects tend to limit the generality of such experiments. In trying to circumvent such problems, experimenters have arranged to present subjects with hypothetical choices between various kinds of gambles (Kahneman and Tversky 1980). However, this approach also has its problems, which include the assumptions (1) that people know how they would behave in actual choice situations and (2) that the people do not disguise their true preferences. We are not aware of systematic investigations of gambling "in the field" (gambles involving real and sizable risk) that comment upon what aspects of gambles are controlling behavior and what variables lead to especially high levels of gambling.

That the substances at issue here can act as reinforcers is of little surprise considering the degree to which they are sought out. Yet given some of their effects, especially on initial use, it is not so obvious that they would be effective positive reinforcers. For example, in addition to euphoria or sense of well-being, opiates often produce nausea; similarly, alcohol is un-palatable to many and can also cause nausea, as can nicotine (Jaffe 1975; Mello and Mendelson 1978). Since it is obvious that these substances are not unique in having reinforcing potential, we might ask why these reinforcers are of particular concern to society. Part of the answer has to do with the fact that society is impressed by dramatic cases in which individuals' lives are dominated by behavior instrumental in gaining access to and consuming such substances and by the consequences of certain levels of substance use on other social behaviors and the individual's health. Having demonstrated that these substances can act as reinforcers, we ask what additional proper-ties cause a reinforcer to be sought out more frequently or in greater amounts.

Acquired Tolerance

Acquired tolerance is defined as a diminution of the ability of a particular amount of a drug to produce some effect, resulting from prior experience with the drug. One consequence of acquired tolerance is that if individuals repeatedly use a drug in order to experience hedonic effects and as a result become tolerant to such effects, increases in the dosage will be required to maintain the level of subjective effect that was initially desired. Having to use greater and greater quantities of the drug could have a number of adverse effects. First, at low doses a drug such as an opiate may gain control over behavior as a result of positive reinforcing properties—that is, without producing signs of physiological dependence (Schuster and Villareal 1968; Woods and Schuster 1971). At higher doses, physiological dependence often develops, thereby further increasing the drug's control over behavior, and thus abstinence becomes more difficult (Deneau et al., 1969). In such cases behavioral control is increased because of two sources of control: the positive reinforcing effects of the drug and the reinforcement gained by es-caping the withdrawal state (see Grabowski and O'Brien 1980). Therefore, tolerance may affect the level of control a substance gains over behavior by making it more likely that, with repeated use, individuals will increase dose size (as they become more tolerant to the initial hedonic effects of the substance), thereby increasing the likelihood of becoming physiologically dependent.

A second consequence of acquired tolerance is that substance use becomes more expensive, especially if the substance is a controlled one, for illicit use is usually expensive. Tolerance acts to increase the cost of main-taining use, thereby making greater demands upon the individual's financial resources. Severely reduced financial resources may, in turn, disrupt the in-dividual's work and other routine activities, which could then produce stress and other emotional consequences that make the sought-after effects of the substance even more attractive. To overcome the difficulty of obtaining larger and larger amounts of the desired drug, an individual may be encouraged to seek out a variety of other drugs in order to obtain similar effects at lower costs, so that acquired tolerance may promote multisubstance use.

Increasing tolerance to a drug may, ironically, increase the likelihood of a drug "overdose." Work by Siegel (1975, 1977, 1979) suggests that tolerance is in part the product of Pavlovian conditioning processes and thus specific to the stimulus context in which the drug is typically administered. That is, if drug tolerant individuals receive the drug in a novel context, they will be less tolerant (more like a drug-naive individual). One consequence of situational specificity of tolerance has been recently demonstrated by Siegel et al. (1982). During a tolerance-conditioning phase, rats received a series of intravenous infusions of heroin in one stimulus context and infusions of saline in a different context. The dose of heroin at the start was 1 mg/kg; at the end of the tolerance phase it was 8 mg/kg. On the test day, half of the rats received 15 mg/kg of heroin in the stimulus context in which heroin was expected (in the presence of stimuli associated with heroin administration during the tolerance-conditioning phase) and the other half of the subjects received the same test dose but in the context in which saline was expected. When heroin was not expected (when the stimuli predicted the administration of saline), 64.3 percent (27 of 42) of the rats died. (In a control group that had received only saline infusions prior to receiving the test dose, 96.4 percent (27 of 28) of the animals died.) When heroin was expected on the basis of the drug associated stimuli, however, only 32.4 percent died (12 of 37). These results suggest that if individuals take large doses of a drug because of previously established tolerance, they may be differentially responsive to the drug effects in different contexts and therefore more prone to overdose compared to nontolerant individuals who would use more reduced doses.

Unquestionably, the data of Siegal et al. (1982) are provocative, calling for further research to assess the boundary conditions under which tolerance to lethal doses can be modulated by conditioning processes.

Alcohol. At effective doses, ethanol has a wide range of behavioral and physiological effects, most noticeably impairment of motor functioning and intellectual functioning as well as relaxation. These effects tend to diminish with prolonged exposure to the substance, either acute or chronic (Mello 1972). This finding is partly the result of the drinker's increased capacity to metabolize ethanol because of increased hepatic microsomal enzyme activity, a capacity that declines after several weeks of abstinence. An acquired pharmacodynamic tolerance can also be observed: with chronic use, higher blood concentrations are needed to produce intoxication and chronic users show less sedation and ataxia than nontolerant subjects at the same blood concentrations of alcohol. Behavioral tolerance, the ability to perform behavioral tasks with no impairment, typically shows rapid increases with repeated use and can be seen at blood alcohol levels as high as 200 milligrams per 100 milliliters of blood and greater (Mello 1972). Grossly observable indices of acquired tolerance and dependence dissipate quickly after cessation of alcohol use (within five to seven days). However, more sensitive measures, such as changes in sleep patterns, EEG, evoked responses, indicate long-lasting changes resulting from chronic use (Cicero 1978). While behavioral tolerance is considerable, some have suggested that acquired tolerance to the lethal effects of alcohol is not as great, and certainly not as dramatic as with opiates (Jaffe 1975).

Evidence is accumulating that shows acquired tolerance to ethanol to be at least in part specific to the stimulus context in which it is typically used. As a result of Pavlovian conditioning processes, the level of tolerance observed can be influenced by stimuli associated with the use of ethanol. The findings of an experiment by Jones (1974) suggest that social drinkers were more tolerant to ethanol when ethanol was expected (in the evening) than when it was unexpected (at a time of day when alcohol was not often consumed). Subjects who had consumed ethanol between 1 and 5 P.M. or between 5 and 10 P.M. were given several cognitive tasks (Raven's Progressive Matrices Test). Subjects who had drunk the ethanol during the afternoon performed more poorly than subjects who drank it during the evening. Control subjects, who were given a nonalcoholic beverage at the same time, showed the reverse—better performance on the cognitive task during the afternoon than in the evening.

Reports from three laboratories have demonstrated that the development of a nonbehavioral effect of ethanol, hypothermia, is in part situation specific (Crowell, Hinson, and Siegel 1980; Lê, Poulos, and Cappell 1979; Mansfield and Cunningham 1980). Although the experiments differ in a number of details, the basic procedure involved giving two groups of rats identical numbers of injections of saline or ethanol (1.3-2.5 g/kg, 12.5-20 percent v/v) in the tolerance training phase. Injection of the drug and the placebo was alternated across days, the two groups differing only with respect to the stimuli associated with administration of ethanol or saline. Group 1 received ethanol and group 2 received saline in a distinctive stimulus context. On alternate days group 1 received saline injections and group 2 received ethanol injections in their home cages. The dependent measure was postinjection changes in core body temperature. During the training phase of the experiment, subjects developed tolerance to the hypothermic effects of ethanol. In test sessions ethanol injections were given in the presence of stimuli previously associated with ethanol injections or cues associated with saline injections. The results from the three separate experiments were uniform in showing that subjects injected with ethanol in the presence of cues associated with ethanol produced *less* hypothermia (showed more tolerance) than subjects injected with ethanol in the presence of stimuli associated with saline injections—even though subjects had received the same number of ethanol injections during the initial training phase.

Additional evidence that the effects of the ethanol-related stimuli were due to associative processes (Crowell et al. 1980; Mansfield and Cunningham 1980) was obtained by demonstrating that tolerance could in part be reversed via a Pavlovian extinction procedure. After the tolerance-development phase, rats were given repeated injections of a placebo (saline) in the presence of stimuli previously associated with ethanol (extinction condition) or in the presence of stimuli previously associated with saline (extinction control). When subjects were subsequently given an injection of ethanol in the presence of cues associated with ethanol during initial training, the extinction group showed reliably less tolerance than did the nonextinction control group.

In a related series of experiments Cappell, Roach, and Poulos (1981) demonstrated that acquired tolerance to the hypothermic effects of pentobarbital and cross tolerance to the hypothermic effects of ethanol in rats are in part due to Pavlovian conditioning procedures. That is, for animals given equivalent exposure to pentobarbital, tolerance to its hypothermic effect was more pronounced when the pentobarbital injection was preceded by stimuli previously paired with its administration than when it was preceded by stimuli previously paired with saline. In addition, when ethanol was administered for the first time, cross tolerance was more pronounced when ethanol was injected in the presence of stimuli associated with pentobarbital than in the presence of stimuli associated with saline.

Although the development of tolerance to the hypothermic effects of ethanol may be of little behavioral consequence, the significance of these studies is that, in using well-controlled procedures they clearly demonstrate that such tolerance can be modulated by stimuli associated with ethanol use. What is important is the implication that what is true of thermic responses may be true of the affective responses to ethanol.

Opiates. Repeated administration of opiates typically results in the development of pronounced tolerance to the euphoric and analgesic effects of the opiate (Haertzen and Hooks 1969; Houde 1974). Other measures of opiate effects show less dramatic increases in tolerance; for example, constriction of pupils and depression of respiration become less pronounced with repeated administration of an opiate, but both effects continue to appear with continued use (Martin and Jasinsky 1969).

As with ethanol, acquired tolerance to opiate effects is in part the result of Pavlovian conditioning processes. Siegel reports that acquired tolerance to the analgesic (Siegel 1975, 1977), thermic (Siegel 1978), and lethal (Siegel, Hinson, and Krank, 1979; Siegel et al. 1982) effects of opiates (morphine and heroin) in rats can be modulated by stimuli associated with the repeated administration of the opiate. Tolerance was more pronounced when the opiate was expected, that is, when it was preceded by drug-associated stimuli, than when it was preceded by stimuli associated with saline injections. Furthermore, the effects of the drug-associated stimuli could be reversed (acquired tolerance could in part be diminished) via a Pavlovian extinction procedure that involved injecting a placebo in the presence of stimuli previously paired with the opiate. (The design was essentially the same as the experiment of Crowell et al. 1980 on ethanol tolerance.)

Several experiments have *not* obtained results in line with Siegel's observations. Sklar and Amit (1978) failed to find an effect of extinguishing drug-associated stimuli on the lethal effects of morphine. However, they provided no independent evidence of stimulus control over acquired tolerance and used an extremely unconventional procedure to evaluate tolerance. Sherman (1979) failed to replicate Siegel's reports on associative modulation of tolerance to the analgesic and thermic effects of morphine. As a result Siegel's and Sherman's labs have recently collaborated in a series of experiments in an effort to resolve some of the differences in their previous reports (Siegel, Sherman, and Mitchell 1980). Using both Siegel's and Sherman's previous methods for extinguishing drug-associated stimuli, the results were consistent with Siegel's previous findings: tolerance to the analgesic effects of morphine was attenuated. The difference between the two labs regarding changes in the thermic effects of the drug are still unresolved.

Nicotine. Evidence that chronic use of nicotine can result in acquired tolerance to some of its effects is indicated by the findings of Jones, Farrell, and Herning (1978), who report that for smokers, intravenous injections of 700 mg of nicotine were not aversive but that, for nonsmokers, doses over 300 mg are usually reported as aversive. In assessing the effects of intravenous infusions of nicotine on heart rate, Jones et al. arranged for smokers to receive four 700-mg infusions of nicotine and for nonsmokers to receive four 300-mg infusions, one infusion per hour. For both groups, the infusion caused a pronounced increase in heart rate, but each succeeding infusion elicited less of a response, indicating the development of acquired tolerance within the session. As expected, smokers showed more tolerance than nonsmokers in that the last two 700-mg infusions for smokers produced less of an increase in heart rate than the last two 300-mg infusions for nonsmokers.

An increased tolerance to behavioral effects of nicotine as a result of acute and chronic exposure to the drug has been demonstrated in rats by

Stolerman, Fink, and Jarvik (1973). Assessing the effects of nicotine on the level of behavioral activity in a runway (where nicotine reduced activity), they found that a second dose of nicotine was less effective in reducing activity, compared to the equivalent-sized initial dose. As the interval between the first and second injection was varied, the acquired tolerance produced by the first injection was greatest two hours after injection and decreased thereafter. When subjects were given repeated injections of nicotine, they showed an increased tolerance that lasted at least ninety days.

Larson and colleagues (1961, 1968, 1971, 1975), in their review of the literature, report that development of tolerance to nicotine is a general phenomenon in that it has been demonstrated in a wide variety of species, including rats, mice, dogs, birds, and human beings. As with alcohol, acquired tolerance to nicotine may be partly the result of an increased ability to metabolize nicotine. For example, the effects of tar (Hunter and Chasseaud 1976) and benzopyrene (Oates et al. 1975) as enzyme inducers, may account for some of the tolerance exhibited to tobacco use. Smokers excrete nicotine faster after a nicotine injection than do nonsmokers (Beckett, Gorrod, and Jenner 1971).

Food. Evidence that tolerance or habituation may play a role in the regulation of feeding behavior is suggested by the work of Rolls (1979 and Rolls et al. 1981). The basic observation is that individuals offered a variety of foods consumed greater amounts than individuals offered comparable amounts of a single preferred food. Beatty (1982) reported similar findings for women (but not men); women given access to several preferred flavors of ice cream consumed over twice as much as women offered a single preferred flavor. Rolls et al. report that "as a particular food is eaten, its taste becomes less pleasant, but the taste of other foods remains relatively unchanged" (1981:215). High consumption in the variable condition results from the fact that exposure to any one food is reduced, thereby diminishing the opportunity for the palatability of each of the foods to habituate and resulting in appetite remaining higher than when only a single food is available. Consistent with this interpretation is the finding that the greater the qualitative differences among foods offered in the variable condition, the greater the difference in amount consumed in the variable versus single food condition, even when overall preferences were equated (Rolls et al. 1981).

One could argue that exposure-produced habituation or tolerance to the palatability of a food acted to decrease consumption. Here, acquired tolerance acts to decrease, rather than increase, consumption of the target food. However, such processes may encourage individuals to seek out a variety of foods in order that the palatability of foods consumed during a meal remain high. Under such conditions, individuals particularly influenced by palatability and other food-related cues, rather than internal cues, in their regulation of food intake may be more likely to overeat than in conditions where variety is more restricted. Habituation processes might also cause the individual to seek out the food in a more concentrated form, with higher sugar content when palatability is governed by sweetness, for example.

Gambling. There appear to be no experiments that address this issue. However, the following report by Barich provides an example of what one might observe.

> My problem was epidemic among small-time gamblers. When you're playing with limited cash—twenty dollars was a big bet for me . . . it's difficult to win decisively, i.e., in quantities large enough to inflate the ego. A two-dollar bettor can pick four or five winners and if they're favorites show a profit of less than twenty dollars. . . . So small-timers make the mistake, as I was beginning to do, of shopping around for long shots. Too often I passed up horses I liked because their odds were short, eight to five, even two to one, and bet instead second or third favorites on the outside chance they'd improve enough to win. They seldom did. *Then, too, I was getting bored, in need of larger shocks, riskier endeavors, to obtain the results (adrenaline rushes, accelerated heartbeat) I'd always gotten freely as a casual bettor. . . . So I decided like so many plungers before me to up the ante. I would bet less frequently . . . but in higher units.* [Emphasis added.] (1981:144-145)

Repeated experience with a substance does not invariably result in the development of tolerance. Repeated experience with cocaine, for example, can result in either tolerance or sensitization (Kilbey and Ellinwood 1977; Stripling and Ellinwood 1977). This is to say that tolerance may not be a property exhibited by all valued or abused substances. Furthermore, one should expect schedule and dose effects to have a profound influence on the development of tolerance (for an informative series of experiments addressing schedule effects on morphine tolerance see Kesner and Baker 1981 and in the related literature on habituation, see Davis 1970).

Withdrawal Effects—Psychological and
Physiological Dependence

Substances such as opiates are commonly considered especially subject to abuse because of the undesirable effects experienced by habitual users denied access to them—the so-called withdrawal syndrome. Withdrawal effects are not unique to substances of abuse, however, but regularly occur when habitually sought-after events are made unavailable. An animal deprived of expected reinforcement becomes highly agitated, highly emotional, and persistently searches for the reinforcer (Tinklepaugh 1928). One factor that distinguishes withdrawal of habitually used substances such as opiates or alcohol or barbiturates from withdrawal of a conventional reinforcer is severity of the effects. When individuals who are accustomed to using large amounts of alcohol or barbiturates are prevented access to the substance, withdrawal reactions can be severe and even lethal. Their physiological well-being depends upon continued access to the substance; they are said to be physiologically dependent upon the substance. Similarly, abstinence from opiates can cause a variety of physiological symptoms. Other effects of abstinence that are of considerable consequence include a craving for the substance, emotional distress, and the ensuing disruption of routine behavior. In such cases the emotional or behavioral well-being of the individual depends upon accustomed access to the substance; the person is said to be psychologically dependent upon the substance. In trying to understand the variables controlling habitual substance use, withdrawal effects are of interest as a source of motivation for continued use.

Alcohol. Victor and Adams (1953) characterized the progression of withdrawal symptoms in humans who were chronic users of alcohol as follows: Within a few hours after the last drink tremulousness, nausea, weakness, anxiety, sweating, cramps, purposive behavior directed toward obtaining alcohol, vomiting, hyperreflexia, alcoholic hallucinations, and grand mal seizures (less common with alcohol abuse than barbiturate abuse) occur; the individual's electroencephalogram (EEG) shows mild but definite dysrythmia; the REM phase of sleep, which is depressed by alcohol, shows a rebound increase during alcohol withdrawal. The state of withdrawal peaks between twenty-four and forty-eight hours after cessation of drinking. With further progress (tremulous delerium) insight is lost, subjects become weaker and more confused, agitated, and disoriented. They may experience vivid hallucinations. Hyperthermia is common and cardiovascular collapse may occur.

Total abstinence is not a necessary condition for the occurrence of withdrawal. Even a relative decline in blood concentration (from 300 to 100 mg per 100 ml blood) may precipitate the withdrawal syndrome, and such declines may occur with changes in the pattern of drinking as well as with decreases in the total daily intake (Jaffe 1975; Mello and Mendelson 1978). The depletion of catecholamines aggravates the alcohol withdrawal syndrome. Only drugs that induce cross dependence or that facilitate the effects of the inhibitory neurotransmitter gama amino butyric acid (GABA) have an ameliorative effect (Goldstein 1973), which is consistent with the observed fall in brain GABA concentration during ethanol withdrawal (Jaffe 1975; Patel and Lal 1973).

Opiates. Chronic use of opiates leads to psychological dependence, which is manifested in such withdrawal symptoms as craving for the drug and persistent efforts to gain access to opiates and emotional reactions such as anger. Physiological dependence is manifested by nausea, cramps, tremors, lacrimation, tachycardia, and increased respiration. As with alcohol, total abstinence is not a necessary condition for withdrawal effects to appear, even a reduction in the dosage can result in the appearance of withdrawal symptoms (Grabowski and O'Brien 1980; Jaffe 1975).

Nicotine. Habitual smoking of tobacco can result in the development of psychological dependence. Abstinence from tobacco typically results in a craving for tobacco (Burns 1969; Fletcher and Doll 1969; Guilford 1966) and increased anxiety and irritability (Frankenhauser et al. 1971; Friedman 1972; Myrsten et al. 1972; Nesbitt 1973). Other effects of abstaining from tobacco include nausea, headache, constipation, and increased appetite (Guilford 1966; Myrsten, Elgerot, and Edgren 1977; Weybrew and Stark 1967).

Food. That everyone is physiologically dependent on food is obvious. Even so, it may be worthwhile to ask what the effects might be of reducing food consumption (that is, dieting) for individuals who have a history of overeating, individuals for whom food could be considered an abused substance. A number of researchers have reported that depression in dieting is very severe and that affective responses to dieting produce anxiety and apathy in some individuals (see Glucksman and Hirsch 1968; Grinker, Hirsch, and Levin 1973; Kollar and Alkinson 1966; Robinson and Winnik 1973; Swanson and Dinello 1970). The most notable features of the dieting depression syndrome are weakness, nervousness and anxiety manifested in restlessness, irritability, fatigue, difficulty in concentrating, general apathy, and downheartedness (Stunkard 1957).

One source of the dieting depression syndrome may be the result of metabolic changes that are induced by significant weight loss (Stunkard 1957). Another possibility is that dieters are people who love to eat. When dieting, they feel deprived and as a result crave food that they can no longer have. For these individuals, the prospects of living on an austere diet and the fact that dieting may have to become a way of life are very depressing. Rodin (1977) has suggested that data from surgical treatment of obesity favor the latter of the two interpretations of dieting-induced depression.

Jejunoilial bypass surgery reduces the effective length of the intestine, which results in a controlled malabsorption of nutrients. This state results in a relatively rapid weight loss; the weight loss is substantial and stabilizes after one to two years. The particular advantages of this surgical procedure for studying the psychological impact of weight loss is that weight loss is rapid and reliable and simultaneously allows individuals an unrestricted diet. Since they can eat all they want, the procedure does not make prolonged demands on the patients' willpower and after their recovery does not interfere with routine activities in the home or work environment. In a study of the psychosocial effects of intestinal bypass surgery for severe obesity, Solow, Silverfarb, and Swift (1974) demonstrated an improvement after surgery and weight loss in mood, self-esteem, interpersonal and vocational effectiveness, body image, and activity level. There was a decrease in depression and also improvements in ego strength and body image that were directly proportional to the magnitude of weight loss. These findings have recently been supported by Halmi, Stunkard, and Mason (1980) and Rodin (1980). Rodin found that when obese individuals who had elected to have bypass surgery lost weight by being placed on a low calorie diet prior to surgery, they experienced diet-induced depression. However, after the same individuals had undergone surgery and began to show considerable weight loss on an unrestricted diet, they showed an improvement in self-esteem and emotional well-being.

Gambling. The establishment of organizations such as Gamblers Anonymous (which is modeled after Alcoholics Anonymous) attests to the fact that for some gamblers, abstinence is very difficult and requires considerable support. We are unaware of any systematic evaluations of abstinence effects in gamblers.

In most explanations of drug abuse, withdrawal typically plays the central role (Wikler 1948, 1973), being considered the primary incentive for further drug use. By administering sufficient amounts of the drug, the individual can quickly escape from the withdrawal state, compared to the more delayed, but more prolonged, escape obtained by continued abstinence. In other words, the choice facing the individual going through withdrawal is either (1) to use the drug and obtain immediate relief but later discomfort or (2) to abstain and obtain immediate discomfort and later relief. As immediate reinforcement and punishment are more effective than delayed, the immediate effects of alternatives (1) and (2) would be more heavily weighted, making (1) the more likely choice.

Recall that the unavailability of habitually sought reinforcers produces adverse withdrawal effects and that the severity of the withdrawal effect is one factor that appears to distinguish substances of abuse from other, less abused reinforcers. Yet another way in which substances of abuse might differ from other reinforcers is the degree to which other substances or events can be substituted without causing adverse results. Individuals who habitually play golf on Saturday afternoons may very much dislike getting rained out, but they can usually substitute a wide variety of alternative activities. However, for individuals who habitually use substances such as opiates, alcohol, or barbiturates, especially in large quantities, the range of substitutable substances or activities is relatively restricted. Using manifestation of physiological dependence as the criterion, it may be that only substances that show cross tolerance to the habitually used substance can be substituted without withdrawal effects appearing (Jaffe 1975). Using manifestations of psychological dependence as a criterion, only substances or activities that prevent the appearance of the affective consequences of withdrawal should serve as satisfactory substitutes. An additional factor determining the range of substances or activities that can be substituted is their availability to the individual. Hence availability of alternative substances and activities acceptable to the individual in part determines the degree of an individual's dependence upon a habitually used substance.

Affective Contrast—Opponent Responses

With chronic use of any one of a variety of substances, the initial hedonic effects (euphoria or a sense of well-being) become attenuated—tolerance develops. When the substance is no longer available, withdrawal produces affective states that oppose the initial effects of the substance (dysphoria). One framework for describing these affective contrasts is the opponent-process model of Solomon (1977, 1980) and Solomon and Corbitt (1974). According to this theory, these contrasting effects are not the consequence of chronic drug exposure but are to be expected when any affective response is elicited. A core assumption of the model is that the later, opposing state increases as the frequency of elicitation increases. As a result, withdrawal effects are more easily *detected* after chronic exposure to events or substances having affective value. Nevertheless, such contrast should be expected at the outset. More formally, Solomon proposes that the nervous system acts to oppose and suppress many types of affect, whether they are pleasurable or aversive. The opposing affective or hedonic processes are automatically elicited by events that psychologists have identified to be effective Pavlovian unconditioned stimuli (UCSs) or operant reinforcers (rfts).

The primary affective processes elicited by strong UCSs or rfts are called *a-process*. The a-process is said to be phasic, to correlate closely with stimulus intensity, quality, and duration of the reinforcer, and show little sensitization or habituation. In Pavlovian terminology, the primary affective processes are emotional or affective UCRs.

A primary (UCR) process [a-process] arouses a *b-process* which then opposes and suppresses the affective strength of the a-process. In contrast to the a-processes, b-processes (the opponent-processes) are thought to be sluggish and inertia-laden. They are (1) of relatively long latency or reaction time, (2) slow to build up to maximum amplitude, and (3) slow to decay after the stimulus input (UCS) is terminated and the a-process (UCR) has ceased. Because the b-process is an opponent-process, it must have an affective or hedonic quality *opposite* to that of the a-process . . . (Solomon 1977:69-70).

With repeated presentation of the UCS, or rft, the repeated elicitation of the b-process by the a-process is said to cause the b-process to grow in strength and to be more rapidly elicited by the a-process. Therefore, as a consequence of repeated exposure to the UCS, the b-process more quickly and fully opposes the a-process, resulting in a diminution of responding to the UCS mediated by the a-process.

Unfortunately, many investigations of the affective states produced by drugs in naive subjects document the magnitude and duration of initial effects but do not continue to assess subjects' reactions after the initial effects have subsided. Demonstrations of biphasic effects typically rely on easily measured responses such as activity, heart rate, and body temperature and comment only remotely if at all upon the affective consequences. What follows is a review of studies commenting on a variety of biphasic effects produced by the substances we have chosen to consider.

Alcohol. Observations of a late, opponent response to alcohol were reported by Mullin and Luckhardt (1934). Using human subjects, they found that oral doses of ethanol caused an initial depression in subjects' sensitivity to pain but "a short-lasting period of increased sensitivity to pain was usually recorded immediately following the depression caused by alcohol" (p. 77).

McQuarrie and Fingl (1958) report that mice given a single oral dose of ethanol followed 4, 8, 12, or 22 hours later by administration of pentylenetetrazol showed an increased seizure threshold at 4 hours, a decreased seizure threshold at 8 and 12 hours, and no change in seizure threshold at 22 hours compared to control subjects who received water instead of alcohol. That is, the initial effect of ethanol was an increased resistance to seizure, followed by a decreased resistance to seizure, followed by a return to the baseline or control level. That a single dose of ethanol can produce a later state of hypersensitivity has been demonstrated by Goldstein (1972). Mice given injections of ethanol showed no susceptibility to ethanol-produced seizures induced by handling, but there was a greater tendency for handling to produce seizures 7 to 10 hours after injection, which thereafter declined to control levels. With chronic use of alcohol, the later state of hypersensitivity becomes more pronounced (e.g., Goldstein 1972; McQuarrie and Fingl 1958).

Opiates. Tatum, Seevers, and Collins (1929) and Seevers and Pfeiffer (1936) report that giving naive (nonaddict) human subjects, as well as other species, a single dose of morphine or heroin produced an initial sedative effect, which was followed by a stimulant effect (hyperreactivity, increased sensitivity to pain).

Nicotine. We are not aware of data that comment on the late effects of acute administration of nicotine.

Food and Insulin. In assessing behavioral consequences of food presentation, Konorski (1967) reports that presentation of small amounts of food results in an initial decrease in activity and excitability (during the consummatory phase), which is followed by an increase in activity and excitability that exceeds baseline levels. One consequence of presenting food or food-related stimuli is the release of insulin (Parra-Covarrubias et al. 1971; Woods et al. 1977), which among its many effects can result in increased hunger and eating (hence we review here some of the literature commenting on the conditioned and unconditioned effects of administration of exogenous insulin). Administration of insulin results in a decrease in blood glucose levels. When blood glucose drops below normal levels, compensatory responses are elicited. For example, hyperinsulinism results in release of growth hormones, which antagonizes peripheral carbohydrate uptake and oxidation and promotes mobilization and utilization of lipids (Bondy 1954; Young and Korner 1960; Williams 1960). A condition of hyperinsulinism also results in the release of glucagon, which accelerates gluconeogenesis, thereby supplying glucose to the blood (L.L. Miller 1961; Wicks 1969). Other investigators have found that insulin administration can produce an initial inhibition of motor activity of the gastrointestinal tract (Bachrach 1953; but that with the subsequent onset of hypoglycemia, there is an increase in motor activity; Quigley, Johnson, and Solomon 1930; Stunkard and Wolf 1954).

Gambling. There appear to be no data that address this issue.

Conditioning Effects

In the section on tolerance, we briefly discussed an experiment by Siegel et al. (1982) demonstrating tolerance to the lethal effects of heroin to be specific to the stimulus context associated with drug administration. These results suggest that conditioning processes play a part in the development of tolerance to opiates—that the administration of a drug can act as a Pavlovian unconditioned stimulus (UCS). An early demonstration of the effectiveness of morphine as a UCS was reported by Pavlov (1927). Dogs given repeated injections of morphine responded as if to the drug (with copious salivation and vomiting) when presented with stimuli that had been repeatedly paired with morphine administration (sight of the experimenter or syringe). More recently, Siegel has demonstrated that repeated injections of morphine can also result in conditioning of compensatory responses, responses that oppose the initial effect of the drug (Siegel 1975, 1976, 1977). It should be noted that Siegel's explanation of context-specific tolerance is based upon such observations, that is, upon drug-associated stimuli eliciting conditioned responses that are antagonistic to the immediate effects of drug administration. Yet given nonassociative accounts such as Solomon's opponent-process model (Solomon 1980), acquired tolerance might well be expected to be an overdetermined phenomenon. If so, exposure to a drug such as morphine could result in a long-lasting, context-specific decrement in effectiveness due to associative learning processes and a more transient decrement due to nonassociative processes (see Donegan 1981; Donegan and Wagner 1983; Pfautz 1980; Wagner 1982 for a more detailed analysis of the ways associative processes, stimulus intensity, and inter trial interval may interact to determine the level of responding observed to a target stimulus).

Experimental evidence supporting the foregoing reasoning was provided by Kesner and Baker in 1981. In a series of experiments, morphine (5 mg/kg) was administered to rats under conditions calculated to affect differentially both associative and nonassociative processes involved in the development of an acquired tolerance to the analgesic effects of the drug. Training trials (morphine injections) were given in a distinctive or a non-distinctive stimulus context and the inter trial interval (ITI) was relatively long (48 hours) or short (12 hours, for spaced versus massed training). Given the findings in the Pavlovian conditioning literature (see Mackintosh 1974; Kimble 1961), the involvement of associative processes should be maximized and the role of nonassociative processes minimized for subjects receiving morphine in the distinctive stimulus context at the long ITI. Conversely, the involvement of associative processes should be minimized and nonassociative processes maximized for subjects receiving morphine in the nondistinctive stimulus context at the short, ITI.

The data are in agreement with these predictions. The contribution of associative processes was evident in the finding that tolerance to the analgesic effects of morphine was greater in groups trained in the distinctive than in the nondistinctive context. Furthermore, this effect was considerably larger when trials were spaced (at 48-hour intervals) than when massed (at 12-hour intervals). Conversely, for groups trained in the nondistinctive context, analgesic tolerance was greater for the group trained at the 12-hour ITI than in the group trained at the 48-hour ITI. That is, the nonassociative basis for acquired tolerance dissipated as the interval between trials was increased from 12 to 48 hours (see Kesner and Baker 1981: figure 2a).

To distinguish further between associative and nonassociative processes underlying acquired tolerance, Kesner and Baker assessed the retention of acquired tolerance in two groups of subjects—one that had received morphine in the distinctive context and one that had received the drug in the nondistinctive context at 12-hour intervals. The authors predicted that subjects trained in the distinctive context would show little loss of tolerance over the retention interval compared to subjects trained in the nondistinctive context because of the greater opportunity for tolerance to be mediated by associative processes in the distinctive-context group. After receiving ten injections of morphine in their assigned contexts, subjects remained in their home cages for two weeks, during which morphine was not administered. Subjects were subsequently returned to the context in which they were trained and were given a test dose of morphine. The results were dramatic; subjects trained and tested in the distinctive context showed no loss of tolerance, whereas subjects trained and tested in the nondistinctive context showed a complete loss of acquired tolerance. The analgesic effectiveness of the morphine had returned to the pretraining level (Kesner and Baker 1981: fig. 3).

Demonstrations such as those of Pavlov and Siegel indicate that stimuli associated with an effective unconditioned stimulus come to elicit responses that mimic or oppose subjects' initial response to the UCS (Grabowski and O'Brien 1980). Put another way, given the biphasic nature of the unconditioned response (UR), sometimes the conditioned response (CR) mimics the initial response to the UCS and sometimes the CR mimics the later, opposing response to the UCS. What is of interest is the role such conditioning processes may play in the development of psychological dependence on a substance—for example, the conditioning of responses that have motivational significance.

The concept of conditioned motivational states is not a new one and the idea that they have important influences on behavior has played a central role in attempts to understand the development of habitual behavior, such as two-factor learning theory (Mowrer 1947; Rescorla and Solomon 1967). Presenting a tone CS to an untrained animal may elicit investigatory behavior or the animal may be indifferent to its presence. However, after repeatedly pairing of the tone with a shock UCS, the tone acquires conditioned aversive properties as evidenced by the fact that the animal will learn to engage in behavior that allows it to escape or avoid the tone (Brown and Jacobs 1949; McAllister and McAllister 1962; N.E. Miller 1948). On the basis of such demonstrations the tone is said to be a conditioned elicitor of a motivational state—fear.

Given demonstrations such as Siegel's that pairings of stimuli with pharmacological UCSs can elicit responses that oppose the initial drug effects (Siegel 1972, 1975, 1977), such stimuli may elicit emotional states that oppose the initial drug effect. If the drug produces euphoria, then stimuli associated with repeated drug use may come to elicit dysphoria. This is to say that components of the withdrawal syndrome may become conditioned.

Such stimuli, in providing a motivational basis for continued drug use (craving for the drug) (Grabowski and O'Brien 1980), may serve to initiate behavior instrumental in escaping the withdrawal state through continued drug use (Wikler 1948, 1973).

Alcohol. A number of authors have suggested that for alcoholics, stimuli associated with the use of alcohol elicit a conditioned motivational state (a craving for alcohol or its effects) that leads to further alcohol consumption and is one of the determiners of relapse (Hinson and Siegel 1980; Keller 1972; Ludwig and Wikler 1974; Marlatt 1978). Hinson and Siegel have described the role that drug related stimuli might play in the maintenance of habitual drinking as follows. Assume that an individual is presented with cues that have been repeatedly associated with alcohol consumption, say a place where the individual frequently drinks or the time of day at which drinking typically occurs. In such circumstances the situational cues may elicit ethanol-compensatory conditioned responses. If alcohol is not being consumed, then these compensatory effects are unaltered by any drug effects. In these situations such responses may constitute withdrawal symptoms. However, given the above premises, the resulting syndrome might be better characterized as drug preparation symptoms, rather than drug withdrawal symptoms:

> the individual is displaying responses that would adaptively cancel the pharmacologically-induced homeostatic imbalance usually experienced in the circumstances. However, since the ethanol stimulation does not occur, the result of the preparatory responding is a homeostatic imbalance of a different sort, which may be generally characterized as responses opposite to those induced by ethanol. These anticipatory responses are presumably uncomfortable, and are attenuated by the administration of ethanol. The alcoholic, then, may have learned that conditioned ethanol responses are ameliorated by ethanol ingestion, and such conditional responses are interpreted as "craving." In a similar vein, Ludwig and Wikler (1974) have suggested that alcohol craving represents "the physiological or cognitive correlate of a 'subclinical' conditioned withdrawal syndrome. (Hinson and Siegel 1980:189)

In a study by Ludwig and Stark (1974), male alcoholics (who were receiving inpatient treatment) were given a questionnaire on drinking and craving, which sought to determine what variables were influencial when the subjects drank. When asked if stimuli customarily associated with the consumption of alcohol give rise to a craving for alcohol, 56 percent reported that their craving for alcohol increased when they were in places in which alcohol is typically found. Given this line of reasoning, the taste of alcohol should be a very effective cue and therefore an especially potent elicitor of conditioned effects. Ludwig and Stark (1974) report that initial drinking increases subjects' craving for alcohol and that under such conditions subjects report that they are unable to stop. Similarly Hodgson and Rankin (1974) reported that the taste of an alcoholic beverage can elicit craving in alcoholics. Given such results, it should be the case that reducing the taste of alcohol should reduce the craving elicited by a primer dose of alcohol. Merry (1966) found that a priming dose of vodka was ineffective in eliciting craving when the taste of alcohol was disguised. Similarly Marlatt, Demming, and Reid (1973) found that nonabstinent male alcoholics' and heavy social drinkers' expectations of receiving an alcoholic or nonalcoholic beverage determined the amount of beverage consumed, but the actual presence or absence of alcohol did not (with one part vodka to five parts well-chilled tonic water, presence of alcohol could not be detected).

Additional evidence that alcoholics' desire for alcohol and consumption of alcohol can be modulated by alcohol-related cues has been reported by Ludwig, Cain, and Wikler (1977). Alcoholic patients were asked to rate their craving for alcohol and allowed to work for alcohol in two different environments. One test room was arranged to simulate a bar and the other a laboratory. Individuals in the bar room reported greater craving for alcohol and pressed a button delivering small amounts of bourbon more frequently than did subjects tested in the mock laboratory devoid of stimuli likely to have been previously associated with alcohol.

Reports from three laboratories have demonstrated the acquisition of conditioned compensatory responses to stimuli associated with an ethanol unconditioned stimulus (Crowell, Hinson, and Siegel 1981, Lê, Poulos, and Cappell 1979; Mansfield and Cunningham 1980). (The basic procedure is described in the section on tolerance to ethanol.) The manipulation of interest was whether or not rats received placebo (saline) injections in the presence of stimuli previously associated with ethanol injections or saline injections. The dependent measure was postinjection core body temperature. The results from the three separate experiments were uniform in showing that in the presence of stimuli signaling ethanol, placebo (saline) injections elicited a conditioned hyperthermia. However, when the placebo was injected in the presence of stimuli signaling saline, no appreciable thermic response was seen.

Although conditioned hyperthermia probably has little significance in the development of habitual use of ethanol, the importance of these studies is that in using well-controlled procedures they clearly demonstrate that stimuli associated with repeated administration of ethanol can come to elicit conditioned responses that oppose the initial consequences of ethanol administration. What is true of thermic responses may be true for responses with motivational significance, that is, the effects underlying the development of a craving for alcohol.

Opiates. Like the explanation of ethanol dependence, explanations of opiate dependence have acknowledged the importance of drug-related stimuli in the maintenance of opiate use and in precipitating relapse (Wikler 1948, 1973; Siegel 1979). That stimuli associated with habitual administration can elicit a variety of compensatory or withdrawal effects has been demonstrated in a number of reports (see table 4-1). The role these conditioned effects play has been summarized by Hinson and Siegel:

> There is a considerable amount of epidemiological and experimental evidence in support of a conditional compensatory response and analysis of so-called withdrawal response symptoms with respect to opiate drugs (reviewed by Siegel 1979). Briefly, (1) opiate withdrawal symptons are, to a great extent, opposite in direction to the effects of the opiates; (2) environmental stimuli which would be expected to have become associated with heroin in human addicts elicit both [signs and symptoms of withdrawal] and subjective reports of craving (O'Brien 1976; Teasdale 1973); (3) following withdrawal in an environment different from that in which they used drugs, release of individuals to an environment rich in cues previously associated with drug use leads to withdrawal symptoms and, usually, relapse (e.g., Brecher 1972, Ch. 10); (4) following withdrawal, release of opiate addicts to an environment very different from that in which they previously used drugs does not usually result in great withdrawal discomfort and relapse (Robins et al. 1974); (5) morphine addicted rats, like humans, display greater relapse if, following withdrawal, they are returned to the same environment in which they were originally addicted than if they are returned to a different environment (Thompson and Ostlund 1965; Weeks and Collins 1968)   (Hinson and Siegel 1980:190)

Stimuli can come to elicit withdrawal effects in two ways, either by pairing the stimulus with the administration of the opiate (Siegel 1977) or by pairing the stimulus with the withdrawal state (O'Brien 1975; O'Brien, Testa, O'Brien, Brady, and Wells 1977). O'Brien and his colleagues arranged for former heroin addicts maintained on methadone to receive repeated pairings of a complex CS (tone and smell of peppermint oil) and the administration of naloxone (0.1 milligram), an opiate antagonist, which elicited withdrawal symptoms. After twelve conditioning sessions, subjects were tested by presenting the CS and following it with a placebo injection. The results of testing showed that the CS had acquired the ability to elicit withdrawal symptoms similar to those produced by the naloxone injection.

It should be noted that with regard to the clinical evidence that conditioned withdrawal responses may precipitate relapse when users return to areas in which they previously had used drugs and experienced withdrawal, there is no evidence that allows one to specify the mechanisms responsible. That is, we do not know whether conditioning of compensatory responses through pairings of the stimulus context with drug administration or conditioning of withdrawal responses through pairings of the stimulus context with previous bouts of withdrawal plays the greater role.

Table 4-1
Conditioned Response Opposite to Opiate Effect

CS	CR	Dose	Subjects	Authors
Saline injection	Hyperalgesia	Morphine, 5 mg/kg	Rats	Siegel 1975
Saline injection	Hypothermia	Morphine, 5 mg/kg	Rats	Siegel 1978
Distinctive preinjection environment	Hypothermia	Morphine, 5-200 mg/kg	Rats	Eikelboom and Stewart 1979
Slides of drug related and drug-taking stimuli	Negative affects usually associated with withdrawal	History of heroin use, dose unknown	Humans	Teasdale 1973
Preinjection rituals	Decreased skin temperature, increased pupil size, tachycardia, subjective reports of craving and withdrawal sickness	History of street opiate use, drug-free or on opiate antagonist	Humans	O'Brien 1975
Self-injection after one or more unreinforced trials (opiate blocked by naltrexone or syringe contains saline)	Increased skin temperature, increased pupil size, tachycardia, increased respiration, subjective reports of craving, sickness, and anger.	Same as above	Humans	O'Brien et al. 1975
Drug objects, slides, video tapes of drug-taking behavior	Decreased skin temperature, increased heart rate, increased scores on withdrawal scales	Two groups of former street opiate users, one stabilized on methadone, one drug-free	Humans	Ternes et al. 1980
Video tapes of drug-related behavior	Tachycardia, subjective reports	Recently detoxified former opiate addicts	Humans	Sideroff and Jarvik 1980
Buzzer	Tachycardia (UCR at this dose was initial heart rate increase, then decrease)	10 mg/kg (lower dose in table 4-2)	Dogs	Rush et al. 1970

Source: J. Grabowski and C.P. O'Brien (1980) Conditioning factors in opiate use. In Nancy K. Mellow, ed., *Advances in Substance Abuse*, vol. 2. Greenwich, Conn.: JAI Press. Reprinted by permission.

In addition to conditioning of compensatory or withdrawal responses, it should be noted that stimuli associated with opiate use have also been shown to produce responses as if to the opiates. Results of studies in which CSs elicited mimicking CRs are summarized in table 4-2. In producing effects like those of drugs, these stimuli should presumably serve as secondary reinforcers, that is, stimuli that have acquired reinforcing properties as a result of their association with a primary reinforcer. In these cases, drug users should be eager to gain access to such stimuli, particularly when experiencing withdrawal. Grabowski and O'Brien (1980) point out that so-called needle-freak behavior is likely to be such a case; to attenuate craving for the drug, some individuals repeatedly inject a placebo, which they report produces a short-lasting effect akin to that normally produced by the drug.

It is not clear what variables determine the kinds of conditioned responses that will develop, that is, whether the CRs will mimic or oppose the initial effects of the drug. The question of what factors determine the products of conditioning trials is of theoretical and practical importance and is likely to receive increased attention in the future (see Eikelboom and Stewart 1982).

Nicotine. It is common lore that abstinent smokers experience craving for tobacco and a greater tendency to relapse when they are in contexts associated with habitual use of tobacco (after a meal, while drinking alcoholic beverages or coffee). However, few studies systematically evaluate the role of smoking-related stimuli on smoking behavior. Herman (1974) assessed the effects of varying how prominently cigarettes were displayed for two classes of smokers, light smokers (with average daily intake of one to fifteen cigarettes) and heavy smokers (with average daily intake of twenty to fifty cigarettes). A robust effect of display condition was found in light smokers: subjects having cigarettes prominently displayed initiated smoking more rapidly and smoked more cigarettes than did subjects for whom cigarettes were less prominently displayed. Interestingly, the heavy smokers in the two display conditions did not differ reliably in their latencies to initiate smoking or the total number of cigarettes smoked. The roles of external and internal cues in the regulation of smoking are discussed in the context of these and related data.

Food. On the basis of research with dogs, Konorski (1967) reports that when a food-deprived animal is repeatedly presented with a food UCS in the experimental room, subsequently exposing the dog to the room typically results in a hunger conditioned response. That is, "we observe the arousal of the motor behavior system manifested by general motor excitement and vocalization and the arousal of sensory system manifested by increased searching behavior—sniffing, exploring the surroundings . . . increased sensitivity to external and taste stimuli and the hunger contractions of the stomach" (p. 277).

Table 4-2
Conditioned Response Resembling Opiate Effect

CS	CR	Dose	Subjects	Authors
Sight of experimenter who previously injected morphine	Salivation, vomiting, sleep	(Not specified)	Dogs	Pavlov 1927
Sight of syringe	Salivation.	Morphine, 30-80 mg/kg	Dogs	Collins and Tatum 1925
Tone	Hyperthermia	Morphine 20 mg/kg	Rats	Miksic et al. 1975
Distinct injection environment	Hyperthermia	Morphine, 5-200 mg/kg	Rats	Eikelboom and Stewart 1979
Tone	Reduction of withdrawal signs ("wet-dog shakes")	Morphine, 15 mg/kg	Rats	Numan, Smith, and Lal 1975
Tone	Resumption of operant behavior suppressed during morphine withdrawal	Morphine, 40 mg/kg	Rats	Tye and Iverson 1975
Buzzer	Increased salivation, gastric secretion, and heart rate	2 mg/kg (higher dose in table 4-1)	Dogs	Rush, Pearson, and Long 1970
Self-injection of saline when opiate expected; or self-injection of opiate in presence of naltrexone	Subjective reports of "taste," "rush," and euphoria; meiosis and increased skin temperature in some subjects, quickly extinguished in most subjects	History of street opiate use; variable dose and duration	Humans	O'Brien 1975-79
Self-injection of heroin (0.5-4.5 mg/dose in presence of naltrexone (75 mg), which effectively blocks pharmacological activity of heroin	Slight decrease in pupil size and decrease in respiratory rate on first few injections, disappeared with later injections. (CR seen only in the 11 of 22 subjects who voluntarily continued to self-inject heroin while receiving naltrexone.)	History of street heroin addiction	Humans	Meyer and Mirin 1979

Source: J. Grabowski and C.P. O'Brien (1980) Conditioning factors in opiate use. In Nancy K. Mello, ed., *Advances in Substance Abuse*. vol. 2. Greenwich, Conn.: JAI Press. Reprinted by permission.

The opinions of other researchers are divided on whether or not stimuli associated with appetitional events elicit a conditioned motivational state. Theorists proposing that stimuli associated with appetitive goal events act to increase motivational states that in turn mediate instrumental behavior include Brown (1961), Hull (1951), Rescorla and Solomon (1967), and Spence (1951). Bolles is slightly more restrictive. He concludes that stimuli associated with food may "make the hungry animal hungrier but has no effect upon the sated animal" (1967:397). At the other extreme, Mackintosh (1974:227) has questioned the need to assume that food-related stimuli have motivational consequences.

With regard to Bolles's conclusion, Konorski (1967) challenged similar statements by describing experiments in which fully sated dogs, when presented with a discriminative stimulus that signaled the availability of food, immediately performed the trained response and often consumed a portion of the food offered. Konorski further suggested that such demonstrations require a strong hunger CS because what he calls the "hunger center" is strongly inhibited in the fully sated animal. As a result, only very effective CSs can overcome the inhibitory processes and elicit the drive state.

Mackintosh's (1974) proposal that stimuli associated with food do not act as a source of appetitive motivation was based upon experiments that evaluated the consequence of presenting a brief CS previously paried with food (CS +) on the vigor of subjects' instrumental responding for food (bar pressing). If the CS + acts to increase the level of motivation (hunger), one would predict that the instrumental behavior should be more vigorous or frequent when the CS + is present than when it is absent. Just the opposite outcome has been reported by several investigators (Konorski and Miller 1937; Azrin and Hake 1969). In the Konorski and Miller experiment, dogs were trained to press a panel for food. When a CS + (a CS previously paired with response-independent delivery of food) was presented during the course of panel-pressing, the dogs stood immobile, looked at the food tray, and salivated copiously.

By making Konorski's distinction between drive (preparatory) reflexes and consummatory reflexes, the picture can be made more clear. Appetitive drive reflexes (hunger) act to arouse the gustatory and olfactory sensory systems and produce motor arousal (general excitement). On the other hand, consummatory reflexes result in mastication and salivation. Importantly, *consummatory reflexes are said to inhibit drive reflexes*. (For example, a hungry, excited animal calms down upon obtaining food: it becomes immersed in eating.) The drive reflex is said to be rapidly conditioned, especially to long-duration on static stimuli—for example, situational stimuli. Consummatory reflexes are more slowly conditioned and come under the control only of stimuli that are of short duration and immediately precede the consummatory reflex.

Given these distinctions, effects of stimuli associated with food presentation become more orderly. The increased level of activity of dogs brought into the experimental room in which they had previously been fed is the result of elicitation of the hunger reflex by the situational stimuli. On the other hand, when Konorski and Miller presented a CS+ having a brief duration, dogs ceased to engage in panel-pressing for food, became quiescent, and salivated copiously. That is, the elicitation of a consummatory CR (salivation) had a inhibitory effect upon the animal's motivational state (hunger).

The proposal that relatively punctuate stimuli will more readily gain control over consummatory CRs and thereby act to decrease levels of motivation, and that relatively longer duration CSs are more likely to gain control over drive (hunger) CRs has received some support. Meltzer and Brahlek (1970) assessed the effects of presenting a CS associated with an appetitive US (sucrose) on the rate at which rats bar pressed for food on a variable-interval schedule of reinforcement. The independent variable was the duration of the CS+, and the dependent measure was rate of bar-pressing. The results indicated that a CS + with a duration of 12 or 40 seconds reliably depressed the rate of bar-pressing compared to baseline rates determined when the CS was not present (the 12-second CS+ almost completely suppressed bar-pressing). On the other hand, presenting a CS+ having a duration of 120 seconds resulted in an increased rate of bar-pressing compared to baseline levels. In a related experiment, Miczek and Grossman (1971) assessed the effects of presenting stimuli (CS+) of different duration that had been paired with response-independent delivery of banana pellets on squirrel monkeys' rate of bar-pressing for regular food pellets on a variable-interval schedule of reinforcement. Conditioned stimuli of 10 and 30 seconds reliably depressed rates of bar-pressing for food. Those of 1 to 3 minutes did not have uniform effects on subjects' responding: bar-pressing occurred in bursts followed by irregular pauses, and the overall rate of bar-pressing was not very different from baseline rates in the presence of the longer duration CSs (also see Edgar, Hall, and Pearce 1981 for a discussion of the role of the schedules of reinforcement maintaining the baseline rate of behavior on the effects of CS+ presentation).

Other variables that are assumed to determine whether a food-related CS will elicit conditioned hunger or conditioned satiety are the amount of food and meal duration. Consuming small portions of food presented frequently (small, frequent meals of short duration) should result in conditioned hunger whereas consuming larger portions of food (large meals of long duration) should result in conditioned satiety (Konorski 1967).

Considering the effects of food cues on insulin secretion, Woods et al. (1977) have demonstrated that rats develop a tendency to secrete insulin in the presence of stimuli that reliably predict the opportunity to eat. With overweight and normal-weight human subjects, Rodin (1978) reports that presenting subjects with the sight and smell of food (a frying steak) resulted in the secretion of insulin. When subjects were classified as high- or low-responsive to external stimuli on the basis of their ratings of food cues, high-responsive individuals (externals) showed larger insulin responses compared to low-responsive (nonexternal) subjects (this pattern was seen in both normal and overweight subjects). It was also the case that overweight subjects in each responsiveness category showed larger insulin responses compared to similarly classified subjects of normal weight. In a second experiment subjects classified as overweight externals and normal-weight nonexternals were shown foods of varying palatability. (Palatability ratings of the foods were obtained from independent pilot studies.) In both of the groups the more palatable the food, the larger was the insulin response. Insulin secretion was greater for overweight externals compared to normal-weight nonexternals when they were shown moderately and highly palatable food. On the basis of such findings, Rodin concluded that if externally responsive people oversecrete insulin in the presence of compelling food cues, then they might eat more calories in order to balance this hormonal and metabolic output and they might also store more of the food in fat. Thus appetite is stimulated and overeating may result as a consequence of increased responsiveness to potent, palatable stimuli.

Effects of Stress, Anxiety, and General
Level of Arousal

In the section on withdrawal effects it was noted that one consequence of withdrawal is an increase in emotional or motivational states. These states are often labeled as a craving for the unavailable substance and said to promote further substance use. In this section we will consider the consequences of emotional or motivational states that have other sources and describe their influence on substance use.

Alcohol. Mello and Mendelson (1966, 1978) report that stress *can* result in an increased intake of alcohol. For example, Clark and Polish (1960) report that chronic shock increases self-administration of alcohol in rhesus monkeys.

Opiates. Whitehead (1974) reports that former heroin addicts maintained on methadone are especially vulnerable to relapse when in stressful situations, as when experiencing marital problems or facing a job interview. What is particularly interesting is that these individuals often interpret their reactions to stress as a need for opiates (compare Schachter and Singer 1962). They report that they are undergoing withdrawal and accuse the physician of reducing their dose of methadone (during these periods their blood level of methadone does not differ from prestress periods). To attenuate the state they *label* as withdrawal, these individuals often resume taking heroin.

Nicotine. In a series of experiments Schachter, Silverstein, Kozlowski, Perlick, Herman, and Liebling (1977) and Schachter, Silverstein, and Perlick (1977) evaluated the relation between stress and smoking. Under various experimental contexts (subjects were told that they were participating in an experiment on tactile sensitivity, with cigarettes available as a courtesy) subjects in the high-stress condition were given periodic painful shocks and subjects in the low-stress condition received just perceptible shocks. Subjects in the high-stress condition tended to smoke more cigarettes and showed a large increases in the number of puffs taken compared to subjects in the low-stress condition. The experimenters also demonstrated that stress increases the acidity of an individual's urine, which in turn affects the rate at which nicotine is excreted. This relationship suggests that subjects in the high-stress condition are excreting nicotine faster than subjects in the low-stress condition and are puffing more in order to maintain a desired level of nicotine. If this is so, then one might be able to reduce or even eliminate the effects of the stress manipulation by experimentally stabilizing urine pH (via bicarbonate of soda). This in fact was the case. Subjects given placebos showed a greater number of puffs in the high-stress compared to low-stress condition. However, when subjects were given bicarbonate of soda prior to the experiment, there were no reliable differences in the number of puffs between the two stress conditions. These results suggest that in stressful situations, individuals smoke more in order to maintain nicotine levels and not in response to stress itself.

Food. In animals a number of stimuli, referred to as nonspecific arousers by certain researchers and stressors by others, have been found to increase intake of food or sweetened fluids during their presentation. Such effects have been produced by buzzers and lights (Drew 1937), noise (Kupferman 1964); tail pinch in sated rats (Antelman et al. 1975; Koob, Fray, and Iverson 1976); and low intensity or short durations of shock (Willis 1968; Blackman 1968; Kupferman 1964; Ullman 1951, 1952). Other agents that have been used to modulate subjects level of arousal are stimulant drugs.

The effects of stimulant drugs on responding for food seem to depend on dose, predrug rate of responding, species, and nutritional state of the animal. For example, while low doses of d-amphetamine increase the rate of lever-pressing (on a fixed-ratio schedule) for food in deprived rats (Glick and Muller 1971), higher doses decrease such responding (Glick and Muller 1971; Owen 1960). Clark and Steele (1966) found that amphetamine decreased high rates of responding and increased low rates.

Amphetamine also increases stereotyped or compulsive behavior such as licking, biting, gnawing, and rapid head movements in rats (Randrup and Munkvad 1967; Stolk and Rech 1967). Given such observations, it is thought that the effects of amphetamine on operant behavior may be the result of an interaction between the operant response and drug-induced locomotor activity (Segal 1962) or specific types of stereotyped behavior (Lyon & Randrup 1972). Lyon and Robbins (1975) propose that the action of amphetamine is such that as the dose response within the CS increases, the repetition rate of all motor activities will increase. The organism will tend to exhibit increasing response rates within a decreasing number of response categories, and as the rate increases, the amount of time spent on each completion of a response sequence continues to shorten until the response sequence is no longer completed.

A number of clinicians have claimed that emotional states (mainly anxiety) may influence overeating and obesity (Kaplan and Kaplan 1957; Bruch 1973). Bruch proposes that overeating may result from inability to discriminate between hunger cues and cues from other emotional states due to an inappropriate feeding schedule in infancy. She believes eating is a learned coping response to emotional upset and may serve as an anxiety reducer because of its early association with the comforting parent who responded to all signs of the infant's distress by feeding the infant.

Experimenters who have attempted to manipulate anxiety report contradictory findings. Abramson and Wunderlich (1972), McKenna (1972), and Schachter, Goldman, and Gordon (1968) found slight or no increases in eating due to anxiety in the obese. However, Slochower (1976) proposes that this hypothesis refers to diffuse or unconscious interal conflicts that produce the anxiety state that elicits eating but that past studies have allowed subjects to identify clearly the source of their emotional state. Thus only unlabeled anxiety is predicted to promote eating. She tested this hypothesis by varying weight (obese versus normal), arousal level (high or low), and ability of subjects to identify the source of arousal. For the high-arousal unlabeled group, the obese subjects ate more than the normal-weight subjects and arousal reduction was reported after eating. Normal-weight subjects ate only in response to internal hunger cues and were not affected by the label manipulation. In a later study Slochower and Kapaln (1980) found that overeating by obese subjects was markedly inhibited by the presence of a label for the arouser and a sense of control over it. The researchers proposed that the label itself was not important but, rather, knowledge about the cause of anxiety and availability of a method of reducing it heighten the subjects' sense of control over the emotional state and thereby decrease the tendency to eat in response to it.

Spitzer, Marcus, and Rodin (1980) have proposed that a stess or arousal model might best apply to binge eating and not all instances of overeating. They suggest that eating may reduce the perceived intensity of some aversive stimulus (via distraction) during eating but that eating does not directly remove or reduce the anxiety or stress, and in fact may be perpetuated because the cessation of eating is usually associated with renewed attention to the stressor.

Food-directed behavior under conditions of stress, when they do occur, may be more the result of arousal than states of negative affect. It would be interesting to pursue this line of thinking in interpreting the results with other substances as well.

In the foregoing sections, we have discussed ways in which various properties might influence the ability of a substance to gain control over behavior and have attempted to document the degree to which these properties are common to various substances. In addition, we have suggested that these properties are not unique to the several substances that we selected. That is, in evaluating events that critically affect other classes of behavior, we would expect to find that such events possess many of the properties we have discussed. As a way of assessing this possibility, we have chosen to consider a class of habitual behavior that falls under the category heading of social attachment.

It is no surprise that affiliative activities comprise much of human behavior. It is interesting that the terms that are sometimes used to describe the control such activities exercise over our behavior are also used to describe the control that other events, even drug use, can exert. It is not unusual for individuals to talk about dependencies upon friends, relatives, and spouses. In the popular press we read about love as an addiction (Peele 1975). When relationships are strong, losses are emotionally devastating. At the same time, as a type of activity, affiliative behavior is valued and very much encouraged by society and abstinence is considered unusual at best. We propose that at a certain level of abstraction a theory of social attachment might not differ markedly from a theory of drug use or other habitual behaviors.

The form of affiliative behavior that has been studied most systematically in the laboratory is imprinting in young birds. For this reason we will review the literature on the ability of imprinting stimuli to influence subjects' behavior.

Exposing a newly hatched duckling to a mother-surrogate or a moving object will result in the surrogate's acquiring a large amount of control over the bird's behavior. For example, ducklings will engage in a wide range of behavior in order to remain in the presence of the surrogate (imprinting stimulus) and separating the bird from the surrogate gives rise to distress calling. What follows is an evaluation of the effects of an imprinting stimulus in terms of the properties we have previously considered.

Reinforcement. Young birds will learn arbitrary responses such as key-pecking, (Hoffman, Searle, Toffey, and Kozma 1966; Peterson 1960) or pole-pecking (Eiserer and Hoffman 1973) to produce brief exposure to the imprinting stimulus. Once trained, the operant will persist many months with the imprinting object as the only source of reinforcement (Hoffman and Kozma 1967). Ducklings also learn to refrain from following the imprinting stimulus when removal of it is made contingent on following (Hoffman, Straton, and Newby 1969).

Tolerance. Results of Hoffman et al. (1974) suggest that the initial excitement that an imprinting stimulus elicits (quick orienting to the imprinting stimulus, rapid approach to the stimulus) declines as the number of exposures increases.

Withdrawal Effects. Removal of an imprinting stimulus typically results in an increase in distress calling (Bateson 1966; Collias 1952; Eiserer and Hoffman 1973; Hoffman 1968; Hoffman and Ratner 1973; Sluckin 1965; Starr 1978). Such distress calling develops gradually with cyclic presentations and removals of the stimulus. The rate at which the withdrawal effects develop and the degree to which they are retained depend upon the interval between presentations of the imprinting stimulus. When the interstimulus intervals are short, the development of distress calling in response to the removal of the stimulus is most rapid and the retention of such effects is longer (Starr 1978). Eiserer and Hoffman (1973) have shown that termination of a long (30- or 180-second) imprinting stimulus results in greater levels of distress calling than termination of a short (3-second) stimulus. It is also the case that birds will attempt to follow a departing imprinting stimulus, even if it must overcome obstacles to do so (Hess 1958).

Affective Contrast—Opponent Responses. Presentation of an imprinting stimulus to a young bird acts to depress the level of distress calling compared to presentation of a novel stimulus or no stimulus. However, removal of the imprinting stimulus results in a short latency burst of distress calling that exceeds baseline levels (Eiserer and Hoffman 1973). It is interesting that the level of distress calling following termination of a 30-second imprinting stimulus was found to be greater than the level of distress calling after termination of a 3-second imprinting stimulus (the larger the dose of the imprinting stimulus, the greater was the opponent response when the stimulus was terminated). With repeated exposure of the imprinting stimulus, the level of excitement elicited by the imprinting stimulus declines; however, the intensity and duration of distress calling elicited by its termination is increased (Hoffman et al. 1974).

Conditioning Effects. Hoffman et al. (1972) have demonstrated that an imprinted stimulus can serve as an effective Pavlovin UCS by showing that a previously neutral stimulus acquired the ability to suppress distress calling as a consequence of its being paired with the imprinted stimulus.

Effects of Stress. Imprinting sessions are more effective (the imprinting stimulus more rapidly gains control over the subject's behavior) when the subject is in a high rather than low state of arousal or stress induced by presentation of shock (Hess 1959; Tolman 1963).

Conclusion

In undertaking the task of identifying commonalities in substance use and habitual behavior, we propose that an understanding of the ways substances gain control over behavior does not require a set of principles unique to each substance. In our discussion of the experimental literature, we were generally able to show that the six properties selected were common to the substances under consideration or were able to point to gaps in the literature and thereby indicate the need for additional research.

At the outset we also propose that the six properties should be important in the development of many habitual behaviors. The fact that we were able to demonstrate that an affiliative behavior such as imprinting is similarly affected by these variables provides support for this proposal.

To say that the six properties we have considered influence the ability of a substance to gain control over behavior is *not* to say that all of them operate in individual cases. Rather, when the task is to modify levels of habitual behavior, one needs to know what variables are controlling the behavior. Given the evidence that these six sources of control are common to the substances we reviewed, we propose that these are among the variables that should be considered when addressing particular cases of substance abuse. The six properties are by no means an exhaustive list of the effects that govern the level of habitual substance use. Other factors peculiar to the individual and the circumstances of use interact to determine the overall level of use or how disruptive abstinence will prove to be. Furthermore, we do not believe that if a substance produces withdrawal effects then it will gain undesired levels of control over the behavior of all individuals who use it. But we do propose that, to the degree that the substance possesses the property, the more likely on the average the substance will gain control over behavior.

Although we have focused on commonalities, variation in the importance of these six properties across substances should be expected: the role of withdrawal effects for habitual use may be greater for opiates than cocaine, for example. We should expect to see differences across the substances in the form of different rank orderings of these properties in their role of influencing habitual use. In considering a wider range of substances than we have, one should similarly expect to see variations in the degree to which these six properties are observed. However, because of the variability in the species of subjects, experimental procedures, and dependent measures used in the experimental literature, the task of identifying commonalities and differences in cross-substance comparisons is a difficult one.

Given the six properties that we chose to consider and the others considered in this volume, we can appreciate that the variables governing substance use are potentially many. The phenomenon is overdetermined. Our increased understanding of the variables that influence substance use reflects progress in the task of solving this difficult problem. At the same time, our appreciation of the complexity of the phenomenon should serve as a caution and prevent our making naive, unfulfillable claims of imminent solutions to the problem of substance abuse.

References

Abramson, E.D., and Wunderlich, R.A. 1972. Anxiety, fear, and eating: A test of the psychosomatic concept of obesity. *J. Abnormal Psychol.* 79:317-321.

Antelman, S.M.; Szechtman, H.; Chin, P.; and Fisher, A.E. 1975. Tail-pinch induced eating, gnawing, and licking behavior in rats: Dependence on the nigrostriatal dopamine system. *Brain Res.* 99:319-337.

Azrin, N.H., and Hake, D.F. 1969. Positive conditioned suppression: Conditioned suppression using positive reinforcers as the unconditioned stimuli. *J. Exp. Anal. Behav.* 12:167-173.

Bachrach, W.H. 1953. Action of insulin on motor and secretory functions of the digestive tract. *Physiol. Rev.* 33:566-592.

Barich, B. 1981. *Laughing in the Hills.* New York: Penguin Books.

Bateson, P.P.G. 1966. The characteristics and context of imprinting. *Biol. Rev. Cambridge Phil. Soc.* 41:177-220.

Beatty, W.W. 1982. Dietary variety stimulates appetite in females but not males. *Bull. Psychon. Soc.* 19:212-214.

Beckett, A.H.; Gorrod, J.W.; and Jenner, P. 1971. The effect of smoking on nicotine metabolism *in vivo* in man. *J. Pharmacy Pharmacol.* 23 (Suppl.):625-675.

Blackman, D. 1968. Conditioned suppression or facilitation as a function of the behavioral baseline. *J. Exp. Anal. Behav.* 11:53-61.

Bolles, R.C. 1967. *Theory of Motivation.* New York: Harper & Row.

Bondy, P.K. 1954. Acute effects of purified crystalline pituitary growth hormone in normal human beings. *Yale J. Bio. and Med.* 26:263-274.

Brecher, E.M. 1972. *Licit and Illicit Drugs.* Boston: Little, Brown.

Brown, J.S. 1961. *The Motivation of Behavior.* New York: McGraw-Hill.

Brown, J.S., and Jacobs, A. 1949. The role of fear in the motivation and acquisition of responses. *J. Exp. Psych.* 39:747-759.

Bruch, H. 1973. *Eating Disorders.* New York: Basic Books.

Burns, B.H. 1969. Chronic chest disease, personality, and success in stopping cigarette smoking. *Brit. J. Prevent. Soc. Med.* 23(1):23-27.

Cappell, H.; Roach, C.; and Poulos, C.X. 1981. Pavlovian control of cross-tolerance between pentobarbital and ethanol. *Psychopharmacology* 74:54-57.

Clark, M.S.G. 1969. Self-administered nicotine solutions preferred to placebo by the rat. *Brit. J. Pharmacol.* 35:376.

Clark, R., and Polish, E. 1960. Avoidance conditioning and alcohol consumption in rhesus monkeys. *Science* 132:223-244.

Clark, F.C., and Steele, B.J. 1966. Effects of d-amphetamine on performance under a multiple schedule in the rat. *Psychopharmacologia* 9:157-169.

Collins, K.H., and Tatum, A.L. 1927. A conditioned salivary reflex established by chronic morphine poisoning. *Am. J. Physiol.* 74:14-15.

Crowell, C.R.; Hinson, R.E.; and Siegel, S. 1981. The role of conditioning in tolerance to the thermic effects of ethanol. *Psychopharmacology* 73:51-54.

Davis, M. 1970. Effects of interstimulus interval length and variability on startle response habituation. *J. Comp. Physiol. Psychol.* 72:177-192.

Deneau, G.A., and Inoki, R. 1967. Nicotine self-administration in monkeys. *Ann. New York Acad. Sci.* 142(1):277-279.

Deneau, G.A.; Yanagita, T.; and Seevers, M.H. 1969. Self-administration of psychoactive substances by the monkey. *Psychopharmacologia* 16:30-48.

Donegan, N.H. 1981. Priming produced facilitation or diminution of responding to a Pavlovian unconditioned stimulus. *J. Exp. Psychol.: Anim. Behav. Process.* 7:295-302.

Donegan, N.H., and Wagner, A.R. 1983. Conditioned diminution and facilitation of the UR: A sometimes opponent process interpretation. In I. Gormezano, W.F. Prokasy, and R.F. Thompson (eds.), *Classical Conditioning III: Behavioral, Neurophysiological, and Neurochemical Studies in the Rabbit.* New Jersey: Lawrence Erlbaum Assoc.

Drew, G.C. 1937. The recurrence of eating in rats after apparent satiation. *Proc. Zool. Soc. London* 107:95-106.

Edgar, D.; Hall, G.; and Pearce, J.M. 1981. Enhancement of food-rewarded instrumental responding by an appetitive conditioned stimulus. *Quart. J. Exp. Psychol.* 33B: 3-19.

Eikelboom, R., and Stewart, J. 1982. Conditioning of drug-induced physiological responses. *Psych. Rev.* 89:507-528.

Eikelboom, R., and Stewart, J. 1979. Conditioned temperature effects using morphine as the unconditioned stimulus. *Psychopharmacology* 61:31-38.

Eisenger, R.A. 1971. Nicotine and addiction to cigarettes. *Brit. J. Addiction* 66:150-156.

Eiserer, L.A., and Hoffman, H.S. 1973. Priming of ducklings' responses by presenting an imprinted stimulus. *J. Comp. Physiol. Psychol.* 82:345-359.

Finnegan, J.K.; Larson, P.S.; and Haag, H.B. 1945. The role of nicotine in the cigarette habit. *Science* 102:94-96.

Fletcher, C., and Doll, R. 1969. A survey of doctors' attitudes to smoking. *J. Prevent. Soc. Med.* 23:145-153.

Frankenhaeuser, M.; Myrsten, A.L.; Post, B.; and Johansson, G. 1971. Behavioral and physiological effects of cigarette smoking in a monotonous situation. *Psychopharmacologia* 22:1-7.

Friedman, J. 1972. Psychopharmacological Aspects of Cigarette Smoking. Unpublished thesis, University of Melbourne, Australia.

Glick, S.D., and Muller, R.O. 1971. Paradoxical effects of low doses of d-amphetamine in rats. *Psychopharmacologia* (Berlin) 22:396-402.

Glucksman, M.L., and Hirsch, J. 1968. The response of obese patients to weight reduction: A clinical evaluation of behavior. *Psychosom. Med.* 30:1-11.

Glucksman, M.L.; Hirsch, J.; and McCully, R.S. 1968. The response of obese patients to weight reduction. II. A quantitative evaluation of behavior. *Psychosom. Med.* 30:359-373.

Goldstein, D.B. 1972. Relationship of alcohol dose to intensity of withdrawal signs in mice. *J. Pharmacol. Exp. Therapeutics* 180:203-215.

Goldstein, D.B. 1973. Alcohol withdrawal reaction in mice: effects of drugs that modify neurotransmission. *J. Pharmacol. Exp. Therapeutics* 186:1-9.

Grabowski, J., and O'Brien, C.P. 1980. Conditioning factors in opiate use. In N.K. Mello (ed.), *Advances in Substance Abuse,* vol. 2. Greenwich, Conn.: JAI Press.

Grinker, J.; Hirsch, J.; and Levin, B. 1973. The affective response of obese patients to weight reduction: A differentiation based on age of onset of obesity. *Psychosom. Med.* 35:57-62.

Guilford, J.S. 1966. Factors Related to Successful Abstinence from Smoking. American Institutes for Research, Pittsburgh, Pa.

Haertzen, A.A., and Hooks, N.T. 1969. Changes in personality and subjective experience associated with the chronic administration and withdrawal of opiates. *J. Nervous Mental Dis.* 148:606-614.

Halmi, K.A.; Stunkard, A.J.; and Mason, E.E. 1980. Emotional responses to weight reduction by three methods: Gastric bypass, jejunoileal bypass, diet. *Am. J. Clin. Nutrit.* 33:446-451.

Hanson, H.M.; Ivester, C.A.; and Morton, B.R. 1977. The effects of selected compounds on the self-administration of nicotine in rats. *Fed. Proc.* 36:1040.

Hanson, H.M.; Ivester, C.A.; and Morton, B.R. 1979. Nicotine self-administration in rats. In N.A. Krasnegor (ed.), *Cigarette Smoking as a Dependence Process.* NIDA Research Monograph No. 23. DHEW pub. no. ADM 79-800. U.S. Dept. of Health, Education, and Welfare, Rockville, Md.

Herman, C.P. 1974. External and internal cues as determinants of the smoking behavior of light and heavy smokers. *J. Pers. Soc. Psychol.* 30:664-672.

Hess, E.H. 1958. Imprinting in animals. *Sci. Am.* 198:81-90.

Hess, E.H. 1959. Imprinting. *Science* 130:133-141.

Hinson, R.E., and Siegel, S. 1980. The contribution of Pavlovian conditioning to ethanol tolerance and dependence. In H. Rigter and J.C. Crabbe (eds.), *The Behavioral Pharmacology of Alcohol Tolerance, Dependence, and Addiction: A Research Handbook.* Amsterdam: Elsevier/North Holland Biomedical Press.

Hodgson, R.J., and Rankin, H.J. 1974. Modification of excessive drinking by cue exposure. *Behav. Res. Therapeutics* 14:305-307.

Hoffman, H.S. 1968. The control of distress vocalization by an imprinted stimulus. *Behaviour* 30:175-191.

Hoffman, H.S.; Stratton, J.W.; and Newby, V. 1969. Punishment by response-contingent withdrawal of an imprinted stimulus. *Science* 163:702-704.

Hoffman, H.S.; Barrett, J.; Ratner, A.; and Singer, D. 1972. Conditioned suppression of distress calls in imprinted ducklings. *J. Comp. Physiol. Psychol.* 80:357-364.

Hoffman, H.S.; Eiserer, L.A.; Ratner, A.M.; and Pickering, V.L. 1974. Development of distress vocalization during withdrawal of an imprinting stimulus. *J. Comp. Physiol. Psychol.* 86:563-568.

Hoffman, H.S., and Kozma, F., Jr. 1967. Behavioral control by an imprinted stimulus: Long term effects. *J. Exp. Anal. Behav.* 10:495-501.

Hoffman, H.S., and Ratner, A.M. 1973. A reinforcement model of imprinting: Implications for socialization in monkeys and men. *Psychol. Rev.* 80:527-544.

Hoffman, H.S.; Schiff, D.; Adams, J.; and Searle, J.L. 1966. Enhanced distress vocalization through selective reinforcement. *Science* 151:352-354.

Hoffman, H.S.; Searle, J.L.; Toffey, S.; and Kozma, F., Jr. 1966. Behavioral control by an imprinted stimulus. *J. Exp. Anal. Behav.* 9:177-189.

Houde, R.W. 1974. The use and misuse of narcotics in the treatment of chronic pain. In J.J. Bonica (ed.), *Advances in Neurology,* vol. 4, *International Symposium on Pain.* New York: Raven Press.

Hull, C.L. 1943. *Principles of Behavior.* New York: Appleton-Century-Crofts.

Hull, C.L. 1951. *Essentials of Behavior.* New Haven, Conn.: Yale University Press.

Hunter, J., and Chasseaud, L.F. 1976. Clinical Aspects of Microsomal Enzyme Induction. In J.W. Bridges and L.F. Chasseaud (eds.) *Progress in Drug Metabolism,* vol. 1, New York: John Wiley and Sons.

Jaffe, J.G. 1975. Drug addiction and drug abuse. In L.S. Goodman and A. Gilman (eds.), *The Pharmacological Basis of Therapeutics.* New York: Macmillan.

Jones, B.M. 1974. Circadian variation in the effects of alcohol on cognitive performance. *Quart. J. Stud. Alcohol* 35:1212-1219.

Jones, R.T.; Farrell, T.R., III; and Herning, R.I. 1978. Tobacco smoking and nicotine tolerance. In N. Krasnegor (ed.), *Self-administration of Abused Substances: Methods for Study.* National Institute on Drug Abuse Research Monograph 20, U.S. Department of Health Education and Welfare Pub. No. (ADM) 78-727. Washington, D.C.: U.S. Government Printing Office.

Kaplan, H.I., and Kaplan, H.S. 1957. The psychosomatic concept of obesity. *J. Nervous Mental Disease* 125:181-201.

Keller, M. 1972. On the loss-of-control phenomenon in alcoholism. *Brit. J. Addiction* 67:153-166.

Kesner, R.P., and Baker, T.B. 1981. Development of morphine tolerance: Behavioral and physiological mechanisms. In J.L. Martinez, Jr., R.A. Jensen, R.B. Messing, H. Rigter, and J.L. McGaugh (eds.), *Endogenous Peptides and Learning and Memory Processes.* New York: Academic Press.

Kilbey, M.M., and Ellinwood, E.H. 1977. Chronic administration of stimulant drugs. In E.H. Ellinwood and M.M. Kilbey (eds.), *Cocaine and Other Stimulants.* New York: Plenum Press.

Kimble, G.A. 1961. *Hilgard and Marqui's Conditioning and Learning* (second edition). New York: Appleton-Century-Crofts.

Kollar, J., and Alkinson, R.M. 1966. Responses of extremely obese patients to starvation. *Psychosom. Med.* 28:227-245.

Konorski, J. 1967. *Integrative Activity of the Brain.* Chicago: University of Chicago Press.

Konorski, J., and Miller, S. 1937. On two types of conditioned reflex. *J. Genetic Psychol.* 16:264-272.

Koob, G.F.; Fray, P.J.; and Iversen, S.D. 1976. Tail-pinch stimulation: Sufficient motivation for learning. *Science* 194:637-639.

Kupferman, I. 1964. Eating behavior induced by sounds. *Nature* 201:324.

Lang, W.J.; Latiff, A.A.; McQueen, A.; and Singer, G. 1977. Self-administration of nicotine with and without a food delivery schedule. *Pharmacol., Biochem., Behav.* 7:65-70.

Larson, P.S.; Haag, H.B.; and Silvette, H. 1961. *Tobacco: Experimental and Clinical Studies.* Baltimore: Williams and Wilkins.

Larson, P.S.; and Silvette, H. 1968. *Tobacco: Experimental and Clinical Studies,* suppl. 1. Baltimore: Williams and Wilkins.

Larson, P.S., and Silvette, H. 1971. *Tobacco: Experimental and Clinical Studies,* suppl. 2. Baltimore: Williams and Wilkins.

Larson, P.S., and Silvette, H. 1975. *Tobacco: Experimental and Clinical Studies,* suppl. 3. Baltimore: Williams and Wilkins.

Lé, A.D.; Poulos, C.X.; and Cappell, H. 1979. Conditioned tolerance to the hypothermic effect of ethyl alcohol. *Science* 206:1109—1110.

Ludwig, A.M.; Cain, R.B.; Wikler, A.; Taylor, R.M.; and Bendfeldt, F. 1977. Physiological and situational determinants of drinking behavior. In M.M. Gross (ed.), *Alcohol Intoxication and Withdrawal. vol. 3b.: Studies in Alcohol Dependence.* New York: Plenum.

Ludwig, A.M., and Stark, L.H. 1974. Alcohol craving: Subjective and situational aspects. *Quart. J. Stud. Alcohol* 35:899-905.

Ludwig, A.M., and Wikler, A. 1974. Craving and relapse to drink. *Quart. J. Stud. Alcohol* 35:108-130.

Ludwig, A.M.; Wikler, A.; and Stark, L.H. 1974. The first drink: psychological aspects of craving. *Arch. Gen. Psychiatry* 30:539-547.

Lyon, M., and Randrup, A. 1972. The dose-response effect of amphetamine upon avoidance in the rat seen as a function of increasing stereotype. *Psychopharmacologia* 23:334-347.

Lyon, M., and Robbins, T.W. 1975. The action of central nervous system stimulant drugs: A general theory concerning amphetamine effects. In W. Essman (ed.), *Current Developments in Psychopharmacology,* vol. 2. New York: Spectrum.

Mackintosh, N.J. 1974. *The Psychology of Animal Learning.* London: Academic Press.

Mansfield, J.G., and Cunningham, C. 1980. Conditioned tolerance to the hypothermic effect of ethanol. *J. Comp. Physiol. Psychol.* 94:962-969.

Marlatt, G.A. 1978. Craving for alcohol, loss of control, and relapse: A cognitive-behavioral analysis. In P.E. Nathan, G.A. Marlatt, and T. Loberg (eds.), *Alcoholism: New Directions in Behavioral Research and Treatment.* New York: Plenum.

Marlatt, G.A.; Demming, B.; and Reid, J.B. 1973. Loss of control drinking in alcoholics: An experimental analog. *J. Abnorm. Psychol.* 81:233-241.

Martin, W.R., and Jasinski, D.R. 1969. Physiological parameters of morphine dependence in man—tolerance, early abstinence, protracted abstinence. *J. Psychiat. Res.* 7:9-17.

McAllister, W.R., and McAllister, D.E. 1962. Role of the CS and of apparatus cues in the measurement of acquired fear. *Psychol. Rep.* 11: 749-756.

McKenna, R.J. 1972. Some effects of anxiety level and food cues on the eating behavior of obese and normal subjects. *J. Pers. Soc. Psy.* 221:311-319.

McQuarrie, D.G., and Fingl, E. 1958. Effects of single doses and chronic administration of ethanol on experimental seizures in mice. *J. Pharmacol. Exp. Therapeutics* 124:264-271.

Meisch, R.A.; Henningfield, J.E.; and Thompson, T. 1975. Establishment of ethanol as a reinforcer for rhesus monkeys via the oral route: Initial results. In M.M. Gross (ed.), *Experimental Studies of Alcohol Intoxication and Withdrawal,* vol. 59, *Advances in Experimental Medicine and Biology.* New York: Plenum.

Meisch, R.A., and Thompson, T. 1971. Ethanol intake in the absence of concurrent food reinforcement. *Psychopharmacologia* 22:72-79.

Meisch, R.A., and Thompson, T. 1974. Rapid establishment of ethanol as a reinforcer for rats. *Psychopharmacologia* 37:311-321.

Mello, N.K. 1972. Behavioral studies of alcoholism. In B. Kissin and H. Begleiter (eds.), *The Biology of Alcoholism,* vol. 2. New York: Plenum.

Mello, N.K., and Mendelson, J. 1964. Operant performance by rats for alcohol reinforcement. *Quart. J. Stud. Alcohol* 25:226.

Mello, N.K., and Mendelson, J.H. 1978. Alcohol and human behavior. In L.L. Iversen, S.D. Iversen, and S.H. Snyder (eds.), *Handbook of Psychopharmacology,* vol. 12. New York: Plenum.

Meltzer, D., and Brahlek, J.A. 1970. Conditioned suppression and conditioned enhancement with the same positive UCS: An effect of CS duration. *J. Exp. Anal. Behav.* 13:67-73.

Merry, J. 1966. The "loss of control" myth. *Lancet* 1:1257-1258.

Meyer, R.E., and Mirin, S.M. 1979. *The Heroin Stimulus: Implications for a Theory of Addiction.* New York: Plenum Medical Book Co.

Miczek, K.A., and Grossman, S.P. 1971. Positive conditioned suppression: Effects of CS duration. *J. Exp. Anal. Behav.* 15:243-247.

Miksic, S.; Smith, N.; Numan, R.; and Lal, H. 1975. Acquisition and extinction of a conditioned hyperthermic response to a tone paired with morphine administration. *Neuropsychobiology* 1:277-283.

Miller, L.L. 1961. Some direct actions of insulin, glucagon, and hydrocortisone on the isolated perfused rat liver. *Rec. Prog. Hormone Res.* 17:539-568.

Miller, N.E. 1948. Studies of fear as an acquirable drive: I. Fear as motivation and fear-reduction as reinforcement in the learning of new responses. *J. Exp. Psychol.* 38:89-101.

Mowrer, O.H. 1947. On the dual nature of learning: A reinterpretation of "conditioning" and "problem solving." *Harvard Ed. Rev.* 17:102-148.

Mullin, F.J., and Luckhardt, A.B. 1934. The effect of alcohol on cutaneous tactile and pain sensitivity. *Am. J. Physiol.* 109:77-78.

Myrsten, A.L.; Elgerot, A.; and Edgren, B. 1977. Effects of abstinence from tobacco smoking on physiological and psychological arousal levels in habitual smokers. *Psychosom. Med.* 39(1):25-38.

Myrsten, A.L.; Post, B.; Frankenhaeuser, M.; and Johansson, G. 1972. Changes in behavioral and physiological activation induced by cigarette smoking in habitual smokers. *Psychopharmacologia* 27(4):305-312.

Nisbitt, P.D. 1973. Smoking, physiological arousal, and emotional responses. *J. Personal. Soc. Psychol.* 25:137-145.

Numan, R.; Smith, N.; and Lal, H. 1975. Reduction of morphine-withdrawal body shakes by a conditional stimulus in the rat. *Psychopharmacol. Commun.* 1:295-303.

Oates, J.A.; Azarnoff, D.L.; Cohen, S.N.; and Melmon, K.L. 1975. Medicinal misadventures. *Emergency Med.* 7:115-137.

O'Brien, C.P. 1975. Experimental analysis of conditioning factors in human narcotic addiction. *Pharmacol. Rev.* 27:533-543.

O'Brien, C.P.; O'Brien, T.J.; Mintz, J.; and Brady, J.P. 1975. Conditioning of narcotic abstinence symptoms in human subjects. *Drug Alcohol Depend.* 1:115-123.

O'Brien, C.P.; Testa, T.; O'Brien, T.J.; Brady, J.P.; and Wells, B. 1977. Conditioned narcotic withdrawal in humans. *Science* 195:1000-1002.

Owen, J.E. 1960. The influence of dl-, d-, and l-amphetamine and d-amphetamine on a fixed ratio schedule. *J. Exp. Anal. Behavior* 3:293-310.

Parra-Covarrubias, A.; Rivera-Rodriguez, J.; and Almarez-Ugalde, A. 1971. Cephalic phase of insulin release in obese adolescents. *Diabetes* 20:800-802.

Patel, G.J., and Lal, H. 1973. Reduction in brain γ-ambinobutyric acid and in barbital narcosis during ethanol withdrawal. *J. Pharmacol. Exp. Therapeutics* 186:625-629.

Pavlov, I.P. 1927. In G. Anrep, (ed.), *Conditioned Reflexes*. London: Oxford University Press.

Peele, S. 1975. *Love and Addiction*. New York: Taplinger Publishing.

Perlick, D. 1977. The Withdrawal Syndrome: Nicotine Addiction and the Effects of Stopping Smoking in Heavy and Light Smokers. (Unpublished Ph.D. dissertation, Columbia University, New York.

Peterson, N. 1960. Control of behavior by presentation of an imprinted stimulus. *Science* 132:1395-1396.

Pfautz, P.L. 1980. Unconditioned facilitation and diminution of the unconditioned response. Unpublished doctoral dissertation, Yale University.

Pradhan, S.N., and Bowling, C. 1971. Effects of nicotine on self-stimulation in rats. *J. Pharmacol. Exp. Therapeutics* 176:229-243.

Quigley, J.P.; Johnson, V.; and Solomon, E.I. 1930. Action of insulin on the motility of the gastrointestinal tract. *Am. J. Physiol.* 91:488-495.

Raiffa, H. 1968. Decision analysis: *Introductory Lectures on Choices under Uncertainty*. Reading, Mass.: Addison-Wesley.

Randrup, A., and Munkvad, I. 1967. Brain dopamine and amphetamine-induced stereotyped behavior. *Acta Pharmacol. Toxicol.* 25 (Suppl. 4):62.

Rescorla, R.A., and Solomon, R.L. 1967. Two-process learning theory: Relationships between Pavlovian conditioning and instrumental learning. *Psychol. Rev.* 74:151-182.

Robins, L.N.; Davis, D.H.; and Goodwin, D.W. 1974. Drug use by US army enlisted men in Viet Nam: A follow up on their return home. *Am. J. Epidem.* 99:235-247.

Robinson, S., and Winnik, H.Z. 1973. Severe psychotic disturbances following crash diet weight loss. *Arch. Gen Psychiat.* 29:559-562.

Rodin, J. 1977. Research on eating behavior and obesity: Where does it fit in personality and social psychology. *Personal. Soc. Psychol. Bull.* 3(3, Summer):333-355.

Rodin, J. 1978. Has the distinction between internal versus external control of feeding outlived its usefulness? In G.A. Bray (ed.), *Recent Advances in Obesity Research* vol. 2. London: Newman.

Rodin, J. 1980. Changes in perceptual responsiveness following jejunotelestomy:their potential role in reducing food intake. *Am. J. Clin. Nutrit.* 33:457-464.

Rolls, B.J. 1979. How variety and palatability can stimulate appetite. *Nutrit. Bull.* 5:78-86.

Rolls, B.J.; Rowe, E.A.; Rolls, E.T.; Kingston, B.; Megson, A.; and Gunary, R. 1981. Variety in a meal enhances food intake in man. *Physio. Behav.* 26:215-221.

Rush, N.L.; Pearson, L.; and Long, W.J. 1970. Conditioned automatic responses induced in dogs by atropine and morphine. *European J. Pharmacol.* 11:22-28.

Schachter, S. 1977. Nicotine regulation in heavy and light smokers. *J. Exp. Psychol.: Gen.* 106:5-12.

Schachter, S. and Singer, J. 1962. Cognitive, social, and physiological determinants of emotional state. *Psychol. Rev.* 69:379-399.

Schachter, S.; Goldman, R.; and Gordon, A. 1968. Effects of fear, food deprivation and obesity on eating. *J. Pesonal. Soc. Psychol.* 10:91-97.

Schachter, S.; Silverstein, B.; Kozlowski, L.T.; Perlick, D.; Herman, C.P.; and Leibling, B. 1977. Studies of the interaction of psychological and pharmacological determinants of smoking. *J. Exp. Psychol.: Gen.* 106:3-49.

Schachter, S.; Silverstein, B.; and Perlick, D. 1977. Psychological and pharmacological explanations of smoking under stress. *J. Exp. Psychol.: Gen.* 106:31-40.

Schuster, C.R., and Villarreal, J.E. 1968. The experimental analysis of opioid dependence. In D.H. Effron (ed.), *Psychopharmacology: A Review of Progress*, Public Health Service Publication no. 1836 pp. 811-828.

Seevers, M.H., and Pfeiffer, C.C. 1936. A study of the analgesia, subjective depression, and euphoria produced by morphine, heroin, diluadid and codine in the normal human subject. *J. Pharmacol. Exp. Therapeutics* 56:166-187.

Segal, E.F. 1962. Effects of dl-amphetamine under concurrent VI DRL nonreinforcement. *J. Exp. Anal. Behav.* 5:105-112.

Sherman, J.E. 1979. The effects of conditioning and novelty on the rat's analgesic and pyretic responses to morphine. *Learning Motivation* 10: 383-418.

Shiffman, S.M. 1979. *The Tobacco Withdrawal Syndrome*. National Institute on Drug Abuse Research Monograph 23, U.S. Department of Health, Education, and Welfare. Pub. N. (ADM) 79-800. Washington, D.C.: U.S. Government Printing Office, pp. 158-184.

Sideroff, S., and Jarvik, M.E. 1980. Conditioned responses to videotape showing heroin-related stimuli. *Int. J. Addictions*.

Siegel, S. 1972. Conditioning of insulin-induced glycemia. *J. Comp. Physiol. Psychol.* 78:233-241.

Siegel, S. 1975. Evidence from rats that morphine tolerance is a learned response. *J. Comp. Physiol. Psychol.* 89:498-506.

Siegel, S. 1976. Morphine analgesic tolerance: Its situation specificity supports a Pavlovian conditioning model. *Science* 193:323-325.

Siegel, S. 1977. Morphine tolerance acquisition as an associative process. *J. Exp. Psychol.: Animal Behav. Proc.* 3:1-13.

Siegel, S. 1978. Tolerance to the hyperthermic effect of morphine in the rat is a learned response. *J. Comp. Physiol. Psychol.* 92:1137-1149.

Siegel, S. 1979. The role of conditioning in drug tolerance and addiction. In J.D. Keehn (ed.), *Psychopathology in Animals: Research and Treatment Implications*. New York: Academic Press.

Siegel, S.; Hinson, R.E.; and Krank, M.D. 1978. The role of predrug signals in morphine analgesic tolerance: Support for a Pavlovian conditioning model of tolerance. *J. Exp. Psychol.: Animal Behav. Proc.* 4:188-196.

Siegel, S.; Hinson, R.E.; and Krank, M.D. 1979. Modulation of tolerance to the lethal effect of morphine by extinction. *Behav. Neural Biol.* 25:257-262.

Siegel, S.; Sherman, J.E.; and Mitchell, D. 1980. Extinction of morphine analgesic tolerance. *Learning Motivation* 11:289-301.

Siegel, S.; Hinson, R.E.; Krank, M.D.; and McCully, J. 1982. Heroin "overdose" death: Contribution of drug associated cues. *Science* 216: 436-437.

Sklar, L.S., and Amit, Z. 1978. Tolerance to high doses of morphine: Lack of evidence of learning. *Behav. Biol.* 22:509-514.

Slochower, J. 1976. Emotional labeling and overeating in obese and normal weight individuals. *Psychosom. Med.* 38:131-139.

Slochower, J., and Kaplan, S.P. 1980. Anxiety, perceived control, and eating in obese and normal weight persons. *Appetite* 1:1-9

Sluckin, W. 1965. *Imprinting and Early Learning*. Chicago: Aldine.

Solomon, R.L. 1977. An opponent-process theory of acquired motivation: The affective dynamics of addiction. In J.R. Maser and M.E.P. Seligman (eds.), *Psychopathology: Experimental models*. San Francisco: W.H. Freeman.

Solomon, R.L. 1980. The opponent process theory of acquired motivation. *Am. Psychologist* 35:691-712.

Solomon, R.L., and Corbit, J.D. 1974. An opponent-process theory of motivation: I. Temporal dynamics of affect. *Psychol. Rev.* 81:119-145.

Solow, C.; Silverfarb, P.M.; and Swift, K. 1974. Psychological effects of intestinal bypass surgery for severe obesity. *New England J. Med.* 290:300-304.

Spence, K.W. 1951. Theoretical interpretations of learning. In S.S. Stevens (ed.), *Handbook of Experimental Psychology*. New York: John Wiley and Sons.

Spitzer, L.; Marcus, J.; and Rodin, J. 1980. Arousal-induced eating: A response to Robbins and Fray. *Appetite* 1:343-348.

Starr, M.D. 1978. An opponent-process theory of motivation: I. Time and intensity variables in the development of separation-induced distress calling in ducklings. *J. Exp. Psychol.: Animal Behav. Proc.* 4:338-355.

Stolerman, I.P.; Fink, R.; and Jarvik, M.E. 1973. Acute and chronic tolerance to nicotine measured by activity in rats. *Psychopharmacologia* 30:329-342.

Stolk, J.M., and Rech, R.H. 1967. Enhanced stimulant effects of d-amphetamine on the spontaneous locomotor activity of rats treated with reserpine. *J. Pharmacol. Exp. Therapeutics* 158:140-149.

Stripling, J.S., and Ellinwood, E.H. 1977. Sensitization to cocaine following chronic administration in the rat. In E.H. Ellinwood and M.M. Kilbey (eds.), *Cocaine and Other Stimulants*. New York: Plenum Press.

Stunkard, A.J. 1957. The dieting depression: incidence and clinical characteristics of untoward responses to weight reduction regimes. *Am. J. Med.* 23:77-86.

Stunkard, A.J., and Wolff, H.G. 1954. Correlation of arterio-venous differences, gastric hunger contractions, and the experience of hunger in man. *Fed. Proc.* 13:147.

Swanson, D.W., and Dinello, F.A. 1970. Follow-up of patients starved for obesity. *Psychosom. Med.* 32:209-214.

Tatum, A.L.; Seevers, M.H.; and Collins, K.H. 1929. Morphine addiction and its physiological interpretation based on experimental evidences. *J. Pharmacol. Exp. Therapeutics* 36:447-475.

Teasdale, J. 1973. Conditioned abstinence in narcotic addicts. *Int. J. Addictions* 8:273-292.

Ternes, J.; O'Brien, C.P.; Grabowski, J.; Wellerstein, H.; and Jordan-Hayes, J. 1980. Conditioned drug responses to naturalistic stimuli. In *Proceedings of the 1979 Committee on Problems of Drug Dependence*, NIDA Research Monograph. Washington, D.C.: U.S. Government Printing Office.

Thompson, T., and Ostlund. W., Jr. 1965. Susceptibility to readdiction as a function of addiction and withdrawal environments. *J. Comp. Physiol. Psychol.* 60:388-392.

Tinklepaugh, O.L. 1928. An experimental study of representative factors in monkeys. *J. Comp. Psychol.* 8:197-236.

Tolman, C.W. 1963. A possible relationship between the imprinting critical period and arousal. *Psych. Rec.* 13:181-185.

Tversky, A., and Kahneman, D. 1974. Judgement under uncertainty: Heuristics and biases. *Science* 185:1124-1131.

Tye, N.C., and Iversen, S. 1975. Some behavioral signs of morphine withdrawal stimuli. *Nature* 255:416-418.

Ullman, A.D. 1951. The experimental production and analysis of a "compulsive eating symptom" in rats. *J. Comp. Physiol. Psychol.* 44:575-581.

Ullman, A.D. 1952. Three factors involved in producing "compulsive eating" in rats. *J. Comp. Physiol. Psychol.* 45:490-496.

Victor, M., and Adams, R.D. 1953. The effect of alcohol on the nervous system. *Res. Pub. Assoc. Ner. Ment. Dis.* 32:526-573.

Wagner, A.R. 1981. SOP: A model of automatic memory processing in animal behavior. In N.E. Spear and R.R. Miller, eds., *Information Processing in Animals: Memory Mechanisms*. Hillsdale, N.J.: Lawrence Erlbaum Assoc.

Weeks, J.R., and Collins, R.J. 1968. Patterns of intravenous self-injection by morphine addicted rats. In A.H. Wikler (ed.), *The Addictive States*. Baltimore: Williams and Wilkins.

Weybrew, B.B., and Stark, J.D. 1967. *Psychological and Physiological Changes Associated with Deprivation from Smoking*. U.S. Naval Submarine and Medical Center Report No. 490.

Whitehead, C. 1974. Methadone pseudowithdrawal syndrome: Paradigm for a psychopharmacological model of opiate addiction. *Psychosom. Med.* 36:189-198.

Wicks, W.D. 1969. Induction of hepatic enzymes by adenosine 3', 5'-monophosophate in organ culture. *J. Biol. Chem.* 244:3941-3950.

Wikler, A. 1948. Recent progress in research on the neurophysiologic basis of morphine addiction. *Am. J. Psychiatry* 105:329-338.

Wilker, A. 1973. Conditioning of successive adaptive responses to the initial effects of drugs. *Conditional Reflex* 8:193-210.

Williams, R.H. 1960. Hypoglycemosis. In R.H. Williams (ed.), *Diabetes.* New York: Paul B. Hoeber.

Winger, G.D., and Woods, J.H. 1973. The reinforcing property of ethanol in the rhesus monkey: I. Initiation, maintenance and termination of intravenous ethanol-reinforced responding. *Ann. New York Acad. Sci.* 215:162-175.

Woods, J.H.; Ikomi, F.; and Winger, G. 1971. The reinforcing property of ethanol. In M.K. Roach, W.M. McIsaac, and P.J. Creaven (eds.), *Biological Aspects of Alcohol.* Austin: University of Texas Press.

Woods, J.H., and Schuster, C.R. 1971. Opiates as reinforcing stimuli. In T. Thompson and R. Pickens (eds.), *Stimulus Properties of Drugs.* New York: Appleton-Century-Crofts.

Woods, S.C.; Vasselli, J.R.; Kaestner, E.; Szakmary, G.A.; Milburn, P.; and Vitiello, M.V. 1977. Conditioned insulin secretion and meal feeding in rats. *J. Comp. Physio. Psych.* 91:128-133.

Yanagita, T. 1973. An experimental framework for evaluation of dependence liability of various types of drugs in monkeys. *Bull. Narcotics* 25:57-64.

Yanagita, T. 1976. Brief review on the use of self-administration techniques for predicting drug dependence potential. In T. Thompson and K.R. Unna (eds.), *Predicting Dependence Liability of Stimulant and Depressant Drugs.* Baltimore: University Park Press.

Young, F.G., and Korner, A. 1960. Growth hormone. In R.H. Williams (ed.), *Diabetes.* New York: Paul B. Hoeber.

5 Addictive Personality: A Viable Construct?

Alan R. Lang

Introduction

Questions abound concerning the viability of the construct "addictive personality." At the simplest level one might ask where the notion of addictive personality originated, why it persists in the absence of supporting evidence, and what might be its utility if there is any. Let us begin with these questions. The critical components of the construct, addictive behavior and personality, will then be defined or characterized and their possible interplay examined. The bulk of the chapter consists of a critical review of the concepts and methods employed in the study of addictive personality, with the major findings highlighted. No pretense of providing an exhaustive coverage of the relevant literature is made. As Freed (1979) observed, considering that Knox's (1976) review of research dealing exclusively with objective psychological test data and behavioral measures of alcoholics and their personalities cited eighty-six references in the two years 1971 and 1972 alone, a comprehensive review would assume epic proportions. The result, moreover, would probably be little more than a trivial annotated bibliography. Thus the focus here is on problems in studying and applying the construct of an addictive personality.

To expedite the review, emphasis will be placed on personality factors in problem drinking. This is justifiable because alcohol-related problems are the most costly and pervasive in this society and because the alcoholic personality has been the most widely studied in the addiction literature. Because other addictive substances have distinctive pharmacological actions and psychosocial significances, however, it is acknowledged that their use and abuse may be associated with uniquely different personality correlates as well. To accommodate this possibility, personality factors related to both marijuana and heroin use will be considered in some detail and occasional reference will be made to other substances.

Origin of the Addictive-Personality Construct

Virtually every theory has as its genesis simple observation. This is no less true of theories in clinical psychology than it is of those in other disciplines. In clinical psychology, however, a good deal of the observation has been carried out by clinicians who, at least historically, have often been steeped in the tradition of psychoanalysis. The practical implications of this state of affairs for the development of a construct of addictive personality are several. First, the observers dealt primarily with psychopathologic rather than normal personalities. Second, they observed addicts on a case-by-case basis in a therapeutic context. Third and most important, their paradigmatic bias led them to look for the cause of addiction within the psyche of the individual. In short, the observers wanted personality to be the basis of addiction and were operating under circumstances that made apparent support for this foregone conclusion rather easy to obtain. Eventually a number of these clinicians, drawing on extensive therapy experience, derived and perpetrated theories to explain the psychic determination of addiction. Not too surprisingly, the esoteric nature of such enterprises resulted in a maze of confusing and contradictory positions (see Pihl and Spiers 1978 for a summary). If the unreliability, method reactance, and biased sampling of serial case studies had not been enough, surely the difficulty of operationalizing psychodynamic concepts and the basically postdictive nature of psychoanalysis would have ensured the scientific untenability of a construct so derived. Given this situation, addiction (or any other complex human phenomenon or syndrome) would hardly be expected to be so constant and so powerful as to influence clinical observations and perceptions in anything approaching a uniform manner.

So it was that the community of scientists threw out the baby (addictive personality) with the bathwater (psychoanalysis). Because of the origin of the construct and the way in which it was (and not infrequently still is) studied, the death knells for addictive personality have been heard—and heard often—over the last three decades or more. For example:

No satisfactory evidence has been discovered that justifies a conclusion that persons of one type are more likely to become alcoholics than persons of another type. (Sutherland, Schroeder, and Tordella 1950:559)

From the psychological standpoint such an assumption (that alcoholics are a homogeneous population) implied that alcoholism was probably the manifestation of a more or less unique constellation of personality characteristics which could be designated the "alcoholic" personality! It is safe to say that a number of different lines of investigation have either demolished these notions or, at any rate, made them inexpedient to entertain as a basis for research. (Popham and Schmidt 1962:3)

The evidence of heterogeneity of personality factors among alcoholics is quite striking. (Stein, Rozynko, and Pugh 1971:258)

The extraordinary variety of personality types found for both heroin and polydrug abusers was interpreted as unequivocally refuting the notion that one personality type is addiction-prone. (Penk et al. 1980:299)

Persistence of the Addictive-Personality Construct

Despite pessimistic conclusions suggesting nonexistence, the search for addictive personalities has continued unabated and has even expanded. What accounts for such staying power is perhaps only that clinicians choose to ignore science or at least question its applicability to what they believe they know about people. But, then again, maybe it is something more than that. Sadava (1978) has suggested that a role for personality in understanding substance abuse may be "theoretically necessary, logically defensible, and empirically supportable." Without some type of addictive personality construct we are left with two rather unsettling null hypotheses: (1) Given comparable environmental factors, every individual is equally vulnerable to addiction. (2) Those who are addicted differ from others only in the particulars of their substance abuse. These statements imply a rather limited range of possible causes for addictive behavior neglecting, for example, constitutional variables. Nevertheless they do point to the need for a consideration of personality factors in any comprehensive theory of addiction. In essence it appears that we must know more about the nature of individuals and their differential motivations if we are ever to understand substance abuse problems fully. Furthermore, if we fail to adopt a perspective broad enough to include individual differences we seem doomed to attempt to control addiction through strictly external means, a tactic that has not proved too effective to date. For these reasons, then, personality seems likely to persist in analyses of the addictions, though it probably will be assigned a contributing role rather than being held up as the primary cause of addiction. The position taken in this chapter is consistent with the former, multivariate point of view.

Utility of the Addictive-Personality Construct

Suppose that some specific connections between personality and addictive behavior could be delineated. What would their utility be? Cox (1979) has suggested a number of possible applications. Besides providing a clearer explanation of etiology and a possible disentangling of certain cause and effect relations, we might be able to classify or subtype deviant populations better. Such separation of addicts according to their personality characteristics could permit development and refinement of differential (optimal) treatment strategies, with corresponding improvement in case disposition and in prediction of outcomes. In another application, discovering personality differences between addicts and other groups could aid in detection of potential or active but surreptitious substance abusers so that more appropriate decisions could be made in areas such as personnel screening and assignment. Finally, a personality-based system for estimating the probability of addictive behavior might allow better identification of high-risk populations so that prevention and early intervention programs could be applied more effectively, before problems reached the critical stage. In general there are good reasons for a continued interest in personality factors in addictive behaviors, over and above the purely academic concerns of basic research scientists. Let us turn then to definition and characterization of the two elements constituting the construct under consideration, namely, addictive behavior and personality.

Addictive Behavior and Personality

Addictive Behavior

In recent years theorists and researchers have begun to examine commonalities among such apparently diverse problems as alcoholism, drug abuse, smoking, overeating, and even compulsive gambling and certain sexual deviations. These behaviors have often been subsumed under the general rubric "addictions" and parallel processes have been identified. Although only alcohol and drug abuse are dealt with in this chapter, it may be instructive to examine some of the general common characteristics of addictive behaviors as well as those specific to the topic at hand.

A number of authors (Marlatt 1980; Miller 1980) have noted that a distinguishing feature of addictive behaviors is that they all involve some form of immediate gratification or pleasure but are accompanied by longer term adverse consequences. The short-term gratification may be referred to as a "high," a "rush," a "trip," a "release," a "relief," or any of a variety of terms that describe an alteration in one's state of consciousness or affect. The long-term negative consequences typically include deterioration of functioning in important life areas such as health, vocation, and social relations.

Another common ground in the addictions is that there appears to be a certain transferability of indulgences, with people often having a cluster of more than one of the problems. Some of the apparent reciprocal relation between smoking and overeating may be accounted for in behavioral terms, and anyone who has ever been on an alcoholism treatment unit can attest to the high rate of nicotine and caffeine consumption among alcoholics. More empirically based reports indicate that polydrug or multidrug abuse, either sequentially (Kandel 1975) or concurrently (Braucht, Kirby, and Berry 1978), are quite prevalent in the world of addictions. Mello (1977) has noted further that it is not uncommon for substance abusers to use two or more drugs with demonstrably different pharmacological effects, say alcohol and methadone or amphetamines as well as barbiturates. Extrapolating from this observation, she has suggested that the common goal that ties many addictions together may be the simple desire for a *change* in one's subjective state, with the direction of that change—up or down—being more or less incidental. In any case it is clear that while most serious addicts have a preferred substance, many freely substitute when their first choice is unavailable. The choice of specific alternatives may in turn be affected by the degree of cross tolerance (reduced responsivity) the individual has developed to certain other substances because of his or her normal usage patterns (Seevers and Deneau 1963). Thus practical as well as theoretical commonalities among the addictions seem apparent.

Among the common elements or defining characteristics more specific to the substance-abuse addictions are those outlined by Schuster and Johansen (1974), including the possibility of (1) physiological dependence, evaluated in terms of tolerance with increasing use and withdrawal symptoms upon cessation of use; (2) behavioral (or psychological) dependence, demonstrated through the disruption of normal behavior patterns when the substance is withheld, with a resumption of them if it is reapplied; (3) behavioral and physiological toxic consequences from substance self-administration, presumably referring to adverse effects of addiction on the important areas of life functioning described earlier; and (4) self-administration of substances for nonmedical purposes, indicating motivations other than those officially approved by the dominant culture.

The substance-abuse disorders are also marked by more or less consistent stages of involvement that might be regarded as separate components to be addressed by any theory of addiction. These stages include (1) initial use, (2) continuation of use, (3) transition from use to abuse, (4) cessation or control of abuse, and (5) relapse (Lettieri, Sayers, and Pearson 1980). Despite these parallels, the substance-abuse disorders are not linked by an single, definitive, and parsimonious etiologic paradigm such as an addictive personality *that has demonstrated validity.* Interestingly, however, progress in the study of each of the addictions has probably been hampered by an ill-advised overemphasis on and stubborn adherence to particular unitary-cause approaches.

Finally, it is evident that substance-abuse disorders share the lack of any treatment method that has a reasonable degree of documented efficacy. This deficiency is underscored by the high relapse rates of those addicts whose indulgences have been temporarily controlled. Hunt and Matarazzo (1973) have presented data revealing remarkably similar and dismal relapse patterns in alcoholics, heroin addicts, and smokers following treatment-induced abstinence. Marlatt (1980) has also identified striking commonalities in the psychosocial stressors that are often antecedents to relapses in the addictions.

Given the preceding, it seems safe to say that the addictive behaviors have a good deal in common. However, as Maisto and Caddy (1981) among others have pointed out, the substance-abuse addictions appear to differ significantly as well. First, the pharmacological properties of the substances themselves vary considerably in their abilities to induce physiological dependence. The amount of time required for addiction to occur, the magnitude of tolerance developed, the intensity of withdrawal symptoms experienced, and the probability that any given individual using a particular drug will become addicted all differ across substances. Moreover, the various drugs often have quite distinctive directions and natures to their particular pharmacological actions. They may be stimulating, depressing, psychedelic, or euphoria-inducing, as well as differing in the duration of their effects, their intrinsic dangerousness or lethality, and the degree to which they interfere with psychosocial functioning.

Predominant models of etiology for addiction reflect decidedly different directions too, including physical disease, underlying psychological problems, and socially learned patterns of behavior. These contrasts in turn have implications for issues of responsibility and control in substance-abuse problems. Perhaps the differences reflect sharp divergences in the general acceptability, social meanings, and practical consequences of use of the various substances. Alcohol consumption, for example, is both legal and normative behavior for adults in the United States, whereas heroin use is illegal and statistically deviant. Certain substances (marijuana) may be associated with particular political reference groups, while others (cocaine) may represent socioeconomic status. Hallucinogens are used primarily for intrapersonal experience, but the use of alcohol has more interpersonal implications. It also might be argued that use of more dangerous drugs is linked to severe personality problems, but nondangerous drug use is simply a social phenomenon. Regardless, the point is that while the similarities among the addictions might suggest general commonalities in personality and other causal or correlated factors, the obvious differences would appear to argue for greater specificity in the role these same factors play in each particular substance-abuse problem. In any event, it would seem wise to keep the multiplicity of variables in mind.

From an empirical standpoint there is a need to specify clearly the phenomena of interest when conducting research on any of the addictive behaviors. The task may seem straightforward, but the multiple dimensions and complexities of substance abuse often make it difficult. To begin with, distinctions among substance use, abuse, and dependence are invariably arbitrary, and the typically inconsistent application of these labels confuses comparisons across studies. In general, simple use denotes consumption without long-term undesirable consequences. As implied earlier, however, the particular characteristics of various substances (say, LSD) may make even a single use problematic, whereas for other substances (say, alcohol) this is less likely. For this reason, choice of substance, itself complicated by differential availability and accessibility and by multi- or polydrug selection and sequencing patterns, needs more precise specification before other classification can be undertaken.

Widely used classification systems, such as the one described in the *Diagnostic and Statistical Manual of Mental Disorders* (DSM III: American Psychiatric Association 1980), have sought to distinguish substance abuse from substance dependence in terms that include the nature of and processes involved in consequences of their use. Abuse is associated only with a pathological pattern of use having a minimum duration and producing adverse effects on social or occupational functioning. Dependence, on the other hand, must also include demonstrable signs of physical dependence, namely, tolerance or withdrawal symptoms. Despite ambiguities in these criteria and conceptual problems in the classification system's attempt to employ discrete categories where a continuum of variation actually exists, the effort at objective definitions considering both consumption and consequences is laudable. Unfortunately, most psychosocial research and particularly that dealing with personality variables has not applied this approach. Instead great confusion continues because investigators do little more than assign esoterically derived labels to widely divergent patterns of substance use, neglecting to consider either the quantity, quality, or variability of use or the attendant consequences of such use. One common assumption seems to be the more *often* one uses a substance or substances, the worse the problem.

To illustrate the flaws in the crude descriptive classification methods currently in use, consider the following. Brill, Crumpton, and Grayson (1971) found the personality characteristics of casual or occasional marijuana users (with use a maximum of twice each month) to be quite similar to those of nonusers but not frequent users. In a subsequent study Knecht et al. (1972) showed the personality attributes of occasional users (who smoked a maximum of four "joints" per week, regardless of frequency) assumed an intermediate position between nonusers and heavy users, differing from both. Finally, Kimlicka and Cross (1978) reported that casual users (with use a maximum of three times each week) did not differ from chronic or daily marijuana users on personality characteristics. Obviously a lack of uniformity in operational definitions may account for these apparently contradictory results regardless of their actual validity. Even employing a more sophisticated rate-over-period-of-time definition would probably not eliminate such misleading conclusions since the massed use of certain substances (as in binge drinking) is usually associated with more problems than regular, spaced usage (a cocktail before dinner each day), despite equivalent rates of consumption across time. Uncertainties about the pharmacological potency of most illicit substances also serves to obscure even further the meaning of simple frequency of use measures.

Still another index of the pervasiveness and significance of a substance use problem is the variety of contexts in which it is used. Sadava (1975) has suggested that, independent of consumption rate or legality issues, substance use that is restricted to solitary or select private settings or special occasions is probably quite different from that which seems to occur in almost any place at nearly any time. A perhaps associated dimension is that of the phase or stage of use. Age of initiation or onset of substance use may be a critical determinant of future drug involvement. Consideration should also be given to one's position in the general life cycle of substance abuse since many patterns seem to be self-limiting, apparently subject to burnout. These aspects of substance abuse are often overlooked in popular descriptions of the problem, which focus on absolute frequency or the like.

In sum it appears that an adequate characterization of the addictive-behaviors phenomena should incorporate multidimensional and multimethod measurement of substance type, quantity/frequency/variability of use of substances with identified potency, stage and context of use, and the adverse consequences associated with the particular pattern. Furthermore, it should be recognized that for the most part each of these factors is best treated as a continuous variable with significant potential for interaction with the others. Obviously such a prescription is idealistic, but a rudimentary application of it might reduce the chaos and equivocation so evident in the literature on personality and addictive behavior.

Personality

In the broadest sense personality is concerned with both the universal characteristics of human beings and the specific differences among them. With such latitude of coverage, there is really little in the experience and behavior of people that personality could not touch. Consequently the variety of possible theoretical perspectives and preferences for conceptualizing the human being and human activities is reflected in the absence of any widespread consensus about how personality should be defined. Given this ambiguity, personality might best be characterized as a complex hypothetical construct that provides a partial framework in which to explore the tenets and systematize the observations of any particular theory of human psychology and behavior. It emphasizes relatively enduring cognitive and behavioral patterns characteristic of the individual, but the goals of its application could be said to parallel those of psychology as a discipline: to *improve understanding* of subjective experience and to *improve prediction* (and perhaps control) of behavior. Unfortunately these two goals often seem incompatible because of the nature of epistemological assumptions and typical research tactics involved in each. The result has been that the frequent paradigm clashes in psychology have had a profound influence on the way personality variables are viewed by practitioners and scientists concerned with substance abuse.

Classical personality theorists, represented largely by psychodynam-ically oriented clinicians, have focused on understanding the internal work-ings of their troubled patients. They postulate that personality in general is a complex product of innate biological instincts or impulses whose expres-sion is modified by early (mostly interpersonal) developmental experiences. Adult personality is regarded as a relatively stable and all-encompassing en-tity whose essence can be understood through intensive study of the indiv-idual (the idiographic method). Verbal accounts, gathered via interview and case history, provide the data. Resulting self-reports and descriptions are re-viewed, analyzed, and interpreted to develop a set of inferences about the organization of and relations among various conscious and unconscious personal characteristics (psychological processes and states) of the subject. The interplay of these underlying instincts and motives is then presumed to be the primary determinant of behavior. For instance, disturbances in libid-inal development and concomitant concerns about homosexuality might yield the personality psychoanalysts term *oral dependent,* which some of them regard as a necessary precondition of alcohol and other drug prob-lems. In any case, as a consequence of the assumption of inner directedness or psychic determinism of behavior, classical personality theorists expect consistency in the actions of individuals across situations.

Global theories of personality in the psychodynamic tradition have as their principal virtue a potential for adding to our understanding of human experience. This attractive characteristic should not be overlooked since it is often absent from the allegedly more scientific theories of psychology. The psychodynamic approach suffers, however, from excessive dependence on isolated, unrepresentative, and unverified idiographic data. Coupled with extensive networks of assumptions and inferences about unobservable inter-nal dynamics, this shortcoming has rendered such theories untestable and unsuitable for most predictive and other practical uses. Finding a referent for the psychodynamic term *addictive personality* would be no mean feat.

Trait theories of personality, unlike psychodynamic ones, have been developed mainly from the study of large groups of adults from the normal population. Most posit a primarily congenital origin for traits (dimensions of personality like that called "extroversion"), though developmental contribu-tions are theoretically possible. The method of trait theorists is to gather data pertinent to a variety of human states, preferences, and behaviors by means of tests, questionnaires, or rating scales. The resulting scores are then factor-analyzed and an individual's rank order or position on a given trait factor or constellation of them provides a personality description or profile. These in turn can be correlated with other attributes or can be used to try to predict behavior.

From a scientific point of view trait theories have a definite advantage over psychodynamic ones in their ability to make direct comparisons across subjects using common metrics collected in a standardized manner. Both approaches share an assumption about the inner directedness of human behavior, however. The practical consequence of this orientation is that behavior is expected to be generally reflective of internal disposition and hence relatively consistent across a variety of situations. These personality theories assume, moreover, the existence of individual differences important in maintaining stable contrasts among people regardless of context. Persons scoring high on traits associated with addiction, for example, should always be more likely to be abusing substances than those low on such traits.

Although alternative ways exist for conceptualizing personality, for example by attempting to arrive at a consensus among observers as to what traits characterize a target individual, the other major force in theories of human behavior is really an antipersonality position termed "situationism." Mischel (1968) has championed this approach by pointing to the fundamental weakness of traditional personality theories—their lack of predictive validity. Citing numerous studies to support his argument, he has contended that the assumption of cross-situational consistency in individual behavior is untenable. Instead of behaving in a stable fashion across time and circumstance, people tend to exhibit remarkable specificity (inconsistency), apparently as part of their efforts to adjust to the unique demands of situations in adaptive ways.

According to situationists, heredity can for the most part account only for individuals' basic response potentials. Beyond this, individual behavior is shaped by situational demands against the backdrop of earlier environmental experience and conditioning history. The assumption is one of outer directedness, the prepotency of the external stimulus configuration, with individual differences cropping up only occasionally to embarrass the paradigm. The primary method of situationist research is the experiment, which has as its goal the development of principles for predicting the behavior of groups of subjects or people in general (the nomothetic method). Implicit in this approach is the assumption that it is not personality that determines addictive behavior but, rather, the stimulus properties and response options of the environment of the individual.

The situationist or environmental determinism viewpoint, with its heritage of experimentation, has a good deal to be said in its favor. It has alerted us to the fact that behavior does not occur in a vacuum and has, through its application, permitted some impressive improvements in prediction. However, its total commitment to empiricism appears to impede the understanding that often comes only from going beyond that which is directly observable. Perhaps more important, the neglect of individual differences or subject variables may have resulted in the unnecessary assignment of some of the variance in predictive efforts to the error category. At least some consideration or reconsideration of the person and personality would seem warranted.

Noting that much of the psychologically interesting variance in human behavior may be found in the interaction between the person and the situation, a number of theorists and investigators (Endler and Magnusson 1976, for instance) have proposed an *interactionist* psychology of personality. This perspective is probably not novel, having forerunners in classical personality theory (see Ekehammar 1974 for a historical review) and even in the "person variables" of Mischel's (1973) revision of the situationist position. Yet its potential for improving not only the accuracy of behavioral prediction but also our understanding of the behavior under consideration remains largely untapped. The interactional approach seeks to supplant both the clinical psychodynamic or trait view (locus of causality in the person) and the situationist or structuralist view (locus of causality in the environment). It does this by positing that actual behavior is the product of continuous and multidirectional interactions of person variables and situation variables.

Acknowledging the importance of situations, interactionist theorists' attention to person variables is predicated on research. In a classic study of personality, Bem and Allen showed "that it is possible to identify on a priori grounds those individuals who will be cross-situationally consistent and those who will not" (1974:506). This being the case, it would seem ill-advised to attend only to the assessment of the situation when trying to predict behavior. Among the factors to be considered is the relevancy of a predictor trait to a particular situation since this will probably mediate its predictive ability. It could make a difference, for example, if the study of personality variables in addictive behavior were restricted to the cognitive realm (beliefs, attitudes, expectations) when individual differences in affective states, psychopathology, or general personality functioning were actually more pertinent to the situation about which the prediction was being made. Several recent reviews (Epstein 1979, 1980) also have concluded that the reliability and predictive value of traits can be increased considerably by indexing and testing them across an aggregate of subjects, stimuli or situations, trials or occasions, and measures, instead of depending on the one-shot evaluations so common in personality research. Finally, again at the level of methodology, there is a need for some sort of combination of idiographic and nomothetic techniques (see Bem and Funder 1978; Kenrick and Stringfield 1980), since the former may be more appropriate to person assessment while the latter has its role in the evaluation of situations.

In considering both personality and situation factors simultaneously we may discover, as Mischel (1977) has suggested, that individual differences strongly determine behaviors in certain ambiguous or loosely structured situations, while strong influences in the immediate environment can overwhelm personality factors in others. Or we may find that only particular kinds of person and situation interactions are important. In any case an adequate evaluation of such propositions will be difficult to make unless researchers are willing to incorporate *both* experimental and subject variables that are theoretically meaningful in the same designs. Sadly, this avenue to achieve better understanding of basic processes as well as better prediction from individual differences has rarely been taken in personality research. Such neglect continues to impede progress in clarifying the role of personality in addictive behavior.

**Conceptual Issues in the Study of
Personality and Addictive Behavior**

What can we reasonably expect to learn about the relation between personality and addictive behavior? So far personal and situational variables have been discussed as the principal determinants of any behavior and by deduction any addictive behavior. Each of these variables can be analyzed further, however. While personality is often viewed as the distinctive psychosocially based behavioral tendencies an individual brings to a situation, it may also reflect genetically transmitted inclinations and propensities. Thus several recent reviews of the familial alcoholism literature (Goodwin 1979) have included considerable speculation about the possible role of genetic predispositions to alcoholic behavior. Other mainly physiologic aspects of individual differences, such as health or organismic status of the person, probably contribute to the likelihood of substance-use problems too.

One cannot ignore the unique long- and short-term effects of situational factors either. Correlational studies by Cahalan and Cisin (1976), among others, have documented a powerful association between sociocultural variables (demographic characteristics, subcultural identification) and drinking patterns. At the same time, experimental research (Pliner and Cappell 1974) has revealed how the immediate circumstances surrounding drinking (solitary versus social) can exert a strong influence on the affective consequences of alcohol consumption. Finally, the environment can have a significant indirect impact or substance use by acting *through* personality, since social psychological elements represent a major component of the personality construct.

Almost regardless of the framework in which they are conceptualized, individual differences clearly interact with addictive behaviors, even when environmental conditions are held constant. Franks (1967), for instance, has shown that the psychological and behavioral effects of both stimulants and depressants vary across several dimensions of personality. Fisher (1970) reported similar findings, and Bachman and Jones (1979) found personality variables could be used to predict withdrawal symptoms following cessation of controlled administrations of cannabis. Moreover, despite the crucial role of learning in substance use, people still choose and perceive their learning environments in idiosyncratic ways. Thus although we may recognize the validity and utility of strictly biological and social or environmental factors, it is incumbent on us to determine the role of psychological personality variables in addictive behaviors. Analogous efforts are already underway in the exploration of biopsychosocial interactions in physical disease processes (Engel 1977); and, an agent-host-environment model for the study of alcoholism was proposed in the 1960s (Mendelson and Mello 1969). How then shall we proceed?

First, we must acknowledge two things: (1) Personality is a developmental and changeable phenomenon, never totally fixed but, rather, in continuous dynamic interaction with other factors, including age, family, other people, culture, health, stress, *and*, substance use, to name a few. (2) Addictive behavior also has a temporal dimension in that it involves a number of distinctive, if not discrete and invariant, stages or phases. The practical implication of these two facts is that the interplay of personality and addictive behavior may take on wholly different complexions at different points in time. There is good reason to believe, for example, that the personal reasons for an individual's initiation into substance use (say, the person's susceptibility to social influence) may be vastly different from those personality factors playing a role in the maintenance of substance abuse (perhaps gross psychopathology) at some later date. Thus it appears there is still validity in Allport's (1937) observation that compulsive behaviors (such as addiction) tend to assume a "functional autonomy," whereby motives originally underlying a behavior often bear little relation to those contributing to its continuation. It is unreasonable to expect that ignoring the dynamic interactions of personality and addictive behavior in the temporal or developmental context can be done without sacrificing both understanding and predictive accuracy relevant to these phenomena.

Given the complexity and multivariate determination of addictive behavior, it would be relatively easy to defend the assertion that discovery of a definitive cause or causes for addictive behavior, whether involving personality or not, is highly unlikely. However, this unlikelihood occurs mostly because in the study of addictive behaviors we cannot ethically attempt to manipulate, by direct experimentation, the variables of interest in order to create the problem. We do not give people certain personality characteristics and see if they become addicts, nor do we stimulate addiction and watch for personality changes. Hence etiological studies are always correlational in nature. This restriction notwithstanding, an array of correlational methods is available, each with a different level of inferential confidence.

The clinical method, utilized in the vast majority of addictive personality studies, is particularly susceptible to the problems of correlational research. Although it can take many specific forms, this approach has two main ingredients: (1) a clinical sample of persons already identified as addicts by some other means such as a psychiatric diagnosis or simply their participation in a treatment program for substance-use problems and (2) one or more personality tests, which may be structured (objective, or having limited response options) or unstructured (projective, or having little or no restriction on responses). Following adminstration of the personality measure(s) to the clinical group (and perhaps to a comparison group of supposed nonaddicts), efforts are made to characterize an addictive personality. This may be done in several ways. First, a descriptive profile can be developed by rational analysis of addicts' test responses on the assumption that they correspond directly to the internal states, feelings, and traits of the individuals who made them. Alternatively, instrumental analysis seeks to distinguish the patterns of addicts' test responses from those of nonaddict comparison subjects on a strictly empirical basis, without inference about the meaning of the items themselves. Finally, substantive analysis presumes that test responses are indicators of personality constructs (theoretical entities hypothetically representing traits postulated to exist within people). Regardless of the method of analysis, if results show a respectable degree of relation between some aspects of personality description or test response pattern and addictive behavior, they are often interpreted as having revealed *the* crucial variable(s) underlying the substance-use problem.

Problems with such a conclusion are manifold. The inherently selected nature of clinical samples and the usually unmatched comparison standards or groups make statistically significant findings relatively easy to obtain. Indeed, Pihl and Spiers (1978) have suggested an inverse relation between methodological rigor and the likelihood of obtaining differences in such studies; and Keller has gone so far as to propose a law about research on the personalities of alcoholics: "The investigation of any trait in alcoholics will show that they have either more of it or less of it" (1972:1147). Cross validation of demonstrated relations using new clinical samples might help detect some spurious results, but many problems of interpretation would still remain. For example, if a given trait or profile associated with addiction were also correlated with everything from baldness to severe menstrual cramps, its explanatory value would be compromised.

The potential contribution of clinical personality studies of addicts to the understanding of etiological processes or the prediction of substance-use problems in the general population is probably quite limited. The obvious

though often overlooked reason for this is that, even if a particular personality trait or characteristic were to be reliably observed in clinical addicts, it
would be impossible to determine whether it preceded, followed, or developed simultaneously with the addictive behavior problem. Each of these
competing interpretations about the sequencing of the variables of interest
is quite feasible given the developmental nature of both personality and addictive behavior. It is not difficult to imagine that a depressed individual
with low self-esteem might find drugs more attractive and might be more
susceptible to social pressures to use various substances, and hence development of a clinical addiction problem would be more probable. On the
other hand, experiencing chronic substance intoxication and a life of failure
and disappointment secondary to substance-abuse problems could easily
lead to depressive low self-esteem as an end state. These two sets of
variables might also complement each other as part of an insidious process
of general deterioration. Such inferential uncertainties, coupled with a
marked tendency toward serious methodological problems, appear to minimize the value of clinical studies for purposes other than personality sub-
typing as a possible aid in treatment planning.

Several alternatives representing efforts to disentangle the sequencing of
personality characteristics and addictive behaviors have been utilized
(Williams 1976). One is the cross-sectional method in which the characteristics of different age groups of addicts are studied simultaneously
(Williams, McCourt, and Schneider 1971). Here it is typically assumed that
the consequences of substance use will be less evident in young addicts than
old ones. A variation of this approach is the comparison of personalities of
known addicts with those of former addicts now in remission, on the
assumption that traits found in active addicts but not present after long
periods of abstinence must be consequences of substance use (Kurtines,
Ball, and Wood 1978). Retrospective longitudinal studies attempt to uncover antecedent personality variables and other characteristics usually by
examining archival data or by querying the addict or informed collateral
sources about what the individual was like prior to the onset of substance
use difficulties (Johnson 1973). A problem all of these strategies have in
common with the clinical study method is that they all begin with identified
addicts and hence may confound personality antecedents with personality
consequents. Other conceptual and methodological weaknesses specific to
each approach, such as biased or incomplete reporting by subjects in
retrospective studies, further erode confidence in these methods, whose
general characteristics already preclude direct inferences about cause and
effect.

Prospective longitudinal studies, in which data on personality and other
variables are collected on the same sample of the population at intervals
before and after any substance use occurs, represent the ideal correlational

method. If appropriate measures are taken, they are capable of accurately specifying the sequence or evolution of personality and addictive behavior, though follow-ups must be sufficiently frequent and long term if they are to capture the essence of these developmental phenomena. The prospective longitudinal study also can avoid problems associated with sampling exclusively from clinical populations. However, cost and convenience often dictate the need to sample from populations not precisely representative of all potential substance users. The low base rates of serious substance-use problems may necessitate selection of subjects from groups thought to be at high risk for addictive behavior. On the other hand, the highest risk individuals (truants and dropouts) may be systematically excluded from studies because they are absent from or underrepresented in the so-called normal institutions such as schools where data can be collected most easily. Attrition of subjects over time may also be biased because addicts often are the most difficult to track and to keep interested in participation. Even though the representativeness of samples bears such impediments, it far outstrips that of the methods discussed previously. And despite the need to consider the impact of historical, cultural, and maturational changes on the variables of interest, the prospective longitudinal study still has the greatest explanatory and predictive potential.

With all the advantages of the prospective longitudinal study, it is important to reiterate that such research cannot be expected to produce complete explanations of addictive behavior or definitive statements about the causal role of personality in it. The results are only correlational, so that while temporal sequencing may be highly suggestive of causality, antecedent events do not in themselves explain subsequent events. There is always the possibility that some third variable or an interaction of variables is responsible for changes in both personality and addiction. Thus it would appear wise to explore personality factors primarily in the context of other variables theoretically relevant to addiction, even when the prospective longitudinal study method is applied.

One promising route to better understanding and prediction is more careful attention to individuals' motives for substance use and to the function such use might serve for them in a given situation, psychological state, and moment. Experimental studies, ideally those considering individual differences along with situational manipulations, could make an important contribution to the elucidation of these factors (Lang et al. 1980). More broadly, the overall strategy needs to be multivariate in nature. Selecting a specific personality trait, or even personality as a construct, and attempting to evaluate its unique impact on addiction in isolation from other potentially causative and interactive factors, seems ill advised. To be meaningful, personality traits must be part of personality theories, which in turn must be part of fundamental psychological theories incorporating biological and social variables.

The explanatory and predictive role of personality in addictive behavior is limited. No unique personality trait or profile is necessary for addiction in general, nor is one consistently associated exclusively with addiction to any substance(s) in a way that would suggest it is a sufficient cause. Even if a broadly defined personality "predisposition" to addiction were to emerge, moreover, two difficult tasks calling for multivariate strategies would remain: (1) discovery of the stressors or other factors that activate it and (2) determination of why in some persons it leads to the choice of one substance, and in others, another. Related to this second issue of specificity is the possibility that the identified predisposition may have outcomes other than substance use. Then there would be a need to ascertain the reasons why some individuals with it have alcohol or other drug problems while others become video game freaks or workaholics. The greater the specificity of the proposed role of personality in addictive behavior, the more prediction is impeded by the natural diversity of people. On the other hand, the greater the generality of the proposed role, the more need to explain occurrences of alternative modes of expression for the personality trait, characteristics, or style.

While personality may be neither a necessary nor sufficient condition for addictive behavior, it is still capable of contributing to it. In order to understand what this contribution is, the extent of it, and how, when, where, why, and for whom it is made requires complex research strategies. A truly multivariate approach, couched in a comprehensive theoretical framework, appears to have the greatest potential for answering these questions. Such studies may call for more sophisticated techniques for data analysis. These might even include new and different (nonlinear) statistical and methodological tactics that individualize prediction for generally homogeneous subgroupings of persons or addictive behavior patterns. This could permit more precise analysis of interactive effects as well as better comparisons across subgroups (Dunnette 1976; Kandel 1978). Unfortunately for purposes of this review, very little of the literature on personality and addictive behavior reflects application of these conceptual and research approaches. Moreover, as the next section demonstrates, the more specific methodological problems of most studies in the existing literature are often so severe that the findings are difficult to interpret even within limited conceptual frameworks. Hence any conclusions drawn about the role of personality in understanding and predicting addictive behavior will necessarily be tentative.

Methodological Issues in the Study of Personality and Addictive Behavior

Personality and addiction, partly because they are constructs lacking clear definitions and having multiple dimensions, are exceedingly difficult to measure. Their developmental and interactive nature complicates this problem further. Yet measurement is the sine qua non if we are to learn about these phenomena and the relation between them. The conceptual issues and broad investigative strategies discussed in the preceding section are important. But regardless of one's perspective, the conclusions drawn from research and their generalizability depend on each study's operational definitions, sampling procedures, methods and circumstances of measurement, and evaluative or data analytic techniques. The present section questions whether research on personality and addictive behavior has dealt adequately with these considerations.

Operational Definitions and Measurements
of Constructs

Ideally, the operational definition and measurement of complex constructs should involve a variety of dimensions and should also employ multiple measures using different measurement methods. This is especially critical if we are to draw valid conclusions about constructs involving psychological components (as personality and addiction do) because of the high level of method variance typically associated with their measurement (Campbell and Fiske 1959). Unfortunately, most addictive personality researchers have ignored these principles. Instead, their tendency has been (1) to select a specific dimension or set of dimensions without providing theoretical justification and (2) to proceed to apply only one of the sometimes problem-ridden measurement methods.

Addictive Behavior Measurement. Whether one considers addiction in a univariate or multivariate framework and whether one is concerned with use, abuse, or dependence, the addiction-relevant terms need operational definitions if they are to be measured. Even very simple and specific definitions are legitimate so long as conclusions drawn from research employing them are limited to the domains they tap. In any event the particular method(s) for measuring the defined constructs may be important determinants of the results obtained.

Self-Reports. Self-report methods are by far the most frequently used measurement techniques for assessing addictive behavior. The commonest forms of this approach are interviews and questionnaires, the latter including both group and individually administered instruments. Self-report methods are convenient and economical to apply and often show a reasonable degree of reliability though obviously this must be evaluated in each case. Self-monitoring, the recording of self-reports by the individual as the

behavior of interest occurs, may provide a check on the reliability of retrospective reports and increment their validity.

Validity is the major problem with self-report measures. In clinical interviews this is always a problem because of interviewer bias regarding inclusion or exclusion of relevant data. Even structured interview data are
generally hard to interpret since published reports about them seldom provide sufficient detail on instrument construction, administration, and scoring. However, the most critical difficulty with self-reports is inaccurate
reporting by the respondents in both interviews and surveys. Because of the
stigma, illegality, and possible untoward consequences associated with detection of substance use and its effects, underreporting is an ever-present
threat to validity when respondents are identified. Despite evidence suggesting anonymity makes little difference to validity (Haberman et al.
1972; Luetgert and Armstrong 1973), some research supports concern about
underreporting. For example, Horan et al. (1974) compared data from separate interviews about either legal or illegal drug use with corresponding
data obtained through anonymous surveys of the same population. They
found consistent reporting of legal substance use across methods, but 23
percent less illegal drug use was acknowledged by those interviewed (identified) than by those completing the survey (unidentified).

Aside from intentional biasing, the validity of self-reports by very
heavy substance users is also open to question because they may not be
capable of accurate reporting due to brain damage, memory impairment, or
other difficulties they suffer secondary to substance abuse. Normal forget-
ting, even in nonclinical populations, can also compromise accuracy. Finally,
a perpetual problem of survey-based research is its dependence on subject
cooperation. Even if return rates exceed 80 or 90 percent, the probability that
those most seriously involved in substance use are overrepresented in the
nonresponding group is high. Hence there is a potential undermining of the
validity of both drug-use prevalence estimates and conclusions about how
substance use relates to other variables included in the survey. This is not to
say self-reports should be discarded, but that the limits of the method should
be realized and supplementary methods employed.

Collateral Reports. One way to verify self-reports would be to compare them
with reports of knowledgeable informants who are in a position to observe
some indications of substance use in the target individuals. This specific
method has not been used extensively for assessing addictive behavior,
though longitudinal studies of adolescents (Kandel, Kessler, and Margulies
1978) report sending questionnaires regarding other matters to parents. While
parents appear to be relatively poor sources of information on their children's
drug use (Kandel 1974), one study (Smart and Jackson 1969) has indicated
that the estimates by classroom representatives of the marijuana use of their

peers corresponded fairly well with self-reports of use by members of the same class. In any case collateral methods deserve consideration. Just as the reliability and validity of self-reports might be increased by self-monitoring, collateral reports could also be improved by having informants record data as the target behaviors actually happen.

Direct Chemical Testing for Substances. It is logical to assume that if one wishes to know about the substance use of an individual, the most valid test of it may come through direct chemical analysis. Urine tests for opiates, for instance, can measure traces up to several days old. Though a useful corroborative indicator in certain situations, such detection methods are impractical in many others because of their cost and intrusiveness. Moreover, most of these tests measure only very recent substance use. Some research (Hollingshead, Marlow, and Rothberg 1974; Hurst, Cook, and Ramsey 1975) has also suggested other flaws in chemical analyses and their application that lead them to underestimate or otherwise to identify substance use inaccurately. Finally, chemical tests are not available for some substances of interest. Although recent technological advances have remedied many of these problems, the expense, analytic skill, and difficulty in obtaining suitable samples for precision testing (Foltz, Fentiman, and Foltz, 1980) appear to limit the applicability of chemical tests. They are probably most appropriate as a cross check on self-reports and other data.

Physiological and Psychophysiological Measures. These measures differ from direct chemical tests in that they examine effects, that is, responses and adaptations to the substances, rather than traces of the substances themselves. Miller (1976) has reviewed the validity of concurrent physiological measures in alcoholism, including tolerance or withdrawal symptoms and such variables as alcohol metabolism, galvanic skin response reactivity, and other effects of chronic alcohol ingestion (changes in hepatic function, memory, sleep, general metabolism). He concluded that these may be useful diagnostic correlates of excessive drinking but cannot stand alone as prima facie evidence of alcoholism. In any case, the costs, including the time and subject discomfort involved, probably prohibit the widespread use of these methods despite the importance of individuals' physical condition or organismic state as a defining component of addiction.

Performance Testing. Known effects of particular substances on performance of various psychomotor, intellectual, and other tasks can provide a basis for measuring substance use. Behavioral tolerance, demonstrated by unimpaired performance on complex tasks despite high substance levels in the bloodstream (200 milligrams of ethanol per 100 milliliters of blood; see

Mello 1972), would suggest extensive experience with the substance in question. Logistical problems of testing and difficulties in controlling for subject motivation, however, reduce the attractiveness of this method.

Archival Data. One often neglected source of data on addictive behavior and its correlates is the records of public institutions. Information gleaned from (1) police or court reports of accidents, arrests, and convictions, (2) school reports of achievement, absenteeism, discipline, and dropout, and (3) clinic or hospital records of illness, psychological problems, and subsequent treatments can all provide corroborative evidence of the pervasiveness of substance-use problems. For both practical and ethical reasons, however, it is sometimes tedious and difficult to obtain these data, which are often incomplete and may be totally lacking for some subjects, particularly those with the most severe problems. Nevertheless, besides validating self-reports and indicating the intensity of addictive behavior, archival data have some potential to provide clues about the etiology of substance use problems.

Direct Observational Measures. A final and obvious method of measuring addictive behavior is through the actual observation of it. This may be accomplished either in the laboratory or in naturalistic settings. Marlatt (1978) has identified a number of ways behavioral methodology can be employed in the laboratory to measure drinking behavior. These techniques could also be applied to populations other than drinkers. First, operant methods require subjects to perform some activity, from simple motor tasks to complex personal or social behaviors, in order to obtain the desired substance. The amount of work an individual will do to obtain the pay-off is taken as an index of motivation for the substance or of its reinforcing value. Similar procedures permit testing of the relative potency of the substance as a reinforcer compared to other sources of reinforcement such as food, money, or social contacts. The operant methods parallel real-life situations in that the addict typically must put out some effort to get the substances he uses in everyday life.

Other behavioral measures of addiction include observation of individuals given free access to specific substances in a research setting. Their behavior may be studied for the brief, circumscribed period of an experiment or over the course of several weeks to investigate conditions related to various patterns of substance use and to determine subjects' routine intake. Finally, detailed observational and rating scale systems have been developed for the natural setting (Reid 1978). These methods permit unobtrusive recording of addictive behaviors, such as drinking, in the situations where they ordinarily occur. Of course, such measures may be easier to obtain for legal than for illegal drugs.

Direct observational measures are generally difficult and expensive to obtain. Furthermore, unless the observation is unobtrusive, there is a distinct possibility that it will affect the behavior under investigation. These methods, however, appear to have a contribution to make in the delineation of individual differences related to addictive behavior.

Summary. There are clearly many ways to operationalize and assess addictive behavior. The point being made here is that single or collected self-report measures, regardless of their multidimensional nature, need to be supplemented with measures involving other methods if construct validity is to be increased significantly. Collateral reports and archival data would appear to be the most likely candidates for large-scale investigations. Few prospective longitudinal studies have employed these alternatives to any great extent, though Kandel et al. (1978) queried parents and Jessor and Jessor (1977) collected information on academic performance in their studies of student drug use. One clinical study of heroin addicts (Platt 1975) was also exemplary in its requirement of multimethod criteria for subject inclusion (agreement of diagnostic interviews, medical and arrest records, and self-reported addiction of minimum six-month duration). Beyond these efforts the selective utilization of at least several other methods (chemical tests and performance testing) on a randomly or specially chosen subgroup of the larger sample under study would be highly desirable. In short, it is maintained that the common practice of defining addictive behavior solely in terms of self-report or involvement in some sort of treatment program is no longer defensible. It simply does not do justice to the complexity of substance-use phenomena nor the variety of people involved in them.

Personality Measurement. A comprehensive analysis and critique of personality measurement is well beyond the scope of this chapter, and others have already performed the service with some eloquence (Wiggins 1973; Sechrest 1976). Thus only a few comments are made under this heading. Many of the same general methods and criticisms discussed in connection with operational definitions of addictive behavior apply to personality measurement as well.

The Nature of Personality Measures (Tests). With very rare exceptions (Smith and Fogg 1978), personality measures used in systematic research on addictive behavior have involved almost exclusively subjects' completion of questionnaires and personality tests. There are other ways to measure personality (peer ratings, behavioral analysis, and other observation-based approaches), but apparently the convenience and tradition of individual self-report methods has made them the overwhelming favorite. As self-reports, however, these measures are susceptible to all the weaknesses associated with overreliance on self-report methods for assessing addictive behavior—and more. Multimethod evaluation is especially critical in personality and addiction research because the role of personality as a causal factor, as well as a complex construct in need of description, is often being scrutinized.

For the most part questionnaire and personality test methods use one of two strategies mentioned earlier: empirical or construct. Empirical approaches, in their purest form, are concerned only with criterion correlations. Test items are selected or retained solely on the basis of their ability to predict or correlate with some criterion behavior of interest. For example, special alcoholism scales of the Minnesota Multiphasic Personality Inventory (MMPI) have been developed by administering the entire inventory to samples of alcoholics and nonalcoholics to determine which items can be used to discriminate between the groups. In empirical tests the items often have low face validity (they bear little surface resemblance) relative to the criterion behavior and consequently the tests are sometimes labeled "indirect." This discrepancy is presumed to reflect the lack of knowledge about how test response verbal behavior relates to other behavior outside the test situation. The item "I like to cook (true or false)," for instance, is on a special MMPI scale for alcoholism (MacAndrew 1965) because alcoholics and neurotics respond to it in different ways. Understanding why responses differ on this particular seemingly irrelevant item is incidental to the criterion correlation goal of the empirical test. Often, however, theorists may propose explanations through content and factor analysis of the items and subsequent development and testing of the inferred personality traits (Finney et al. 1971).

In any case, there are two important things to remember about the application of empirical personality tests: (1) Unless the users explicitly indicate that they view test responses only as samples of verbal behavior, they usually implicitly assume the items represent signs of internal personality characteristics that are elements of or determinants of the criterion behavior. (2) As measures these tests are only as good as the validity of the criteria with which they are being correlated. If the criterion behavior is alcoholism, for example, but its operational definition is poorly conceived or unrepresentative (based on self-report or participation in alcoholism treatment only), then the test will probably be of limited utility.

Construct approaches by definition assume that item responses on personality tests represent manifestations of an underlying personality construct. Construct approaches focus on specifying or understanding that underlying trait or quality, however, rather than on correlations with criterion behavior. Personality constructs generally refer to some attribute that is not fully operationally defined because no criterion or universe of content adequately captures its essence. Nevertheless, scores on personality construct tests like the Personality Research Form, or PRF (Jackson 1967), can be correlated with behaviors such as substance use for purposes of description or prediction as well as construct validation. When such efforts are made, they too will be limited by the adequacy of the criterion, as was the case with empirical tests.

Uses of Personality Tests. Whether empirical or construct, the two main applications of tests for investigation of personality factors associated with addictive behavior are in clinical studies and predictive studies. In clinical studies, differences between the test results of identified substance users and nonusers are analyzed in an effort to identify unique attributes of users. If these differences are robust, they may be useful in the later diagnosis and classification of new, mixed groups of individuals when alternative methods for identification are unavailable, uneconomical, difficult to apply, or of questionable validity for some reason. Results of clinical studies may also provide some basis for the understanding of personality functioning in addicted individuals. Whatever the application, however, it is important to note the contemporary character of clinical studies. They are useful primarily as descriptors of persons who are *already* experiencing addictive behavior, which was or could have been measured by some other means. Obviously, what is described may be an effect or simple correlate of substance use rather than its cause.

Predictive studies involve the measurement of personality sometime prior to the onset of addictive behavior. Most often the subjects are subsequently followed over time so the development of substance use can be monitored. Then, earlier personality measures are correlated with later data on addictive behavior to determine which personal qualities or characteristics appeared to contribute to addiction proneness. Here, the traits of the preaddictive personality might be analyzed and compared to those found in individuals not developing problems to help explain how personality is involved in substance use. An interesting corollary would be the study of traits that appear to insulate people against addiction.

Selection of Personality Tests. Literally thousands of personality tests, both objective and projective, purport to characterize the whole of personality, to measure psychopathology, or to identify specific needs, attitudes, values, propensities, and moods that might be related to addictive behavior. Other psychological tests are alleged to measure intellectual functioning, perceptual processes, and various attributes regarded by some as elements of personality and possible correlates of substance use. How does one choose and evaluate the best test for clinical description or longitudinal prediction? In the construct approach, a theoretical rationale for selection of some particular trait(s) as primary should be provided, though often it is not. Regardless, just as in the empirical approach, there will be a need to demonstrate that the test works. But then, what exactly does it mean to say it works?

First, a test must be *appropriate* or *applicable* for the entire population of interest. It should not discriminate against some subgroup in the way many have maintained that commonly used intelligence tests are unsuitable for blacks. Everyone to whom one wishes to apply the results of a study must be represented in both the study at hand *and* the standardization sample used in developing the test measures if test norms are to be the basis for comparison.

Second, the test should be reliable: it should provide consistent results. Reliability can be determined in a number of ways, but for purposes of addictive personality research, the criterion of relative constancy of measurement over time and testings should suffice. Some perspectives on personality would permit exceptions to this if an individual has experienced developmental events believed to be capable of altering basic patterns of personality. Changes in test results occurring rapidly or without dramatic circumstances, however, would lead to the conclusion that the test is unreliable or that it measures states rather than traits.

Finally, validity or the ability of a test to measure what it says it measures, is essential. One very significant type of validity is criterion-related validity, which can take two forms. When independent assessment devices are found to be measuring the same thing at the same time, they are said to have concurrent validity. An example would be the essentially simultaneous identification of addicts using an indirect personality scale and self-report measures of addictive behavior. Obviously, concurrent validity is most relevant to clinical studies. On the other hand, predictive validity refers to the ability of a measure to predict the occurrence of the criterion behavior of interest at some time in the future. Showing, for instance, that scores on a rebelliousness scale obtained in junior high school correlate highly with the same individuals' initial use of marijuana some years later would provide evidence of predictive validity. Predictive validity is clearly more difficult to demonstrate but offers greater utility both in practical and theoretical terms.

Another perspective on validity is the dichotomy between convergent and discriminant validity. The simplest way to think of test validity is as the correlation between a test score and some independent indicator of the criterion behavior. This is convergent validity. Discriminant validity, however, is quite important to establishing the exclusiveness of a construct like "addictive personality." A personality trait that is highly correlated with substance use *but not with anything else* (delinquency, gambling, sexual promiscuity) would have a high degree of specificity and hence high discriminant validity. On the other hand, if a trait correlated with substance use and also with a marked inclination toward self-indulgence, criminality, or general maladjustment, it would lack discriminant validity and at best would characterize a general tendency toward addictive behavior. Obviously then, additional explanatory and causative factors specific to substance use would need to be identified.

Problems of Personality Tests. Difficulties with applicability, reliability, and the various forms of validity, of course, threaten the utility of personality tests. We know that situational and environmental variables account for a large portion of the variance in behavior, and since test-taking is a behavior, it should be influenced accordingly. Although data concerning the specific effects of setting on test results are lacking, it would be logical to assume that individuals being evaluated in police stations, schools, clinics, or their own homes might respond somewhat differently in each place. Perhaps these differences would reflect their inferences about the purposes and implications of the testing, and the consequent mental sets or motivations could distort responses in specific ways.

There can be little doubt that intentional distortion and other sources of invalidity are both possible and evident in personality testing. The use of empirical tests with low face validity can help reduce such problems to below the level seen in self-reports of substance use, but difficulties still remain. Teasdale, Segraves, and Zacune (1971) showed that the profiles of addicts whose identities were associated with their responses to a personality test turned out more benign than those produced anonymously by addicts from the same sample. In a similar vein, the common use of test administrators and scorers not blind to subjects' condition introduces the possibility of experimenter bias (Rosenthal 1969). Research on both manipulated instructional sets (Hoffman and Nelson 1971) and confusion over instructions when addicts cannot decide if they are to respond as "intoxicated" or "drug free, sober" (Henrigues et al. 1972; Partington 1970) suggests a potential role for experimenter and respondent alike in producing unreliable and invalid test results.

One approach to coping with distortion and invalidity problems is through inclusion of indices of them right in the personality assessments. The MMPI and a number of other tests include such features, though even these validity scales can be circumvented by sophisticated respondents (Kroger and Turnbull 1975). While the successful validity scale might permit selection of only good scores for analysis, it should be noted that such selection is not without liabilities. First, it introduces a source of subject attrition that may also reduce the representativeness of the samples utilized in the study. This in turn diminishes the instrument's coverage, its ability to classify all cases of interest. For example, Lester and Narkunski (1978) found 44 percent of their heroin addict subjects produced invalid profiles on one or both personality tests used in their research and hence could not be described. Second, the accuracy figures or classification and description might be distorted by excluding invalid profiles from analyses. This is especially problematic if, as is often the case, exclusions are not equally distributed across addict and comparison groups (MacAndrew 1979b; Wallace and Hinder 1974). Some researchers (Apfeldorf and Hunley 1976) have challenged the significance of invalidity exclusions by showing the discriminating power of an MMPI alcoholism scale was not diminished much by including invalid profiles; but the potential for problems is still evident.

Reliability and validity might also be affected by the time of the testing. In clinical studies testing is usually done only once, very shortly after admission to treatment facilities. Unfortunately, available data (Libb and Taulbee 1971; Page and Linden 1974) suggest that, at least where alcoholics are concerned, a waiting period of two weeks or more should precede testing if results of personality assessment are to be stable. Apparently, detoxification is incomplete or the events leading up to the admission so intense that signs of psychopathology are significantly higher on early than on later testing.

Summary. Clearly, personality measurement is not without its problems. An infusion of multiple methods, perhaps including physiological and behavioral indices to supplement self-reports, would be helpful to construct validity. Likewise, more careful attention to the legitimate uses of data from clinical (concurrent validity) and predictive studies is advised. Special consideration of discriminant validity is also essential for evaluating the generality and specificity of any addictive personality construct. Ideally, tests should be selected for their theoretical relevance and employed in such a way that problems of extraneous influence, distortion, and invalidity are minimized.

Sampling and Comparison Groups.

Selective Sampling. Assuming one has identified an adequate set of criterion measures and predictor variables relevant to addictive behavior and personality, the next step is to select population samples for testing and measurement. The most common source of subjects for addictive personality studies is institutions. Reasons for this choice are obvious: easy access, convenient data gathering, and (in clinical studies) presence of confirmed substance users. But exclusive dependence on institutionally identified persons is accompanied by serious compromises in the interpretation of research data. The severity of problems associated with samples from institutions, of course, is a function of the nature of the institution and the method of sampling. These factors tend to vary with the type of study.

Longitudinal studies concerned with personality and addictive behavior often sample from schools. Schools represent a fairly broad-based cross section of supposedly normal populations and hence are more representative than are prisons, which cater to special groups. School samples are not without problems, however. First, schools demand a reasonable level of social adjustment, and the restrictiveness of this requirement and other correlates of school involvement tend to increase as the level of schooling increases. Exclusion of absentees and dropouts reduces the representativeness of samples, and research has shown that each of these groups has a higher than average rate of illicit substance use (Smith and Fogg 1976; Johnston 1974). Differential user versus nonuser attrition rates in follow-ups also compound problems of representativeness. At the college level, the undue homogeneity of school samples is particularly critical. College students have a relatively narrow range of IQ, distractibility, and impulsivity, which diminishes the predictive power of these personality-relevant characteristics. Although the ideal of probability sampling, an equal chance that each individual in the population of interest will be included in the sample, is rare indeed, even for simple surveys (Cahalan 1970), it needs to be utilized more widely if generalizable results are to be obtained.

The sampling bias of clinical studies tends to be much worse than that of longitudinal research. In excess of 90 percent of the clinical studies reviewed for this chapter employed subjects who were hospitalized or at least in some form of institutionally based treatment. Individuals who are in treatment constitute a group that is unique in many ways and that may be grossly unrepresentative of the general population of substance users. First, it is important to note that addicts in treatment, whether attempting to ameliorate their substance-abuse problems or serving time for drug-related offenses, are there because they have problems. Whether these problems are a cause or effect of addictive behavior is a moot point. In either case they are correlated with substance use *for these individuals*. But are identified problems typical of everyone engaged in addictive behavior? It is an empirical question; however, anecdotal reports suggest that addicts who admit to problems are the exception rather than the rule. Regardless, the fact that having problems led to in-treatment status, which in turn led to inclusion in addictive personality research, has important implications for interpretation of clinical studies.

To illustrate these problems of interpretation, consider the clinical studies of addicts, employing the MMPI as well as some of its special scales. Reports from such research have frequently characterized alcoholics in treatment as psychopathic or antisocial characters, sometimes having depressive or neurotic features (Megargee 1982). Some (MacAndrew 1979a, 1981) have further suggested two subtypes of alcohol and drug abusers: 85 percent characterological unstable extroverts (pleasure seekers) and 15 percent depressive neurotic introverts (pain avoiders), classifications reminiscent of those observed by Whitelock, Overall, and Patrick (1971). Given such descriptions one could easily trace the likelihood of in-treatment status and the proportional representation of subtypes in clinical samples to associated problem behaviors. Antisocial personalities are highly visible troublemakers with a propensity for conflicts with authority, the law, and family, which often occur in connection with substance use. When such problems do occur, the likelihood of institutional treatment specifically related to addictive behavior is high. Hence, antisocial personalities may be overrepresented in clinical studies. Neurotic depressives, on the other hand, generally attract little attention to themselves. Their substance use problems need to be extraordinary for them to be assigned to treatment for addiction. Thus they may be underrepresented in clinical populations.

A related issue is that of the impact volunteering for treatment has on the representativeness of clinical samples. A number of studies have compared the tested levels of psychopathology of volunteer alcoholics (McArdle 1974) and heroin addicts (Gendreau and Gendreau 1973; Penk and Robinowitz 1976) with those of persons coerced into treatment for substance-use problems or those remaining on the street despite such problems. Results suggested that persons volunteering for treatment either actually have more psychological problems or at least are more willing to report them. In either case the overreliance on addict volunteers in treatment appears capable of distorting the picture of personality characteristics of those involved in addictive behavior.

Other methods of identifying known addicts for research purposes need to be developed. Some could be derived from comments made earlier on measuring addictive behavior. Other available options include advertisements, personal referrals by persons with knowledge of addicts (Becker 1968), recruitment in areas where substance use is prevalent (Allen and West 1968), and demographic quota sampling (Chein et al. 1964). Probability sampling could also be utilized. Obviously none of these methods is foolproof. All require subject cooperation, and some are more broadly representative than others. However, each offers an increment in the opportunity to study personality variables in relation to the addictive behaviors of persons not necessarily, by definition, suffering emotional or legal problems. Less reliance on selective, particularly institutional, sampling is essential to better understanding and prediction of addiction and its personality correlates.

Comparison Groups. Once measures of addictive behavior and personality are collected on some sample, they have meaning only in a relative sense. In other words, results need to be compared to those obtained using some other group(s) if legitimate conclusions about the significance of the data are to be drawn. Thus, in his review Craig (1979) called it astonishing that 40 percent of the personality studies on heroin addicts were interpreted without reference to any specified external referrent. Another 9 percent were compared only to test norms, a totally inappropriate strategy since the tests' standardization samples invariably did not include identified heroin addicts. Craig's figures square nicely with the finding here that just over half the clinical studies employed no comparison group at all. The results of such research are of little value except perhaps in hypothesis generation. The same can be said of retrospective longitudinal studies that do not include control groups.

When comparisons have been made in addictive personality research, they typically have employed one or more of the following groups: college students, other so-called normals such as hospital staff or community groups, groups addicted to some other substance, patients with physical or psychiatric illnesses, and prisoners. The obvious question arising in connection with these comparison groups is to what extent they introduce additional sources of variance, other than addictive behavior itself, that might contribute to different personality test results. To answer this question one must understand the factors that could influence group differences in personality assessment and in addictive behavior diagnosis. We have already seen that volunteering for treatment might be a biasing factor. Another factor potentially quite important, but difficult to control, is access to the substance(s) of interest. Accessibility or availability of alcohol and other drugs is enmeshed in a complex array of demographic and social variables yet must be controlled because it is obviously a necessary prerequisite for substance use. Moreover, because it is correlated with certain characteristics of the individual, his reference group, and his environment, it may also be associated with personality test results.

Age and intelligence have been shown to correlate with personality test results of alcoholics (Hoffman and Nelson 1971) and thus they must be controlled too. Age is especially critical when comparisons are made among groups of addicts, since the average age of alcoholic samples is in the forties, while for most illicit drug users it is in the twenties.

Race is another demographic variable that apparently must be controlled. A number of studies show systematic racial differences on both construct personality tests (Sutker, Archer, and Allain 1978) and empirical tests (Penk et al. 1978), using polydrug abusers and heroin addicts, respectively. Zager and Megargee (1981) also found that MMPI special scales for alcohol and drug abuse showed systematic racial bias in a youthful offender sample. As was the case with age and intelligence, the direction of racial bias in psychological tests has not always been clear, but it seems to be an ever-present danger. Marital status and personality test results in addicts reveal a similarly complex pattern of interrelationships (Hoffman, Jansen, and Wefring 1972).

A host of other variables might be candidates for matching across addict and comparison group because they predict differences in personality test results or addictive behavior. Among these are socioeconomic status, educational level, religiosity, criminal record, cultural background or ethnicity, health status or history, peer or family relations. Finally, gender could be a critical factor. It obviously affects MMPI test results because a separate profile is used for each sex. This variable was not mentioned earlier because it rarely comes up in addiction research, the vast majority of studies having been done using only males as subjects. Whatever the reason for this bias, when research does include both sexes, control for gender will probably be necessary.

The challenge for researchers is to discover which extraneous group differences make a difference so that they can be eliminated as sources of variance. Boscarino (1979) showed that controlling for sex, age, income, marital status, and education effectively eliminated differences in the prevalence rates of abusive drinking between veterans (11 percent) and nonveterans (5 percent). Two exemplary studies of personality factors in addiction proneness, by Gendreau and Gendreau (1970) and Platt (1975), also showed that systematic personality differences between heroin addicts and comparison groups were all but eliminated when factors like age, IQ, socioeconomic status, criminal record, educational achievement level, religion, marital status, and opportunity for drug use were either matched for or statistically controlled (by analysis of covariance), respectively.

In summary, most clinical studies in the published literature fail to attend to even the simplest of matching procedures when selecting comparison groups. Even sophisticated attempts at matching may be inadequate, however, because of the impossibility of matching for all the potentially important variables, given the post hoc nature of such research. As a result, clinical studies are of limited value in determining the role of personality in addictive behavior since tested differences are likely to reflect factors other than those attributable to personality. Empirical studies suffer a related problem in that their ability to distinguish addicts from one group (neurotics) may compromise their ability to differentiate addicts and another group (criminals). This limited discriminant validity minimizes what can be learned about personality contributions to addictive behavior through the study of already addicted individuals. Longitudinal studies, while much more difficult to carry out, have far greater potential for understanding and prediction.

Miscellaneous Design and Analysis Considerations

A few methodological issues remain that did not fit neatly in one of the preceding sections. Most apply to design and conduct of clinical studies, with a few comments pertaining to data analysis. These are briefly summarized below without comment or pertinent citations.

1. Adequate research design for group comparisons demands that the number of subjects studied be sufficiently large to rule out significant biasing by theoretically meaningless idiosyncracies of one or more individuals. Moreover, to the extent possible all subjects should be treated in a like manner. Designs must not create systematic (but spurious) differences between groups, whether by design (one group gets paid and the other does not) or accident (test administrators or scorers are not blind to subjects' group and hence may behave differently toward each).

2. The ability of empirical tests to discriminate clinical populations from comparison groups should be expressed as percentages of accurate classification, and data on rates of false positives and false negatives should be provided so the costs of each of these types of errors can be weighed against the benefits of using the test. Simple presentation of mean differences between clinical and comparison groups, even when accompanied by statistical significance data, is inadequate for most practical purposes.

3. In the development of empirical tests, attention to base rates of the phenomenon of interest in the comparison group is essential. Data on the accuracy of classification may be distorted if the comparison group is not large enough to be expected (on a probabalistic basis) to contain a number of true positives equal to the number of subjects in the clinical group.

4. Before the adequacy of an empirical test is established, it has to be cross validated on a new sample *totally* independent of that used in its development.

5. Statistical procedures applicable only to random samples should be used only when random selection has occurred.

6. Selection of legitimate statistical procedures sometimes involves subjective factors that might influence outcomes (in subtyping groups through factor analytic or related techniques). When this is the case investigators are obliged to justify their selection of data analysis methods.

Summary

Methodological problems in the existing literature on personality and addiction severely limit the conclusions that can be drawn from it. Particularly critical are inadequacies in the operational definitions and confounds in the measurement methods for the basic addictive behavior and personality constructs. Selective, unrepresentative sampling from the populations of interest and ill-conceived group comparisons also plague interpretation of research results. Finally, design and analysis flaws further erode confidence in the validity of reported findings. All these problems do not, however, rule out a potential role for personality in understanding and predicting addictive behavior. They simply make it impossible to determine at this time much about what that role might be.

Highlighting of the Personality and Addictive
Behavior Literature

Several major principles guided this summary of the empirical evidence published on the addictive-personality construct. First, the review was organized around alcohol, marijuana, and heroin as the preferred or primary substance used by the target individuals. These three drugs have been the most widely researched and represent a cross section of substances ordinarily identified with addictive behavior. But research on these drugs differs in potentially critical ways. Alcohol research and heroin research both have a relatively long history and have been conducted mostly with severely addicted subjects. In contrast, the great majority of marijuana and other nonopiate drug studies took place in the late 1960s and early 1970s and focused mainly on simple use by adolescents and college students.

Two basic types of research on personality and addictive behavior are recognized here: longitudinal and clinical. The emphasis is on longitudinal studies because such studies are the most informative, providing data on preaddictive personality characteristics as well as individual attributes present in clinically addicted persons. Information and conclusions from major published reviews were relied on heavily for all but the most recent studies.

Finally, the studies selected for review are merely described and summarized, with little comment and little conceptual or methodological critique. To the extent that the analysis presented to this point has been successful, readers will be sufficiently well aware of the multiplicity of issues and problems to be able to assess and evaluate the implications for themselves.

Alcohol

Alcohol consumption is, of course, a legal activity in U.S. society and as such differs from the use of other substances to be discussed, though many alcoholics abuse other drugs as well. (See Freed 1973 for a review.) It is also a substance whose use is normative, with the great majority of adults being at least occasional imbibers. As a consequence of these two facts, problematic use of alcohol is far more likely to be defined in terms of quantity used and attendant problems than is the case with illegal drugs, for which *any* use may characterize one as having an addictive behavior problem. Applying the quantity-consequence criterion, a probability sample survey by Cahalan and Room (1974) described 15 to 43 percent of adult males and 4 to 17 percent of adult females as having at least some drinking problem. With such a large portion of the population accounted for in these figures, one might anticipate that finding specific personality factors relevant to problem

drinking would be difficult. Reducing the numbers by tightening requirements for inclusion may help somewhat, but any behavior problem directly
affecting an estimated 10 million individuals is bound to involve considerable diversity across personality dimensions. Yet clinicians and other
observers see some commonalities in the personalities of alcohol abusers.

Longitudinal Studies.

Prospective. Though there were some earlier attempts at retrospective self-
report (Wittman 1939) and archival demographic (Wahl 1956) studies of
alcoholics, the first major prospective longitudinal study to look at precursors and developmental factors in alcoholism was by McCord and Mc-
Cord (1960, 1962). These psychoanalytically oriented researchers used
trained social workers in a five-year observation of 225 lower class Boston
boys (aged nine to fourteen), their families, and others with whom the boys
had frequent contact. Archival data were also obtained. Twenty-nine of the
boys later developed alcoholism problems as defined by community records
of alcoholism referral or treatment or more than one arrest for public intoxication. Their personalities were compared with those of 158 boys who
had no alcoholism or criminal record. The prealcoholic boys were characterized as active, self-confident, lacking abnormal fears, high in unrestrained
aggression, somewhat sadistic, sexually anxious, and disapproving of their
mothers. The authors interpreted these findings as suggestive of a facade of
intense masculinity with underlying dependency conflicts. Based on a later
follow-up study (McCord 1972), including eleven more boys who as adults
now fit the alcoholism criteria, the McCords hypothesized that a poor self-
concept born of maternal ambivalence, weak parental expectations, and less
affectionate mothering may predispose boys to alcoholism.

The next significant longitudinal study was that by Jones (1968), who
followed predominantly middle-class children in the Oakland Growth Study
through three assessments (junior high, high school, and adulthood). As
adults (aged thirty-eight to forty-three) all fifty-two of the subjects were
classified as problem, heavy, moderate, or light drinkers or as abstainers,
using detailed frequency data from two self-report interviews and medical
records to arrive at categorizations. Results of California Q-sort personality
measures, interviews, observational ratings, and projective tests showed the
pre-problem-drinker boys were more expressive, hostile, limit-testing, self-
indulgent, undercontrolled, and less fastidious than the other groups. These
ratings were consistent across the three assessments. The authors noted no
evidence of depression, isolation, self-pity, or destructive urges in pre-
problem drinkers.

Jones (1971) also examined female subjects from the Oakland Growth
Study and found that extreme groups (later problem drinkers and abstainers)

shared traits suggesting inadequate coping mechanisms. Heavy-drinking women were social but manipulative as girls, while moderates and lights shared positive social attributes. The key, however, was that women with extreme patterns of either drinking or nondrinking exhibited a comparable rigidity or lack of flexibility, which has often been cited as a precursor of maladaptive behavior of many kinds.

Robins, Bates, and O'Neal (1962) selected a cohort of 524 white children who were referred to a child guidance clinic for behavior problems, comparing this group with a normal public school sample. Agency records were the primary data source for descriptions of the children, all of whom were interviewed as adults. Comparing the 15 percent of problem children who later had serious alcohol problems (three times as many males as females) with problem children who did not, the former group was found to have a history of antisocial behavior often serious enough to yield legal consequences. They also differed on a number of childhood sociocultural and demographic factors and measures of their parents' adjustment, suggesting multiple causality of alcoholism. The selection of persons with childhood behavior problems as having high risk for problem drinking was supported by the almost 4 to 1 ratio of later alcoholism in the problem child versus the normal child sample.

More recent prospective longitudinal studies have shifted toward prediction of problem drinking in the adolescent and college years, rather than advanced stages of alcoholism in later adulthood. These projects typically have assumed a broader social psychological perspective in which personality variables play just one part along with behavioral, sociocultural, and other environmental factors. Often the use of drugs other than alcohol has been measured simultaneously. Different age groups have been followed for various periods of time in such studies.

Kellam and his colleagues started by collecting data on 705 first graders in a poor, black Chicago neighborhood, and then these children were reexamined at four points in a ten-year follow-up (Kellman, Ensminger, and Simon 1980). Criterion measures were any use of drugs (from a list of thirteen, including alcohol and tobacco): (1) ever and (2) within the last two months. Frequency data were taken on the second measure and *heavy, moderate,* or *no use* scores were derived. Predictor variables included teacher ratings of social adaptation status and tested scores for IQ and school readiness. Results showed heavy (frequent) drug use was predicted by high IQ or school readiness scores (for both sexes), by being male, and by rated aggressiveness (as opposed to shyness). The best adapted first graders were most likely to be moderate drug users as adolescents. Generally these outcomes were clearer for males and were to some extent mediated by involvement in antisocial behavior as a teenager.

In a report dealing exclusively with the development and onset of adolescent drinking and its psychosocial correlates, Jessor and Jessor (1975) discussed findings of a four-year study of 432 junior and senior high students. Self-reports of drinking behavior at each of four points were collected along with personality, perceived social-environmental, and behavioral system measures. A theoretical framework of transition-proneness was supported by data showing that the onset of drinking correlated with personality measures indicating lower value on achievement relative to independence (unconventionality), lower expectations for success, higher tolerance for deviance, lower religiosity, and reduced perceptions of drinking as negative. Interacting social-environmental and behavioral systems also were implicated. From a developmental point of view, unconventional patterns of motivation, alienation, and a minimum of personal controls tended to be increased by initiation into drinking. In other words, they changed with as well as predicted the onset of drinking. It was also noteworthy that involvement in other behavior labeled deviant (sexual experimentation, marijuana use, activist protest participation) correlated with problem drinking in this population. These findings supported a psychosocial commonality in the basis for each of these fairly common expressions of adolescent assertiveness or striving for autonomy. This study essentially replicated earlier work by Jessor, Collins, and Jessor (1972). Later theorizing by Jessor (1978) and Jessor and Jessor (1977) further suggested individual difference correlates of problem versus normal drinking may lie in the extent of deviance-proneness, coupled with the functions of alcohol use (to escape or cope with problems) and the pervasiveness of reasons for drinking in one's life.

The preceding sample of prospective longitudinal studies of drinking reflects remarkable diversity in the populations studied, methods of measurement, and theoretical perspectives. Particularly salient are differences in the psychopathology orientation and interview or observation methods of early research, contrasted with a later focus on cognitive aspects of personality (beliefs, values, expectations) in a psychosocial framework using survey methodology. Despite the mix, one might discern a pattern of nontraditional or unconventional values and nonconformist acting out behavior patterns in those most prone to substance use. Whether these characteristics are a manifestation of underlying conflicts, reflect a need for stimulation, represent a rejection of the dominant society, or are indicative of some as yet unspecified variable, the commonality is striking. The ability of such a vague predisposition to predict alcohol problems specifically, however, is suspect.

Retrospective and Other Life History Approaches. One series of retrospective longitudinal projects was based on the serendipitous discovery that 100 alcoholics in two Minnesota treatment facilities had taken the

MMPI an average of thirteen years earlier while freshman at the University of Minnesota. In the first two studies (Kammeier, Hoffman, and Loper 1973: Loper, Kammeier and Hoffman 1973) about one-third of the alcoholics' college MMPIs were located and found to be scorable. Results of these tests were compared with profiles obtained on the alcoholics' admission to the alcohol treatment units (Kammeier et al. 1973) and with the profiles of 148 randomly selected freshman classmates who also had taken the MMPI during college admission orientation (Loper et al. 1973). Unfortunately no follow-up testing was conducted on the controls. The authors reported a general increase in all the clinical scales across the two testings of the alcoholic group. All the differences were significant except scales 8 (schizophrenia) and 9 (hypomania), suggesting a broad-based increase in psychopathology. The modal high point code for clinical alcoholics was a 2-4 (depressed psychopathic deviate), but there was great diversity over all. Looking at contrasts between the college scores of prealcoholics and their classmates, it was found that prealcoholics' profiles were different (higher) on only two of ten clinical scales. They were seen as more rebellious, impulsive, aggressive, unconventional, energetic, and nontraditional (a 4-9 profile) but *not* generally more maladjusted.

Later in a related MMPI study, Hoffman, Loper, and Kammeier (1974) examined the scores of prealcoholics and controls on a number of empirically derived special scales designed to discriminate between clinical alcoholics and other groups. They found that prealcoholics scored higher than controls on both the MAC (MacAndrew 1965) and the ARos (Rosenberg 1972) MMPI alcoholism scales *before* the onset of drinking problems and that these scores differed little from those obtained at follow-up. In fact, 72 percent of persons in these groups could be accurately classified (prealcoholic or control) based on the MMPI data obtained on them as college freshmen.

Taken together, results from longitudinal MMPI studies of problem drinkers suggest that (1) much of the psychopathology observed in the MMPI scores of clinical alcoholics may represent a change concomitant with increased drinking, though the absence of follow-up data on control subjects makes even this documented increase in signs of psychopathology difficult to interpret; (2) premorbid clinical scale profiles of later alcoholics were generally benign, yielding minimal evidence of deviance; and (3) at least for this sample of the population, certain special alcoholism scale scores seemed to tap a relatively stable dimension of personality that exhibited a significant correlation with later involvement in alcoholism treatment.

In a mixed cross-sectional study, Williams, McCourt, and Schneider (1971) compared the psychological test responses of alcoholics (mean age, thirty-eight) in two kinds of treatment facilities with those of heavy-drinking college students and heavy/moderate/light/no drinking medical clinic and psychiatric hospital patients. All subjects completed a battery of personality inventories including the MMPI, the California Psychological Inventory, and the Omnibus Personality Inventory. Alcoholics and heavy drinkers were similar in scoring high on impulsivity, antisocial behavior, order, aggressive sociability and excitement, most of which distinguished both groups from the normal drinkers. Generally alcoholics were more moralistic and socially apprehensive than the heavy drinkers. The authors argued that these data were strong enough to indicate similar personality makeups in all heavy drinkers, whether alcoholic or not.

Cahalan and Room (1974) reported results of a retrospective study of selected personality attributes of problem drinkers identified in their national probability sample alcohol use study. Respondents with drinking problems indicated their earlier life was characterized by impulsive acting-out and sad, difficult childhoods often with disrupted family units.

Fillmore (1975), working with the same research group, analyzed twenty-year follow-up data on college men and women who had reported some heavy drinking problems. She found that early histories of frequent heavy drinking or psychological dependence on alcohol were the best predictors of later alcoholism. Early exposure to alcohol-related legal or accident consequences, however, attenuated this relation in a significant minority of the subjects. Clark and Cahalan (1976) also observed spontaneous but inconsistent changes in alcohol problems in their four-year study of drinkers.

Finally a number of researchers have attempted to use personality variables to predict outcomes of alcoholism treatment. In one example O'Leary, Rohsenow, and Chaney (1979) tested Rotter's Internal-External Locus of Control scale and five factor-analytically derived measures from the MMPI. They found high levels of pretreatment depression predicted patient attrition, as did internal locus of control to a lesser extent. This sort of study makes a practical contribution to treatment planning, while offering a theoretical clue to personality or psychopathology factors in the cessation-relapse phase of addictive behavior.

Before turning to the clinical studies of alcohol use, abuse, and dependence, let us consider the contributions of longitudinal and related research and assess the prospects for future answers to questions about personality and drinking (Freed 1979). First, this research has made it clear that personality factors do not arise or express themselves in a vacuum. Consideration of environmental factors and their interactions with personality is essential. Second, the data suggest a general rather than specific vulnerability to alcohol problems. The variables controlling the timing, direction, and precipitation of alternate expressions of the predisposition must be determined. Third, many of the personality attributes antecedent to clinical alcoholism appear to be quite different from those concurrent with it. Little is known about the transitional stages in this change process. There is also a paucity of clues about what qualities of individuals prevent drinking problems. Some evidence (Jones 1971 and Kellam et al. 1980) suggested that total abstinence from alcohol may indicate rigidity of personality structure potentially as maladaptive as problem drinking itself. Perhaps the principle of moderation should be more widely applied! Finally, if we may be optimistic, recent improvements in data storage and retrieval could reduce the need for lengthy and expensive prospective studies. Instead we might tap into massive data sets documenting the developmental and personal histories of many individuals (if a way could be found to protect their privacy, of course).

Clinical Studies. Clincial studies of the alcoholic are of two basic types: those using tests empirically simply to distinguish alcoholics from other populations and those adding to this a theoretically based description of how and why the groups differ besides the fact that they use and perhaps respond to alcohol differently. A significant literature also utilizes each of these approaches as they pertain to various subtypings of alcoholic populations. For the most part, empirical classification studies use indirect (low face validity) tests like the MMPI, or direct inquiries about drinking and alcohol-related consequences such as those tapped by the Michigan Alcoholism Screening Test, or MAST (Selzer 1971). The latter, direct tests probably reveal little about personality and so will not be discussed here.

Personality description studies, because tied to theory typically employ tests relevant to either a particular dimension of personality under scrutiny or a broad personality structure of interest. Hence much of this research is organized around dynamic or other etiologic themes often linked to specific personality tests. Examples of themes and their testing strategies are many. Some projective tests explore unconscious factors, as do Thematic Aperception Tests (TAT) of power or dominance needs (McClelland et al. 1972). Others focus on more straightforward testing of characteristics like mood, for example by examining the Beck Depression Inventory (Levine and Zigler, 1981) for signs of depression. Finally, survey researchers often use questions about attitudes, values, or beliefs to examine cognitive aspects of personality, such as rebelliousness, which might fit a social-psychological perspective on alcohol use and addiction. Evidence from each approach will be examined.

The range and the confusing and contradictory nature of studies of personality and problem drinking is truly amazing, as indicated by Miller's tongue-in-cheek observation that what we are looking for in the typical alcoholic is "a passive, overactive, inhibited, acting-out, withdrawn, gregarious psychopath with a conscience, defending against poor defenses as a result of excessive and insufficient mothering" (1976:657). The following brief summary does not address all these themes or all the relevant evidence, but merely samples from the vast literature on psychological testing of clinical alcoholic populations. The reader interested in more detail is directed to recent comprehensive reviews by Barnes (1979) and Cox (1979), among others. As a guide to evaluating alcoholic personality research employing psychological tests, one might keep two things in mind: the tests should identify commonalities among alcoholics (convergent validity), and the tests should distinguish alcoholics from other groups (discriminant validity) (Barnes 1979). Discriminant validity should be demonstrable for comparison groups of appropriately matched nonalcoholics and other clinical groups. For our purposes, tests' ability to separate alcoholics from other substance abusers may not be too important because a failure to do so might simply suggest a broader addictive-personality construct.

MMPI. Since the relevance of the widely used MMPI to problem drinking has been the subject of several comprehensive reviews in recent years (Apfeldorf 1978; Butcher and Owen 1978; Clopton 1978; Owen and Butcher 1979), and since the utility of the MMPI in predicting and identifying substance abuse is the primary focus of a companion paper (Megargee 1982), only a brief overview of it is provided here. Attention is called to common approaches, findings, and problems of interpretation in MMPI-alcoholism research.

The MMPI is a 566 item true/false inventory that yields scores on ten clinical scales empirically correlated with psychiatric diagnoses of mental patients. The scales include (1) hypochondriasis (Hs), (2) depression (D), (3) hysteria (Hy), (4) psychopathic deviance (Pd), (5) masculinity-femininity (Mf), (6) paranoia (Pa), (7) psychasthenia (Pt), (8) schizophrenia (Sc), (9) hypomania (Ma), and (10) social introversion (Si). Several validity scales indexing omitted items, probable lying, unusual responses, and defensive response styles are also included to assist in making accurate discriminations between normal and abnormal respondents. Subsets of items found to identify certain characteristics of groups of individuals have frequently been used to form special scales. In any case, it should be borne in mind that the MMPI is psychopathology-based, though it has often been used for general personality description. Interpretation of MMPI scores is both art and science and ranges from simple comparison of single-scale elevations to complex discriminant function or multiple regression type analyses of profile patterns that control for interscale correlations.

Research on the characteristic average clinical profile of alcoholics has indicated that scale 4 (Pd) is the most commonly elevated, though it is by no means always the highest in any given sample of alcoholics (Owen and Butcher 1979). High scorers on this scale would appear to share common characteristics (including impulsivity, readiness to manipulate or act out, social deviance) with individuals who probably would receive a psychiatric diagnosis of antisocial personality. However, the Pd scale also measures guilt and self-punitive remorse, which are not associated with such a diagnosis. Other scales frequently elevated in alcoholics' profiles are 2 (D) and 7 (Pt), adding elements of psychic distress (anxiety or depression) and rigid, obsessive-compulsive traits to the clinical picture (Barnes 1979). Indeed, sophisticated statistical analyses of profiles (Spiegel, Hadley and Hadley 1970) suggest an elevation of scales 2, 4, and 7 is best for discriminating alcoholics from normals and psychiatric controls. Megargee (1982) among others has pointed out, however, that this configuration lacks specificity, being associated with many other clinical groups besides alcoholics, and is based on *average* profiles of alcoholics, who actually show quite diverse individual patterns. The only valid conclusion is that there is no single typical alcoholic profile on the MMPI.

Recognizing this, a number of researchers have attempted to find homogeneous subtypes of alcoholic personalities (Conley 1981); Donovan, Chaney and O'Leary 1978; Eshbaugh, Hoyt and Tosi 1978; Goldstein and Linden 1969). While some of these efforts have replicated the clustering found in the others, this has not always been the case, and the number of subtypes has varied from two to seven. Perhaps such distinctions are useful in case treatment, but they only attest to the diversity of alcoholics' personality or psychopathology as measured by the MMPI.

Special MMPI scales designed specifically for diagnosing alcoholism now number at least eight: Atsaides, Neuringer, and Davis (ICAS 1977), Finney et al. (ALF, 1971), Hampton (Al, 1953), Holmes (Am, 1953), Hoyt and Sedlacek (Ah, 1958), MacAndrew (MAC, 1965), Rich and Davis (ARev, 1969), and Rosenberg (ARos, 1972). Some of these scales were constructed by using the most discriminating items from previous scales in cross validations on different samples. The researchers have contrasted scores of mostly middle-aged alcoholics with those of one or more diverse populations including normals, criminals, other addicts, and either inpatient or outpatient psychiatric groups. In many cases observed differences could have resulted from the frequent failure to match comparison groups on age as pointed out by Sutker et al. 1979. But, perhaps the most remarkable finding in the research on these special scales is their lack of convergence with one another. In Zager and Megargee's (1981) validity study, using a sample of youthful offenders, it was shown that five of these special scales clustered in two *negatively* correlated groups, neither of which was very successful at separating problem from nonproblem drinkers in this population. The authors observed that certain items common to several of the empirically derived scales were sometimes scored in *opposite* directions. Apparently this

was a consequence of unique characteristics of comparison group samples
or the alcoholic samples themselves.

Finney et al. (1971) have attempted a factor analysis of the personality
variables tapped by special alcoholism scales and have noted that their factor loadings differed. The role of comparison groups was implicated in this
difference. For example, psychiatric outpatients generally are high in anxiety and relatively low on the boldness and compulsiveness factors, while
criminals or heroin addicts might tend to be high in both anxiety and
boldness and low in compulsiveness. As a result, the MAC, designed to
distinguish alcoholics from neurotics, naturally gives more weight to different personality factors than a scale designed to separate alcoholics from
criminals and addicts (Haertzen, Hill, and Monroe 1968). Accordingly the
MAC makes alcoholics and heroin addicts look alike but different from
neurotics (Burke and Marcus 1977; Lachar et al. 1976). On the other hand,
the Haertzen et al. (1968) scale makes neurotics and criminals and addicts
look alike. Thus the special alcoholism scales, typically designed to differentiate alcoholics' personality characteristics from those of only one or
two other groups generally do little more than just that. They break down
when new comparison groups are introduced, sometimes making apparently simple cross validations quite difficult. In short, these scales reveal no
consistent picture of either a unique alcoholic or a general addictive personality. Sometimes, depending on comparison groups, a general propensity for antisocial deviance (alcohol and drug abuse, delinquency and
criminality, etc.) has been detected but nothing more specific that that
(MacAndrew 1981a; Rathus, Fox and Ortins 1980). While such findings can
be theoretically useful, they need much refinement before successful integration into predictive formulae can be expected.

California Psychological Inventory (CPI). The CPI shares nearly half of its
items with the MMPI, so it should not be too surprising that results of
clinical studies using it generally parallel those of the MMPI. Williams et al.
(1971) showed that an antisocial personality profile was most characteristic
of the alcoholic sample they studied. Otherwise the most common finding
was a variety of subtypes in alcoholic personalities, perhaps with distinctive
patterns of psychological and adjustment evident at each stage of recovery
(Kurtines, Ball, and Wood 1978).

Sixteen Personality-Factor Questionnaire (16 PF). Another true/false inventory type instrument is Cattell's 16 PF, which also correlates highly with
the MMPI. The 16 PF has been used in a number of studies, mostly lacking
comparison groups. Lind (1972) was perhaps most optimistic in suggesting
that underlying anxiety manifested in weak, passive-dependent, inadequate,
low-self-concept personalities described most alcoholics. Unfortunately, no

data have been presented that would appear to support the ability of the 16 PF to make discriminations between alcoholics and other clinical groups, especially neurotics, whose personalities probably overlap considerably with the so-called alcoholic traits. Moreover, a sampling of recent reports on 16 PF alcoholic personality research suggested a trend toward using the test to subtype alcoholics rather than find commonalities among them (Costello et al. 1978; Neriano 1976; Replogle and Hair 1977). These studies, identifying from three to seven alcoholic subtypes, would appear to discourage talk of a general alcoholic personality.

Edwards Personal Preference Scale (EPPS) and the Jackson Personality Research Form (PRF). Both the EPPS and PRF are rationally, as opposed to empirically, derived inventories intended to survey motivations and needs patterned after Murray's (1938) system. Comparisons among alcoholics, nonalcoholic psychiatric patients, and normals using the EPPS have yielded only a few largely unreplicated results (Fitzgerald, Pasework, and Tanner 1967; Gross, Morosko, and Sheldon 1968; Pryer and Dietefano, 1970). However, Reiter (1970) did show many differences between heavy and light drinkers, with heavy drinkers having more hostile and aggressive needs. Early PRF research (Hoffman 1971) called attention to the role of alcoholics' dependency needs, lack of self-confidence, and need for close social contacts. These results were partially corroborated by Carroll (1980), who characterized his sample of alcoholics as high in affiliative needs with a tendency for self-blame following failure. They also showed a greater conformity to societal norms, so that together these traits suggested a passive-dependent personality. Unfortunately, this apparent convergence was not reliable across different age groups of alcoholics in the Hoffman study and would appear to have little discriminant validity when applied to clinical populations versus normals. Other problems with the instability of PRF tests results in alcoholic populations due to varying instructional set, time of testing, and intelligence have also been noted (Pihl and Spiers 1978).

Differential Personality Inventory (DPI). The DPI, like the PRF, is a construct personality test, but it is designed to measure psychopathology rather than motivational needs. Hoffman and Jackson (1974) used the DPI to contrast the problems associated with alcoholism in men (character disorders) with those accompanying alcoholism in females (neurotic disorders). Members of this same research team (Hoffman, Nelson, and Jackson 1974) noted further that while detoxification reduced psychopathology on the DPI, the basic character structure of the individuals remained constant. However, their claim that these personality traits represented a unitary configuration in alcoholics was inconsistent with earlier work by Johnson (1969), who found five distinct DPI subtypes in a large alcoholic sample.

Eysenck Personality Inventory (EPI). The EPI was designed to measure two basic dimensions of personality: introversion-extroversion (actually, an index of the ease with which one acquires and loses conditioned responses) and neuroticism (a measure of the ease with which one becomes emotionally aroused). Alcoholics have been shown to be more neurotic than normals (Keehn 1970; Orford 1976), but this contrast is not particularly distinctive. Moreover, alcoholics did not differ on introversion-extroversion though they reported perceiving themselves as more impulsive and outgoing while intoxicated (Keehn 1970). Brain damage attendant to chronic alcoholism may also produce greater extroversion in the individual. While the results of EPI clinical testing have been generally disappointing, MacAndrew (1981b) has proposed that the EPI personality dimensions might enhance understanding of alcoholic subtypes identified by other means, such as special scales of the MMPI. He argued that high scorers on the MAC (MacAndrew 1965) are unstable extroverts (reward- or stimulation-seekers similar to antisocial personalities); and low scorers are unstable introverts (punishment-avoiders not unlike neurotics). Although this constitutes only a hypothesis, its merits make it one worthy of further consideration.

Rotter's Internal-External Locus of Control (I-E). Given alcoholics' difficulty in controlling their drinking and theories of their passive-dependency, it is natural to predict that they might attribute control of events to forces external to themselves. Attempts to demonstrate such a perception using Rotter's I-E Scale have, however, produced very equivocal results. In their review of the relevant literature, Rohsenow and O'Leary (1978) noted that a number of studies (Costello and Manders 1974) found just the opposite, with highly significant *internal* locus of control scores evident in many alcoholics. Butts and Chotlos (1973), however, criticized these counterintuitive results by pointing out methodological weaknesses such as nonexistent or poorly matched control groups. Indeed, better designed studies have produced strong externality findings for heavy- versus light-drinking army recruits (Naditch 1975), youths (Jessor et al. 1970), and others, though some studies have shown no differences at all (Carman 1974). In sum it appears that the popularity of I-E and related measures in personality and addictive behavior research is not supported by any decisive results they have produced. Such narrowly conceived indices of personality would appear to be of limited value, especially when studied in isolation.

Projective Tests. Overall, neither the convergent nor the discriminant validity of projective personality tests (those using ambiguous or unstructured stimuli to elicit relatively free-ranging responses hypothesized to "project" unconscious psychic processes) applied to clinical alcoholics has been impressive. These results may be more a product of poor research strategies, the generally low reliability and validity of projective tests, and the difficulties in empirically grounding psychodynamic theories underlying projective tests than they are a reflection of the absence of real personality differences. Moreover, methodological problems such as experimenter bias due to nonblind individual administration and scoring of these instruments often confound the clincial studies.

In his 1976 review of the alcoholism and Rorschach Inkblot Test literature, Freed noted a general tendency toward testing specific content responses of theoretical relevance to drinking. "Oral" and "water" themes, for example, have sometimes been reported more frequently in the protocols of alcoholics than in those of normals (Weiss and Masling, 1970), though there are many contradictory findings. Signs of alleged latent homosexuality and dependency conflicts have also been investigated, with mixed results. Even if such constructs were supported, their vague referents would limit their descriptive or explanatory value, and their predictive utility (though not tested to date) would still be suspect. Perhaps more general dimensions like high anxiety and perceptual field dependence, suggested by Barnes (1979), would be more meaningful than specific content analysis. In sum, any Rorschach-based conclusion of a unitary oral, dependent personality in alcoholics is unwarranted given the looseness of the construct and the variety of results on potentially relevant indicators.

The Thematic Aperception Test (TAT) more than other projective tests has been employed in investigations of a fairly well worked out theory of problem drinking. McClelland et al. (1972) hypothesized that men drink to excess because intoxication increases their (often minimal) sense of personal power or ability to dominate others in the social arena. These researchers tested their hypotheses by administering alcohol to male subjects with various drinking histories and then having them complete TAT testing. The results of several studies suggested that aggressive or dominance power fantasies increased after drinking. Others (Key et al. 1972) have stressed the role of alcoholics' inhibition level as the major determinant of their drinking and have produced some confirmatory TAT results showing increased action or power orientation after drinking, though it was not specifically dominant or aggressive in nature. Wilsnack (1974) extrapolated from dominance theories of male drinking to hypothesize that female alcoholism accompanies women's feelings of uncertainty about their femininity. Drinking is seen as an attractive time out from sex-role conflicts in these individuals since Wilsnack has shown that it leads to increased feelings of womanliness as measured by TAT responses. Thus, despite questions of the psychometric characteristics of the TAT, there does appear to be a modest convergence in alcoholic personality research employing it: persons who drink excessively may do so to gain access to a state of congruence with traditional sex-role stereotypes. Whether this pattern is an antecedent, concomitant, or consequent of problem drinking, however, is unknown.

Projective techniques involving picture drawing have yielded a number of significant differences between alcoholics and normals in such things as portrait size and the ordering of multiple drawings, but the relevance of these contrasts to alcoholics' personalities is unclear (Cox 1979). However, one study of young Norwegian sailors (Irgens-Jensen 1971) included subjects' drawing both male and female figures so an examination of their relationship could be made. Problem drinking was shown to correlate with portrayals showing such things as incomplete, obscene, dominant, larger, and poorly delineated female figures. The author speculated that such differences might suggest greater sex-role conflicts and lower self-confidence in heterosexual relations for the men who were problem drinkers. These kinds of results and their accompanying conjectures summarize the role of projective tests in the study of alcoholic personalities. They may have some heuristic value, but in and of themselves are not likely to produce much of consequence.

Tests of Affect and Self-Concept. Research into the moods and self-perceptions of alcoholics is predicated on the assumption that these individuals drink to escape aversive states. This theory really has two assumptions: (1) alcoholics are more anxious and depressed than normals and have lower self-concept and (2) alcohol consumption will alleviate these states at least temporarily. A variety of psychological tests have been used in both simple assessment and experimental examinations of these assumptions. A few examples should be sufficient to illustrate the paradigms and findings.

Some research on the self-concepts of alcoholics has employed the Tennessee Self-Concept Scale (TSCS), to differentiate alcoholics from others. It showed they have a below-normal view of their bodies, their health, their physical appearance, and their sexuality, and that alcoholics' commitment to moral religious principles was below average (Yakichuk 1978). Alcoholics' self-descriptions also yield some fairly consistent patterns in terms of their tendency to view themselves in the context of a primary relationship with another and to reveal a generally disorganized and disintegrated self (Connor 1962). Other analyses of collegiate male problem drinkers (Kalin 1972) and female alcoholics (Herzog and Wilson 1978) have shown men in the first of these groups describe themselves as acting out, lively, and disorganized, while drinking by women in the second group correlated only with acting out. Carroll (1980) and Carroll, Klein, and Santo (1978) compared the self-concepts of alcoholics with those of other drug addicts and found striking similarities in their moral-ethical guilt related to family, their general sense of inadequacy or failure, and other concepts. Alcoholics did appear to be more acquiescent and less positive about themselves, showing more signs of psychic distress, though this difference may reflect incomplete matching of the comparison groups. Greater discrepancies between the real and the ideal self in alcoholics compared to normal and even psychiatric comparison groups are common too (Berg 1971). Overall, there is a reasonable research consensus that alcoholics report low self-esteem, often correlated with increased anxiety and depression. In many cases, however, the social-behavioral incompetence of alcoholics would appear to justify their views of themselves as inadequate, particularly where social skills are involved (O'Leary, O'Leary, and Donovan, 1976).

Regardless of the consistency or legitimacy of low self-esteem found in alcoholics, the impact of drinking on the affect of these individuals is a question surrounded by considerable controversy. Alcoholics themselves often report that they are more assertive and less inadequate when drinking (MacAndrew and Garfinkel 1962; Blume and Shepard 1967). However, experimental research (Mayfield and Allen 1967) has revealed that alcoholics actually experience increases in self-reported anxiety and depression almost immediately after they begin drinking in a laboratory setting. Indeed, comprehensive reviews of the literature on alcohol and stress reduction (Brown and Crowell 1974; Cappell and Herman 1972; Higgins 1976) provide little support for theories of the tension-reducing properties of ethanol. Likewise, although people may drink more when depressed (Noel and Lisman, 1980), it does not appear to reduce depression significantly.

In sum, it seems safe to assert that alcoholics are often anxious and depressed and have low self-concepts. Moreover, they appear to drink partly because they believe it will alleviate these aversive conditions. However, in the absence of pertinent longitudinal data it is impossible to determine if these emotional dispositions predated problem drinking, were concomitants or consequences of it, were present only in alcoholics seeking treatment, and so on. Furthermore, experimental data indicating that drinking may reduce anxiety or depression only in certain, circumscribed situations underscores the need for further research clarifying the conditions necessary for these effects.

Tests of Perceptual Processes. Two measures of perceptual style, the Rod and Frame Test (RFT) and the Embedded Figures Test (EFT), have been among the most discriminating tests applied to alcoholic and normal samples. Developed by Witkin and his colleagues (Witkin et al. 1954), these instruments were designed to measure the construct of field-dependence/independence in perception, a construct presumably related to personality. High scorers on field-independence view parts of the perceptual field as distinct from the background and hence perform better on tasks requiring this ability (adjusting a rod in a complex perceptual field). Field-independence is alleged to be associated with clearer perceptions of body image, and more differentiated, independent personalities. Field-dependent persons, on the other hand, are expected to have distorted self-images, and undifferentiated, dependent personalities more likely to be controlled by external forces. Dependency theories of the alcoholic personality (Blane 1968) naturally would predict that alcoholics are field-dependent in their perceptual styles.

Witkin, Karp, and Goodenough (1959) were among the first to demonstrate the high field-dependence of alcoholics. Using the RFT, EFT, and a third measure, the Body Adjustment Test, they differentiated alcoholics from nonalcoholic psychiatric controls. A half-dozen other studies have replicated this difference in new samples of alcoholics and controls. The field-dependence quality of problem drinkers has also been shown to be relatively stable over time, drinking history, and even experimental intoxication treatments. Some data suggest field-dependence may predispose people to a variety of addictive behaviors, including heroin addiction (Arnon, Kleinman, and Kissin 1974), though no prospective longitudinal studies of this trait have as yet been undertaken and there are contradictory findings in other drug abusers (Weckowicz and Janssen 1973). This is important since a few reports have challenged the stability of field-dependence traits. Goldstein and Chotlos (1965, 1966), for example, showed alcoholics' field-dependence could be reduced by several months of psychiatric treatment and also presented data suggesting that field dependence in this population may be an artifact of brain damage secondary to excessive alcohol intake. Further, there are indications the trait is age-related, with field-dependence increasing with age (Schwartz and Karp 1967).

A fair summary of the research on field-dependence/independence testing would be that it produces remarkably reliable differences between alcoholics and some other groups, though test norms of questionable representativeness have often been used in comparisons. In addition, the differences appear to be relatively stable and may even predate problem drinking. A critical question, however, is what does this difference mean? Tests of the dependent personality theory of alcoholism (Blane and Chafetz, 1971) have found predicted field-dependence/independence differences, but failed to get convergent validity on more direct tests of personal dependency (the Dependency-Situation Test). It may well be that the field-dependence/independence measure is of little theoretical or practical significance because it merely reflects one of many possible, but trivial, differences between a highly select population (inpatient alcoholics) and the more general population. Additional research will be needed to resolve this question.

Two final aspects of perception that fit only marginally well under this heading are "stimulus intensity modulation" and "sensation-seeking." They do, however, deserve some mention in this context. First, there appear to be individual differences in the ways in which persons modulate the intensity of stimuli producing pain and other sensations. Petrie (1967), showed that those with high sensitivity ("augmenters") can be differentiated from those with low sensitivity ("reducers") based on their size estimations of physical objects they touch after receiving tactile stimulation (the kinesthetic figural after-effect test). It was also demonstrated by Petrie that augmenters experience a marked decrease in sensitivity to pain or other stimulation when intoxicated. Reducers, on the other hand, maintain fairly constant pain perceptions when given ethanol. One study has shown that alcoholics tend to be augmenters and it has been theorized that they may imbibe alcohol to get some relief from their hypersensitivity; in other words, they may drink to self-regulate. This intriguing hypothesis seems worthy of further exploration.

In a possibly related theory, Zuckerman (1979) has proposed that individuals differ in their need or desire for novel, varied, or complex experiences. The Sensation Seeking Scale (SSS) was developed to measure characteristic preferences for cognitive and emotional activity and positive emotional tone. It has been hypothesized that persons indulge in sensation-seeking behaviors in part to attain optimal levels of psychophysiologic arousal. Those scoring high on the SSS naturally are expected to engage in more sensation-seeking behavior, and accordingly might be viewed as less conforming (deviance is exciting) and more likely to experiment with alcohol and other drugs to alter states of consciousness and physical sensations. In a significant study employing the SSS, along with a variety of other personality measures (Kilpatrick, Sutker, and Smith 1976), the sensation-seeking index performed as the best discriminator of different levels of substance use. SSS scores were highest for regular drug users, followed by (in declining order) problem drinkers, occasional alcohol and other drug users, and nonusers of substances. Others (Segal 1975), have replicated this finding with enough consistency to make it worth pursuing as a personality factor in addictive behavior. Again, it is suggested that some substance use may be a form of self-regulatory behavior. In all probability, if sensation-seeking is a valid predictor, it will be as a generalized predisposer to deviant behaviors, of which substance use is only one type.

Surveys: Value and Attitude Correlates. A final set of psychological factors perhaps relevant to personality and alcohol use are those cognitive and psychosocial variables often explored in survey research. Two illustrative large-scale studies have examined the role of personal values and attitudes in alcohol use and abuse. First, in a national survey of over 15,000 junior and senior high school students, Donovan and Jessor (1978) collected data on frequency of drunkenness and frequency of negative alcohol-related consequences to define their "problem drinker" criterion group. Other questions asked about personality, environmental, and behavioral systems theoretically relevant to problem drinking. Students prone to problem drinking (as well as other deviance) were found to value independence more and achievement less and to have lower expectations for academic achievement. These persons also had fewer personal controls against deviance (greater tolerance of transgressions, less religiosity, and less emphasis on negative effects or functions of drinking). In short, the youthful problem drinkers were unconventional, not conforming to the established institutional goals and values, but instead emphasizing personal autonomy. Environmental systems (drinking models) and behavioral systems (general deviant activity) had independent and interactive effects, forming a multivariate network accounting for a substantial portion of the variance in adolescent drinking. The results were remarkably consistent across different definitions of problem drinking and various segments of the overall population. Interestingly, an almost identical set of psychosocial correlates of marijuana use was found in a related survey (Jessor, Chase, and Donovan 1980), with behavior-specific environmental factors such as the particular type of substance available and usage modeled by parents or peers accounting for differences in choice of drug.

Wingard, Huba, and Bentler (1979) surveyed 1,634 Los Angeles junior high students, inquiring about the use of thirteen different substances, including cigarettes and three forms of alcoholic beverages as well as various illicit drugs. A five-point scale of usage frequency was employed. In this age group fewer than 10 percent had ever used illicit drugs. In order, beer, wine, cigarettes, and liquor had been tried by in excess of 50 percent, with marijuana about 30 percent. Personality assessment was carried out using the Bentler Personality Inventory, a twenty-eight-dimension index of personal characteristics, interests, attitudes, etc. A cross-validation procedure was conducted within the sample. General substance use in this adolescent population was found to correlate with the dimensions of "non-abidance with the law, liberalism, leadership, extraversion, lack of diligence, and lack of deliberateness" (p. 139). There was a fairly high overlap of personality factors and drug use overall, but the ability of personality characteristics to account for specific substance choice was relatively low. In general, the personality attributes found important to substance use (mostly alcohol use) in this study could be described as nonconformity and unconventionality. Two theoretical themes accounting for such a connection are (1) substance use is part of a broad socialization into adulthood that often involves problem behaviors in the service of developing identity and autonomy (Jessor and Jessor 1977), and (2) substance use is tied to the sensation-seeking quest described by Zuckerman (1979) and, as such, there may be unique significance to both actual drug effects and nonconformity, each of which has exciting, arousing properties (Segal, Huba, and Singer 1978). Both these hypotheses, however, clearly involve the combination of social-environmental and behavioral variables in interaction with individual difference forces.

Summary. Can anything definitive be said in defense of a distinctive prealcoholic or alcoholic-personality construct? The answer is probably no, largely because of the conceptual and methodological flaws in virtually all the available research. However, if we adopt a metaanalytic approach and examine the literature as a whole, assuming the errors of one researcher to some extent cancel out those of another, a few suggestions can be ventured. First, alcoholics appear to be different from others throughout their life spans. More specifically, they often seem to act out, showing signs of undercontrol or impulsivity, sometimes accompanied by aggression. Nontraditional and unconventional attitude and action is a common theme. Affectively, they seem troubled by anxiety or depression in the clinical setting, though the origin of these moods in unknown. Sexual concerns, independence conflicts, and lack of self-confidence are implicated in a number of theories.

Despite some apparent consensus, all of the preceding comments are tentative and are tainted with contradictory or at least inconclusive research findings. Perhaps there are lessons to be learned. Single-trait explanations of problem drinking, whether power or dependency or orality or whatever, are not compelling when taken in isolation. Integration and interaction are what personality research in general and alcoholic personality research in particular is missing. The best evidence of a role for personality variables in addictive behavior points to general predispositions toward problem drinking. The key to understanding how these types of variables operate is through examining the *function* of substance use for any given individual, considering his or her social learning and the time, place, and circumstance of use. There may be a commonality in such function or perhaps a few subfunctions or subtypes. Indeed, a variety of lines of research seemed to converge on two subtypes: (1) anxious, depressed neurotic and (2) unstable antisocial personality. The function of drinking for the first might be analgesia (time out for the augmenter?), while for the second it could be thrills and excitement for self-regulation of arousal (sensation-seeking?). Such theoretical perspectives need refinement, though creating many more subtypes is probably not the answer, for in doing so the advantages of clustering and aggregation are lost. We are only now at the threshold of understanding how personality influences addiction. The volumes of research that have preceded us probably contribute little substantively, but can be invaluable if we learn from the mistakes chronicled therein.

Marijuana

Little more than a decade ago, there was neither any widespread concern nor even any survey data on marijuana use (National Commission on Marijuana and Drug Use 1972). It was, of course, an illegal substance, but one used primarily by jazz musicians and other small groups. More recent national survey statistics (Parry 1979), however, indicate that 28 percent of youths aged twelve to seventeen have used marijuana (16 percent in the last month), and the figures for young adults aged eighteen to twenty-five (60 percent ever; 28 percent last month) suggest that "some use" is approaching cultural normalcy in many youthful groups. For these persons, smoking "pot" may be a casual and socially acceptable activity. In sharp contrast, among older adults (aged twenty-six and up) only 15 percent have ever tried marijuana and 3 percent or fewer have used it in the last month. So what we are examining here is a youth phenomenon perhaps tied to recent social change, whereas with alcoholism the research focus was on middle-aged populations, as it has been for many years. These differences alone could be enough to overwhelm any personality commonalities that may exist in alcohol and marijuana use, at least as they might be revealed by the existing literature.

Other differences between alcohol and marijuana research further complicate comparisons of findings across these two most heavily abused substances. Obviously the legal dimension is important, leading operational definitions of "marijuana abuse" to emphasize simple use-versus-nonuse categorizations with less consideration of quantity, frequency, consequences, and other factors. This in turn influences the nature of research tactics. Alcohol studies are mostly clinical, but since there are few marijuana treatment units, this convenient way of accessing subjects is not available. Thus nearly all the marijuana-use literature is survey-based, an outcome that despite obvious weaknesses has some advantages in terms of representative sampling.

Partly because of its nonclinical orientation, marijuana research investigating personality factors has stressed sociocognitive variables (attitudes, beliefs, expectations, values), rather than affective measures and underlying dynamics of personality traditionally associated with psychopathology. In other words, personality has been more broadly defined as a relatively constant set of general attributes or styles that play a role in determining not only substance-use behavior but many other behaviors as well. When investigations have explored preexisting or concomitant signs of maladjustment in marijuana users, the results have typically been rather weak and equivocal. Paton, Kessler, and Kandel (1977) found, for instance, that depression was a modest predictor of transitions from nonuse to use of marijuana and of further experimentation with other illicit drugs. O'Malley (1975), on the other hand, found no connection between "psychological problems" and later drug use. McGuire and Megargee (1974) found that, among youthful offenders, regular marijuana users (more than weekly use) were the *best* adjusted according to the MMPI scores, though heavy users (daily use with other drugs) showed the most psychopathology. Given its widespread use and acceptance as a recreational drug, one could hardly expect simple use of marijuana to be any more of an index of maladjustment than social drinking. It is the high quantity and frequency and the consequences of substance use one might properly associate with psychopathology. Indeed, very heavy users of marijuana have been shown to exhibit more psychological problems, but even then the comparison is confounded by their almost inevitable use of other, more dangerous drugs at the same time (Cross and Davis 1972).

Finally, it appears that for the most part, marijuana research is more sophisticated than alcohol research. It is characterized by broader psychosocial perspectives and interactional models and sports more well-conceived longitudinal studies, though these are still few in absolute number. Developmental studies of marijuana and other drug use are also evident and potentially quite important in efforts to uncover phases and stages of usage patterns.

The highlighting of the marijuana literature that follows draws heavily on points made in several excellent reviews. Braucht et al. (1973) provided an overview of deviant drug use in adolescents. Gorsuch and Butler (1976) examined psychosocial factors in *initial* drug use. Kandel (1978) has summarized and integrated the major longitudinal studies dealing mainly with marijuana. Finally, Jessor (1979) provided an overview of recent marijuana-psychosocial factors research. The specific clinical or concurrent correlates literature has not been reviewed separately in the past several years, so a few more original sources were sampled where appropriate. This section is organized around themes and the findings relevant to those themes, rather than around designs and methods, as was the case with alcohol. Marijuana research has greater convergence, so this is more efficient. A variety of personality characteristics related to marijuana use have been suggested by other authors, including rebelliousness, independence, poor sense of psychological well-being, low self-esteem, and low academic aspirations and motivation (Kandel 1978), unconventional, nontraditional and nonconforming values, flexibility and openness to experience, and low expectations for achievement or satisfaction (Jessor 1979). The themes presented here more closely parallel Jessor's but emphasize the function of marijuana use in connection with each trait cluster. Persons having the personality dispositions and expectations about marijuana outlined would be predicted to be users more often than others in comparable environments.

An Expression of Poor Socialization. One common predictor and concomitant of marijuana use is an individual's lack of conventional or traditional values. This attribute is indicative of poor socialization by the dominant culture, and marijuana use may hence be viewed as one way of expressing the consequent nonconformity. Naturally, as marijuana use becomes more accepted and normative, its value in this capacity may diminish.

In one of the most extensive longitudinal studies of personality and adolescent marijuana use, Smith and Fogg (1978) collected both self- and peer-ratings of the personalities of 651 junior and senior high school students whose self-reported drug use was followed for up to five years. Early onset, frequency, and extent of drug use were all positively correlated with self- and peer-descriptions of subjects as "rebellious" prior to initial drug use. Similarly, low scores on "obedient/law abiding" were excellent predictors of the degree of later marijuana involvement. Jessor, Jessor and Finney (1973) also found high school and college students who subsequently used marijuana were more critical of society and expressed a greater sense of alienation from it. Both a tendency toward acting out aggressively and a high value and expectation for, and self-description of, independence were evident in youthful marijuana users studied by O'Malley (1975). Further, as already noted for alcohol use, a lack of religiosity (Jessor 1976) and a greater tolerance for deviance (Brook, Lukoff and Whiteman 1980) were characteristic predictors of initiation into substance use, including marijuana. So was a liberal or left-wing political stance (Gordon 1972). In a prospective study of college students covering their four years of matriculation, Kay et al. (1978) showed marijuana use was consistently correlated with lower scores on responsibility, socialization, and conformity as measured by the CPI and other standardized psychological tests. Finally, the tendency of prospective marijuana users to shun a societally promoted achievement orientation and especially to value independence highly relative to achievement have been amply demonstrated in both high school and college populations (Jessor et al. 1973). In sum, the potential role of marijuana use in the expression of general nonconformity borne of incomplete socialization seems well documented by prospective longitudinal studies of college and secondary school populations.

A few retrospective and clinical-survey studies might also be mentioned in the context of the expression of the poor socialization theme. Gulas and King (1976) showed that college seniors who were marijuana users had scored higher than nonusers on scales of "ascendency" (independence) and "irresponsibility" taken earlier in their academic careers. Brill et al. (1971) examined the MMPI scores of eighteen and nineteen year-old students as a function of their level of marijuana use and found heavier use correlated with rebelliousness (elevated Pd) and higher scores on an "ego strength" special scale. In a similar study of undergraduates, Knecht et al. (1972) reported that increasing marijuana use was associated with lower social conformity scores on the CPI. Thus, several divergent methodologies produced analogous results showing the part marijuana use might play in expressing nonconformity or the lack of socially inculcated values and controls.

An Alternative Coping Response. Jessor (1979) noted that research on prospective and current users of marijuana suggests that they not only reject traditional values about achievement but also express lower expectations about their ability to attain satisfaction through pursuit of achievement-oriented goals. Thus marijuana use may represent identification with an alternate set of goals, or it may be viewed as a way of coping with the perception that frustration and failure are imminent (Carman 1974). Within the latter perspective, below average self-esteem and a reduced sense of psychological well-being to accompany the perceived lack of self-efficacy might be expected. For such individuals marijuana use may serve as a "self-handicapping strategy" (Jones and Berglas 1978) designed to obscure the meaning and hence diminish the impact of failure. It provides a convenient excuse or rationalization for any untoward outcome because of the widespread belief that being high reduces motivation and ability to perform many personally and socially significant tasks. In this way marijuana may function to insulate users against potentially aversive information about themselves. Naturally, marijuana might also be used more directly to cope with tension, anxiety, or depression. In either case the theory is predicated on the assumption that degree of marijuana use is correlated with one's sense of psychological comfort and self-efficacy.

Few studies of marijuana use have included measures of affective aspects of personality or psychopathologic states. When they have, the results have not been impressive in either predicting or correlating them with marijuana use. A critical variable seems to be the level of marijuana use. Haagen's 1970 retrospective study of college students showed frequent users tested two years earlier had been more anxious, apprehensive, conflicted, and generally dissatisfied than infrequent users. Kilpatrick et al. (1976) found regular drug users (mostly marijuana) were more anxious (both state and trait measures) than occasional users in a random sample of male veterans admitted to a VA hospital. And McGuire and Megargee (1974) noted that maladjustment appears to occur mainly in those youthful offenders who used drugs to extremes. Other data, however, even including some from studies with level of usage controls (Orive and Gerard 1980), have produced no differences in anxiety, depression, and so on. Yet Segal (1977) found that a substantial portion of collegiate marijuana users he sampled indicated that a frequent reason for their use was to deal with psychological conflicts and cope with poor self-concepts.

Looking more specifically at self-esteem and self-efficacy, Haagen (1970) noted that "frequent" users had previously suffered from low self-esteem. Kaplan (1975) assessed junior high students at three points and found a lowering of self-esteem between the first two times predicted greater drug involvement during the next time interval. Smith and Fogg (1978) observed that adolescent marijuana use often reflected a low sense of capability. Finally, cross-sectional research (Norem-Hebeisen 1975) found a sense of well-being, based mainly on a standard self-esteem measure, contrasted normal adolescents and those with drug use problems. Some studies, however, have not replicated the finding of lower self-esteem in marijuana users, though the reasons for this are unclear (Jessor and Jessor 1978; Kandel, Kessler, and Margulies, 1978; Naditch 1975; O'Malley 1975). Perhaps changes in self-efficacy are rather transient and situationally determined, making them difficult to assess. In any case Segal's (1977) finding that many marijuana smokers indicate their drug use is related to psychological stress, would appear to make the theme of marijuana use as a coping response worth pursuing.

An Indication of Desire for New Experiences. So far the two themes discussed as personality predictors or correlates of marijuana use have a pejorative ring. Nonconformity is generally frowned upon and the implication that some people need to use drugs to cope is not flattering to them. Kandel (1978) has also pointed out that beliefs about substance use leading to criminality or "amotivational syndrome" (lethargy, loss of interest) enjoy a large audience despite some contrary evidence for each (Johnston, O'Malley, and Eveland 1978; Brill and Christie 1974, respectively). It is no wonder drug use has a bad name. Yet there are some positive correlates as well. Creative and artistic people have a reputation for substance use and represent a sharp contrast to the stereotypic conservatism, rigidity, and closed-mindedness of the abstainer (Grant 1981). One personality characteristic that may underlie the apparent spontaneity and openness to experience of drug users is sensation-seeking. Segal (1977) found that, in addition to using marijuana to deal with conflict and poor self-concepts, the majority of users indicated that they sought its effects to change and enhance social relations and to intensify positive experiences. Altering one's state of consciousness may be intrinsically reinforcing. Many people comment in a very positive way on the "high" they get from meditation, jogging, or skiing. Perhaps people simply differ in their desire for such stimulation and hence find marijuana and other drug use attractive to varying degrees.

In their longitudinal study of college students, Kay et al. (1978) found marijuana users were more spontaneous, flexible, and desirous of change than nonusers as indexed by the CPI and an adjective checklist measure. In two retrospective studies of college marijuana users, Goldstein and Sappington (1977) showed that preusers' MMPIs suggested adventurous pleasure-seeking, while Haagen (1970) found infrequent marijuana users to be spontaneous, insightful, and seeking change and new experience.

Surveys correlating scores on the Sensation Seeking Scale with marijuana use corroborate the findings cited. Results of the Kilpatrick et al. (1976) study of hospitalized veterans have already been mentioned, and

Segal (1975) also found sensation-seeking was correlated with marijuana use in college students. Finally, Brill et al. (1971) found the more frequent the marijuana use, the higher the SSS scores. More supportive studies could be cited and no significant contradictory evidence was turned up in the present review. Thus, it would appear that sensation-seeking or the desire for new experiences is a fairly robust correlate of marijuana use.

Summary. Though internal-external locus of control (I-E), introversion-extroversion, field dependence-independence, and a number of other personality traits outside the three themes or clusters discussed here have been investigated, each has received no better than marginal support. Even the dimensions or themes noted here (expression of nonconformity, coping response, and sensation seeking) all appear to be continuously distributed in the population, resulting in quantitative rather than qualitative differences among people. Indeed, as Jessor (1979) has pointed out, comparative studies of the personalities of marijuana users and nonusers (Huba, Segal and Singer 1977), have turned up no difference in their organization of traits, only in the magnitude of their various attributes.

In assessing the role of personality factors in marijuana use, several conclusions can be drawn. First, users' profiles tend to be fairly benign with respect to traditional psychopathology, though some marijuana use is probably stress-related. Second, even considering personality as a complex system of beliefs, motives, instigators, and personal controls (Jessor and Jessor 1977), its total contribution to prediction of high school and collegiate marijuana use is not more than 25 percent. This amount is substantially less than environmental contributions, which seem to increase as the level of schooling rises, presumably because in college drugs are more available and their use is more normative. Related to this is the following notion of Nurco's:

> The earlier the onset of deviant behaviors, the more malignant the process invoked and the more ominous the prognosis . . . The younger the age of onset, the more intense and committed the addictive career (1979:321)

Thus it should not be too surprising to learn that Lucas (1978), among others, has demonstrated that the personality and other variables salient in initial drug use at various ages and times differed significantly. Moreover, since the social meaning (and hence the pleasure and utility) of a substance like marijuana is not likely to remain static (Kovacs 1976), it is unlikely that proponents of even the most sophisticated formulae for relating person and situation variables to its use will be able to stand pat. Still, consideration of personality factors can help us to understand and predict substance use, and may even help us prevent its abuse, so their contribution cannot be ignored.

Other Illicit Drugs: Heroin

Much no doubt separates heroin from other illicit drugs (besides marijuana), yet it is the representative chosen here because it is not so subject to fads, trends, and transient social meanings as, say, hallucinogens. Like many other illicit drugs (for example, amphetamines, sedatives) heroin is undoubtedly a dangerous substance and a highly addictive one (though not inevitably addictive; see Zinberg 1979). It is also associated with severe penalties for possession, sale, or use. Finally, it represents a sort of end point in substance use—there is no further step to take. As Kandel (1975) has demonstrated, the usual sequence of involvement in drug use (for adolescents) starts with beer or wine, progresses through hard liquor and cigarettes to marijuana, and finally terminates with other illicit drugs. At this fourth phase one finds heroin use but with frequent substitutions of other drugs when the preferred one is unavailable. Hence the typical heroin user has at least tried other dangerous, illicit drugs if he or she is not a polydrug or multidrug user as a rule.

One more characteristic that ties heroin and illicit drugs (other than marijuana) together is the low base rate of their usage. According to Parry's (1979) national survey, no substance in this group was reportedly used by more than 4 percent of *any* age group in the preceding month. This fact, coupled with the other exceptional characteristics of illicit drugs other than marijuana, has important implications for research. First, it means that research subjects will be exceedingly difficult to locate except through treatment or correctional institutions. Furthermore, social sanctions applied to those using heroin and the high cost of addiction are liable to force users into very deviant subcultures and life-styles. Finally, the low base rates of such illicit drug use all but rule out prospective longitudinal studies as impractical. Indeed only a handful of longitudinal studies of any kind, including long-term follow-ups of heroin rehabilitation patients (Valliant 1966), has ever been conducted. And unfortunately for our purposes, the best longitudinal study of opiate use, Robins' (1973) work with Vietnam veterans, did not collect data on personality variables.

The literature on heroin and illicit drugs, and their personality or psychopathology correlates, is in a sorry state. Most subjects examined were incarcerated at the federal treatment facility at Lexington, Kentucky, and the vast majority of studies consist of methodologically confounded efforts to use the MMPI for (1) clinical descriptions or subtyping of the psychiatric status of addicts or (2) discrimination between heroin addicts and other groups (polydrug abusers, alcoholics, criminals, psychiatric patients). Let us examine what has been learned from these endeavors.

Clinical Profiles. Perhaps the greatest consensus in the heroin and personality literature is that these addicts exhibit psychopathology in excess of that observed in the other substance use groups we have reviewed. Sutker (1971) reported that only 12 percent of her heroin addict sample produced normal MMPI profiles. Monroe, Ross, and Berzins (1967) noted similar findings in a major MMPI study of four sources of patients for the National Institute of Mental Health center at Lexington: (1) civil commitment admissions, (2) prisoners from federal courts, (3) volunteers, and (4) probationers from municipal court proceedings. Committed patients were the most severely disturbed, but all groups had substantial representation of diverse clinical syndromes: neuroses, psychoses, antisocial personalities, and other personality disorders. Elevated 4 scales (psychopathic deviate) were common, with some high 2 scales (depression) as were seen among alcoholics. However, greater evidence of psychosis was also evident in a pattern of elevated 8 (schizophrenia) and 9 (mania) scales commonly associated with disorganized and expansive thinking. Similar, though even more extreme 4-8-9 patterns have been seen in polydrug abusers, evaluated in a variety of settings (Megargee 1982). Again, however, the profile heterogeneity underlying these average high points was both statistically and practically significant, as evidenced by repeated efforts to develop multiple personality subtypes within addicted samples. These have ranged from just two subtypes with 60 percent or more unclassifiable (Berzins et al. 1974) to seventeen or eighteen subtypes of heroin or polydrug abusers, respectively (Penk et al 1980). To complicate matters further, it has been shown that the profiles produced by addicts may be systematically biased by subjects' race (Penk et al., 1978) and volunteer status (Penk and Robinowitz 1976). It would be safe to say that addicts in institutional settings manifest psychopathology at an above-average rate though with considerable diversity in its expression. In this heterogeneous group, a small but significant bias toward classic antisocial personality characteristics, but with considerable anxiety, might be distilled from available data (Craig 1979).

Other Personality Characteristics. Platt and Labate (1976) have reviewed the heroin-personality literature through 1975 and little has been added since then. A brief, updated sampling of the more popular traits investigated follows.

Low self-esteem and low self-concept have been associated with addiction in the theories of many authors, who believe heroin use is a way to minimize threats to the self (Laskowaitz 1961). However, early research by Schift (1959), using a Q-sort procedure to detect discrepancies in real and ideal self, showed young addicts' self-esteem did not differ from young nonaddicts but that both these groups had *higher* self-esteem than corresponding older groups. In a related study Ogborne (1974) inquired about the effects of heroin use on psychological and interpersonal functioning and found two subtypes of respondents. There were "enhancers" who used heroin to increase awareness and general well-being, and there were "avoiders" who took it to reduce awareness and responsibilities and to escape problems. Perhaps, these functions also change with age in a way that would account for the findings of Schift (1959).

Needs, values, and attitudes have also received some attention in the heroin and personality literature. Application of the EPPS of needs suggested that addicts wished to be free from restraint and responsibility and also desired new experiences more than nonusers (Sheppard et al. 1974). However, Miller, Sensenig, and Reed (1972) found that desire for new experience did not extend to risk-taking situations. Instead, avoiding losses and putting one's own safety ahead of that of loved ones were characteristic values of addicts. These individuals also ranked trust very low (Blumberg et al. 1974) seemed very short-sighted (Laskowitz 1961). Overall, such needs, attitudes, and values would seem to characterize an antisocial personality style.

Locus of control issues and consequent use of Rotters' I-E scale for measurement are second only to psychopathology and the MMPI in the heroin addiction literature. Craig (1979) reviewed nine studies of locus of control in addicts, five showing addicts more internal, three more external, and one no different. On closer inspection it can be noted that the studies producing externality results had no control groups, whereas those with internality findings all did. Interestingly, addicts move even more toward internality after treatment, apparently feeling even greater power, self-satisfaction, confidence, and independence. All these posttreatment traits again seem consistent with the egocentricism and antisocial, self-indulgence of addicts (Berzins and Ross 1973).

In perhaps the best-designed study in the heroin and personality literature, Platt (1975) investigated sensation-seeking, among other attributes in a sample of youthful offenders. Fifty-eight consecutive cases yielded complete data on twenty-seven addicts and twenty nonaddicts, with addiction defined by multimethod criteria. Blind data collection and analysis were carried out on thirty-four personality variables, including measures of self-evaluation, social self-esteem, anomie, locus of control, death concern, self-description (using an adjective checklist), and sensation-seeking. Potentially confounding variables (Gendreau and Gendreau 1970) such as age at first arrest, number of arrests, IQ, achievement test scores, religion, and marital status were controlled as covariates in the analysis. Results showed addicts differed from the comparison group by having higher sensation- and experience-seeking, greater death concern, and more heterosexuality, exhibitionism, and autonomy. In discussing these findings Platt argued that they did not provide sufficient evidence of an addictive personality because (1) the significant results did not fit a coherent theory, (2) many predicted results did not materialize, and (3) the results offered no clues about which came first, the addiction or the traits.

Summary. In general it would appear that no distinct addictive personality is evident in the literature on heroin addiction. Moreover, attempted sub-typing by psychopathology has produced many divergent groups. Only a broadly defined personality style with antisocial or psychopathic elements, such as selfishness and sensation-seeking, and a significant level of general psychopathology seems to capture much of the variance in clinical heroin addiction. The absence of prospective longitudinal data makes it impossible to say any more.

Similarities and Differences in Substance Use

At this point one can only be pessimistic about finding a unique set of personal characteristics to associate with any particular substance. Indeed, even attempts to tie psychological conditions to drugs whose pharmacological actions should logically benefit them have met with little success. Using the MMPI, for example, Henrigues et al. (1972) failed to find anxiety in heroin or barbiturate users or depression in amphetamine users. Fitzgibbons, Berry, and Shearn (1973) found mainly general maladjustment in the various drug users they tried to match in a similar effort. Gordon (1980) had the same problem in trying to get sharp distinctions between sedative or hypnotic abusers and polydrug abusers using the Rorschach. Others, however, have claimed a bit more success. For instance, Overall (1973) was able to differentiate the clinical profiles of alcoholics and narcotics addicts, with only a 15 percent case overlap. Penk et al. (1979) replicated his finding for heroin addicts, but Trevithick and Hosch (1978) did not. Further, deterioration in the reliability of drug-specific clinical profiles seems to occur as the populations of addicts diverge. Thus, the subtype patterns for drug abusing prisoners (Holland 1977) were different again, in still other ways. The lesson seems to be that it is not too difficult to arrive at clinical decision rules for classifying drug abusers so long as one does not try to apply them while visiting another institution.

An alternative approach is to look for personality commonalities across many drugs, trying to contrast them with attributes of nonusers of drugs. Special scales derived from the MMPI have been the major vehicle for this endeavor. Especially significant was MacAndrew's (1965) MAC alcoholism scale, which has been reasonably successful at identifying both alcoholics and drug abusers in broader psychiatric populations where it was developed (Burke and Marcus 1977; Kranitz 1972; Lachar et al. 1976; Lachar, Gidowski, and Keegan 1979). Unfortunately, when this scale is applied to youthful samples, especially those containing delinquents and criminals (Rathus et al. 1980; Zager and Megargee 1981), the MAC loses its discriminant validity specific to substance use. Analogous problems have been encountered with special heroin abuse scales, such as He (Cavior, Kurtzberg and Lipton 1967) or drug abuse scales, DaS (Panton and Brisson 1971). These scales work fairly well in the correctional settings where they were developed but may not be capable of discriminating alcoholics from neurotics in a psychiatric population. Thus it appears that a problem with such special scales is they are too special.

Summary, Conclusions, and Implications

Is the addictive-personality construct viable? Despite the serious conceptual and methodological problems characterizing most research in the area, the answer must certainly be that no single, unique personality entity is a necessary or sufficient condition for substance use. Moreover, the claims of theorists like Spotts and Shontz (1980) notwithstanding, specific types of personalities have not been consistently linked to individuals' preferences for particular drugs. Part of the reason these conclusions are so evident is that such hypotheses are at least tacitly predicated on the assumption that the construct personality represents a set of discrete types rather than an aggregation of continuous variables. Such a conceptualization and the pursuit of related personality-type main effects on behavior seems indefensible in the light of what we know and are learning about the interactions between person and situation that affect human actions.

But if we look at personality as a contributor, a predispositional component to or concurrent dimension of substance use and abuse, the picture appears to be somewhat different. The complexities of operationally defining addictive behavior become critical. Different personality characteristics or styles may make different contributions, depending upon the type, frequency, time, consequences, and stage of substance involvement under consideration. The social psychologies of moderate usage and abusive substance involvement, for example, seem very likely to be divergent. The need for a theoretical framework for dealing with these variables thus seems obvious.

Substance use is behavior that first of all demands availability and access to substances, and multiple sociocultural factors undoubtedly interact to determine the level of this variable. Beyond this, other aspects of the environment are also important. A disengagement from proscriptions against substance use or some experience with a context that supports use (permissive parental models, high levels of peer involvement, drug subcultures) make a clear contribution. Finally, individual perceptions, attitudes and values, and personal traits or styles can explain why, given comparable environments, people vary in their substance use. What are some of the significant personality factors?

A high value on independence and nonconformity, concomitant with a weak commitment to societally promoted achievement goals is common among both addiction-prone and addicted individuals. A sense of social alienation and a general tolerance for deviance have also frequently been identified in connection with substance use and, for obvious reasons, these attitudes appear to increase as substance use continues. Personal characteristics of impulsivity, difficulty delaying gratification, and perhaps even an antisocial personality style have also been identified to varying degrees across alcohol, marijuana, and heroin use. Perhaps closely tied to these factors is a disposition toward sensation-seeking that may be relatively independent of environmental conditions.

In the arena of psychopathology, there is some evidence to suggest that role strain or other forms of stress predispose one to substance use, at least acutely. Also, an earlier initiation to drugs seems to predict more severe substance-use problems, perhaps indicating a greater general vulnerability to stress or the stressfulness of substance use itself. These relations may in part explain why adolescent and other transitions are often associated with the most severe substance abuse problems, among other behaviors considered deviant (Jessor and Jessor 1977). Beyond simple adjustments to life stresses, the level of psychopathology observed in clinical addicts seems to increase with the dangerousness and level of involvement with the drug. Polydrug abusers and heroin addicts, showed much more psychopathology than marijuana users. The specific nature of psychopathology, however, is not consistent, and issues of causality and directionality of these correlations remain to be worked out. Finally, a potentially critical issue in the personality-addictive behavior nexus is the expected function of substance use for the individual. Use of drugs to escape or avoid problems rather than to increase sensations would appear to be a more foreboding pattern.

The ideas and data reviewed in this chapter suggest that personality contributions to addictive behavior are not specific. They represent a potential for deviance that has many forms, the expression of which can only be predicted through consideration of environmental variables in a relation as yet little understood. The optimal research strategies of the future must be multivariate and interactional, using a variety of methods for personality assessment to specify more clearly the aspects of addictive behavior that are of interest.

References

Allport, G. 1937. The functional autonomy of motives. *A.J. Psychol.* 50:141-156.

American Psychiatric Association. 1980. *Diagnostic and Statistical Manual of Mental Disorders,* 3rd ed. Washington, D.C.: APA.

Apfeldorf, M. 1978. Alcoholism scales of the MMPI: Contributions and future directions. *Int. J. Addictions* 13:17-53.

Apfeldorf, M., and Hunley, P. 1976. Exclusion of subjects with F scores at or above 16 in MMPI research on alcoholism. *J. Clin. Psychol.* 32:498-500.

Arnon, D.; Kleinman, M.; and Kissin, B. 1974. Psychological differentiation in heroin addicts. *Int. J. Addictions* 9:151-159.

Atsaides, J.; Nueringer, C.; and Davis, K. 1977. Development of an institutional chronic alcoholic scale. *J. Consulting Clin. Psychol.* 45:609-611.

Bachman, J., and Jones, R. 1979. Personality correlates of cannabis dependence. *Addictive Behav.* 4:361-371.

Barnes, G.E. 1979. The alcoholic personality: A reanalysis of the literature. *J. Stud. Alcohol* 40:571-634.

Becker, H. 1968. Marijuana: A sociological overview. In D. Solomon (ed.), *The Marijuana Papers.* New York: Signet Books.

Bem, D., and Allen, A. 1974. On predicting some of the people some of the time: The search for cross situational consistencies in behavior. *Psychol. Rev.* 81:506-520.

Bem, D., and Funder, D. 1978. Predicting more of the people more of the time: Assessing the personality of situations. *Psychol. Rev.* 85:485-501.

Bentler, P., and Eichberg, R. 1975. A social psychological approach to substance abuse construct validity: Prediction of adolescent drug use from independent data sources. In D. Lettieri (ed.), *Predicting Adolescent Drug Abuse.* NIDA Research Issues Series (No. 11), Rockville, MD.

Berg, N. 1971. Effects of alcohol intoxication on self-concept: Studies of alcoholics and controls in laboratory conditions. *Quart. J. Stud. Alcohol* 32:442-453.

Berzins, J., and Ross, W. 1973. Locus of control among opiate addicts *J. Consulting Clin. Psychol.* 40:84-91.

Berzins, J., & Ross, W., English, G., and Haley, J. 1974. Subgroups among opiate addicts: A typology investigation. *J. Abnormal Psychol.* 83:65-73.

Berzins, J., Ross, W., and Monroe, J. 1971. A multivariate study of the personality of hospitalized narcotic addicts on the MMPI. *J. Clin. Psychol.* 27:174-181.

Blane, H. 1968. *The personality of the alcoholic: Guises of dependency.* New York: Harper & Row.

Blane, H., and Chafetz, M. 1971. Dependency conflict and sex role identity in drinking delinquents. *Quart. J. Stud. Alcohol* 32: 1025-1039.

Blumberg, H.; Cohen, S.; Dronfield, B.; Mordecai, E.; Roberts, J.; and Hawks, D. 1974. British opiate users: II. Differences between those given an opiate script and those not given one. *Int. J. Addictions* 9:205-220.

Blume, S., and Sheppard, C. 1967. The changing effects of drinking on the changing personalities of alcoholics. *Quart. J. Stud. Alcohol* 28:436-443.

Boscarino, J. 1979. Alcohol abuse among veterans: The importance of demographic factors. *Addictive Behav.* 4:323-330.

Braucht, G.; Brakarsh, D.; Follingstad, D.; and Berry, K. 1973. Deviant drug use in adolescence: A review of psychosocial correlates. *Psychol. Bull.* 79:92-106.

Braucht, G.N.; Kirby, M.W.; and Berry, G.J. 1978. Psychosocial correlates of empirical types of multiple drug abusers. *J. Consulting Clin. Psychol.* 46:1463-1475.

Brill, N., and Christie, R. 1974. Marijuana use and psychosocial adaptation. *Arch. Gen. Psychiatry,* 31:713-719.

Brill, N.; Crumpton, E.; and Grayson, H. 1971. Personality factors in marijuana use. *Arch. Gen. Psychiatry,* 24:163-165.

Brook, J.S.; Lukoff, I.F.; and Whiteman, M. 1980. Initiation into adolescent marijuana use. *J. Genetic Psychol.* 37:133-142.

Brown, J., and Crowell, R. 1974. Alcohol and conflict resolution: A theoretical analysis. *Quart. J. Stud. Alcohol* 35:66-85.

Burke, H., and Marcus, R. 1977. MacAndrew MMPI alcoholism scale: Alcoholism and drug addictiveness. *J. Psychol.* 96:141-148.

Butcher, J., and Owen, P. 1978. Objective personality inventories. In B. Wolman (ed.), *Clinical Diagnosis of Mental Disorders: A Handbook.* New York: Plenum.

Butts, S., and Chotlos, J. 1973. A comparison of alcoholics and nonalcoholics on perceived locus of control. *Quart. J. Stud. Alcohol* 34:1327-1332.

Cahalan, D. 1970. *Problem Drinkers.* San Francisco: Jossey-Bass.

Cahalan, D., and Cisin, I. 1976. Epidemiological and social problems associated with drinking problems. In R. Tarter and A. Sugerman (eds.), *Alcoholism: Interdisciplinary Approaches to an Enduring Problem.* Reading, MA: Addison-Wesley, 1976.

Cahalan, D., and Room, R. 1974. *Problem Drinking among American Men.* New Brunswick, N.J.: Rutgers University Center of Alcohol Studies.

Campbell, D., and Fiske, D. 1959. Convergent and discriminant validation by the multitrait-multimethod matrix. *Psychol. Bull.* 56:81-105.

Cappell, H., and Herman, C. 1972. Alcohol and tension reduction: A review. *Quart. J. Stud. Alcohol* 33:33-64.

Carman, R. 1974. Internal-external locus of control, alcohol use, and adjustment among high school students in rural communities. *J. Commun. Psychol.* 2:219-133.

Carroll, J. 1980. Similarities and differences of personality and psychopathology between alcoholics and addicts. *Am. J. Drug Alcohol Abuse* 7:219-236.

Carroll, J.; Klein, I.; and Santo, Y. 1978. Comparison of the similarities and differences in the self-concepts of alcoholics and addicts. *J. Consulting Clin. Psychol.* 46:545-576.

Cavior, N.; Kurtzburg, R.; and Lipton, D. 1967. The development and validation of a heroin addiction scale with the MMPI. *Int. J. Addictions* 2:129-137.

Chein, I.; Gerard, D.; Lee, R.; and Rosenfeld, E. 1964. *The Road to H: Narcotics, Delinquency and Social Policy.* New York: Basic Books.

Clark, W., and Cahalan, D. 1976. Changes in problem drinking over a four-year span. *Addictive Behav.* 1:251-259.

Clopton, J. 1978. Alcoholism and the MMPI. *J. Stud. Alcohol* 39:1540-1558.

Conley, J. 1981. An MMPI typology of male alcoholics: Admission, discharge and outcome comparisons. *J. Personal. Assessment* 45:33-39.

Connor, R. 1962. The self-concepts of alcoholics. In D. Pittman and C. Snyder (eds.), *Society, Culture and Drinking Patterns.* New York: Wiley.

Costello, R. M.; Lawlis, G. F.; Manders, K. R.; and Celistino, J. F. 1978. Empirical derivation of a partial personality typology of alcoholics. *J. Stud. Alcohol* 39:1258-1266.

Costello, R., and Manders, K. 1974. Locus of control and alcoholism. *Brit. J. Addiction* 69:11-17.

Cox, W. 1979. The alcoholic personality: A review of the evidence. *Prog. Exp. Personal. Res.* 9:89-148.

Craig, R. 1979. Personality characteristics of heroin addicts: A review of the empirical literature with critique—Part I. *Int. J. Addictions* 14:513-532.

Craig, R. 1979. Personality characteristics of heroin addicts: A review of the empirical literature with critique—Part II. *Int. J. Addictions* 14:607-626.

Cross, H., and Davis, G. 1972. College students' adjustment and frequency of marijuana use. *J. Counseling Psychol.* 19:65-67.

Donovan, D.; Chaney, E.; and O'Leary, M. 1978. Alcoholic MMPI subtypes. Relationships to drinking styles, benefits, and consequences. *J. Nervous Mental Disorders* 166:553-561.

Donovan, J., and Jessor, R. 1978. Adolescent problem drinking: Psychosocial correlates in a national sample study. *J. Stud. Alcohol* 39:1056-1524.

Dunette, M. 1975. Individual prediction as a strategy for discovering demographic and interpersonal/psychosocial correlates of drug resistance and abuse. In D. Lettieri (ed.), *Predicting Adolescent Drug Abuse.* NIDA Research Issues Series (No. 11), Rockville, Md.

Ekehammar, B. 1974. Interactionism in personality from a historical perspective. *Psychol. Bull.* 81:1026-1048.

Endler, N., and Magnusson, D. 1976. Toward an interactional psychology of personality. *Psychol. Bull.* 83:956-974.

Engel, G. 1977. The need for a new medical model: A challenge for biomedicine. *Science* 196:129-136.

Epstein, S. 1979. The stability of behavior. I. On predicting most of the people much of the time. *J. Personal. Soc. Psychol.* 37:1097-1126.

Epstein, S. 1980. The stability of behavior II: Implications for psychological research. *Am. Psychologist* 35:790-806.

Eshbaugh, D.M.; Hoyt, C.; and Tosi, D.J. 1978. Some personality patterns and dimensions of male alcoholics: A multivariate description. *J. Personal. Assessment* 42:409-417.

Fillmore, K. 1975. Relationships between specific drinking problems in early adulthood and middle age. *J. Stud. Alcohol* 36:882-907.

Finney, J.; Smith, D.; Skeeters, D.; and Auvenshire, C. 1971. MMPI alcoholism scales: Factor structure and content analysis. *Quart. J. Stud. Alcohol* 32:1055-1060.

Fisher, S. 1970. Nonspecific factors as determinants of behavioral responses to drugs. In A. DiMascio and R. Shoder (eds.), *Clinical Handbook of Psychopharmacology.* New York: Science House, 1970.

Fitzgerald, B.; Pasewark, R.; and Tanner, C. 1967. Use of the Edwards Personal Preference Schedule with hospitalized alcoholics. *J. Clin. Psychol.* 2:194-195.

Fitzgibbons, D.; Berry, D.; and Shearn, C. 1973. MMPI and diagnosis among hospitalized drug abusers. *J. Commun. Psychol.* 1:79-81.

Foltz, R.; Fentiman, A.; and Foltz, R. 1980. *GC/MS assays for abused drugs in body fluids.* NIDA Research Monograph Series (No. 32), Rockville, Md.

Franks, C. 1967. The use of alcohol in the investigation of drug-personality postulates. In R. Fox (ed.), *Alcoholism: Behavioral Research, Therapeutic Approaches.* New York: Springer.

Freed, E. 1973. Drug abuse by alcoholics: A review. *Int. J. Addictions* 8:451-473.

Freed, E. 1976. Alcoholism and the Rorschach test: A review. *J. Stud. Alcohol* 37:1163-1154.

Freed, E. 1979. *An alcoholic personality?* Thorofare, N.J.: Charles B. Slack.

Gendreau, P., and Gendreau, L. 1970. The "addiction-prone" personality. A study of Canadian heroin addicts. *Can. J. Behav. Sci.* 2:18-25.

Gendreau, P., and Gendreau, L. 1973. A theoretical note on personality characteristics of heroin addicts. *J. Abnorm. Psychol.* 82:139-140.

Goldstein, G., and Chotlos, J. 1965. Dependency and brain damage in alcoholics. *Perceptual Motor Skills* 21:136-150.

Goldstein, G., and Chotlos, J. 1966. Stability of field dependence in chronic alcoholic patients. *J. Abnorm. Psychol.* 71:420.

Goldstein, J.W., and Sappington, J.T. 1977. Personality characteristics of students who become heavy drug users: An MMPI study of an avant-garde. *Am. J. Drug Alcohol Abuse* 4:401-412.

Goodwin, D. 1979. Alcoholism and heredity: A review and hypothesis. *Arch. Gen. Psychiatry* 36:57-61.

Gordon, L. 1972. Value correlates of student attitudes on social issues: A multination study. *J. Appl. Psychol.* 56:305-311.

Gordon, L. B. 1980. Preferential drug abuse: Defenses and behavioral correlates. *J. Personal. Assessment* 44:345-350.

Gorsuch, R., and Butler, M. 1976. Initial drug use: A review of predisposing social psychological factors. *Psychol. Bull.* 83:120-137.

Goss, A.; Morosko, T.; and Sheldon, R. 1968. Use of the Edwards Personal Preference Schedule with alcohol in a vocational rehabilitation program. *J. Psychol.* 68:287-289.

Grant, M. 1981. Drinking and creativity: A review of the alcoholism literature. Unpublished manuscript, Alcohol Education Centre, London.

Gulas, I., and King, F. 1976. On the question of pre-existing personality differences between users and nonusers of drugs. *J. Psychol.* 92:65-69.

Haagen, C. 1970. Social and psychological characteristics associated with the use of marijuana by college men. Mimeographed paper, Wesleyan University.

Haberman, P.; Josephson, E.; Zanes, H.; and Elinson, J. 1972. High school drug behavior: A methodological report on pilot studies. In S. Einstein and S. Allen (eds.), *Proceedings of the First International Conference on Student Drug Surveys.* Farmingdale, N.Y.: Baywood.

Haertzen, C.; Hill, H.; and Monroe, J. 1968. MMPI scales for differentiating and predicting relapse in alcoholics, opiate addicts, and criminals. *Int. J. Addictions* 3:91-106.

Hampton, P. 1953. A psychometric study of drinkers: The development of a personality questionnaire for drinkers. *Genetic Psychol. Monograph* 48:55-115.

Henriques, E.; Arsenian, J.; Cutter, H.; and Samaraweera, A. 1972. Personality characteristics and drug of choice. *Int. J. Addictions* 9:73-76.

Herzog, M.A., and Wilson, A.S. 1978. Personality characteristics of the female alcoholic. *J. Clin. Psychol.* 34:1002-1004.

Higgins, R. 1976. Experimental investigations of tension reduction models of alcoholism. In G. Goldstein and C. Neuringer (eds.), *Empirical Studies of Alcoholism.* Cambridge, Mass.: Ballinger, 1976.

Hoffman, H., and Jackson, D. 1974. Differential personality inventory for male and female alcoholics. *Psychol. Rep.* 34:21-22.

Hoffman, H.; Jansen, C.; and Wefring, L. 1972. Relationships between admission variables and MMPI scale scores of hospitalized alcoholics. *Psychol. Rep.* 31:659-662.

Hoffman, H.; Loper, R.; and Kammeier, M. 1974. Identifying future alcoholics with MMPI alcoholism scales. *Quart. J. Stud. Alcohol* 35:490-498.

Hoffman, H., and Nelson, J. 1971. Personality characteristics of alcoholics in relation to age and intelligence. *Psychol. Rep.* 29:143-146.

Hoffman, H.; Nelson, P.; and Jackson, D. 1974. The effects of detoxification on psychopathology for adults as measured by the Differential Personality Inventory (DPI). *J. Clin. Psychol.* 30:89-93.

Holland, T. R. 1977. Multivariate analysis of personality correlates of alcohol and drug abuse in a prison population. *J. Abnorm. Psychol.* 86:644-650.

Hollinshead, W.; Marlowe, D.; and Rothberg, J. 1974. *Defining Drug Involvement in an Army Population.* Unpublished paper, Department of Psychiatry, Walter Reed Army Institute of Research.

Holmes, W. 1953. The Development of an Empirical MMPI Scale for Alcoholism. Unpublished masters thesis, San Jose State College.

Horan, J.; Westcott, T.; Vetovich, C.; and Swisher, J. 1974. Drug usage: An experimental comparison of three assessment conditions. *Psychol. Rep.* 35:211-215.

Hoyt, D., and Sedlacek, G. 1958. Differentiation of alcoholics, normals and abnormals with the MMPI. *J. Clin. Psychol.* 14:59-74.

Huba, G.; Segal, B.; and Singer, J. 1977. Organization of needs in male and female drug and alcohol users. *J. Consulting Clin. Psychol.* 45:34-44.

Hunt, W., and Matarazzo, J. 1973. Three years later: Recent developments in the experimental modification of smoking behavior. *J. Abnorm. Psychol.* 84:107-114.

Hurst, P.; Cook, R.; and Ramsey, D. 1975. Assessing the prevalence of illicit drug use in the Army. U. S. Army Research Institute for the Behavioral and Social Sciences, Technical paper 264.

Irgens-Jensen, O. 1971. *Problem Drinking and Personality: A Study Based on the Draw-a-Person Test.* Oslo: Universitetsforlaget.

Jackson, D. 1967. *Personality Research Form Manual.* Goshen; N.Y.: Research Psychologists Press.

Jessor, R. 1976. Predicting time of onset of marijuana use: A developmental study of high school youth. *J. Consulting Clin. Psychol.* 44:125-134.

Jessor, R. 1978. Psychosocial factors in the patterning of drinking behavior. In J. Fishman (ed.), *The Bases of Addiction.* Berlin: Dahlem Konferenzen.

Jessor, R. 1979. Marijuana: A review of recent psychosocial research. In R. Dupont, A. Goldstein and I. O'Donnell (eds.), *Handbook on Drug Abuse.* Washington, D.C.: U.S. Government Printing Office.

Jessor, R.; Chase, J.; and Donovan, J. 1980. Psychosocial correlates of marijuana use and problem drinking in a national sample of adolescents. *Am. J. Pub. Health* 70:604-613.

Jessor, R.; Collins, M.; and Jessor, S. 1972. On becoming a drinker: Social psychological aspects of an adolescent transition. *Ann. New York Acad. Sci.* 197:199-213.

Jessor, R., and Jessor, S. 1975. Adolescent development and the onset of drinking. *J. Stud. Alcohol* 36:27-51.

Jessor, R., and Jessor, S. 1977. *Problem behavior and psychosocial development: A longitudinal study.* New York: Academic Press.

Jessor, R., and Jessor, S. 1978. Theory testing in longitudinal research on marijuana use. In D. Kandel (ed.), *Longitudinal Research on Drug Use.* Washington, D.C.: Hemisphere.

Jessor, R.; Jessor, S.; and Finney, J. 1973. A social psychology of marijuana use: Longitudinal studies of high school and college youth. *J. Personal. Soc. Psychol.* 26:1-15.

Jessor, R.; Young, H.; Young, E.; and Tesi, G. 1970. Perceived opportunity, alienation, and drinking behavior among Italin and American youth. *J. Personal. Soc. Psychol.* 15:215-222.

Johnson, B. 1973. *Marijuana Users and Drug Subcultures.* New York: Wiley.

Johnston, L. 1973. *Drugs and American Youth.* Ann Arbor, Mich.: Institute for Social Research, The University of Michigan.

Johnston, L.; O'Malley, P.; and Eveland, L. 1978. Drugs and delinquency: A search for causal connections. In D. Kandel (ed.), *Longitudinal Research on Drug Use.* Washington, D.C.: Hemisphere.

Jones, E., and Berglas, S. 1978. Control of attributions about the self through self-handicapping strategies: The appeal of alcohol and the role of underachievement. *Personal. Soc. Psychol. Bull.* 4:200-206.

Jones, M.C. 1968. Personality correlates and antecedents of drinking, drinking patterns in adult males. *J. Consulting Clin. Psychol.* 321:2-12.

Jones, M. 1971. Personality antecedents and correlates of drinking patterns in women. *J. Consulting Clin. Psychol.* 36:61-69.

Kalin, R. 1972. Self-descriptions of college problem drinkers. In D. McClelland, W. David, R. Kalin, and E. Wanner (eds.), *The Drinking Man.* New York: Free Press.

Kammeier, M.; Hoffman, H.; and Loper, R. 1973. Personality characteristics of alcoholics as college freshman and at time of treatment. *Quart. J. Stud. Alcohol* 34:390-399.

Kandel, D. 1974. Interpersonal influences on adolescent illegal drug use. In E. Josephson and E. Carroll (eds.), *Drug Use: Epidemiological and Sociological Approaches.* Washington, D.C.: Hemisphere.

Kandel, D. 1975. Stages of adolescent involvement in drug use. *Science* 190: 912-914.

Kandel, D. (ed.) 1978. *Longitudinal Research on Drug Use: Empirical Findings and Methodological Issues.* Washington, D.C.: Hemisphere-Halsted.

Kandel, D.; Kessler, R.; and Margulies, R. 1978. Antecedents of adolescent initiation into stages of drug use: A developmental analysis. In D. Kandel (ed.), *Longitudinal Research on Drug Use.* Washington, D.C. Hemisphere-Halstead.

Kaplan, H. 1975. Increase in self-rejection as an antecedent of deviant responses. *J. Youth Adolescence* 4:281-292.

Kay, E.; Lyons, A.; Newman, W.; Mankin, D.; and Loeb, R. 1978. A longitudinal study of the personality correlates of marijuana use *J. Consulting Clin. Psychol.* 46(3):470-477.

Keehn, J. 1970. Neuroticism and extroversion: Chronic alcoholics' reports on effects of drinking. *Psychol. Rep.* 27:767-770.

Kellam, S.; Ensminger, M.; and Simon, M. 1980. Mental health in the first grade and teenage drug, alcohol and cigarette use. *Drug Alcohol Dependence,* 5:273-304.

Keller, M. 1972. The oddities of alcoholics. *Quart. J. Stud. Alcohol* 33: 1143-1148.

Kenrick, D., and Stringfield, D. 1980. Personality traits and the eye of the beholder: Crossing some traditional philosophical boundaries in the search for consistency in all people. *Psychol. Rev.* 87:88-104.

Key, J.; Cutter, H.; Rothstein, E.; and Jones, W. 1972. Alcohol, power, and inhibition: A factor analytic evaluation of McClelland's hypothesis with a construct validation of the factors. *J. Health Soc. Behav.* 13:337-346.

Kilpatrick, D.G.; Sutker, P.B.; and Smith, A.D. 1976. Deviant drug and alcohol use: The role of anxiety, sensation seeking, and other personality variables. In M. Zuckerman and C.D. Speilberger (eds.), *Emotions and Anxiety: New Concepts, Methods, and Applications.* Hillsdale, N.J.: Lawrence Erlbaum.

Kimlicka, T.M., and Cross, H.J. 1978. A comparison of chronic vs. casual marijuana users on personal values and behavioral orientations. *Int. J. Addictions* 13:1145-1156.

Knecht, S.; Cundick, B.; Edwards, D.; and Gunderson, E. 1972. The prediction of marijuana use from personality scales. *Ed. Psychol. Measurement* 32:1111-1117.

Knox, W. 1976. Objective psychological measurement and alcoholism. A review of the literature 1971-1972. *Psychol. Rep.,* 1976, *1023,* 1050.

Kovacs, M. 1975. A psychological approach toward the meanings of drug use. In D. Lettierei (ed.), *Predicting Adolescent Drug Abuse.* NIDA Research Issues Series (No. 11), Rockville, Md.

Kranitz, L. 1972. Alcoholics, heroin addicts and nonaddicts: Comparisons on the MacAndrew alcoholism scale of the MMPI. *Quart. J. Stud. Alcohol* 33:807-809.

Kroger, R., and Turnbull, W. 1975. Invalidity of the validity scales: The case of the MMPI. *J. Consulting Clin. Psychol.* 43:48-55.

Kurtines, W.; Ball, L.; and Wood, G. 1978. Personality characteristics of long-term recovered alcoholics: A comparative analysis. *J. Consulting Clin. Psychol.* 46:971-977.

Lachar, D.; Berman, W.; Gisell, J.; and Schoof, K. 1976. The MacAndrew alcoholism scale as a general measure of substance abuse. *J. Studies Alcohol* 37:1069-1615.

Lachar, D.; Gdowski, C. I.; and Keegan, J. F. 1979. MMPI profiles of men alcoholics, drug addicts and psychiatric patients. *J. Stud. Alcohol,* 40:45-56.

Lang, A.R., Searles, J; Lauerman, R.; and Adesso, V. 1980. Expectancy, alcohol, and sex guilt as determinants of interest in and reaction to sexual stimuli. *J. Abnorm. Psychol.* 89:644-653.

Laskowitz, D. 1961. The adolescent drug addict: An Alderian view. *J. Individual Psychol.* 17:68-79.

Lester, D., and Narkunski, A. 1978. Methodological problems in describing the addictive personality. *Psychol. Rep.* 43:134.

Lettieri, D.; Sayers, M.; and Pearson, H. 1980. *Theories on drug abuse: Selected contemporary perspectives.* NIDA Research Monographs #30, 1980.

Levine, J., and Zigler, E. 1981. The developmental approach to alcoholism: A further investigation. *Addictive Behav.* 6:93-98.

Libb, J., and Taulbee, E. 1971. Psychotic-appearing MMPI profiles among alcoholics. *J. Clin. Psychol.* 27:101-102.

Lind, C. 1972. 16 PF screening instrument for alcoholics. *J. Clin. Psychol.* 28:548-549.

Loper, R.; Kammeier, M.; and Hoffman, H. 1973. MMPI characteristics of college freshman males who later became alcoholics. *J. Abnorm. Psychol.* 82:159-162.

Lucas, W. 1978. Predicting initial use of marijuana from correlates of marijuana from correlates of marijuana use: Assessment of panel and cross-sectional data 1969-1976. *Int. J. Addictions* 13:1035-1047.

Luetgert, M., and Armstrong, A. 1973. Methodological issues in drug usage surveys: Anonymity, recency, and frequency. *Int. J. Addictions* 8:683-689.

MacAndrew, C. 1965. The differentiation of male alcoholic outpatients from nonalcoholic psychiatric outpatients. *Quart. J. Stud. Alcohol* 26: 238-246.

MacAndrew, C. 1979a. Evidence for the presence of two fundamentally different age-independent characterological types within unselected runs of male alcohol and drug abusers. *Am. J. Drug Alcohol Abuse* 6:207-221.

MacAndrew, C. 1979b. On the possibility of the psychometric detection of persons who are prone to the abuse of alcohol and other substances. *Addictive Behav.* 4:11-20.

MacAndrew, C. 1981a. What the MAC scale tells us about alcoholic men: An interpretative review. *J. Stud. Alcohol* 42:604-625.

MacAndrew, C. 1981b. Similarities in the self-depictions of men alcoholics and psychiatric outpatients: An explanation of Eysenck's dimension of emotionality. *J. Stud. Alcohol* 42:421-432.

MacAndrew, C., and Garfinkel, H. 1962. A consideration of changes attributed to intoxication as common sense reasons for getting drunk. *Quart. J. Stud. Alcohol* 23:252-266.

Maisto, S., and Caddy, G. 1981. Self-control and addictive behavior: Present status and prospects. *Int. J. Addictions* 16:109-133.

Marlatt, G. 1978. Behavioral assessment of social drinking and alcoholism. In G. Marlatt and P. Nathan (eds.), *Behavioral Approaches to Alcoholism.* New Brunswick, N.J.: Journal of Studies of Alcohol Inc.

Marlatt, G. 1980. Relapse prevention: A self-control program for addictive behaviors. Unpublished manuscript, Department of Psychology, University of Washington.

Mayfield, D., and Allen, D. 1967. Alcohol and affect: A psychoparmacological study. *Am. J. Psychiatry* 123:1346-1351.

McArdle, J. 1974. Impression management by alcoholics. *Quart. J. Stud. Alcohol* 35:911-916.

McClelland, D.; Davis, W.; Kalin, R.; and Wanner, E. 1972. *The Drinking Man.* New York: Free Press.

McCord, J. 1972. Etiological factors in alcoholism: Family and personal characteristics. *Quart. J. Stud. Alcohol* 33:1020-1027.

McCord, W., and McCord, J. 1960. *Origins of Alcoholism.* Stanford, Calif.: Stanford University Press.

McCord, W., and McCord, J. 1962. A longitudinal study of the personality of alcoholics. In D.J. Pittman and C. Snyder (eds.), *Society, Culture, and Drinking Patterns.* New York: John Wiley and Sons.

McGuire, J., and Megargee, E. 1974. Personality correlates of marijuana use among youthful offenders. *J. Consulting Clin. Psychol.* 42:124-133.

Megargee, E. 1982. Screening army enlistees to identify individuals with potential substance abuse problems. Unpublished paper prepared for the Committee on Substance Abuse and Habitual Behavior, National Research Council, Washington, D.C.

Mello, N. 1972. Behavioral studies of alcoholism. In B. Kissin and H. Begleiter (eds.), *Biology of Alcoholism,* vol. 2. New York: Plenum Press.

Mello, N. 1977. Stimulus self-administration: Some implications for the prediction of drug use liability. In P. Thompson and K. Unna (eds.), *Predicting Dependence Liability of Stimulant and Depressant Drugs.* Baltimore: University Park Press.

Mendelson, J., and Mello, N. 1969. A disease as an organizer for biochemical research: Alcoholism. In A. Mandell and M. Mandell (eds.), *Psychochemical Research in Man.* New York: Academic Press.

Miller, W. 1976. Alcoholism scales and objective assessment methods: A review. *Psychol. Bull.* 83:649-674.

Miller, W. 1980. *The Addictive Behaviors.* Oxford: Pergamon Press.

Miller, J.; Sensenig, J.; and Reed, T. 1972. Risky and cautious values among narcotic addicts. *Int. J. Addictions* 7:1-7.

Mischel, W. 1968. *Personality and Assessment.* New York: Wiley.

Mischel, W. 1973. Toward a cognitive social learning reconceptualization of personality. *Psychol. Rev.* 80:252-283.

Mischel, W. 1977. The interaction of person and situation. In D. Magnusson and N. Endler (eds.), *Personality at the Crossroads.* New York: Halstead.

Monroe, J.; Ross, W.; and Berzins, J. 1967. The decline of the addict as "psychopathy": Implications for community care. *Int. J. Addictions,* 2:601-608.

Murray, H. 1938. *Explorations in personality.* New York: Oxford, 1938.

Naditch, M. 1975. Ego mechanisms and marijuana usage. In D. Lettieri (eds.), *Predicting Adolescent Drug Abuse.* NIDA Research Issues Series (No. 11), Rockville, Md.

Naditch, M. 1975. Locus of control and drinking behavior in a sample of men in Army basic training. *J. Consulting Clin. Psychol.* 43:96.

National Commission on Marijuana and Drug Use. 1972. *Marijuana: A signal of misunderstanding, Appendix,* vol. 1. Washington, D.C.: U.S. Government Printing Office.

Nerviano, V. 1974. Common personality patterns among alcoholics. *J. Consulting Clin. Psychol.* 44:104-110.

Noel, N., and Lisman, S. 1980. Alcohol consumption by college women following exposure to unsolvable problems: Learned helplessness or stress-induced drinking? *Behav. Res. Therapy* 18:429-440.

Norem-Hebeisen, A. 1975. Self-esteem as a predictor of adolescent drug abuse. In D. Lettieri (ed.), *Predicting Adolescent Drug Abuse.* NIDA Research Issues Series (No. 11), Rockville, Md.

Nurco, D. 1979. Etiological aspects of drug abuse. In R. DuPont, A. Goldstein, and J. O'Donnell (eds), *Handbook on Drug Abuse.* Rockville, Md: National Institute on Drug Abuse.

Ogborne, A. 1974. Two types of heroin reactions. *Brit. J. Addictions* 69: 237-242.

O'Leary, D.; O'Leary, M.; and Donovan, D. 1976. Social skills acquisition and psychosocial development of alcoholics: A review. *Addictive Behav.* 1:111-120.

O'Leary, M., Rohsenow, D., & Chaney, E. 1979. The use of multivariate personality strategies in predicting attrition from alcoholism treatment. *J. Clin. Psychol.* 40:190-193.

O'Mally, P. 1975. Correlates and consequences of illicit drug use. Unpublished Ph.D. dissertation, University of Michigan, Ann Arbor, Mich.

Orford, J. 1976. A study of the personalities of excessive drinkers and their wives using approaches of Leary and Eysenck. *J. Consulting Clin. Psychol.* 44:534-545.

Orive, R., and Gerard, H. 1980. Personality, attitudinal and social correlates of drug use. *Int. J. Addictions* 15:869-881.

Overall, J. 1973. MMPI personality patterns of alcoholics and narcotics addicts. *Quart. J. Stud. Alcohol* 34:104-111.

Owen, P., and Butcher, J. 1979. Personality factors in problem drinking: A review of the evidence and some suggested directions. In R. Pickens and L. Heston (eds.), *Psychiatric Factors in Drug Abuse.* New York: Grune and Stratton.

Page, R., and Linden, J. 1974. "Reversible" organic brain syndrome in alcoholics: A psychometric evaluation. *Quart. J. Stud. Alcohol* 35:98-107.

Panton, J., and Brisson, R. 1971. Characteristics associated with drug abuse within a state prison population. *Corrective Psychiatry J. Soc. Therapy* 17:3-33.

Parry, H. 1979. Sample surveys of drug use. In R. DuPont, A. Goldstein and I. O'Donnell (eds.), *Handbook on Drug Abuse.* NIDA Research Issues Series (No. 11), Rockville, Md.

Partington, J. 1970. Dr. Jekyll and Mr. High: Multidimensional scaling of alcoholics' self-evaluations. *J. Abnorm. Psychol.* 75:131-138.

Paton, S.; Kessler, R.; and Kandel, D. 1977. Depressive mood and illegal drug use: A longitudinal analysis. *J. Genetic Psychol.* 131:267-289.

Penk, W.E.; Fudge, J.W.; Robinowitz, R.; and Neman, R.S. 1979. Personality characteristics of compulsive heroin, amphetamine, and barbiturate users. *J. Consulting Clin. Psychol.* 47:583-585.

Penk, W., and Robinowitz, R. 1976. Personality differences of volunteer and nonvolunteer heroin and nonheroin drug users. *J. Abnorm. Psychol.* 85:91-100.

Penk, W.E.; Woodward, W.A.; Robinowitz, R.; and Hess, J.L. 1978. Differences in MMPI scores of black and white compulsive heroin users. *J. Abnorm. Psychol.* 87:505-153.

Penk, W.; Woodward, W.; Robinowitz, R.; and Parr, W. 1980. An MMPI comparison of polydrug and heroin abusers. *J. Abnorm. Psychol.* 89:299-302.

Petrie, A. 1967. *Individuality in Pain and Suffering.* Chicago: University of Chicago Press.

Pihl, R., and Spiers, P. 1978. The etiology of drug abuse. In B. Maher (ed.), *Progress in Expermental Personality Research,* vol. 8. New York: Academic Press.

Platt, J. 1975. "Addiction proneness" and personality in heroin addicts. *J. Abnorm. Psychol.* 84:303-306.

Platt, J., and Labate, C. 1976. *Heroin Addiction: Theory, Research, and Treatment.* New York: Wiley, 1976.

Pliner, P., and Cappell, H. 1974. Modification of affective consequences of alcohol: A comparison of social and solitary drinking. *J. Abnorm. Psychol.* 83:418-425.

Popham, R., and Schmidt, W. 1962. *A Decade of Alcoholism Research.* A review of the research activities of the Alcoholism and Drug Addiction Foundation of Ontario, 1951-1961. Toronto: University Press.

Pryer, M., and Distefano, M. 1970. Further evaluation of the EPPS with hospitalized alcoholics. *J. Clin. Psychol.* 26:205.

Rathus, S.A.; Fox, V.A.; and Ortins, V.B. 1980. The MacAndrew scale as a measure of substance abuse and delinquency among adolescents. *J. Clin. Psychol.* 36:579-583.

Reid, J. 1978. Study of drinking in natural settings. In G. Marlatt and P. Nathan (eds.) *Behavioral Approaches to Alcoholism.* New Brunswick, N.J.: Rutgers Center of Alcohol Studies.

Reiter, H. 1970. Note on some personality differences between heavy and light drinkers. *Perceptual Motor Skills* 30:762.

Replogle, W.H., and Hair, V.F. 1977. A multivariable approach to profiling alcoholic typologies. *Multivar. Exp. Clin. Res.* 3:157-164.

Rich, C., and Davis, H. 1969. Concurrent validity of MMPI alcoholism scales. *J. Clin. Psychol.* 25:425-426.

Robins, L. 1973. *A Follow-up of Vietnam Drug Users.* Washington, D.C.: U.S. Government Printing Office.

Robins, L.; Bates, W.; and O'Neal, P. 1962. Adult drinking patterns in former problem children. In D. Pittman and C. Snyder (eds.), *Society, Culture and Drinking Patterns.* New York: Wiley.

Rohsenow, D.J., and O'Leary, M.R. 1978. Locus of control research on alcoholic populations: A review. I. Development, scales, and treatment. *Int. J. Addictions* 13:55-78.

Rohsenow, D.J., and O'Leary, M.R. 1978. Locus of control research on alcoholic populations: A review. II. Relationships to other measures. *Int. J. Addictions* 13:213-226.

Rosenberg, N. 1972. MMPI alcoholism scales. *J. Clin. Psychol.* 28:515-522.

Rosenthal, R. 1969. Interpersonal expectations: Effects of the experimenter's hypothesis. In R. Rosenthal and R. Rosnow (eds.), *Artifact in Behavioral Research.* New York: Academic Press.

Sadava, S. 1975. Research approaches in illicit drug use: A critical review. *Genetic Psychol. Monographs* 91:3-59.

Sadava, S.W. 1978. Etiology, personality and alcoholism. *Can. Psychol. Rev.* 19:198-214.

Schiff, S. 1959. A self-theory investigation of drug addiction in relation to age of onset. Unpublished PhD dissertation, New York University.

Schuster, C., and Johansen, C. 1974. The use of animal models for studying drug abuse. In R. Gibbins et al. (eds.), *Research Advances in Alcohol and Drug Problems,* vol. 1. New York: Wiley, 1974.

Schwartz, D., and Karp, S. 1967. Field dependence in a geriatric population. *Perceptual Motor Skills* 24:495-504.

Sechrest, L. Personality: 1976. In *Annual Review of Psychology,* 1976.

Seevers, M., and Deneau, G. 1963. Physiological aspects of tolerance and physical dependence. In W. Root and F. Hofmann (eds.), *Physiological Pharmacology.* New York: Academic Press, 1963.

Segal, B. 1975. Personality factors related to drug and alcohol use. In D. Lettieri (ed.), *Predicting Adolescent Drug Abuse.* NIDA Research Issues Series (No. 11), Rockville, Md.

Segal, B. 1977. Reasons for marijuana use and personality: A canonical analysis. *J. Alcohol Drug Ed.* 22:64-67.

Segal, B.; Huba, G.; and Singer, J. 1978. The prediction of college drug and alcohol use from personality and day dreaming tendencies. *Int. J. Addictions* 13:34-44.

Selzer, M. 1971. The Michigan Alcoholism Screening Test: The quest for a new diagnostic instrument. *Am. J. Psychiatry* 127:1653-1658.

Shepphard, C.; Ricca, E.; Fracchia, J.; and Merlis, S. 1974. Psychological needs of suburban male heroin addicts. *J. Psychol.* 87:123-128.

Smart, R., and Jackson, D. 1969. *A Preliminary Report on the Attitudes and Behavior of Toronto Students in Relation to Drugs.* Toronto: Addiction Research Foundation.

Smith, G., and Fogg, C. 1978. Psychological predictors of early use, late use, and nonuse of marijuana among teenage students. In D. Kandel (ed.), *Longitudinal Research on Drug Use.* Washington, D.C.: Hemisphere-Halstead.

Spiegel, D.; Hadley, A.; and Hadley, R. 1970. Personality test patterns of Rehabilitation center alcoholics, psychiatric inpatients, and normals. *J. Clin. Psychol.* 26:366-371.

Spotts, J., and Shontz, F. 1980. A life theme theory of chronic drug abuse. In D. Lettieri, M. Sayers, and H. Pearson (eds.), *Theories on Drug Abuse.* NIDA Research Issues Series (No. 11), Rockville, Md.

Stein, K.; Rozynko, V.; and Pugh, L. 1971. The heterogeneity of personality among alcoholics. *Brit. J. Soc. Clin. Psychol.* 10:253-259.

Sutherland, E.H.; Schroeder, H.G.; and Tordella, C.L. 1950. Personality traits and the alcoholic. *Quart. J. Stud. Alcohol* 11:547-561.

Sutker, P. 1971. Personality differences and sociopathy in heroin addicts and nonaddict prisoners. *J. Abnorm. Psychol.* 78:247-251.

Sutker, P.B.; Archer, R.P.; and Allain, A.N. 1978. Drug abuse patterns, personality characteristics, and relationships with sex, race, and sensation seeking. *J. Consulting Clin. Psychol.* 46:1374-1378.

Sutker, P.; Archer, R.; Brantley, P.; and Kilpatrick, D. 1979. Alcoholics and opiate addicts: A comparison of personality characteristics. *J. Stud. Alcohol* 40:635-644.

Teasdale, J.; Segraves, R.; and Zacune, J. 1971. "Psychoticism" in drug users. *Brit. J. Soc. Clin. Psychol.* 10:160-171.

Trevithick, L., and Hosch, H.M. 1978. MMPI correlates of drug addiction based on drug of choice. *J. Consulting Clin. Psychology* 46:180.

Vaillant, G. 1966. A twelve year follow-up of New York narcotic addicts: Some social and psychiatric characteristics. *Arch. Gen. Psychiatry* 15:599-609.

Wahl, C. 1956. Some antecedent factors in the family histories of 109 alcoholics. *Quart. J. Stud. Alcohol* 17:643-654.

Wallace, D., and Hiner, D. 1974. Some descriptive measures of 100 consecutive VA hospital drug abuse admissions. *Int. J. Addictions* 9:465-473.

Weckowitz, T., and Janssen, D. 1973. Cognitive functions, personality traits, and social values in heavy marijuana smokers and nonsmoker controls. *J. Abnorm. Psychol.* 81:264-269.

Weiss, L., and Masling, J. 1970. Further validation of a Rorschach measure of oral imagery: A study of six clinical groups. *J. Abnorm. Psychol.* 76:83-87.

Whitelock, P.; Overall, J.; and Patrick, J. 1971. Personality patterns and alcohol use in a state hospital population. *J. Abnorm. Psychol.* 78:9-16.

Wiggins, J. 1973. *Personality and Prediction: Principles of Personality Assessment.* Reading, Mass.: Addison-Wesley.

Williams, A. 1976. The alcoholic personality. In B. Kissin and H. Begleiter (eds.), *The Biology of Alcoholism: Social Aspects of Alcoholism.* New York: Plenum Press.

Williams, A.; McCourt, W.; and Schneider, L. 1971. Personality self-descriptions of alcoholics and heavy drinkers. *Quart. J. Stud. Alcohol* 32:310-317.

Wilsnack, S. 1974. The effects of social drinking on women's fantasy. *J. Personal.* 42:43-61.

Wingard, J.A.; Huba, G.V.; and Bentler, P.M. 1979. The relationship of personality structure to patterns of adolescent substance use. *Multivar. Behav. Res.* 14:131-143.

Witkin, H.; Karp, S.; and Goodenough. D. 1959. Dependence in alcoholics. *Quart. J. Stud. Alcohol* 20:493-504.

Witkin, H.; Lewis, H.; Hertzman, M.; Machover, K.; Meissner, P.; and Wapner, S. 1954. *Personality through Perception: An Experimental and Clinical Study.* New York: Harper.

Wittman, P. 1939. Developmental characteristics and personalities of chronic alcoholics. *J. Abnorm. Soc. Psychol.* 34:361-377.

Yakichuk, A.J. 1978. A study of the self-concept evaluations of alcoholic's and nonalcoholics. *J. Drug Ed.* 8:41-49.

Zager, L., and Megargee, E. 1981. Seven MMPI alcohol and drug abuse scales: An empirical investigation of their interrelationships, convergent and discriminant validity, and degree of racial bias. *J. Personal. Soc. Psychol.* 40:532-544.

Zinberg, N. 1979. Nonaddictive opiate use. In R. DuPont, A. Goldstein, and J. O'Donnell (eds.), *Handbook on Drug Abuse.* Rockville, Md: National Institute on Drug Abuse.

Zuckerman, M. 1979. *Sensation-seeking: Beyond the Optimal Level of Arousal.* Hillsdale, N.J.: Lawrence Erlbaum.

**Part III
Biological Commonalities**

Opiate Receptors: Properties and Possible Functions

Eric J. Simon

Explosive progress in the field of opiate research has occurred since the biochemical demonstration of opiate receptors in 1973. This was followed about two years later by the discovery and identification of endogenous opioid peptides, the enkephalins and endorphins, the putative natural ligands of the opiate receptor. This chapter deals with developments in the understanding of opiate receptors. The enkephalins and endorphins will be mentioned only in regard to their interactions with the receptors (see chapter 7 for discussion of the opioid peptides).

Receptor Postulate and Discovery of Stereospecific Opiate Binding Sites

The hypothesis that opiates must bind to specific sites located on the surface of or inside nerve cells in order to exert their effects has been put forth by investigators for several decades. These putative binding sites were termed *receptors* in line with the nomenclature used by endocrinologists for specific binding sites for hormones. The concept of a receptor includes, in addition to the binding site, a transducing factor that allows binding to be translated into physical or chemical sequelae that lead ultimately to the observed responses.

The reason for postulating receptors for morphine and related natural and synthetic narcotic analgesics was the high degree of steric and structural specificity inherent in many of the actions of opiates. Thus for a large number of morphinelike analgesics studied, only one enantiomer is active, (usually the levorotatory), while the dextrorotatory isomer has little or no analgesic or addiction-producing activity. Small alterations in molecular structure can frequently result in profound changes in pharmacological potency. The most interesting and most studied structural change is the substitution of the N-methyl group by a larger alkyl group such as allyl or cyclopropylmethyl. Such a substitution frequently results in the formation of a molecule with potent, specific antagonistic activity against morphine and related narcotic analgesics. Antagonist activity is most easily explained by competition for a receptor site. Binding of an antagonist is presumed not to produce the subsequent changes necessary to evoke a response. The finding that many such opiate antagonists retain some of their analgesic potency but little of their addiction liability has spurred the synthesis of a large number of such mixed agonist-antagonist drugs for clinical trial as safer analgesics. Antagonists, especially the pure antagonists naloxone and naltrexone (called "pure" because devoid of analgesic, addicting, and other opiate agonist properties) are also used for the treatment of addicts.

The search for the putative opiate receptors was complicated by the difficulty of distinguishing nonspecific binding to various tissue components from specific binding to receptors. It was relatively easy to demonstrate the binding of tritiated dihydromorphine to brain and other tissue homogenates. However, attempts by Van Praag and Simon (1966) to distinguish specific binding by its sensitivity to displacement by the antagonist nalorphine were unsuccessful. Ingoglia and Dole (1970) were the first to use the principle of stereospecificity in an attempt to identify opiate receptors. They injected l-and d-methadone into the lateral ventricle of rats but found no difference in the rate of diffusion of the enantiomers into brain tissue.

In 1971 Goldstein, Lowney, and Pal (1971) used stereospecificity as the criterion of receptor binding in brain homogenates. They incubated mouse brain homogenates with ^{3}H-levorphanol in the presence of a large excess of unlabeled levorphanol or of its inactive enantiomer dextrorphan. Since dextrorphan has neither agonist nor antagonist activity, it is presumed not to be recognized by the receptor. Stereospecific binding was therefore defined as the portion of binding of the labeled drug that is prevented by levorphanol but not by dextrorphan. In their experiments Goldstein's group found only about 2 percent of the total binding to be stereospecific. This stereospecific material was purified and found to be cerebroside sulfate.

In 1973 the laboratories of Simon, Terenius, and Snyder, each using similar modifications of the Goldstein procedure, independently and simultaneously reported the observation of stereospecific opiate binding in rat brain homogenate that represented the major portion of total binding (Simon, Hiller, and Edelman 1973; Terenius 1973; Pert and Snyder 1973). The modifications involved the use of very low concentrations of labeled ligand, made possible by high specific activity, and the washing of homogenates after incubation with cold buffer to remove contaminating unbound and loosely bound radioactivity. Since that time these results have been confirmed in many laboratories and much evidence has accumulated suggesting that these stereospecific binding sites indeed represent receptors to which opiates must bind in order to produce their pharmacological responses. They have been found in human beings and in all vertebrates so far studied. Recently they have also been reported in invertebrates.

Properties of Opiate Binding Sites and Evidence
that They Are Pharmacological Receptors

The stereospecific binding sites are found in the central nervous system and in the innervation of certain smooth muscle systems such as the myenteric plexus of the guinea pig ileum. They have not been observed in nonnervous tissues. They are tightly associated with membrane fractions of tissue homogenates and have been reported to be most concentrated in the synaptosomal cell fraction, suggesting a location in the vicinity of synapses.

Stereospecific opiate binding is saturable, and binding at saturation amounts to about 0.25 picomoles per milligram (pmol/mg) of brain protein in brain membrane preparations. Both agonists and antagonists bind with high affinity. Affinities, as defined by dissociation constants, range from 0.025 nanomolar for the most potent fentanyl derivative known, to low or no measurable affinity for drugs that possess little or no opiatelike activity. The striking discrimination between stereoisomers is best exemplified by levorphanol and dextrorphan, which differ by four orders of magnitude in their affinities.

The pH optimum for opiate binding is fairly broad, ranging from 6.5 to 8. The addition of various salts to the incubation medium tends to reduce binding. Sodium represents an exception that is dealt with in some detail in the subsequent section on conformational changes in opiate receptors.

The inhibition of stereospecific opiate binding by proteolytic enzymes and a wide variety of protein reagents, including sulfhydryl reagents, strongly suggests that one or more proteins are involved in opiate binding. The role of lipids is less clear since binding is inhibited by treatment with phospholipase A (from some sources but not from others) but is virtually unaffected by phospholipases C and D. Ribonuclease, deoxyribonuclease, and neuraminidase are without effect on opiate binding.

The most convincing evidence indicating that the observed binding sites represent pharmacological receptors comes from the close correlation between binding affinities and pharmacological potencies observed for a large number of drugs in several studies. Thus good correlation was found for a homologous series of ketobemidones differing only in the length of their alkyl substitution on the nitrogen. Creese and Snyder (1975) found excellent correlation between binding of a series of opiate agonists and antagonists to receptors in the guinea pig ileum and their pharmacological potency in this system.

We studied a series of twenty-six coded drugs from the repertory of Janssen Pharmaceutica (Stahl et al. 1977). The binding affinities of these drugs were assessed by competition with labeled naltrexone for stereospecific binding. These affinities were compared to analgesic potencies measured by the tail withdrawal reaction following intravenous administration of drug. In this series, in which the drugs varied in pharmacological potencies over six orders of magnitude, a rank correlation coefficient of 0.9 was found.

The drugs studied included a number of neuroleptics, such as haloperidol and droperidol, which were found able to compete with labeled opiates for binding in the micromolar range, in agreement with reports by others. Van Nueten, Janssen, and Fontaine (1976) have found that similar concentrations of neuroleptic drugs will inhibit the electrically stimulated contractions of the isolated guinea pig ileum in a manner reversible by naloxone.

Loperamide, an antidiarrheal drug with little effect on the central nervous system, has high affinity for opiate receptors. Experiments were presented suggesting that this drug does not readily penetrate the blood-brain barrier, a property that may explain the separation of antidiarrheal and central effects of this drug. The stereospecificity, saturability, and high affinity of the opiate binding sites and, above all, the excellent correlation between pharmacological potency and binding affinity for a large number of opiates and antagonists support the hypothesis that these sites represent the binding portion of pharmacologically relevant receptors.

Regional Distribution of Opiate Receptors in the Central Nervous System

The regional distribution of stereospecific opiate binding in the central nervous system (CNS) is of considerable interest because it might reveal a relation between opiate receptor localization and regional brain function. Hiller, Pearson, and Simon (1973) therefore embarked on a detailed study of regional distribution of stereospecific ^{3}H-etorphine binding in human brain obtained at autopsy from the office of the chief medical examiner of the City of New York. Stereospecific binding could be demonstrated in autopsy material, and the level of binding for a given anatomical site from one brain to another showed remarkably good reproducibility. Over forty anatomical regions were examined for opiate receptor levels. Receptors are not distributed uniformly. There are large differences in levels of etorphine binding ranging from 0.4 pmol/mg protein in, for example, the olfactory trigone, amygdala, and septal nuclei, to virtually no binding in cerebral white matter, dentate nucleus of the cerebellum, tegmentum, and other areas. A similar study was carried out by Kuhar, Pert, and Snyder (1973) in monkeys with strikingly similar results.

Since that time very detailed mapping of ^{3}H-diprenorphine binding after intravenous administration in rats was done by Atweh and Kuhar (1977a, 1977b, 1977c) in the rat CNS. All these data can be summarized by stating that high levels of opiate receptors are present in all areas of the CNS that have been implicated in pain perception and pain modulation, such as the substantia gelatinosa of the spinal cord, the thalamus, and the periaqueductal gray region. High binding levels are also found in virtually all parts of the limbic system, such as the amygdala, septal nuclei, hypothalamus, and frontal cortex. These are all regions that had previously been implicated as possible sites of action of the opiates. The presence of high levels of opiate receptors in the corpus striatum is at present more difficult to explain. Very high levels of receptors are also present in the locus coeruleus, a finding of considerable interest, especially in view of the recent success in the treatment of heroin addicts with the α-adrenergic agonist, clonidine. A composite of all these studies is presented in figure 6-1.

It should be pointed out that recent studies have shown that the distribution of the enkephalins is rather well correlated with the distribution of opiate receptors. This is not the case for β-endorphin.

Early effects in mammals after acute morphine administration include changes in behavior. While depressive behavior is observable in many species including the dog, monkey, and human being, excitatory behavior is elicited in the cat, sheep, and cow among others. In an effort to ascertain whether the species difference in behavior caused by morphine is reflected in the distribution pattern of opiate binding sites in the brain, Hiller and Simon (1976) undertook a survey of the levels of stereospecific binding of ³H-etorphine in selected areas of the brains of the species. There was reasonably good reproducibility of binding levels for any given anatomical region of all six species studied. The only areas that exhibited consistent differences were the amygdala and the frontal cortex, which were at least twofold higher in receptor level for the species that exhibit depression than for the species that show an excitatory response to opiates.

These consistent differences between the two groups of animals, though based on a small number of species, are intriguing; their interpretation is difficult, however. Both the amygdala and frontal cortex are part of the limbic system, wherein most of the regions of high opiate binding in human and monkey are located. It has been reported that bilaterally amygdalectomized monkeys were rendered placid, whereas the same procedure performed on cats produced a sustained ferocity. Thus amygdaldectomy mimics the effects seen in acute morphine administration to these species. The removal of the frontal cortex in man may leave the perception of pain unaffected while the anxiety associated with pain is markedly diminished. This observation has also been made in patients in pain who are receiving morphine.

Ontogeny of the Opiate Receptor

The ontogenetic development of opiate receptors in the brain of rat and guinea pig was investigated by Clendennin, Petraitis, and Simon (1976). In

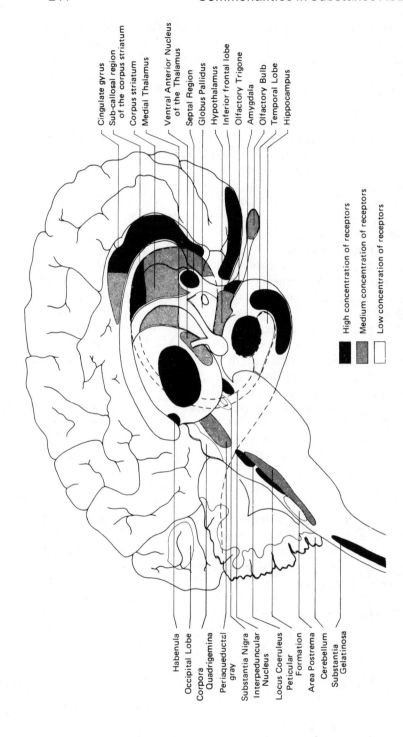

Cingulate gyrus
Sub-callosal region of the corpus striatum
Corpus striatum
Medial Thalamus
Ventral Anterior Nucleus of the Thalamus
Septal Region
Globus Pallidus
Hypothalamus
Inferior frontal lobe
Olfactory Trigone
Amygdala
Olfactory Bulb
Temporal Lobe
Hippocampus

Habenula
Occipital Lobe
Corpora Quadrigemina
Periaqueductal gray
Substantia Nigra
Interpeduncular Nucleus
Locus Coeruleus
Peticular Formation
Area Postrema
Cerebellum
Substantia Gelatinosa

High concentration of receptors
Medium concentration of receptors
Low concentration of receptors

Source: Eric J. Simon (1977) Le recepteur de la morphine. *La Recherche* 8 (78):416-423. Reprinted by permission.

Figure 6-1. Section of the Brain Showing Concentration of Opiate Receptor Sites

the rat the rate of increase of opiate binding is greatest between the midfetal stage and three weeks postpartum (three- to fourfold). Thereafter, until adulthood (from ten to twenty weeks) the rise is more gradual (about twofold). Scatchard analysis of saturation curves for naltrexone binding in rat brain from one day after birth to the age of ten weeks has shown that the increase in binding is due to an increase in number of receptors rather than to greater affinity.

Opiate binding to guinea pig brain homogenates has demonstrated no significant difference in either receptor number or binding affinity between late fetal life and adulthood in this species. Binding in brain homogenate from a midterm fetus is about one-half that observed late in gestation and in adult guinea pigs. The fact that guinea pigs are born with a full complement of receptors is well correlated with previous reports that the guinea pig is an animal with almost full brain development before birth, whereas the rat is an animal in which a significant portion of brain development continues for at least three weeks after birth. In rat brain, the percentage increase of opiate receptors from newborn to adults in various regions of the brain differs widely. For example, receptor binding in the hippocampus and parietal cortex increases by 830 percent and 690 percent, respectively, but in the medulla pons and corpus striatum by only 270 percent and 300 percent (Coyle and Pert 1976). The development of the opiate receptor in both rat and guinea pig closely parallels the development of other major neurological and biochemical components of the nervous system, suggesting that these receptors are themselves important components of the CNS.

Conformational Changes in Opiate Receptors

The studies discussed so far do not permit distinction of a potent agonist from an equally potent antagonist by a receptor binding assay. The two types of drug compete with each other for the same receptor and show identical binding characteristics. A way that permits the distinction of agonists from antagonists by their binding characteristics came from what appeared to be an experimental discrepancy between two laboratories. Pert and Snyder (1973) reported that the addition of salt had little effect on binding, while Simon, Hiller, and Edelman (1973) reported profound inhibition. Since the New York University group (Simon) was using the potent agonist etorphine and the Johns Hopkins University group (Snyder) was using the so-called pure antagonist naloxone, Simon et al. suggested that the apparent discrepancy might represent a general difference in the manner in which agonists and antagonists bind to the receptor. It was indeed found that the binding of all agonists examined was inhibited by salt whereas the binding of antagonists was augmented. It was also shown that this ability to discriminate between agonists and antagonists was not a general effect of salts, but a unique property of the cation Na^+. The effect is not shown by the other alkali metals, K^+, Rb^+, and Cs^+, but Li^+ does exhibit this action, though to a much smaller degree. No other inorganic cations nor a number of organic cations studied were found to exhibit this property. This ability of sodium ions to distinguish between such closely related molecules as an opiate and its corresponding antagonist (allyl or cyclopropylmethyl analogue) is of considerable interest, especially in light of the uniqueness of Na^+ in this respect. The effect of sodium reaches its maximum at 100 mM and is completely reversible upon removal of sodium from the incubation medium.

Manganese and magnesium salts have been reported to increase agonist binding while they depress antagonist binding. This effect is observed most clearly when sodium is also present and may represent a reversal of the sodium effect by the divalent cations.

Studies of the mechanism of the sodium effect were carried out. The first question asked was whether the differences in binding represented changes in the number of sites or in the affinity of binding. Pert and Snyder (1974) reported that sodium caused an increase in the number of high affinity binding sites for naloxone and a decrease of binding sites for dihydromorphine. Simon et al. (1975b), on the other hand, found that sodium increased the affinity for the receptor of naltrexone and other antagonists while reducing the affinity of agonists. No change in number of binding sites was noted. These results were consistent with a model involving a conformational change of the opiate receptor in the presence of sodium ions. The experimental discrepancies have never been completely resolved. Studies carried out in both laboratories involving competition experiments favor the changes in affinity, however. When a relatively pure antagonist is allowed to compete for binding with a labeled antagonist there is little or no change in the IC_{50} of the competitor when sodium is added to the incubation mixture. When an unlabeled agonist is allowed to compete with a labeled antagonist the IC_{50} for the agonist is increased drastically in the presence of sodium (tenfold to sixtyfold). Such a shift in IC_{50} reflects a change in affinity but not in the number of binding sites.

The best evidence for an alteration in receptor conformation by sodium ions came unexpectedly from a study of the kinetics of receptor inactivation by the sulfhydryl alkylating reagent, N-ethylmaleimide (NEM) by Simon and Groth (1975). When a membrane fraction from rat brain was incubated with NEM for various periods followed by inactivation or removal of unreacted NEM, there was a progressive decrease in the ability of the membranes to bind opiates stereospecifically. The rate of receptor inactivation followed pseudo-first-order kinetics consistent with the existence of one

SH-group per receptor essential for binding. Protection against inactivation was achieved by the addition of low concentrations of opiates or antagonists during the preincubation with NEM, suggesting that the SH-group is located near the opiate binding site of the receptor.

Considerable protection was observed (the half-time of inactivation was increased to thirty minutes from eight minutes) when inactivation was carried out in the presence of 100 mM NaCl. Since sodium salts were without effect on the alkylation of model SH-compounds, such as cysteine or glutathione, this suggested that the SH-groups were made less accessible to NEM by a conformational change in the receptor protein. The fact that this protection exhibited the same ion specificity (Na^+ protects; Li^+ protects partially; K^+, Rb^+, or Ca^+ not at all) and the same dose-response to Na^+ as the differential changes in ligand affinities, suggests that the conformational change that masks SH-groups is the same as that resulting in increased affinity of antagonists and decreased affinity of agonists.

These studies illustrate that the opiate receptor can alter its shape. The physiological function of this plasticity is not yet clear. A role in the coupling of opiate binding to subsequent physical or chemical events has been suggested, as has a role for Na^+ ions in the action of opiates.

It should be mentioned that similar changes have been observed as a consequence of changes in the temperature at which binding takes place. This was first shown by Creese et al. (1975) and confirmed by Hiller and Simon (1976).

A simple model for the allosteric effect of sodium on opiate receptors is shown in figure 6-2. In line with the observed cooperativity the receptor is represented as a dimer. When sodium ions are bound to the allosteric site there is a change in the shape of the receptor molecule. This in turn results in an alteration in the binding site, which now binds antagonists with

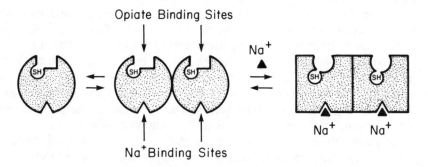

Figure 6-2. Model for the Allosteric Effect of Sodium Ions on the Conformation of Opiate Receptors

greater affinity and agonists with reduced affinity. It also results in a masking of the SH-group of the receptor that makes it less accessible to inactivation by SH-reagents.

A Tissue Culture Model for the Study of Opiate Receptors: Presynaptic Location of Receptors

For the investigation of problems related to the mode of action of opiates in the CNS, organotypic cultures of central nervous tissue would clearly provide advantages over tumor-derived established cell lines as well as over whole animals. Such cultures derived from fetal mouse spinal cords and attached sensory ganglia have recently been found useful for studies for opiate action. Crain et al. (1977) demonstrated that the sensory-evoked synaptic networks in the dorsal horn regions of these explants can be selectively depressed by exposure to analgesic concentrations of morphine and other opiates as well as by enkephalins and endorphins. These effects are reversed by naloxone. The dextrorotatory form of naloxone has recently been found to be ineffective (Crain and Simon, unpublished) demonstrating the stereospecificity of the naloxone reversal.

Measurements of opiate receptor binding levels in these spinal cord-dorsal root ganglion cultures as well as in cultures of isolated dorsal root ganglia and defferented cord explants were made by Hiller et al. (1978). In these cultures profuse neuritic outgrowth develops primarily as a result of the stimulation by nerve growth factor of the dorsal root ganglia and extends for several millimeters beyond the explant zone. In some cases separate determinations of opiate binding were made on explant and outgrowth zones. Homogenates of these cultures were found to exhibit stereospecific binding of the potent opiate antagonist diprenorphine. It was apparent that the greatest amount of binding was present in the neuritic outgrowth of both isolated dorsal root ganglion cultures and cord-ganglion cultures. Four to seven times more binding per milligram of protein was seen in the neuritic outgrowth of the cultures than in the explant area.

The central afferent branches of the neuritic arborization from the dorsal root ganglion explant have been shown in cord-ganglion cultures to establish synaptic connections within the dorsal horn of the spinal cord explant. The high level of opiate receptors in the neuritic outgrowth constitutes strong evidence for a presynaptic location of these receptors.

Experiments in rhesus monkeys (La Motte et al. 1976) demonstrated a reduction in opiate receptor binding in the upper dorsal horn of the spinal cord following dorsal root section. This result also supports a presynaptic location on primary afferent terminals in the spinal cord. However, as pointed out by the authors, a postsynaptic localization of receptors cannot be ruled out since the rhizotomy-induced decrease in opiate binding could result from transsynaptic degenerative changes.

We have recently found that exposure of spinal cord-DRG cultures to morphine (1 μM) for two to three days results in the development of tolerance (S.M. Crain et al. 1979). Inhibition of sensory-evoked dorsal cord responses in treated cultures required from tenfold to a hundredfold more morphine than in naive cultures. Tolerance also developed to the enkephalin analogue Sandoz FK 33-284, and those cultures exhibited strong cross tolerance to morphine and to the enkephalins. Simultaneous exposure to low levels of naloxone (0.1 μM) prevented tolerance development.

Tolerance was observed even if the cord-DRG cultures were incubated with 1 μM morphine in a simple balance salt solution. However, incubation of cultures at 20°C, even in complete growth medium, did not result in tolerance. Such results obviously cannot be obtained in studies with intact animals.

Biochemical Events Following Opiate Binding

As indicated earlier, the binding of opiates to their receptors must trigger chemical or physical events that ultimately result in the observed pharmacological responses. The nature of these events remains a black box. However, efforts have been made to penetrate the box.

Cyclic 3',5'-adenosine monophosphate (cAMP) has been shown to act as second messenger in a number of hormonally controlled phenomena. The finding that cAMP and the phosphodiesterase inhibitor, theophylline, antagonize the antinociceptive action of morphine suggested to Collier and Roy (1974) that cAMP may have a role in the action of opiates. These authors have shown that the stimulation of cAMP formation by prostaglandins E_1 or E_2 in rat brain homogenate is inhibited by morphine and other opiates. There is no inhibition of the basal production of cAMP. This inhibition was seen at concentrations of opiates comparable to those required for analgesia and was antagonized by naloxone. The study of a series of opiates led to the finding that inhibition of prostaglandin-stimulated formation of the cAMP was well correlated with antinociceptive potency, opiate receptor binding affinity, and inhibition of electrically simulated contraction of the isolated guinea pig ileum. Specificity for E-prostaglandin stimulation was suggested by the absence of inhibition of fluoride-stimulated cAMP production. Involvement of E prostaglandins is further supported by the finding of Ehrenphreis, Greenberg, and Belman (1973) that they reverse inhibition by morphine of contractions of the guinea pig ileum.

Similar results were obtained in the neuroblastoma X glioma hybrid cells in culture previously shown to contain opiate receptors. Here, however, there appears to be less specificity since Sharma et al. (1975) have found that opiates inhibit basal as well as adenosine and PGE_1-stimulated adenylate cyclase. The parental cell lines from which the hybrid cells are derived contain few, if any, opiate receptors. Their adenylate cyclase is not inhibited by opiates.

In apparent contradiction to the results of Collier's group, Puri, Cochin, and Volicer (1975) have reported that morphine sulfate produced a dose-dependent increase in the adenylate cyclase of rat corpus striatum when given in vivo or added to the enzyme in a striatal homogenate. This effect is not stereospecific, however, and cannot be reversed by naloxone. Iwatsubo and Clouet (1975) reported that the addition of morphine and other opiates (3-300 mM) to crude synaptosomal membranes from rat caudate nucleus had no effect on the dopamine stimulation of adenylate cyclase. When morphine was administered subcutaneously to rats at a dose of 60 mg/kg, however, significant increases were found in basal and dopamine-stimulated adenylate cyclase in the caudate nucleus from 15 to 120 minutes after injection.

Bonnet (1975) has reported that systemic injections of morphine produced dose-dependent increases in the level of cAMP and adenylate cyclase in the striatum and thalamus of rat brain, whereas in the substantia nigra and the periventricular gray area the level of cAMP was found to be reduced. More recently Bonnet and Gusik (1976) have demonstrated that the increases in thalamic adenylate cyclase were reversible by naloxone, suggesting the involvement of opiate receptors in this effect. They also found that the level of Ca^{2+} was of great importance. Physiological levels of Ca^{2+} (up to 1.3 mM) tended to increase the opiate stimulation of adenylate cyclase in the thalamus, whereas high levels of Ca^{2+} tended to suppress it.

Minneman (1977) reported in a very recent communication that morphine, at concentrations from 10^{-7} to 10^{-4}M, caused a 30-50 percent decrease in cAMP levels of striatal slices. He also found a highly specific and complete inhibition of dopamine-stimulated cAMP levels in the slices. Morphine, up to a concentration of 10^{-3}M, had no effect on the stimulation of cAMP levels elicited by isoprenaline, adenosine, or PGE_1. This selective inhibition of dopamine-sensitive adenylate cyclase, as well as the depression of basal cAMP, was not seen in striatal homogenate and appears, therefore, to require intact cells. Both effects were blocked by naloxone ($1v$ M), suggesting that they are mediated via specific opiate receptors.

The finding by Ho, Loh, and Way (1973) that the administration of cAMP accelerated the development of tolerance and physical dependence stimulated exploration as to whether raised levels of cAMP could produce behavioral patterns in naive rats resembling the morphine-withdrawal syndrome. Collier and collaborators (Butt et al. 1979) approached this by administration of large doses of phosphodiesterase inhibitors such as theophylline and other methyl-xanthines. Such behavior, termed by the authors *quasimorphine-withdrawal-syndrome* (QMWS), was indeed observed, as was intensification of the syndrome by opiate antagonists and its stereospecific suppression by agonists. It has not been proven that the observed effects are indeed the result of raised brain levels of cAMP. However, the testing of seven phosphodiesterase inhibitors showed that ability to elicit the QMWS was correlated with their potency as inhibitors of cAMP hydrolysis. Moreover, there is a report by Mehta and Johnson (1974) that total brain content of cAMP increases sharply during naloxone-precipitated withdrawal from opiates. For the effect of long-term morphine treatment and withdrawal on cAMP production in neuroblastoma X glioma hybrid cells in culture, see subsequent section on opiate receptors and opiate addiction.

Assuming that opiates (and endorphins) can indeed produce changes in the cellular level of cAMP and assuming that some of the contradictory results are sorted out and reconciled, the manner in which these changes are implicated in either acute or chronic effects of opiates is still unclear. However, results from several laboratories (personal communications from K.A. Bonnet, D.H. Clouet, P. Greengard) suggest that the cAMP-dependent phosphorylation of membrane proteins may be affected by chronic morphine treatment of animals.

The results suggesting that the opiate receptor can exist in alternate conformations make it attractive to postulate that similar physical changes may occur that could mediate opiate effects by causing modifications in the neighboring synaptic membrane. To date, the evidence for such alterations during acute or chronic treatment with opiates is scant. Kang, Sessa, and Green (1973) reported that synaptosomal membranes, isolated from rat brain cortex, undergo a characteristic structural change accompanied by a time-dependent increase in ultraviolet absorption (at 265 and 220-230 nm) and a decrease in intrinsic fluorescent intensity. Morphine sulfate appears to block this transition as shown by inhibition of the optical density increase at 265 namometers. This effect, however, required relatively high concentrations of morphine (95 μg/ml) and was not tested for stereospecificity. Preliminary results obtained here at NYU indicate that quencing of fluorescence in partly purified synaptosomal membranes can be produced by the addition of levorphanol but not of dextrorphan (N. Clendeninn and E.J. Simon, unpublished results).

Evidence for the Existence of Multiple Opiate Receptors

Receptors for neurotransmitters usually exist in multiple forms. Thus, there is a muscarinic and a nicotinic receptor for acetylcholine, at least two receptors for dopamine and multiple receptors for norepinephrine and serotonin. This realization, along with the many pharmacological responses elicited by the opiates, stimulated keen interest in the question whether more than one opiate receptor exists.

The earliest evidence for heterogeneity of opiate receptors came from the work of Martin and coworkers (1976) in chronic spinal dogs. Striking differences in pharmacological responses to different types of narcotic analgesics and their inability to substitute for each other in suppression of withdrawal symptoms in addicted animals led them to postulate the existence of at least three types of receptors. These were named for the prototype drugs that gave rise to the distinction: μ for morphine, $\varkappa$ for ketocyclazocine and s for SKF 10047. These results, though of great interest, suffer from the disadvantage that in such animal studies other interpretations of the results are possible.

Kosterlitz's group (Lord et al. 1977) has published results indicating that the receptor present in the mouse vas deferens are different from those in the guinea pig ileum, as shown by the different rank order of potencies of opiates, enkephalins, and endorphins in the two systems. These investigators have also reported results that suggest heterogeneity of opiate receptors in rat brain. Opiate alkaloids were found to be considerably more effective in displacing other alkaloids than labeled enkephalins, whereas enkephalins were more effective in replacing labeled enkephalins. Based on these results Kosterlitz suggested that there are receptors with relatively high affinity for morphine and related opiates, which he named μ (in the hope that they may be identical to Martin's μ receptors) and another type of receptor that exhibits preferential affinity for enkephalins, which he named δ (for vas deferens, which seems to have a preponderance of receptors resembling the enkephalin receptors in the CNS).

Competition experiments, while they point to a possible receptor multiplicity, can also be explained by evoking differences in the way opiates and enkephalins bind to the same receptor. Further work was, therefore, carried out in a number of laboratories, including our own, on the question whether there are indeed several kinds of opiate receptors. J. Smith and I (1980) examined receptor inactivation of opioid binding by N-ethylmaleimide and protection from such inactivation by receptor ligands. Enkephalin binding is inactivated by NEM and the half-time of inactivation is very similar to that for inactivation of opiate alkaloids. However, cross-protection studies revealed that preincubation with opiates leads to much better protection of opiate binding than of enkephalin binding. The reverse was found when membranes were pretreated with enkephalin analogues. Enkephalinamide, which had previously been reported to bind equally well to both μ and δ receptors, was found to protect ^{3}H-naltrexone and ^{3}H-Dala^{2}-D-leu^{5} enkephalin binding about equally well.

These results support the notion of at least two receptors. Similar results were obtained in Kosterlitz's laboratory (Robson and Kosterlitz 1979) using the irreversible inhibitor phenoxybenzamine. The fact that opiate and enkephalin binding are both sensitive to sulfhydryl reagents and exhibit similar degrees of sensitivity to NEM, as well as to proteolytic enzymes and phospholipases suggests that the differences between the morphine and enkephalin receptors are quite subtle.

Studies in Cuatrecasas's laboratory (Chang et al. 1979) and in our own (Simon et al. 1980) have shown regional differences in binding indicative of differences in the distribution of μ and δ receptors. The most striking result was obtained in the thalamus. Here saturation kinetics as well as competition studies demonstrated that there seemed to be a predominance of μ receptors. For example, while in most brain regions naloxone is from six-fold to tenfold more potent in competition with ^{3}H-naloxone than with ^{3}H-leu enkephalin, no such difference was found in the thalamus. We have recently obtained similar results in the human brain (Bonnet et al. 1981).

Pert has reported differentiation of receptors by the degree of their inhibition by GTP and has suggested that there are two classes of opiate receptors, which she has called type 1 (GTP-sensitive) and type 2 (GTP-resistant). Herkenham and Pert (1980) have reported autoradiographic evidence for a difference in their regional distribution in the CNS.

This research area is obviously still in its infancy. However, the evidence does seem to be accumulating that there may be two or more opiate receptors. If this can indeed be proven and if the receptors mediate different responses, considerable theoretical and practical benefit could be derived from these studies.

Progress in Receptor Solubilization and Purification

Progress in the solubilization of opiate receptors, normally tightly bound to cell membranes, has been even slower than for some other hormone and neurotransmitter receptors. One of the major reasons is the extreme sensitivity of opiate receptors to detergents, including the nonionic variety frequently used for the solubilization of membrane proteins. A significant advance was made by Simon, Hiller, and Edelman (1975a) when a method was found for solubilizing an etorphine-macromolecular complex that has properties suggesting that it may be an etorphine-receptor complex. This was accomplished with a nonionic detergent called BRIJ-36T. All attempts to bind opiates to this macromolecular material in solution after dissociation of the etorphine and removal of the detergent have been unsuccessful. Zukin and Kream (1979) have repeated this work with identical results and have shown that the method works equally well for solubilization of an enkephalin-macromolecular complex. They succeeded in cross linking some of the enkephalin (or stable enkephalin analogue) covalently to the solubilized receptor, a technique that may prove very useful for purification.

Recently some success has been obtained in the solubilization of active opiate binding sites. We have succeeded in demonstrating stereospecific opiate binding following detergent solubilization of toad (*Bufo marinus*) brain (Ruegg et al. 1980; Ruegg et al. 1981) and, very recently, our laboratory and others have solubilized active opiate receptors from mammalian brain (Howells et al. 1982).

Opiate Receptors and Opiate Addiction

It was research on the biochemical mechanism of opiate addiction (or at least tolerance and physical dependence) that resulted in the discovery of opiate receptors and their putative ligands, the endogenous opioid peptides. It was therefore of immediate interest to determine how the endogenous opioid system might explain chronic morphine effects, in particular, the development of tolerance and dependence. To date, the efforts toward this end have led to largely negative results. Klee and Streaty (1974) reported very early that they were unable to observe differences in either receptor number or binding affinity between the brains of naive and addicted rats. It occurred to K. Bonnet and me that such differences might occur in relatively small regions and not be detectable when binding is measured in the whole brain. Bonnet, Hiller, and Simon (1976) studied opiate binding in three brain areas, the periventricular gray area, the medial thalamus, and the caudate nucleus. All of these regions have high levels of opiate binding and at least the first two have been implicated in opiate action. No difference in either receptor number or binding affinity, in the presence or absence of sodium, was detectable in any of the three areas. Attempts to show differences in enkephalin and β-endorphin levels have been equally unfruitful to date.

An encouraging result was recently obtained in clinical studies by Su et al. (1978) in Taiwan. The intravenous administration of 4 milligrams of β-endorphin to human addicts resulted in dramatic improvement in their extremely severe withdrawal syndrome. Moreover, the relief lasted for several days, whereas relief of abstinence by opiates lasts only a few hours. This result suggests that the endorphins may indeed have a role in the mechanism of addiction to opiates.

An interesting result that may or may not prove to be applicable to what happens in the CNS has been obtained in a cell line of neuroblastoma x glioma hybrid cells. In these cultures chronic treatment with opiates leads to an increase in the activity of the adenylate cyclase coupled to opiate receptors. This results in an increase in opiate required to inhibit, a form of tolerance. Removal of opiates from the medium or treatment of the chronically morphinized cultures with naloxone results in a dramatic over-production of cAMP, which Klee and Nirenberg (1976) have suggested may be the cellular equivalent of dependence. If this mechanism is indeed operative in the CNS it would explain the absence of changes in the binding site of the opiate receptor and in the level of peptides.

There is little doubt in the minds of most investigators in this area that the opiate receptor-endorphin system will ultimately be shown to have an important role in the development of opiate addiction. Further work is needed to establish this connection.

Future Directions of Research

The discovery of opiate receptors is still very recent, as is that of the endogenous opioid peptides. A great deal of work must be done before scientists can understand the physiological significance of this system and its role in opiate addiction. Several areas of future research should prove very fruitful.

Investigation of Receptor Multiplicity

This very active though young research area is of considerable interest. If several receptors exist and if they mediate different pharmacological responses it would become much easier to design useful drugs, especially nonaddictive analgesics. Moreover, all of the studies of receptor number and properties in addicted animals were done before anything was known regarding multiple types of receptors. They will have to be repeated with this in mind.

Study of the Sequellae of Opiate or Endorphin Binding

Virtually nothing is known about the steps that intervene between opioid binding and the observed responses. Is the opiate receptor coupled to an adenylate cyclase, as it seems to be in a tumor cell line? This knowledge would be of great importance. Does conformational change in the receptor or the nearby cell membrane play a part in opiate action? Is there a change in ion fluxes produced by these membrane changes? An understanding of this black box is essential to the understanding of addiction, pain modulation, and probably other aspects of mood and behavior.

Isolation and Purification of the Receptor(s)

This research area is of great importance because a purified receptor will permit scientists to know its molecular structure and subunit composition. Antibodies could be made to the receptor and the injection of such antibodies may shed light on what goes wrong when these receptors are inactivated in situ quite specifically and therefore what their physiological role may be. Finally, much can be learned by reinserting the purified receptors into suitable membranes and observing how this alters membrane behavior. Purified receptors can also be used to study receptor-ligand interactions by a variety of physical-chemical techniques, such as fluorescence and electron spin resonance.

Functions of Opiate Receptors

Evidence for the involvement of opiate receptors in a given brain function is generally based on the reversibility of that function by an opiate antagonist such as naloxone. This widely accepted test is clearly imperfect and indirect. Based on naloxone-reversibility a large number of physiological and pharmacological effects seem to be mediated via opiate receptors. They include physical dependence, tolerance, analgesia (exogenous as well as endogenous), catatonia, appetite, sexual activity, certain types of behavior, various types of shock, and possibly some mental illnesses, such as schizophrenia and depression. It will be important in future research to obtain more direct evidence that will permit determination of the degree of participation of opiate receptors and their ligands in any or all of the aforementioned conditions. Ultimately we wish to know the molecular mechanism of opiate receptor function.

As for possible commonalities between different kinds of addiction and other compulsive behavior, it is too early to say whether the endogenous opioid system may play a role in alcohol, barbiturate, amphetamine, and other addictions or even in compulsive overeating (all of which have been suggested in the literature). It is likely that all kinds of behavior will involve complex interactions between different neurotransmitter systems, including the endorphinergic and enkephalinergic system. In every case it will be necessary to differentiate between primary effects, secondary effects, and effects even farther removed from the primary event.

The approach that has been so successful in the opiate field can be and has already been generalized. Other drugs that lead to compulsive abuse have properties that suggest that they bind to specific receptors. In these cases it becomes important to detect the existence of such receptors and to find out whether (as in the cases of amphetamine and LDS) these binding sites are the receptors for already known neurotransmitters. This knowledge can be very helpful to our understanding of the action of the drug. In cases in which the receptors do not appear to serve any of the known brain chemicals, a search for endogenous analogues of the drug should be instituted. The best example of such a study, based on the opiate experience, is the discovery of specific binding sites for benzodiazepines and the search now in progress for endogenous anxiolytic agents.

Alcohol and other abused solvents do not show the kind of specificity that suggests their binding to specific receptors. In these cases other approaches must be used.

Reviews

Comprehensive bibliographies can be found in the following review articles:

Höllt, V. 1978. Opiate receptors. In A. Herz (ed.), *Developments in Opiate Research*, chap. 1. *Modern Pharmacology-Toxicology*, vol. 14, New York and Basel: Marcel Dekker.

Simon, E.J., and Hiller, J.M. 1978. The opiate receptors. *Ann. Rev. Pharmacol. Toxicol.* 18:371-394.

Simon, E.J. and Hiller, J.M. Opiate peptides and opiate receptors. In G.J. Siegel, R.W. Albers, R. Katzman, and B.W. Agranoff (eds.), *Basic Neurochemistry*, 3rd ed. Boston: Little Brown, 1981.

Snyder, S.H.; Pasternak, C.W.; and Pert, C.B. 1975. Opiate receptor mechanisms. In L.L. Iverson, S.D. Iversen, and S.H. Snyder (eds.), *Handbook of Psychopharmacology*, vol. 5, New York: pp. 329-360, Plenum.

References

Atweh, S.F., and Kuhar, M.J. 1977a. *Brain Res.* 124:53-67.

Atweh, S.F., and Kuhar, M.J. 1977b. *Brain Res.* 129:1-12.

Atweh, S.F., and Kuhar, M.J. 1977c. *Brain Res.* 134:393-406.

Bonnet, K.A. 1975. *Life Sci.* 16:1877-1882.

Bonnet, K.A., Groth, J.; Gioannini, T.L.; Cortes, M.; and Simon, E.J. 1981. *Brain Res.* 221:437-440.

Bonnet, K.A., and Gusik, S. 1976. *Neurosci. Abstr.* 2:849.

Bonnet, K.A.; Hiller, J.M.; and Simon, E.J. 1976. pp. 335-343. In H.W. Kosterlitz (ed.), *Opiates and Endogenous Opioid Peptides.* Amsterdam: Elsevier.

Butt, N.H.; Collier, H.O.J.; Cuthbert, N.J.; Francis, D.L.; and Saeed, S.A. 1979. *Eur. J. Pharmacol.* 53:375-378.

Chang, K.J.; Cooper, B.R.; Hazum, E.R.; and Cuatrecasas, P. 1979. *Mol. Pharmacol.* 16:91-104.

Clendeninn, N.J.; Petraitis, M.; and Simon, E.J. 1976. *Brain Res.* 118: 157-160.

Collier, H.O.J., and Roy, A.C. 1974. *Prostaglandins* 7:361-376.

Coyle, J.T., and Pert, C.B. 1976. *Neuropharmacol.* 15:555-560.

Crain, S.M.; Crain, B.; Finnegan, T.; and Simon, E.J. 1979. *Life Sci.* 25: 1797-1802.

Crain, S.M.; Peterson, E.R.; Crain, B.; and Simon, E.J. 1977. *Brain Res.* 133:162-166.

Creese, I.; Pasternak, G.W.; Pert, C.B.; and Snyder, S.H. 1975. *Life Sci.* 16:1837-1842.

Creese, I., and Snyder, S.H. 1975. *J. Pharmacol. Exp. Ther.* 194:205-219.

Ehrenpreiss, S.; Greenberg, J.; and Belman, S. 1973. *Nature* 245:280-282.

Goldstein, A.; Lowney, L.I.; and Pal, B.K. 1971. *Proc. Natl. Acad. Sci. USA* 68:1742-1747.

Herkenham, M., and Pert, C.B. 1980. *Proc. Natl. Acad. Sci. USA* 77:5532-5536.

Hiller, J.M.; Pearson, J.; and Simon, E.J. 1973. *Res. Commun. Chem. Pathol. Pharmacol.* 6:1052-1062.

Hiller, J.M., and Simon, E.J. 1976. pp. 335-353. In D.H. Ford and D.H. Clouet (eds.), *Tissue Responses to Addictive Drugs*. New York: Spectrum Publications, Inc.

Hiller, J.M.; Simon, E.J.; Crain, S.M.; and Peterson, E.T. 1978. *Brain Res.* 145:396-400.

Ho, I.K.; Loh, H.H.; and Way, E.L. 1973. *J. Pharmacol. Exp. Ther.* 185: 347-357.

Howells, R.D.; Gioannini, T.L.; Hiller, J.H.; and Simon, E.J. 1982. *J. Pharmacol. Exp. Ther.* 222:629-634.

Ingoglia, N.A., and Dole, V.P. 1970. *J. Pharmacol. Exp. Ther.* 175:84-87.

Iwatsubo, K., and Clouet, D.H. 1975. *Biochem. Pharmacol.* 24:1499-1503.

Kang, S.; Sessa, G.; and Green, J.P. 1973. *Res. Commun. Chem. Pathol. Pharmacol.* 5:359-388.

Klee, W.A., and Nirenberg, K. 1976. *Nature* 263:609-612.

Klee, W.A., and Streaty, R.H. 1974. *Nature* 248:61-63.

Kuhar, M.J.; Pert, C.B.; and Snyder, S.H. 1973. *Nature* 245:447-450.

La Motte, C.; Pert, C.B.; and Snyder, S.H. 1976. *Brain Res.* 112:407-412.

Lord, J.A.H.; Waterfield, A.A.; Hughes, J.; and Kosterlitz, H.W. 1977. *Nature* 267:495-499.

Martin, W.R.; Eades, C.G.; Thompson, J.A.; Huppler, R.E.; and Gilbert, P.E. 1976. *J. Pharmacol. Exp. Ther.* 197:517-532.

Mehta, C.S., and Johnson, W. 1974. *Fed. Proc.* 33:493 (Abstr.).

Minneman, K.P. 1977 *Br. J. Pharmacol.* 59:480p-481p (Abstr.).

Pert, C.B., and Snyder, S.H. 1973. *Science* 179:1011-1014.

Pert, C.B., and Snyder, S.H. 1974. *Mol. Pharmacol.* 10:868-879.

Puri, S.K.; Cochin, J.; and Volicer, L. 1975. *Life Sci.* 16:759-768.

Robson, L.E., and Kosterlitz, H.W. 1979. *Proc. R. Soc. London.* B. 205: 425-432.

Ruegg, U.T.; Cuenod, S.; Hiller, J.M.; Gioannini, T.L.; Howells, R.D.; and Simon, E.J. 1981. *Proc. Natl. Acad. Sci. USA* 78:4635-4638.

Ruegg, U.T.; Hiller, J.M.; and Simon, E.J. 1980. *Eur. J. Pharmacol.* 64: 367-368.

Sharma, S.K.; Klee, W.A.; and Nirenberg, M. 1975. *Proc. Natl. Acad. Sci. USA* 72:3092-3096.

Simon, E.J.; Bonnet, K.A.; Crain, S.M.; Groth, J.; Hiller, J.M.; and Smith, J.R. 1980. pp. 335-346. In E. Costa and M. Trabucchi, (eds.). *Neural Peptides and Neuronal Communication.* New York: Raven Press.

Simon, E.J., and Groth, J. 1975. *Proc. Natl. Acad. Sci. USA* 72:2404-2407.

Simon, E.J.; Hiller, J.M.; and Edelman, I. 1973. *Proc. Natl. Acad. Sci. USA* 70:1947-1949.

Simon, E.J.; Hiller, J.M.; and Edelman, I. 1975. *Science* 190:389-390.

Simon, E.J.; Hiller, J.M.; Groth, J.; and Edelman, I. 1975. *J. Pharmacol. Exp. Ther.* 192:531-537.

Smith, J.R., and Simon, E.J. 1980. *Proc. Natl. Acad. Sci. USA.* 77:281-284.

Stahl, K.D.; van Bever, W.; Janssen, P.; and Simon, E.J. 1977. *Eur. J. Pharmacol.* 10:183-193.

Su, C.Y.; Lin, S.H.; Wang, Y.T.; Li, C.H.; Hung, L.H.; Lin, C.S.; and Lin, B.C. 1978. *J. Formosan Med. Assoc.* 77:133-141.

Terenius, L. 1973. *Acta Pharmacol. Toxicol.* 32:317-320.

Van Nueten, J.M.; Janssen, P.A.J.; and Fontaine, J. 1976. *Life Sci.* 18: 803-809.

Van Praag, D.; and Simon, E.J. 1966. *Proc. Soc. Exp. Biol. Med.* 122:6-11.

Zukin, R.S., and Kream, R.M. 1979. *Proc. Natl. Acad. Sci. USA* 76:1593-1597.

7

Endorphins: Cellular and Molecular Aspects for Addictive Phenomena

Floyd E. Bloom

An explosion of recent scientific reports has dealt with the endorphin peptides [1-3], the nonpeptidic endorphins [4,5], the actions of opiates [6,7], and the effects of these materials on the radioreceptor-displaceable opioid ligand binding assays [8,9].[a] These topics have become the subject of some of the most rapidly expanding chapters in the history of neuroscience, including those earlier explosions dealing with the discovery of the hypothalamic hypophysiotrophic peptides [10,11]. The following survey provides a detailed overview of the current status of work on the several frontiers of this research. Several detailed reviews are available for further pursuit [2-4,6,8,12,13].

At the time of the original molecular identification of met[5]-enkephalin (M-e) and leu[5]-enkephalin (L-e) [14], the possibility of one or more other endorphins of pituitary origin had already been suggested [15-19] when sequencing studies of the purified M-e revealed it to be the N-terminal pentapeptide [20] of the erstwhile pituitary hormone β-Lipotropin (β-LPH) [21-23]. The possibility that β-LPH was the prohormone of pituitary M-e was temporarily viable. That possible relationship appeared to be strengthened by the subsequent isolation, purification, sequencing, and synthesis of -endorphin (A-E) [24-26], β-endorphin (B-E) called also C-fragment, [23,27-31,17,32-35] γ-endorphin (G-E) [25,26,35], and δ-endorphin (D-E) called also C'-fragment [17,36]. All of these fragments of B-LPH were found in extracts of brain and pituitary, exhibited some action as specific opioid agonists, and contained M-e as their N-terminal pentapeptide. When subsequent tests in vitro [27,30,37] and in vivo [27,29,32,38,39] revealed that B-E was by far the most potent and longest acting of the natural peptides, some workers concluded that the transient opioid actions of M-e and L-e indicated that these substances were merely weakly active breakdown produces of the naturally active hormone, B-E [16,29,36,40,41]. Others interpreted the same data to mean that the natural neurotransmitter opioid peptides were the succinctly acting M-e and L-e [42,43] and regarded B-E exclusively as a pituitary product whose longer duration of action arose from proteolytic protection afforded by the greater length of its peptide

---

[a]These reports are cited by number in this chapter because they are too numerous to cite by author and date.

chain. Curiously, this greater length did not improve the potency or duration of A-E, D-E, or G-E [44]. Nevertheless, all workers seemed agreeable to the idea that opiate receptors in innervated tissues really represented the natural receptors to the endorphins and enkephalins.

Better definition of the functional roles and relations among these peptides required the development of perfected methods for the optimal preservation and extraction [45-50] of the individual peptides and the development of specific antisera for RIA [24] and immunocytochemical localization of their storage sites in brain and pituitary [19,51,52]. The results of such studies lead to the conclusion that cells containing B-E exist independently from enkephalins and from pituitary endorphins [19,51-53]. Furthermore, comparison of the actions of B-E with those of enkephalin on central and peripheral receptors has led to the postulation that there may not be simply a single monolithic class of endorphin receptors used by all the peptides but, rather, subclasses of opioid receptors that are peptide-specific [54-56].

Much recent work attests to the view that M-e is not derived from B-E at all and that L-e may also have its own precursor peptide that is completely unrelated to the molecules of the B-LPH derived endorphin series [253-255]. In addition, a very active opioid peptide, dynorphin [255] isolated from pituitary sources by Goldstein and associates, contains the L-e pentapeptide at its N-terminus, with at least eight more amino acid residues extending from the leucine in the C-terminal direction. Although the full sequence of dynorphin has not yet been reported, current evidence suggests that because of its potency greater than that of L-e on the assays of guinea pig iluem and mouse vas deferens, dynorphin is unlikely to be a simple precursor of L-e. Whether the reduced activity of L-e indicates instead that the short peptide is a by-product of dynorphin remains to be determined. However, preliminary tests in the Salk Institute laboratory in which dynorphin is applied by iontophoresis to cells of the hippocampus indicate that the longer peptide lacks the potent excitatory action produced by enkephalins and by B-E (S. Henriksen and F. Bloom, unpublished). The latter observation suggests from yet another direction the potential diversity of central endorphin receptors and the futility of attempting to base mechanisms of opiate addiction on studies of receptor processes before the nature of the true endogenous agonist is known.

Actions of Endorphins via CSF

The endorphins, particularly B-E, exhibit several very potent actions that emulate various elements of the pharmacological profile of opiates. These actions after intracerebroventricular injection to rodents consist of akinesia [38,39,54,55,57-66] hypothermia [38,67] and hyperglycemia [60,68]. At threshold doses for analgesia, respiratory depression is more pronounced in primates than it is in rodents [69; F. Bloom, S. Foote, S. Henriksen, and K. Ommaya, unpublished observations]. Cats also show cardiovascular responses, especially elevation of blood pressure [70].

Analgesia

Many workers have examined the ability of the natural and synthetic endorphins and enkephalins [see 29,56,71] to produce analgesia, an antinocisponsive effect. (The term *nocisponsive* was suggested by Clineschmidt and McGuffin [72] to reflect more accurately what is measured in such tests, namely responsiveness to noxious stimuli.) Analgesia is a complicated pharmacological action that may be the result of many independent receptor events at various levels of the nervous system. Nevertheless, the results [28,38,39,60,73-75] support the general contention that B-E is the most potent and longest acting natural endorphin and that it is thirty or more times more potent than morphine on a molar basis. The transient nature of the enkephalin effects in these tests makes the comparisons complicated, however.

Pharmacokinetics and Routes of Administration

Two related pharmacological issues concern the importance of route of administration and tolerance-development [61,66,76]. Tseng et al. [77] have observed that B-E can produce modest analgesia in the mouse tail flick after intravenous administration in the dose range of 8-20 milligrams per kilogram (mg/kg), a dose level at which some peptide may be presumed to have entered certain portions of the CNS, although this remains to be determined. When expressed on a molar basis, even these seemingly larger amounts of B-E still indicate it to be three to four times more potent in producing analgesia than morphine [38,77,78]. In cats (tail-pinch test), Feldberg and Smyth [40] have also reported that B-E (250 μg/kg) administered intravenously produced some analgesia that lasted about 20 minutes.

In the rat, subcortical EEG recordings have been found to be a highly sensitive index of central endorphin actions, with the limbic electroconvulsive activity being detectable earlier and at lower dosages than analgesia to tail pinch or loss of corneal reflexes [42,54,55,62,79]. With this index, in the rat, B-E produced no detectable actions by the intravenous route at cumulative doses up to 20 mg/kg [51,54].

Therefore, after systemic administration, B-endorphin may not accumulate in the rat brain in amounts sufficient to produce opiatelike changes.

However, even in the rat, intravenous B-E and enkephalin will cause the release of vasopressin [68], prolactin [80,81], and growth hormone [80,81] although these central effects could result from activating peripheral autonomic receptors or central receptors that are outside the blood brain barrier, such as those in median eminence and other circumventricular organs.

Tolerance to B-E administered by continuous intraventricular infusion was reported early in the course of research, when analgesia and locomotor depression were used as the primary indices [61,66,75,78, 82]. As with morphine, dependence is minimal if 24 hours of drug-free state elapse between test doses [38]. If the EEG activity is employed as the index, tolerance is not seen with intertest intervals of 8-12 hours [54]. Since the electroconvulsive activity of even a single low dose of B-E may last for as long as 4 hours [54,62] it may be difficult to distinguish between "tolerance" and reduced effectiveness due to refractoriness from a recent response. Other studies employing analgesia and withdrawal symptoms as indices have been interpreted as indicating that rats made dependent on morphine by continuous subcutaneous release show cross tolerance to the effects of centrally administered B-E [61,66,75,78,82]. However, as mentioned earlier, the meaning of withdrawal signs such as the wet dog's shaking behavior may need some reevaluation since this response is produced in opiate-naive animals on the first central injection of B-E and M-e [38,64,65].

Although little pharmacological work has been directed toward modifying the rate of synthesis or degradation of B-E by brain peptidases [36,53,83,84], available evidence suggests that B-E is relatively resistant to degradation in both plasma and CSF [48]. Structural manipulations of the endorphins have generally been directed toward synthetic pentapeptides in order to stabilize the molecule or improve its penetrance into CNS target areas. Although these developments may well lead to significant pharmacological improvements, it is not yet clear how well the synthetic analogs follow specificity differences in endorphin receptors.

Effects on Other Central Neurotransmitters

Opiates have been shown to inhibit release of transmitter from electrically activated autonomic nerve fibers [85,86]. Similar actions of M-e have been demonstrated for acetylcholine [87], noradrenaline [88], and Substance P [89] release from brain slices, and B-E shows a similar presynaptic effect on dopamine release [90,91]. In addition, intracerebroventricular injection of B-E in doses that produce akinesia, analgesia, and muscular rigidity [see below; 38,92] produces slight elevations of midbrain serotonin levels and a slight decrease in the "turnover" of midbrain DA [90,92-94]. After injections of small analgesic doses of B-E, a decrease in the turnover of acetylcholine has also been observed in cerebral cortex, hippocampus, globus pallidus, and nucleus accumbens [95,96].

Presence of Endorphins in CSF: Physiology and Pathophysiology

The pharmacological effects of the various natural and synthetic endorphins produced after injection into the CSF provide a strong basis for examining the physiological role of the natural substances in the CSF and their possible involvement in pathological states. However, before proceeding to examine the available measurements of endorphins in human CSF, some consideration must be given to what such measurements may mean. The detection of a substance in the CSF may have at least one of two major interpretations: (1) the substance escapes or is secreted into CSF only during periods of extreme activity (such as the extremes to which some experiments or disease states perturb the system), or (2) alternatively, the substance may normally be secreted into CSF by nerve fibers adjacent to or penetrating into the ventricular system, as one means of reaching targets to which intrinsic central fibers have not been extended. In the case of the maps of the endorphins [44,52,77] and enkephalins [97,98,46,99,100-103], no fibers have been observed to extend into CSF, but in every case fibers have been seen close to the ependyma. The possibility that the first explanation of CSF-measured materials may hold does not necessarily exclude the second explanation and vice versa. Nevertheless, the tenability of the escape view also raises the possibility that materials not detected within CSF (such as the enkephalins, based upon present reports [20,104,105, but also see Sarne et al. 106] may also still perform functional roles within the substance of the brain.

With combined RIAs to detect N-terminal and C-terminal segments of B-E or B-LPH, Jeffcoate et al. have reported that the lumbar CSF of normal humans does indeed contain B-endorphin (rather than possible B-LPH, which is also read by all C-terminally directed anti B-E sera). However, the amounts present are in the 50-150 picomolar (pM) range. In their subjects, Jeffcoate et al. observed more endorphinlike material in CSF than in plasma. That observation, together with substantial evidence from direct assay of normal and hypophysectomized animal brains strongly suggests the conclusion that CSF B-E arises from brain [49].

Akil et al. [104] also reported bioassay data indicating that in patients with chronic pain syndromes, electrical activation of the periaqueductal gray, a region rich in both enkephalins and endorphins, releases into the third ventricular CSF an opiatelike material originally thought to be immunoreactive enkephalin. However, repetition of these studies by the same authors employing a B-E radio-immunoassay system revealed that the material released was in fact B-E, which rose from below their limit of detectability (25 pM) to amounts in the range of hundreds of femtomols/milliliter [105]. This reinterpretation was more in keeping with the work of Hosobuchi and Li [20,63,107], who have observed in some humans that periaqueductal gray stimulation for intractable pain is naloxone-sensitive [107]; analgesia can be produced in these patients with third ventricular injections of B-E but not with enkephalin [63].

In more recent studies [20], Hosobuchi et al. found that electrical stimulation induced pain relief associated with elevated CSF levels of radio-immunoassayed B-E in those patients with periaqueductal gray stimulating electrodes. Basal levels (140-210 pg/ml; 46-70 fmol/ml; or 46-70 pM) rose twofold to sevenfold between 5 and 15 minutes after onset of stimulation. A second group of intractable pain patients obtained maximal pain relief with electrodes placed in internal capsule. This relief is not naloxone-sensitive. CSF samples from these patients showed equal basal levels to the first group but no rise during stimulation. More recent clinical studies have provided additional information on the nature of the systems regulating endorphin-mediated central analgesia. Hosobuchi et al. [256] have demonstrated that the tolerance that develops in some patients with periaqueductal gray (PAG) stimulation is associated with diminished release or immunoreactive B-E into the cerebrospinal, rather than diminished responsiveness of any neuronal receptors. Furthermore, the ability to release and the response to the implanted stimulator can be restored in these patients by treatment with 5-hydroxytryptophan. In studies done on patients with extensive chronic pain syndromes from carcinomatosis, some of whom were already tolerant to morphine, prolonged pain relief (24 hours and longer) has been achieved by the introduction of B-E into the epidural space in milligram amounts; in these patients the onset of the pain relief is very rapid, whether or not the patient was already tolerant to morphine [257]. Other recent studies [264,265] further indicate a disparity between tolerance to opiates and effectiveness of endorphine peptides.

The antisera produced in various laboratories against B-E, L-e, and M-e were obtained after coupling these antigens to bovine serum albumin [45,49,108,109,97], ovalbumin [110], hemocyanin [111,112], or other hapten carriers. The antisera prepared against B-LPH by C.H. Li did not require any coupling, because B-LPH is a large molecule (91 amino acids) with sufficient intrinsic immunogenicity [113,114].

Most sera obtained in different laboratories against M-e cross react heavily (1-10 percent cross reactivity) with L-e and vice versa. Because of the absence of a monospecific serum we still do not know if the enkephalins M-e and L-e are stored in different neurons or if they are both stored in the same set of neurons. However, by combining RIAs with HPLC-methods for peptide separation direct assessments of each pentapeptide can be made despite cross-reaction of antisera [115].

Distribution of Enkephalins

Using antisera developed independently in several laboratories against N-terminally conjugated enkephalins, a series of progressively refined reports have described the quantitative and cytological distribution [97,98,116,108,99,117] of these pentapeptides in the nervous system and other tissues.

Central Nervous System. Distributional studies on the content of enkephalins in brain were reported [50,101,118,119] before the availability of the specific radioimmunoassay. These data, obtained through the use of radioreceptor displacement assays on unpurified extracts, provided numbers that can now be considered of doubtful significance. In retrospect, the original methods gave poor recovery of endogenous peptides because of both incomplete inactivation of degrading peptidases or suboptimal extraction procedures [48].

Simantov and Snyder [101] were the first to report the results of a regional assessment of rat brain with an enkephalin radioimmunoassay in which the antisera showed at least 10 percent cross reactivity between L-e and M-e immunogens. These values were tenfold less than reported by Yang et al. [103] with results on rats killed with focused microwave irradiation. Both of these studies indicated that the amounts of M-e were some five to ten times greater than L-e, that enkephalins were generally low in cortical regions and highest in diencephalic regions, and that they were highest of all in the corpus striatum. Similar results were also obtained by others [109,110,120] but not by Simantov and Snyder [50,101], who reported that in cow brain the ratio of M-e/L-e was 0.1. More recent studies have shown that the ratio of M-e/L-e in cows was around five to ten [121] as it is in other species (rat, rabbit), that the amounts of M-e were some five to ten times greater than L-e, that enkephalins were generally low in cortical regions and highest in diencephalic regions, and that they were highest of all in the corpus striatum. Similar results were also obtained with results obtained by chemical methods. In chemical essays, L-e and M-e are separated by various chromatographic methods and then each one is separately assayed by radioimmunoassays [115,123], by radioreceptorassay [121], or by biological assay [122]. Alternatively, M-e activity is destroyed by treatment with cyanogen bromide, while L-e values remain unaffected. By differential assays before and after treatment, values for both M-e and L-e were obtained [122]. The brain region containing the lowest immunoreactive (ir) enkephalin levels is the cerebellum. Since no enkephalinergic fibers or enkephalinergic cell bodies have been reported by immunocytology in any layer of the cerebellum, one must question whether the presence of authentic enkephalin there has been established. A nonpeptidic morphinelike material has been reported to exist in cerebellum, however [124].

The estimates of enkephalins by RIAs are in general agreement with the recent quantitative regional and histological estimates of the distribution of the opiate receptors [125-127]. Nevertheless the distribution of the enkephalins and B-E system does not always parallel the opiate receptors.

Immunohistochemistry of Enkephalins in CNS. Although there have been some more detailed studies on enkephalin-containing regions [46], the best guide to the distribution of enkephalin content in brain has derived from immunohistochemistry. All of the studies that have described immunocytochemical distribution patterns are largely in agreement on the location of nuclear groups exhibiting nerve terminals in untreated rats and immunoreactive perikarya in rats pretreated with colchicine [98,108]. The following descriptions are based largely on the results of detailed studies by Uhl et al. [118] Sar et al. [99] and at the Salk Institute [unpublished results with antisera donated by R.J. Miller, University of Chicago]. Such general agreement eliminates the necessity to dwell on the possibility that slight differences in immunogens, in tissue fixation, antibody detection, or other covert causes or artifactual result have any significant bearing on the results. All of the results are to be considered as specific for enkephalins, although none alone is fully capable of absolute discrimination between M-e and L-e. The reasons underlying the reproducible finding that colchicine pretreatment facilitates the localization of enkephalin-containing perikarya remain unclear; the unproven assumption is that by disaggregating microtubules and depressing cellulofugal transport of stored peptide, immunoreactive materials accumulate within the perikaryon.

If observations are restricted to colchicine-pretreated rats, enkephalin immunoreactive cells and fibers are detected throughout the central nervous system [98,99,116,118,128, and Salk Institute results]. With four exceptions discussed separately below, no specific pathways have linked immunoreactive perikarya with specific sets of nerve terminals.

In forebrain, enkephalin-reactive neurons are found in n. accumbens, the caudate nucleus, and putamen (especially at the caudal pole) the interstitial nucleus of the stria terminalis, and the central nucleus of the amygdala. Nerve-terminal-like patterns of immunoreactivity are densest in the globus pallidus and central nucleus of the amygdala, and show generally heavy innervation of the n. accumbens, the bed nucleus of the stria terminalis, and occasional patches of intense fiber staining around pyramidal cells in the posterior cingulate gyrus and in restricted patches within the hippocampus.

In diencephalon, immunoreactive neurons are found in both the supraoptic and paraventricular nuclei and in scattered smaller cells in the perifornical region and more diffusely, in the lateral hypothalamus. Fibers have been seen in almost all hypothalamic nuclei but are especially dense in the periventricular area, in the external layer of the median eminence, and the ventromedial nucleus. Thalamic nuclei exhibit mainly nerve fibers, which are less dense than in hypothalamic areas; in thalamus reactive fibers are present within the anterior intralaminar nuclei but not in the paraventricular nuclei [99].

Within the more ventral and caudal portions of the midbrain, positively reactive perikarya have been reported for interpeduncular nucleus, the dorsal cochlear nucleus, the medial vestibular nucleus, and the spinal portion of the vestibular nucleus, as well as in isolated small neurons throughout the pontine central gray and within the general confines of the reticular zone of the brain stem. Nerve fibers are found throughout the central gray as well, and specifically innervate those nuclei made popular by their monoamine content: the zona compacta of dopamine cells in the substantia nigra, the noradrenergic neurons of the locus coeruleus, and the serotonergic neurons of the midline raphe nuclei. Reactive fibers penetrate into the fourth, seventh, tenth, and twelfth cranial nerve motor nuclei as well as the n. tractus solitarius, and the spinal portion of the trigeminal nucleus and the substantia gelatinosa. In spinal levels, enkephalin-reactive fibers are pronounced in the dorsal laminae I and II; some immunoreactive perikarya can also be seen within the dorsal horn.

Possible Enkephalin Circuits in CNS. Although the technology for tracing connectivity patterns of neuronal circuits is currently undergoing a renaissance due to the advent of new orthograde and retrograde markers, only four possible enkephalin-containing circuits have as yet been proposed from the details of cells and fibers that are immunoreactive. These proposed circuits have been based either on the results of large transecting lesions or direct tracing: none has been tested physiologically.

Hokfelt et al. [116] proposed on the basis of lesions that the enkephalin reactive neurons of the dorsal horn and of the spinal trigeminal nucleus are the source for the immunoreactive fibers of the spinal-cord dorsal horn and superficial layers of the spinal trigeminal nucleus. Cuello and Paxinos [129] also used transsections to propose that the enkephalinergic innervation of the globus pallidus may arise from the reactive neurons of the caudate nucleus and putamen, which had been suggested earlier on radioimmunoassay results [130]. Similarly, Uhl et al. [118] have proposed on the basis of transection studies that the enkephalinergic innervation of the bed nucleus of the stria terminalis arises from central nucleus of the amygdala, based also on a pathway demonstrated earlier by De Olmos [131] without chemical designation. However, after transsections of the stria terminalis, Gros et al. [132] were unable to observe any decrease of (ir) M-e levels in the bed nucleus of the stria terminalis. Direct retracing of pathways already known to exist also underlies the proposal [133] by my colleagues and me that the enkephalinergic neurons of the paraventricular and supraoptic nucleus provide the enkephalin-reactive fibers to the neural lobe. These fibers and neural lobe enkephalin content can also be shown to parallel functional or genetic changes in vasopressin content, and it was proposed that hypothalamic pars nervosa enkephalinergic pathway may modulate neurohypophysial neurosecretion [133].

Enkephalin Fibers and Opiate Receptors. These general immunocyto-chemical results can then be compared with the distribution of the chemically detected or autoradiographically detected opiate-binding properties. As acknowledged by Simantov et al. [100], at least five major discrepancies are still unexplained: (1) Receptors are very dense in caudate and putamen but not in globus pallidus where the heaviest fibers are seen. (2) Similarly the caudate and putamen are perplexingly slight in immunoreactivity for fibers, although some perikarya are seen here after colchicine treatments. (3) Cerebral cortex, which shows receptors by binding and electrophysi-ologic studies [134] shows almost no immunoreactivity. (4) Although nerve cells and fibers are exceedingly dense in the central nucleus of the amygdala, receptors are distributed more or less evenly throughout the entire amygdaloid complex. (5) Within the spinal cord the fibers of the ventral gray regions are not represented by equivalent opiate receptor values. Finally, the colchicine injections required to demonstrate enkephalin-reactive perikarya in rodents have been shown to result in a redistribution enkephalin content in only one case [262]. Enkephalin immunoreactive perikarya are visible in avian brain by standard methods and without col-chicine [263].

Distribution of Enkephalins in PNS

Gut. Although guinea pig intestinal muscle has been a primary bioassay target for detection and isolation of all the endorphins, determination of the presence of one or more of the endorphins there has received little attention [138] until quite recently. Puig et al. [139] suggested that an endogenous opiate could be undergoing release in vitro on the basis of a naloxone-induced reduction in the recovery from the decreased responsiveness to electrical stimulation shown by guinea pig ileum after high-frequency trains of stimuli. Subsequently Elde [97] made direct immunocytochemical recognition of enkephalinlike immunoreactivity in guinea pig myenteric plexus, and soon thereafter Polak et al. [140] reported that human pyloric antrum and duodenal musosal cells showed immunoreactivity within antienkepha-lin sera.

Linnoila et al. [141] have recently reported a region-by-region analysis of the guinea pig and rat intestinal tract with both immunocytochemistry and radioimmunoassay of enkephalins. Immunopositive fibers but no cell bodies were most prevalent in stomach, duodenum, and rectum of the guinea pig; concentration and number of fibers were tenfold less in the rat. Radioimmunoassay values roughly paralleled the increased fiber density seen in the stomach and rectum but with less marked variations. Interestingly, the fibers were considerably more reactive with anti-M-e sera than with anti-L-e sera; by radioimmunoassay, the M-e / L-e ratio was greater than ten. These differences were less marked in the duodenum and rectum. Within the small intestine the fibers were seen to surround the ganglion cells of the Meissner's plexus and were occasionally seen in the circular muscle; relatively few fibers were observed in the longitudinal muscle layer. Jejunum and ileum were even more sparsely innervated than duodenum. Fibers in the circular muscle layer of the colon were more reactive to anti-L-e sera than to anti-M-e sera. A few immunopositive fiber were also observed in the walls of the common bile duct and gall bladder. These observations fail to indicate why isolated myenteric longitudinal muscle strip of the guinea pig has evolved into such a sensitive in vitro bioassay system. Nevertheless, the immunoreactive intestinal nerve fibers reported in these studies would seem definitely to be intrinsic to the gut, as intestinal fibers continue to exhibit immunoreactivity in fetal mouse intestines after three weeks in organotypic cultures [142]. Recently methods for the simultaneous localization of L-e and M-e by non-cross-reacting antisera have been applied to the localization of these peptides in neurons of the myenteric plexus [258]. These results further support the independent localization and presumptive specialized function for the two enkephalins or their yet to be discovered true precursor agonists.

In 1978 Schultzberg et al. [143] reported that rat, cat, and guinea pig adrenomedulla cells contained (ir) enkephalins. By immunofluorescence all the cells of the cat adrenomedulla were strongly visualized. Moreover, nerve terminals arising from the splanchnic nerves, as shown by transsection studies, exhibited also (ir) materials. Extensive neurochemical work on the adrenal medullary peptides exhibiting enkephalinlike properties on radioimmunoassay or by bioassay indicates that this may well be a Pandora's box of unfolding discoveries: at least five such molecules have been found to contain either L-e or M-e or both [259]! In addition, human plasma immunoreactive enkephalins have been measured accurately by chemically modifying the M-e to a more antigenic sulfoxide form; although present in very low amounts, this immunoreactivity fluctuates in a circadian rhythm similar to that known for plasma catecholamines [260]. It should be realized, however, that the content of enkephalinlike peptides in adrenal medullary cells and within the catecholamine-containing storage granules from which the peptides can be released is only 1/1,000th that of the molar concentration of catecholamine [261].

Distribution of β-endorphin

Radioimmunoassay of B-E. The radioimmunoassay system used for measurement of B-E is specific for the Leu[14]-His[27] segment of the molecule. Because B-E is the COOH-terminal 31 amino acid fragment of B-LPH, this antiserum also binds on an equimolar ratio B-E, B-LPH and the 31,000 molecular weight prohormone [144-146]. In attempts to separate the immunoreactive components by gel filtration, extracts of whole rat brains were passed through a Bio-Gel P-60 column. Consistently, two peaks of immunoreactivity were resolved. One peak coincided precisely with the location of synthetic B-E; the other peak was eluted in a broad zone of larger molecular weight (10,000-30,000) that did not coincide closely with the elution pattern of either B-LPH or the 31,000 prohormone. Smyth and associates have reported similar results on porcine hypothalamus [147]. When the same brain regions are compared for B-E and enkephalin content two classes of opioid peptides vary independently from region to region [49]. Globus pallidus and caudate nucleus, which contain large numbers of immunocytochemically detected enkephalin fibers, contained virtually no B-E. Thus these data strongly suggest that B-E and enkephalin are segregated within different neuronal systems in the brain.

B-E in CNS. Using the well-characterized anti-B-E serum RB 100 of Guillemin, Ling, and Vargo [45], we have examined in detail the distribution of B-E immunoreactivity in the rat and mouse central nervous system [151]. Even in untreated rats, immunoreactive neurons and neuronal processes exhibit immunoreactivity, which is most pronounced within the diencephalon. The immunoreactive neurons exist exclusively within two adjacent clusters of the basal tuberal zone of the hypothalamus; these neurons are 10-20 micra in size, fusiform in shape, and extend from dorsolateral portions of the middle of the arcuate mucleus anterolaterally below the ventromedial nucleus, reaching almost to the lateral border of the hypothalamus. No other immunoreactive cells are observed, even after colchicine pretreatment sufficient to reveal enkephalin-immunoreactive neurons. Extensive nerve-fiber-like processes can be traced away from the B-E immunoreactive neurons into the anterior hypothalamic area, were they turned dorsally into the stria medullaris to extend along the dorsal midline of the thalamus as far caudally as the dorsal raphe nucleus. From this level the fibers extend into the central gray, moving caudally and laterally toward the locus coeruleus. Caudal to the locus coeruleus, fibers become extremely difficult to detect. Specific nuclei in which there would appear to be extensive arborization of B-E immunoreactive fibers are the supraoptic, periventricular, paraventricular, and suprachiasmatic nuclei of the hypothalamus, the dorsal and along the dorsal midline of the thalamus as far caudally as the dorsal raphe nucleus. From this level, the fibers extend into the central gray, moving caudally and laterally toward the locus coeruleus. Caudal to the locus coeruleus, fibers become extremely rare. Dorsal raphe and locus coeruleus are both innervated, but substantia nigra receives only a few fibers in the most lateral zone.

Enkephalins and Endorphins: Contrasting Distributions

Those regions most dense in enkephalin fibers show no reactivity with the antiendorphin sera; globus pallidus, central nucleus of the amygdala, and interpeduncular nucleus are all negative for B-E immunoreactivity, as is the whole of the substantia gelatinosa and dorsal horn. Direct comparisons of the B-E reactive nerve fibers and those reacted in serial sections with anti-L-e sera (from R.J. Miller, University of Chicago) indicate that B-E fibers are larger and longer in a given region the L-e reactive fibers in the same region. Observations in serial sections of staining patterns with anti sera to ACTH fragments (provided by D. Krieger, New York, by R. DiAugustine, National Institute of Environmental Health Sciences, or R. Benoit, Salk Institute) indicate that the regional distribution of this immunoreactions of the B-E reactive nerve fibers and those reacted in serial sections with anti-L-e sera indicate that B-E fibers are larger and longer in a given region than L-e-reactive fibers in the same region. Observations in serial sections of staining patterns with anti-sera to ACTH fragments showed that B-E is synthesized within a common precursor of ACTH [144,145]. The anti-B-E sera recognize B-LPH as well as B-E. Patterns of immunoreactivity with antisera to unconjugated human B-LPH are similar—if not identical—to those observed by us with RB 100 [151] and [52] with anti-ACTH serum. These data may be most conservatively explained, as we have proposed [151]: namely, that B-LPH, B-E and ACTH (or alpha MSH) may well coexist within the same neurons of the rat CNS as they are known to do within the cells of the intermediate lobe and within the corticotroph cells of the adenohypophysis. The cells and fibers observed in the human hypothalamus with antisera to human B-LPH [153] are in keeping with this idea as well. Nevertheless, the question must be regarded as incomplete pending more detailed studies of the precise patterns and ultrastructural details of the neuronal elements stained with each of these antisera.

For example, in our hands antisera to ovine or porcine B-LPH show no reactivity with rat pituitary or brain; such lack of reactivity may indicate that differences exist in the human hypothalamus with antisera to human B-LPH [153]. Nevertheless, the question must be regarded as incomplete pending more detailed studies of the precise patterns and ultrastructural details of the neuronal elements stained with each of these antisera.

In our hands, antisera to ovine or porcine B-ᵉ needed more peptide to displace 100 percent of the ^{125}I B-LPH trace, while 10 μ gm/ml of synthetic B-E gave approximately 55 percent displacement of the B-LPH trace; it seems quite possible that the antihuman B-LPH (raised against unconjugated B-LPH) also reads B-E, and that therefore this uncharacterized B-LPH antiserum cannot be used to prove or disprove the nature of the tissue reagent that exhibits immunoreactivity in rat brain. Sizing experiments on the immunoreactivity of rat brain [48] indicate that more than 67 percent of the B-E immunoreactive material coelutes with synthetic B-E, while the remainder was in some as yet uncharacterized form of larger molecular weight.

Yet another controversial aspect of the distribution of endorphins is also associated with the relationship between pituitary endorphins and brain endorphins. Yalow and her colleague Moldow have suggested that brain ACTH arises not from brain but from diffusion from the pituitary [154]. This view stems from the correlation between ACTH tissue content and distance from the basal hypothalamus and infundibulum, and from her finding that certain commercially prepared hypophysectomized animals still exhibited ACTH-immunoreactivity in plasma and in tissue scrapings from the sella turcica. This speculation on the nature of the brain ACTH source would therefore also be presumably leveled at the brain's B-E content if it could be firmly established that B-E and ACTH were made in (and released simultaneously from) the same cells. We have recently reinvestigated this problem to determine the validity of our earlier observations that brain and pituitary endorphine content were unrelated [49,146]. That conclusion was drawn on the basis of results obtained in rats that were maintained for several months after commercial hypophysectomy and also on the basis of endocrine manipulations found to result in increases or depletions of adenohypophyseal endorphin and ACTH content. Devoting special attention to the issue of basal secretion in animals that showed no plasma B-E or ACTH, and no detectable increase after ether stress, we also found no detectable ACTH or (ir) B-E in scrapings of the sella turcica; yet these animals showed a distribution of B-E and ACTH immunoreactivity indistinguishable from normal rats [Guillemin et al., in preparation].

Effects of Opioid Peptides on Neuronal Activity

Electrophysiologic research on opiates and opioid peptides has used extracellular, and more rarely intracellular, single unit recordings directed in CNS areas with either a high density of opiate receptors or involvement in nociception. To document that neuronal responses to opioids involve stereospecific opiate binding sites, two tests have been relied upon: (1) blockade of effects with an antagonist like naloxone and (2) mimicry of actions by agonists like levorphanol but not by its inactive D + enantiomer, dextrophan.

In general, the effects of opioid peptides ae the same as the effects of opiate alkaloids [however, see 155-157]. Most of these stereospecific, naloxone-antagonizable actions are inhibitions of single-unit discharge that are qualitatively similar throughout the mammalian central and peripheral nervous system. However, some major exceptions exist: naloxone-reversible excitatory responses were seen with pyramidal cells in the hippocampus [158,159], Renshaw cells in the spinal cord, and some less well identified cells in various parts of the CNS [158,160-163]. The excitatory responses of hippocampal neurons may now be viewed as a primary inhibitory effect resulting in excitation by disinhibition.

Cerebral Cortex

Only the frontal cortex contains notable concentrations of opiate binding sites [164] and relatively modest to negligible amounts of enkephalin-immunoreactivity [98,165]; neurons in frontal or parietal areas are depressed by opiate agonists via stereospecific naloxone-reversible opiate receptors [166-168]. Like opiate alkaloids, met- and leu-enkephalin depress spontaneous and l-glutamate-induced discharge of most units tested in this part of the cortex [169].

Striatum

Despite the high concentration of opiate binding sites, the role of the straitum in the pharmacology or physiology of opiates and opioid peptides remains unclear. Striatal neurons are depressed by opioid and opiate agonists applied microiontophoretically [158,170-173] or systemically [174,175]. The speeding of some neurons in substantia nigra by systemic applications [176] would be in accord with neurochemical evidence that opiates increase the synthesis and release of dopamine at striatal nerve terminals. Iontophoretic studies indicate that the inhibitions produced by opioid or by dopamine are mediated by separate receptors [171,172].

Thalamus

Noxious thermal and mechanical stimulation excites cells in the ventrobasal complex and the nucleus lateralis anterior of the thalamus. The responses are depressed by phoretically or systemically administered opiates or opioids

[177-182]. Some of these effects were antagonized by systemic naloxone; phoretically applied antagonists gave strong spike blocking side-effects [183]. In contrast to the results in the rat [180], Duggan et al. [162] found that morphine caused a naloxone-reversible increase of spontaneous and acetylcholine-induced discharge activity of neurons in the nucleus lateralis anterior of the thalamus, which is clearly not due to an interaction with the muscarinic cholinergic input to pyramidal cells [186]. This type of hippocampal unit is the most frequently encountered species when conventional multibarreled electrodes are employed [158]. However, all hippocampus studies report both excitations and inhibitions to opioids. Because some authors were unable to antagonize these excitations with phoretically applied naloxone, the specificity of the opiate-related effects, and other unspecific actions remained uncertain [187,157]. Interestingly, on some hippocampal neurons, inhibitory effects were stereospecific, and tolerance developed to the excitatory effect of opiate agonists in morphine-tolerant or morphine-dependent animals [187].

Experiments employing single and simultaneous double unit recordings from hippocampal pyramidal and basket cells have revealed that some of the excitatory responses were brought about by naloxone-sensitive inhibitory actions of opiate agonists (morphine, met-enkephalin, D-ala^2-enkephalin, β-endorphin) on nearby inhibitory interneurons, leading to disinhibition of pyramidal cells. These results indicate that the effects of a phoretically applied drug depend not only on the receptors involved but also on the circuitry in a given brain region.

Spinal Cord

Extracellular Recordings. Although most neurons located in the dorsal horn of the spinal cord are involved in somatosensory perception or in processing nociception, neurons in lamina 1 and 5 are considered to play the major role in nociceptive processes [see 188,189]. Opiate binding sites and the enkephalin-containing small neurons are concentrated in lamina 2 and 3 [97,98,100,108]. Some but not all inhibitory responses to phoretically and systemically applied opiates and opioid peptides were antagonized by naloxone, whereas some but not all excitatory responses and other effects were obviously not mediated via stereospecific opiate receptors. The dorsal horn neurons are particularly sensitive to inhibition when the opiate agonists are applied to the lamina 2 and 3 (corresponding to the substantia gelatinosa of Rolandi [160,162,155]). The mechanism of these inhibitory effects is unknown. The data would support a primary distal dendritic action of opiates, although an excitatory action on inhibitory interneurons in this layer or an effect directly on primary afferent terminals cannot now be excluded. Renshaw cells in the ventral horn of the spinal cord [190-192] are most likely not involved directly in nociception. Recent studies showed that excitations induced by opiate alkaloids [161] are mimiced by opiate peptides and are stereospecific [160,162,163]. This excitatory effect seems to be a unique property of these specialized interneurons, because here naloxone also antagonizes the excitatory (nicotinic) actions of acetylcholine.

Intracellular Studies. Early studies of morphine agonists in the spinal cord showed that intravenous administration depressed polysynaptic EPSPs (excitatory postsynaptic potential). This effect was reduced by opiate antagonists [193,194]. More recent studies employing intracellular recording and simultaneous extracellular microiontophoretic application revealed that morphine and opioid peptides do not change membrane potential or resting membrane resistance [173,195]. Nevertheless, opiates still decrease the rate of rise of the postsynaptic excitatory potential in motoneurons, interneurons, and neurons in the dorsal horn involved in somatosensory perception. These effects are antagonized by naloxone and are stereospecific.

In addition, opiates and opioids also depress the l-glutamate-induced depolarization [195]. Microiontophoretically applied l-glutamate is considered to cause an increase of the permeability of the postsynaptic membrane to sodium ions [196]. Zieglgansberger has proposed that the opiates interfere with the chemically excitable sodium channel. Since these depolarizing responses are clearly antagonized by opiate agonists, the opiate receptors involved in this effect must be located on the postsynaptic membrane.

The in vivo antiglutamate actions of opiates and opioids have recently been confirmed with spinal neurons grown in tissue culture [197]. The analysis of the kinetics of the action indicates that the inhibitory action of the opiate peptides are brought about by a noncompetitive mechanism on the postsynaptic sodium conductance mechanism. A similar interpretation was also suggested by effects of opiates upon the depolarizing response seen in neuroblastoma/glioma hybrid cells [198].

Myenteric Plexus

The analgesic potency of opiates correlates with their depressant effect upon the electrically induced twitch of the guinea pig ileum and is accurately reflected in single-unit studies [199-205]. The stereospecific depressant effect can be seen also in Ca + + free/high Mg + + solution, indicating a postsynaptic effect [206,207]. Gut is relatively rich in enkephalins, and the peptide produces actions identical to opiates: hyperpolarizing actions occasionally associated with decreased input resistance [138]. This effect is at variance to the data obtained in central neurons [173,195]. However, a common mechanism of both central and peripheral opiate receptors could still exist. If the central neurons (altered spinal neurons or intact cord neurons in vivo) were encountered while at or close to the ionic equilibrium potential for the opiate receptor, neither a shift in membrane potential or conductance might be expected. Second, nonlinearity in the current/voltage characteristic of the gut neurons (anomalous rectification) could account for the fall in membrane input resistance seen [138].

Tolerant and Dependent Animals

When animals are pretreated with increasing doses of morphine for several days, the primarily inhibitory responses [166-168] of cortical and striatal [169,173] neurons are either absent or are inverted into naloxone-insensitive excitatory responses. Increased sensitivity to the excitatory effects of opiates also occurs in Renshaw cells [163]. Cross tolerance seems likely between morphine and the opioid peptides, while the sensitivity to phoretically administered l-glutamate and acetylcholine was markedly increased in these animals [208].

Endorphins and Narcotic Addictive Phenomena

The wealth of facts from the rapidly produced flood of investigative reports on the actions of endorphins, their neuroanatomy, receptor pharmacology, and behavior-altering properties may obscure what are the truly pertinent bits of information relative to questions of narcotic abuse. Despite early reports to the contrary [232], studies on opiate receptor numbers or affinity have failed to reveal any quantitative changes in opiate binding after the development of opiate addiction or withdrawal in whole animals [233-235] although some signs of altered cell function not directly associated with opiate binding can be seen in isolated cell systems [236]. At the electrophysiological level, opiate tolerance is associated with loss or qualitative reversal of responsivity to iontophoretically applied opioids in cerebral cortex and striatum [7,168,195]. Opiate-dependent animals show cross tolerance to the analgesic and to other actions of intracerebroventricular opioid peptides [66,78]. In human narcotic addicts on methadone replacement programs, systemic B-endorphin in milligram quantities relieves some subjective symptoms of methadone withdrawal [237], but the site (central or peripheral) of this effect is not known. The neuroanatomy of the enkephalins and endorphins links endogenous opiate receptors with systems that are involved in neuronal function at almost all levels of the CNS, including many diencephalic and forebrain structures, and in particular the limbic regions, which are less likely to be involved in the perception of pain and more likely to be related (in an as yet unclear manner) with integrative or affective components of brain function.

In addition, a recent series of developments pertinent to the issue of narcotic addiction and the symptoms of narcotic withdrawal stems from a wholly unrelated line of research on the central catecholamine neurons of the locus coeruleus [LC]. Based on the behavioral effects of LC stimulation and ablation on the facial and emotional responses of stumptail macaque monkeys [238], Redmond and associates have proposed a role for this central NE nucleus in anxiety [239]. They have reported that clonidine, a drug with the properties of an alpha-2 adrenergic receptor agonist (among its other pharmacologic actions) relieves anxiety. They correlate this effect with clonidine actions on neuronal discharge of the locus coeruleus. In rats, parenteral or iontophoretic administration of clonidine depresses LC cell firing [240] presumably by the somatic receptors through with recurrent noradrenergic inhibition is mediated [241]. Piperoxane, an alpha-2 antagonist drug, accelerates firing of LC neurons in rats [241] and produces in stumptail monkeys an anxiety-type response that is reversed by clonidine [238]. Recently Aghajanian has reported that opiate dependence also alters the discharge properties of LC cells and has proposed that this shift may relate to the ability of clonidine to treat the anxiety of narcotic withdrawal [240]. In normal rats, Aghajanian confirmed the reports [242] that opiates produce potent inhibition of LC discharge and that this inhibition is naloxone-sensitive; he further observed the opiate inhibition to be independent of the receptors by which clonidine and adrenergic agonists affect LC discharge [240]. In opiate-tolerant rats, however, morphine depressions of LC neurons are reduced in potency (with different pipets in different animals, the same iontophoretic current produces 87 percent inhibition in controls and only 50 percent inhibition in morphine-dependent rats). Pertinent to the question of the role of the locus coeruleus in the central changes that follow naloxone-precipiated opiate withdrawal were the following observations: The discharge rate of locus coeruleus neurons was initially slowed by parenteral injections of morphine. Within twenty-four hours after implantation of subcutaneous morphine pellets, LC neurons adapt to the presence of the circulating opiate and resume normal rates of discharge. After four or five days of opiate exposure and when challenged with parenteral naloxone, LC units show a prompt acceleration. (Naloxone was reported not to produce speeding of LC units in control rates.) Furthermore, iontophoretic or parenteral clonidine was still able to reduce the accelerated firing of the LC neurons during the naloxone-induced withdrawal from the opiate-dependent state [240]. Based on these observations, Redmond and associates report reduced withdrawal symptoms and lessened narcotic craving in addicts treated with anxiety-reducing doses of clonidine [239].

Like the effects of 6-hydroxydopamine treatment, long-term exposure to morphine leads to an increase of beta noradrenergic receptivity in cortex and an increase in the ability of NE to activate adenylate cyclase [243]. However, this effect is not easily predicted from the normal or enhanced firing seen by Aghajanian in his rats treated with different doses of morphine for different durations. Furthermore, the response of LC neurons to opiates [242] or to opioid peptides at naloxone-reversible receptors, would presumably represent the postsynaptic receptors for the enkephalin- or endorphin-containing nerve fibers that project to LC [97,99,151,244]. If these endorphin peptide circuits are at all tonically active, however, it is difficult to understand why naloxone treatment in normal rats does not "disinhibit" the LC cells. Another potential source of confusion derives from reports that clonidine may act as a histamine H-2 receptor agonist [245], and as an antagonist to the direct depressant effects of adenosine and other adenine nucleotides [246]. In other reports, clonidine actions have also been classified as an alpha antagonist [247]. Nevertheless, one might conclude from this line of research that chronic treatment with opiates does lead to alterations of physiological activity within the central noradrenergic neurons and may therefore by indirect evidence also act on their target cells. Whether such effects also apply to other circuits bearing detectable opiate receptors remains to be determined.

Although very few studies of receptor sensitivity changes have been carried out on neurons that are known to be the targets of one or another endorphin-mediated circuit, the present situation with regard to opiate receptor numbers after chronic treatment with opiate alkaloids makes these receptors somewhat different from other hormone and transmitter receptors that have been studied dynamically [234,235,245,248]. In the instances of other transmitters and hormones, experimental changes that increase transmitter occupation of postsynaptic receptors, such as loading with precursors or long-acting agonists or preventing re-uptake or catabolism all lead to decreased numbers of transmitter binding sites and to decreased sensitivity [248-251]. Conversely changes in receptor occupancy caused by diminished release or response to the natural ligand generally result in more ligand binding sites and more responsiveness [248-251]. The latter set of findings makes it difficult to understand how it is that naloxone produces the immediate withdrawal symptoms in the morphine-dependent animal and suggests that additional studies focused on sites of endorphinergic transmission may be important.

Neurochemical Basis of Behavior: General Considerations

How might cellular and molecular pharmacological evidence relate to possible explanations of behavioral pehnomena in terms of specific chemical transmitters. For example, over the past two decades brain monoamines have been implicated as "the" critical chemical mediators of a variety of physiological-behavioral outputs of the brain, ranging from feeding, drinking, thermoregulatory and sexual behavior on the one pole to pleasure, reinforcement, attention, motivation, memory, learning-cognition, the major psychoses and their chemotherapy at the other. Although many such hypotheses have been put forth, and to variable degrees supported, negated, and endlessly debated with experimental and correlative evidence, it seems fair to admit that even among diehard supporters of monoamines, there is no conclusive proof that a monoamine mediates any behavior. In fact, the same general conclusion could be given with regard to every defined transmitter system, with very few possible exceptions.

Why is it so hard to establish a behavioral-level mediator role for a chemically defined transmitter substance? Confronting this question seriously may illuminate some of the obstacles to be faced when trying to apply similar strategies to more recently discovered transmitters like the neuropeptide endorphins. At the molecular level, most neurotransmitters are still undefined and unidentified, and their sites and mechanisms of action unresolved. At the cellular level, the precise wiring diagrams are still not comprehensively mapped for even those brain regions composed of redundant, similarly constructed modular cell ensembles such as are recognized in cerebellum, hippocampus, olfactory bulb, or retina; nor do we understand very much about how these cell ensembles work together to process information and communicate the results to the other near or distant regions to which they are directly connected. However, even when the criteria can be satisfied to document that a specific chemical does transmit between two given neurons and, in turn, that cellular step can be integrated into the *overall* functional circuitry of the connected micro- or macroregions, there are no generally accepted criteria that could be satisfied experimentally to establish that such an X-ergic circuit mediates a behaviorally defined phenamenon.

What criteria could establish the neurochemical basis of regulatory events underlying normal behaviors? Could analogous criteria be devised for the more complex questions of the neurochemical basis underlying the neuropathology of an abnormal behavior? For the purpose of exposition, the argument requires several primary assumptions that in fact cannot now withstand critical analysis without considerably more evidence.

1. Let us define the basic operational unit of behavior as a response and assume that any given behavior B may be executed through different levels of complexity within the nervous system. Let us further assume that each B must be operationally defined within each complexity examined, and that the antecedents of B, generated either by internal or external stimuli, can be clearly defined.

2. We must also assume that populations of nerve cells able to have a role in behavior can be reliably designated under normal conditions. In fact, some experienced analysts of human and animal behavior might be moved to the view that the brain does not really generate normal behavior but, rather, simply reacts in predetermined or predisposed ways to general classes of exogenous or endogenous stimuli. If that view were valid, we refer here to the neural ensembles responding to a defined class of stimuli with an output leading to performance of a defined behavior.

3. We next assume that these nerve cells are organized within a processing module capable of receiving and transmitting information to an output system that executes the subroutine of skeletal muscular coordination necessary to perform B.

Given these assumptions, one could then reason that under a standard condition, behavior B is mediated by transmitter T, when the following relationship can be demonstrated:

1. T is the transmitter for any of the neuron ensembles that participate in the processing between input and output.

2. Spatially and temporally appropriate enhancement of the availability of T within the brain elicits B ("appropriate" here is hard to specify).

3. Elimination of T or its specific antagonism prevents the elicitation of B by stimulation of T.

4. Activity in the neuron ensembles containing T predicts B.

It is also immediately obvious that if the cells responsible for B are widely dispersed and a certain number of this subpopulation must be active simultaneously before B occurs, appropriate simulation by delivery of exogenous T into the CNS may not be possible. Similarly if T also occurs in other cellular arrays (is not unique to B or to B-activating stimuli) replication even with appropriate delivery may not be precise or selective.

Having made these stipulations and having set up these criteria, the next step is to apply these concepts to our analysis of the function of the endorphins in the nervous system. First, endorphins have been identified in secreting organs such as the pituitary and in neurons, and, in general, these sites have been shown to have a role in pain relief, locomotor activation (central nervous system), and stress (both central nervous system and pituitary), and learning (central nervous system and pituitary).

Second, opiates and endorphins injected intraventricularly or intracerebrally have clearly identified effects in pain relief and locomotor activation. Opiates peripherally and centrally also appear to inhibit the performance or memory of aversively motivated learning, a phenonemon not generally shared by low doses of endorphins themselves, however.

Third, elimination or blockade of endorphins by naloxone prevents morphine and endorphin pain relief and blocks the activation due to opiates. Identification of the specific pathways involved remains for future research. In learning situations, naloxone clearly blocks the effects of morphine: yet the interaction with the effects of endorphins themselves remains confused at best. In fact, in certain situations naloxone and low doses of endorphins appear to produce the same results.

Finally, no studies to date have successfully demonstrated a direct relationship between the amounts of endorphin released during a behvioral effect and, the amount of endorphin available to elicit a behavioral effect.

Thus, as with the monoamines (perhaps even more so because of the potentially large neuroendorcrinological contribution), identification of all specific roles for the endorphins in behavior remains a challenge. It is the satisfaction of these criteria that needs to be met before one can speculate about the role of endorphins in normal and pathophysiological behavior.

Having gone through this exercise in logic and experimental design and matched the cellular and molecular observations to those of behavioral phenomena within the limited scope on which such data can be compared, yet another exercise of possible strategic importance may envisioned. Noted previously, within the body of the initial assumptions, was the virtually implicit tenet that there is "a neurochemical basis underlying the neuropathology of behavior." Indeed the relatively new field of biological psychiatry generally rests upon this tenet and its corollary that the pathological process may be detected through objective measurements on neurotransmitters or their by-products in biological fluids or tissues of mentally ill patients (or, in the present case, drug abusers). In fact, what the soundest of these neurochemical observations gives us are correlations between a given behavioral syndrome and a given neurotransmitter. In contrast, the foregoing exercise has been designed to pursue the kinds of experimental evidence that would be required to establish causal relations between a system of neurons operating through secretion of an identifiable transmitter and an abnormal behavioral state. Nevertheless, whether dealing with a epiphenomenal correlate or a direct causative neurochemically specifiable process, all of the foregoing has assumed that there will eventually be found a chemically or functionally demonstrable pathology in the hardware of the brain (its cells and molecules). At present there is no obvious reason why an abnormality expressed as abnormal behavior could not be based upon instead upon a problem in the "software" of the brain, if there is one (the unconscious cell system interaction sequences that form the strategies for recognizing, analyzing, and acting upon information of the external or internal environment). Those software abnormalities could in fact be easily viewed as leading to abnormalities in transmitter formation or utilization, without that chemical step itself being a direct pathological

pathological phenomenon but, rather, more properly its epiphenomenal correlate. Perhaps it is not too soon to begin thinking of strategies by which these two rather different views could be contrasted and tested.

References

1. Kosterlitz, H.W., and Hughes, J. 1978. *Adv. Biochem. Psychopharmacol.* 18:31-44.
2. Childers, S.W.; Schwarcz, R.; Coyle, J.T.; and Snyder, S.H. 1978, *Adv. Biochem. Psychoparmacol.* 18:161-174.
3. Terenius, L. 1978. *Ann. Rev. Pharmacol.* 18:189-204.
4. Terenius, L. 1978. *Adv. Biochem. Psychopharm.* 18:321-332.
5. Gintzler, A.R.; Gershon, M.D.; and Spector, S. 1978. *Science* 199:477-478.
6. Bloom, F.E.; Rossier, J.; Battenberg, E.L.F.; Bayon, A.; French, E.; Henriksen, S.J.; Siggins, G.R.; Siegal, D.; Browne, R.; Ling, N.; and Guillemin, R. 1978. *Adv. Bioch. Psychopharmacol.* 18:89-110.
7. Zieglgansberger, W., et al. 1978. In J.M. Van Ree and L. Terenius (eds.), *Characteristics and Functions of Opioids,* Amsterdam: Elsevier. pp. 75-86.
8. Simon, E., and Hiller, J.M. 1978. *Ann. Rev. Pharmacol.* 18:371-394.
9. Hollt, V., and Herz, A. 1978. *Fed. Proc.* 37:158-161.
10. Guillemin, R. 1978. *Science* 202:390-401.
11. Schally, A. 1978. *Science* 202:18-28.
12. Snyder, S.H. 1978. *Am. J. Psychiatry* 135:645-652.
13. Goldstein, A. 1976. *Science* 193:1081-1086.
14. Hughes, J.; Smith, T.W.; Kosterlitz, H.W.; Fothergill, L.A.; Morgan, B.A.; and Morris, H.R. 1975. *Nature* 258:577-580.
15. Cox, B.M.; Opheim, K.E.; Teschemacher, H.; and Goldstein, N.A. 1975. *Life Sci.* 16:1777-1782.
16. Goldstein, A. 1976. *Science* 193:1081-1086.
17. Graf, L.; Ronai, A.Z.; Bajusz, S.; Cseh, G.; and Szekely, J.I. 1976. *Febs. Lett.* 64:181-185.
18. Ross, M.; Dingledine, R.; Cox, B.M.; and Goldstein, A. 1977. *Brain Res.* 124:523-532.
19. Teschemacher, H.; Opheim, K.E.; Cox, B.M.; and Goldstein, A. 1976. *Life Sci.* 16:1771-1775.
20. Hosobuchi, Y.; Rossier, J.; Bloom, F.E.; and Guillemin, R. 1979. *Science* 203:279-381.
21. Li, C.H. 1964. *Nature* 201:924.
22. Li, C.H.; Barnafi, L.; Chretien, M.; and Chung, D. 1965. *Nature* 208:1093-1094.

23. Li, C.H., and Chung, D. 1976. *Proc. Natl. Acad. Sci. U.S.A.* 73:1145-1148.
24. Guillemin, R.; Ling, N.; and Burgus, R. 1976. *Comptes Rendus Acad. Sci. Paris Ser. D.* 283:783-785.
25. Ling, N. 1977. *Biochem. Biophys. Res. Commun.* 74:248-256.
26. Ling, N.; Burgus, R.; and Guillemin, R. 1976. *Proc. Natl. Acad. Sci. U.S.A.* 73:3942-3946.
27. Bradbury, A.F.; Feldberg, W.F.; Smyth, D.G.; and Snell, C.R. 1976. In H.W. Kosterlitz (ed.), *Opiates and Endogenous Opioid Peptides, pp. 9-17.* Amsterdam: Elsevier.
28. Bradbury, A.F.; Smyth, D.G.; Snell, C.R.; Birdsall, N.J.M.; and Holme, E.C. 1976. *Nature* 260:793-795.
29. Bradbury, A.F.; Smyth, D.G.; Snell, C.R.; Deaken, J.F.W.; and Nendlandt, S. 1977. *Biochem. Biophys. Res. Commun.* 74:748-754.
30. Doneen, B.A.; Chung, D.; Yamashiro, D.; Law, P.Y.; Loh, H.H.; and Li, C.H. 1977. *Biochem. Biophys. Res. Commun.* 74:656-662.
31. Dragon, N.; Seidah, N.G.; Lis, M.; Routhier, R.; and Chretien, M. 1977. *J. Biochem.* 55:666-670.
32. Graf, L.; Szekely, J.I.; Ronai, A.Z.; Dunai-Kovacs, A.; and Bajusz, S. 1976. *Nature (London)* 263:240-242.
33. Li, C.H.; Lemaire, S.; Yamashiro, D.; and Doneen, B.A. 1976. *Biochem. Biophys. Res. Commun.* 71:19-25.
34. Li, C.H.; Yamashiro, D.; Tseng, L.F.; Loh, H.H. 1977. *Med. Chem.* 20:325-328.
35. Ling, N., and Guillemin, R. 1976. *Proc. Natl. Acad. Sci. U.S.A.* 73:3308-3310.
36. Smyth, D.G., and Snell, C.R. 1977. *Febs. Lett.* 78:225-228.
37. Lazarus, L.H.; Ling, N.; and Guillemin, R. 1976. *Proc. Natl. Acad. Sci. U.S.A.* 73:2156-2159.
38. Bloom, F.E.; Segal, D.; Ling, N.; and Guillemin, R. 1976. *Science* 194:630-632.
39. Loh, H.H.; Tseng, L.F.; Wei, E.; and Li, C.H. 1976. *Proc. Natl. Acad. Sci. U.S.A.* 73:2895-2898.
40. Feldberg, W., and Smyth, D.G. 1977. *J. Physiol. (London)* 265:25-27 P.
41. Geisow, M.J.; Deakin, J.F.W.; Dostrovsky, J.O.; and Smyth, D.G. 1977. *Nature* 269:167-168.
42. Urca, G.; Frenk, H.; Liebeskind, J.C.; and Taylor, A.N. 1977. *Science* 197:83-86.
43. Volavka, J.; Marya, A.; Baig, S.; and Perez-Cruet, J. 1977. *Science* 106:1227-1228.
44. Bloom, F.; Rossier, J.; Battenberg, E.; Vargo, T.; Minick, S.; Ling, N.; and Guillemin, R. 1977. *Neurosci. Abstr.* 3:286.

45. Guillemin, R.; Ling, N.; and Vargo, T.M. 1977. *Biochem. Biophys. Res. Commun.* 77:361-366.
46. Kobayashi, R.M.; Palkovits, M.; Miller, R.J.; Chang, K.J.; and Cuatrecasas, P. 1978. *Life Sci.* 22:527-530.
47. Krieger, D.T.; Liotta, A.; Suda, T.; Palkovits, M.; and Brownstein, M.J. 1977. *Biochem. Biophys. Res. Commun.* 26:930-936.
48. Rossier, J.; Bayon, A.; Vargo, T.; Ling, N.; Guillemin, R.; and Bloom, F. 1978. *Life Sci.* 21:847-852.
49. Rossier, J.; Vargo, T.M.; Minick, S.; Ling, N.; Bloom, F.; and Guillemin, R. 1977. *Proc. Natl. Acad. Sci. U.S.A.* 74:5162-5165.
50. Simantov, R., and Snyder, S.H. 1976. *Proc. Natl. Acad. Sci. U.S.A.* 73:2515-2519.
51. Bloom, F.; Battenberg, E.; Rossier, J.; Ling, N.; Leppaluoto, J.; Vargo, T.M.; and Guillemin, R. 1977. *Life Sci.* 20:43-48.
52. Bloom, F.E.; Rossier, J.; Battenberg, E.L.F.; Bayon, A.; French, E.; Henriksen, S.; Siggins, G.R.; Segal, D.; Browne, R.; Ling, N.; and Guillemin, R. 1978. In E. Costa (ed.), *Endorphins,* 141-157. New York: Raven Press.
53. Austen, B.M., and Smyth, D.G. 1977. *Biochem. Biophys. Res. Comm.* 26:86-94.
54. Henriksen, S.J.; Bloom, F.E.; McCoy, F.; Ling, N.; and Guillemin, R. 1978. *Proc. Natl. Acad. Sci. U.S.A.* 75:5221-5225.
55. Henriksen, S.J.; McCoy, F.; French, E.; and Bloom, F.E. 1978. *Soc. Neurosci. Abstr.* 4:408.
56. Lord, J.A.H.; Waterfield, A.A.; Hughes, J.; and Kosterlitz, H.W. 1977. *Nature (London)* 267:495-499.
57. Belluzzi, J.D.; Garnt, N.; Garsky, V.; Safrantakis, D.; Wise, C.D.; and Stein, L. 1976. *Nature* 260:625-626.
58. Bhargava, H.N. 1978. *J. Pharm. Sci.* 67:136-137.
59. Buscher, H.H.; Hill, R.C.; Romer, D.; Cardinaux, F.; Closse, A.; Hauser; D., and Pless, J. 1976. *Nature* 261:423-425.
60. Feldberg, W., and Smyth, D.G. 1976. *J. Physiol.* 260:30-31P.
61. Gispen, W.H.; Wiegent, V.M.; Bradbury, A.F.; Hulme, E.C.; Smyth, D.; Snell, C.R.; and de Wied, D. 1976. *Nature* 264:792-794.
62. Henriksen, S.J.; Bloom, F.E.; Ling, N.; and Guillemin, R. 1977. *Soc. Neurosci. Abstr.* 3:293.
63. Hosobuchi, Y., and Li, C.H. 1978. *Comm. Psychopharmacol.* 2:33-37.
64. Leybin, L.; Pinsky, C.; La Bella, F.S.; Havlicek, V.; and Rezek, M. 1976. *Nature* 264:458-459.
65. Segal, D.S.; Browne, R.G.; Bloom, F.; Ling, N.; and Guillemin, R. 1977: *Science* 198:411-414.
66. Tseng, L.-F.; Loh, H.H.; and Li, C.H. 1976. *Proc. Natl. Acad. Sci. U.S.A.* 73:4187-4189.

67. Holaday, J.W.; Law, P.-Y.; Tseng, L.-F.; Loh, H.H.; and Li, C.H. 1977. *Proc. Natl. Acad. Sci. U.S.A.* 74:4628-4632.
68. Guillemin, R.; Bloom, F.E.; Rossier, J.; Minick, S.; Henriksen, S.; Burgus, R.; and Ling, N. 1977. In I. McIntyre (ed.), *Sixth International Conferences on Endocrinology,* pp. 221-2235. Amsterdam: Elsevier.
69. Moss, I.R., and Friedman, E. 1978. *Life Sci.* 23:1271-1276.
70. Feldberg, W., and Wei, E. 1978. *J. Physiol.* 280:18P.
71. McGregor, W.H.; Stein, L.; and Belluzzi, J.D. 1978. *Life Sci.* 23:1371-1378.
72. Clineschmidt, B.V.; McGuffin, J.; and Bunting, P.B. 1979. *Europ. J. Pharmacol.* 54:129-141.
73. Meglio, M.; Hosobuchi, Y.; Loh, H.H.; Adams, J.E.; and Li, C.H. 1977. *Proc. Natl. Acad. Sci. U.S.A.* 74:774-776.
74. Roemer, D.; Buescher, H.H.; Hill, R.C.; Pless, J.; Bauer, W.; Cardinaux, F.; Closse, A.; Hauser, D.; and Hugenin, R. 1977. *Nature* 268:549-574.
75. Szekeley, J.I.; Ronai, A.Z.; Dunai, R.; Kovacs, Z.; Miglecz, E.; Bajusc, S.; and Graf, L. 1975. *Life Sci.* 20:1259-1264.
76. Wei, E., and Loh, H.H. 1976. *Science* 193:1262-1264.
77. Tseng, L.-F.; Loh, H.H.; and Li, C.H. 1976. *Nature* 263:239-240.
78. Tseng, L.F.; Loh, H.H.; and Li, C.H. 1977. *Biochem. Biophys. Res. Commun.* 74:390-396.
79. Frenk, H.; Urca, G.; and Liebeskind, J.C. 1978. *Brain Res.* 147: 327-337.
80. DuPont, A.; Cusan, L.; Garon, M.; Labrie, F.; and Li, C.H. 1977. *Proc. Natl. Acad. Sci. U.S.A.* 74:358-359.
81. Rivier, C.; Vale, W.; Ling, N.; Brown, M.; and Guillemin, R. 1977. *Endocrinology* 100:238-241.
82. Wei, E.; Loh, H.H.; and Way, E.L. 1973. *J. Pharmacol. Exp. Therapeutics* 185:108-115.
83. Austen, B.M., and Smyth, D.G. 1977. *Biochem. Biophys. Res. Comm.* 76:447-482.
84. Kosterlitz, H.W.; Hughes, J.; Lord, J.A.H.; and Waterfield, A.A. 1977. In W.M. Cowan and J.A. Ferrendelli (eds.), *Society for Neuroscience, Symposia, vol. 2,* pp. 291-301. Bethesda, Md.: Society for Neuroscience.
85. Kosterlitz, H.W.; Lord, J.A.H.; and Watt, A.J. 1973. In H.O.J. Collier and J.E. Villareal (eds.), *Agonist and Antagonist Actions of Narcotic Analgesic Drugs,* pp. 45-61. Baltimore, Md.: University Park Press.
86. Paton, W.D.M. 1957. *Brit. J. Pharmacol. Chemother.* 12:119-137.
87. Jhamandas, K.; Sawynok, J.; and Sutak, M. 1977. *Nature* 260:433-434.

88. Taube, H.D.; Borowski, E.; Endo, T.; and Starke, K. 1976. *European J. Pharmacol.* 38:377-380.
89. Jessel, T.M., and Iversen, L.L. 1977. *Nature* 268:549-551.
90. Berney, S., and Hornykiewicz, O. 1977. *Comm. Psychopharmacol.* 1:597-604.
91. Loh, H.H.; Brase, D.A.; Sampath-Khanna, S.; Mar, J.B.; Way, E.L.; and Li, C.H. 1976. *Nature* 264:567-568.
92. Jacquet, Y.F., and Marks, N. 1976. *Science* 194:632-635.
93. Van Loon, G.R., and De Souza, E.B. 1978. *Life Sci.* 23:971-978.
94. Van Loon, G.R. and Kim, C. 1978. *Life Sci.* 23:961-970.
95. Moroni, F.; Cheney, D.L.; and Costa, E. 1977. *Nature* 267:267-269.
96. Moroni, F.; Cheney, D.L.; and Costa, E. 1978. *Neuropharmacol.* 171:191-198.
97. Elde, R.; Hokfelt, T.; Johansson, O.; and Terenius, L. 1976. *Neurosci.* 1:349-351.
98. Hokfelt, T.; Elde, R.; Johansson, O.; Terenius, L.; and Stein, L. 1977. *Neurosci. Lett.* 5:25-31.
99. Sar, M.; Stumpf, W.E.; Miller, R.J.; Chang, K.J.; and Cuatrecasas, P. 1978. *J. Comp. Neurol.* 182:17-38.
100. Simantov, R.; Kuhar, M.J.; Uhl, G.R.; and Snyder, S.H. 1977. *Proc. Natl. Acad. Sci. U.S.A.* 74:2167-2171.
101. Simantov, R., and Snyder, S.H. 1976. In H.W. Kosterlitz (ed.), *Opiates and Endogenous Peptides,* pp. 41-48. Amsterdam: Elsevier.
102. Watson, S.J.; Akil, H.; Richards, C.W., III; and Barchas, J.D. 1978. *Nature* 275:225-227.
103. Yang, H.Y.; Hong, J.S.; and Costa, E. 1977. *Neuropharmacol.* 16:303-307.
104. Akil, H.; Richardson, D.E.; Hughes, J.; and Barchas, J.D. 1978. *Science* 201:463-465.
105. Akil, H.; Richardson, D.E.; Barchas, J.D.; and Li, C.H. 1978b. *Proc. Natl. Acad. Sci. U.S.A.* 75:5170-5172.
106. Sarne, Y.; Azov, R.; and Weissman, B.A. 1978. *Brain Res.* 151:399-403.
107. Hosobuchi, Y., Adams, J.E., and Linchitz, R. 1977. *Science* 197:183-186.
108. Watson, S.J.; Akil, H.; Sullivan, S.; and Barchas, J. 1977. *Life Sci.* 21:733-738.
109. Miller, R.J.; Chang, K.J.; Cooper, B.; and Cuatrecasas, P. 1978. *Biol. Chem.* 253:531-538.
110. Gros, C.; Pradelles, P.; Rougeot, C.; Bepoldin, O.; Dray, F.; Fournie-Zaluski, M.C.; Roques, B.P.; Pollard, H.; Llorens-Cortes, C.; and Schwartz, J.C. 1978. *J. Neurochem.* 31:29-39.
111. Hong, J.S.; Yang, H.Y.; Fratta, W.; and Costa, E. 1977. *Brain Res. 134:383-386.*

112. Childers, S.; Schwarcz, R.; Coyle, J.; and Snyder, S. 1978. In E. Costa and M. Trabucchi (eds.), *Endorphins,* pp. 161-174. New York: Raven Press.

113. Rao, A.J., and Li, C.H. 1977. *Peptide Protein Res.* 10:167-171.

114. Watson, S.J.; Barchas, J.D.; and Li, C.H. 1971. *Proc. Natl. Acad. Sci. U.S.A.* 74:5155-5158.

115. Bayon, A.; Rossier, J.; Mauss, A.; Bloom, F.E.; Iversen, L.L.; Ling, N.; and Guillemin, R. 1978. *Proc. Natl. Acad. Sci. U.S.A.* 75:3503-3506.

116. Hokfelt, T.; Ljungdahl, A.; Terenius, L.; Elde, R.; and Nilsson, G. 1977. *Proc. Natl. Acad. Sci. U.S.A.* 74:3081-3085.

117. Pasternak, G.W.; Simantov, R.; and Snyder, S.H. 1976. *Mol. Pharmacol.* 12:504-513.

118. Uhl, G.; Kuhar, M.; and Snyder, S. 1978. *Brain Res.* 149:223-228.

119. Hughes, J. 1975. *Brain Res.* 88:295-308.

120. Gillin, J.C.; Hong, J.S.; Yang, H.Y.T.; and Costa, E. 1975. *Proc. Natl. Acad. Sci. U.S.A.* 75:2991-2993.

121. Lewis, R.V.; Stein, S.; Gerber, L.D.; Rubinstein, J.; and Udenfriend, S. 1978. *Proc. Natl. Acad. Sci. U.S.A.* 75:3473-3477.

122. Hughes, J.; Kosterlitz, H.W.; and Smith, T.W. 1977. *Brit. J. Pharmac.* 61:639-647.

123. Hong, J.S.; Yang, H.Y.T.; Fratta, W.; and Costa, E. 1978. *J. Pharmacol. Exp. Therapeutics* 205:141-147.

124. Gintzler, A.R.; Gershon, M.D.; and Spector, S. 1978. *Science* 199:447-448.

125. Atweh, S., and Kuhar, M. 1977. *Brain Res.* 124:53-67.

126. Atweh, S., and Kuhar, M. 1977. *Brain Res.* 129:1-12.

127. Atweh, S., and Kuhar, M. 1977. *Brain Res.* 124:393-405.

128. Barchas, J.D.; Akil, H.; Elliott, G.R.; Holman, R.B.; and Watson, S.J. 1978. *Science* 200:964-973.

129. Cuello, A.C., and Paxinos, G. 1978. *Nature* 271:178-180.

130. Hong, J.S.; Yang, H.Y.T.; and Costa, E. 1977. *Neuropharmacology* 16:451-453.

131. De Olmos, J. 1972. B. Eleftheriou (ed.), *The Neurobiology of Amygdala,* pp. 145-204. New York: Plenum Press.

132. Gros, C.; Pradelles, P.; Dray, F.; Le Gal La Salle, G.; and Ben-Air, Y. 1978. *Neurosci. Lett.* 10:193-196.

133. Rossier, J.; Pittman, Q.; Battenberg, E.; Pittman, Q.; Bayon, A.; Koda, L.; Miller, R.; Guillemin, R.; and Bloom, F. 1979. *Nature* 277:653-655.

134. Zieglgansberger, W.; French, E.; Siggins, G.R.; and Bloom, F.E. 1979. Pp. 75-86. *Proc. Int. Narcotic Club,* Amsterdam.

135. De Bodo, R.C. 1944. *J. Pharmacol. Exp. Therapeutics* 82:74-85.

136. Tseng, L.-F.; Loh, H.H.; and Li, C.H. 1978. *Int. J. Peptide Res.* 12:173-176.
137. Simantov, R., and Snyder, S. 1977. *Brain Res.* 124:178-184.
138. Smith, T.W.; Hughes, J.; Kosterlitz, H.W.; and Sosa, R.P. 1976. In H.W. Kosterlitz (ed.), *Opiate and Endogenous Opioid Peptides,* pp. 57-62. Amsterdam: Elsevier.
139. Puig, M.H.; Gascon, P.; Craviso, G.L.; and Musacchio, J.M. 1977. *Science* 195:419-420.
140. Polak, J.M.; Bloom, S.R.; Sullivan, S.N.; Facer, P.; and Pearse, A.G.E. 1977. *Lancet* 1:972-974.
141. Linnoila, R.I.; DiAugustine, R.P.; Miller, R.J.; Chang, K.J.; and Cuatrescasas, P. 1978. *Neuroscience* 4 (3):1187-1196.
142. Schultzberg, M.; Dreyfus, C.F.; Gershon, M.D.; Hokfelt, T.; Elde, P.; Nilsson, G.; Said, S.; and Goldstein, M. 1978. *Brain Res.* 155:239-248.
143. Schultzberg, M.; Lundberg, J.M.; Hokfelt, T.; Terenius, L.; Brandt, J.; Elde, R.P.; and Goldstein, M. 1978. *Neuroscience* 3:1174-1186.
144. Mains, R.E.; Eipper, B.A.; and Ling, N. 1977. *Proc. Natl. Acad. Sci. U.S.A.* 74:3014-3018.
145. Roberts, J.L., and Herbert, E. 1977. *Proc. Natl. Acad. Sci. U.S.A.* 74:5300-5304.
146. Rossier, J.; French, E.; Rivier, C.; Ling, N.; Guillemin, R.; and Bloom, F. 1977. *Nature* 170:618-620.
147. Smyth, D.G.; Snell, C.R.; and Massey, D.E. 1978. *Biochem. J.* 175:261-270.
148. Liotta, A.S.; Suda, T.; and Krieger, D.T. 1979. *Proc. Natl. Acad. Sci. U.S.A.* 75:2950-2954.
149. Yoshimi, H.; Matsukura, S.; Sueoka, S.; Fukase, M.; Yokota, M.; Hirata, Y.; and Imura, H. 1978. *Life Sci.* 22:2189-2196.
150. Rubinstein, M.; Stein, S.; and Udenfriend, S. 1977. *Proc. Natl. Acad. Sci. U.S.A.* 74:4969-4972.
151. Bloom, F.; Battenberg, E.; Rossier, J.; Ling, N.; and Guillemin, R. 1978. *Proc. Natl. Acad. Sci. U.S.A.* 75:1591-1595.
152. Watson, S.J.; Richard, C.W., III; and Barchas, J.D. 1978. *Science* 200:1180-1182.
153. Pelletier, G.; Desy, L.; Lissitszky, J.C.; Labrie, F.; and Li, C.H. 1978. *Life Sci.* 22:1799-1804.
154. Moldow, R., and Yalow, R.S. 1978. *Proc. Natl. Acad. Sci.* 75:994-998.
155. Duggan, A.W.; Hall, J.G.; and Headley, P.M. 1976. *Nature* 264:456-458.
156. Carette, B., and Poulain, P. 1978. *Neurosci. Lett.* 7:137-140.
157. Segal, M. 1977. *Neuropharmacol.* 16:587-592.

158. Nicoll, R.A.; Siggins, G.R.; Ling, N.; Bloom, F.E.; and Guillemin, R. 1977. R.: *Proc. Natl. Acad. Sci. U.S.A.* 75:1591.

159. Hill, R.G.; Mitchell, J.F.; and Pepper, C.M. 1976. *J. Physiol.* (London) 272:50-51.

160. Davies, J., and Dray, A. 1978. *Brit. J. Pharmacol.* 63:87-96.

161. Davies, J., and Duggan, A.W. 1974. *Nature New Biol.* 250:70-71.

162. Duggan, A.W.; Davies, J.; and Hall, J.G. 1976. *J. Pharmacol. Exp. Therapeutics* 196:107-120.

163. Davies, J. 1976. *Brain Res.* 112:311-326.

164. Pert, C.B.; Kuhar, M.J.; and Snyder, S.H. 1974. *The Opiate Narcotics,* New York: Pergamon Press, pp. 97-101.

165. Uhl, G.R.; Kuhar, M.J.; and Snyder, S.H. 1977. *Proc. Natl. Acad. Sci. U.S.A.* 74:4059-4063.

166. Satoh, M.; Zieglgansberger, W.; Fries, W.; and Herz, A. 1974. *Brain Res.* 82:378-382.

167. Satoh, M.; Zieglgansberger, W.; and Herz, A. 1975. *Life Sci.* 17:75-80.

168. Satoh, M.; Zieglgansberger, W.; and Herz, A. 1976. *Brain Res.* 115:99-110.

169. Zieglgansberger, W.; Fry, J.P.; Herz, A.; Moroder, L.; and Wunsch, E. 1976. *Brain Res.* 115:160-164.

170. Frederickson, R.C.A., and Norris, F.H. 1976. *Science* 194:440-442.

171. Bradley, P.B., and Gayton, R.J. 1976. *Brit. J. Pharmacol.* 57:425-426.

172. Gayton, R.J., and Bradley, P.B. 1976. In H.W. Kosterlitz (ed.), *Opiates and Endogenous Opioid Peptides,* pp. 213-219. Amsterdam: Elsevier.

173. Zieglgansberger, W., and Fry, J.P. 1976. In H.W. Kosterlitz (ed.), *Opiates and Endogenous Opioid Peptides,* pp. 213-238. Amsterdam: Elsevier.

174. Bigler, E.D., and Eidelberg, E. 1976. *Life Sci.* 19:1399-1406.

175. Chan, S.H.; Lee, C.M.; and Wong, P.C.L. 1977. *Fed. Proc.* 36:688.

176. Iwatsuto, K., and Clouet, D.H. 1977. *J. Pharm. Exp. Therapeutics* 202:429.

177. Frederickson, R.C.A.; Norris, F.H.; and Hewes, C.R. 1975. *Life Sci.* 17:81-82.

178. Hill, R.G.; Pepper, C.M.; and Mitchell, J.F. 1976. *Nature* 262:604-606.

179. Hill, R.G.; Pepper, C.M.; and Mitchell, J.F. 1976. In H.W. Kosterlitz (ed.), *Opiates and Endogenous Opioid Peptides,* pp. 225-230. Amsterdam: Elsevier.

180. Hill, R.G., and Pepper, C.M. 1976. *Brit. J. Pharmacol.* 58:459-460.

181. Hill, R.G., and Pepper, C.M. 1977. *J. Physiol. (London)* 269:378.

182. Hill, R.G., and Pepper, C.M. 1977. In R.W. Ryall and J.S. Kelly (eds)., *Microiontophoresis and Transmitter Mechanisms in the Mammalian Central Nervous System.* Pp. 329-331 Amsterdam: Elsevier.

183. Duggan, A.W., and Hall, J.G. 1977. *Brain Res.* 122:49-57.

184. Chou, T., and Wang, S.C. 1976. *Fed. Proc.* 35:357.

185. Henriksen, S.J.; Bloom, F.E.; Ling, N.; and Guillemin, R. 1977. *Soc. Neurosci. Abstr.:*293.

186. French, E.D.; Siggins, G.R.; Henriksen, S.J.; and Ling, N. 1977. *Soc. Neurosci. Abstr.:*291.

187. Fry, J.; Zieglgansberger, W.; and Herz, A. 1980. *Brit. J. Pharmacol.* 68:585-592.

188. Yaksh, T.L., and Rudy, T.A. 1977. *J. Pharm. Exp. Therapeutics* 202:411-428.

189. Yaksh, T.L., and Rudy, T.A. 1978. *Pain* 4.

190. Curtis, D.R., and Duggan, A.W. 1969. *Agents Actions* 1:14-19.

191. Duggan, A.W., and Curtis, D.R.: 1972. *Neuropharm.* 11:189-196.

192. Felpel, L.P.; Sinclair, J.G.; and Yim, G.K.W. 1970. *Neuropharmacology* 9:203-210.

193. Jurna, I. 1966. *Int. J. Neuropharmacol.* 5:117-123.

194. Jurna, I.; Grossman, W.; and Theres, C. 1973. *Neuropharmacol.* 12:983-993.

195. Zieglgansberger, W., and Bayerl, H. 1976. *Brain Res.* 115:111-138.

196. Zieglgansberger, W., and Puil, E.A. 1972. *Exp. Brain Res.* 17:35-49.

197. Barker, J.L.; Neale, J.H.; Smith, T.G., Jr.; and MacDonald, R.L. 1978. *Science* 199:1451-1453.

198. Myers, P.R.; Livengood, D.R.; and Shain,W. 1975.*Nature*257:238-240.

199. Dingledine, R.; Goldstein, A.; and Kendig, J. 1974. *Life Sci.* 14:2299-2309.

200. Dingledine, R., and Goldstein, A. 1975. *Life Sci.* 17:57-62.

201. Dingledine, R., and Goldstein, A. 1976. *J. Pharmacol. Exp. Therapeutics* 196:97-106.

202. Sato, T.; Takayanagi, I.; and Takagi, I. 1973. *Jap. J. Pharmacol.* 23:665-671.

203. North, R.A., and Henderson, G. 1975. *Life Sci.* 17:63-66.

204. North, R.A. 1976. *Neuropharmacol.* 15:1-9.

205. North, R.A., and Tonini, M. In H.W. Kosterlitz (ed.), *Opiates and Endogenous Opioid Peptides,* pp. 205-212. Amsterdam: Elsevier.

206. North, R.A., and Williams, J.T. 1976. *Nature* 264:460-461.

207. North, R.A., and Williams, J.T. 1977. *Fed. Proc.* 36:3667.

208. Satoh, M.; Zieglgansberger, W.; and Herz, A.1976. *Naunyn-Schmiedeberg's Arch. Pharmac. Exp. Path.* 293:101-103.

209. Browne, R.G.; Derrington, D.C.; and Segal, D.S. 1979. *Life Sci.* 24:933-942.

210. Browne, R.G., and Segal, D.S. 1978. In J.M. Van Ree and L. Terenius (eds.), *Characteristics and Function of Opioids, Developments in Neuroscience,* vol. 5, pp. 413-414. Amsterdam: Elsevier.

211. Izumi, K.; Motomatsu, T.; Chretien, M.; Butterworth, R.F.; Lis, M.; Seida, N.; and Barbeau, A. 1977. *Life Sci.* 20:1149-1156.

212. Motomatsu, T.; Lis, M.; Seidah, N.; and Chretien, N. 1977, *Can. J. Neurol. Sci.* 4:49-52.

213. Fog, R. 1972. *Acta Neurol. Scand.* 48 (suppl. 50):10-66.

214. Belluzzi, J.D., and Stein, L. 1977. *Nature* 266:556-558.

215. de Wied, D.; Bohus, B.; Van Ree, J.M.; and Urban, I. 1978. *J. Pharmac. Exp. Therapeutics* 204:570-580.

216. de Wied, D.; Kovacs, G.L.; Bohus, B.; Van Ree, J.M.; and Greven, H.M. 1978. *Eur. J. Pharmacol.* 49:427-436.

217. Gispen, W.H.; Van Ree, J.M.; and de Wied, D. 1977. *Int. Rev. Neurobiol.* 20:209-248.

218. de Wied, D. 1977. *Life Sci.* 20:195-204.

219. Kastin, A.J.; Scollan, E.L.; King, M.G.; Schally, A.V.; and Coy, D.H. 1976. *Pharmacol. Biochem. Behav.* 5 (Suppl 1):691-695.

220. Gunne, L.M..; Lindstrom, L.; and Terenius, L. 1977. *J. Neural Transmission* 40:13-19.

221. Davis, G.C.; Bunney, W.E., Jr.; de Fraites, E.G.; Kleinman, J.E.; Van Kammen, D.P.; Post, R.M.; and Wyatt, R.J. 1977. *Science* 197:74-77.

222. Janowsky, D.S.; Segal, D.S.; Abrams, A.; Bloom, F.; and Guillemin, R. 1977. *Psychopharmacology* 53:295-297.

223. Janowsky, D.S.; Segal, D.S.; Bloom, F.; Abrams, A.; and Guillemin, R. 1977. *Am. J. Psychiatry* 134:926-927.

224. Gilbert, P.E., and Martin, W.R. 1976. *J. Pharmacol. Exp. Therapeutics* 198:66-82.

225. Martin, W.R.; Eades, C.G.; Thompson, J.A.; Huppler, R.E.; and Gilbert, P.E. 1976. *J. Pharmacol. Exp. Therapeutics* 197:517-532.

226. Emrich, H.M.; Cording, C.; Piree, S.; Killing, A.; Zerssen, D.; and Herz, A. 1977. *Pharmakopsychiat.* 10:265-270.

227. Watson, S.; Berger, P.A.; Davis, K.; and Barchas, J. 1978. *Science* 201:73-76.

228. Schenk, G.K.; Enders, P.; Engelmeier, M.P.; Ewert, T.; Hendermerten, S.; Kohler, K.-H.; Lodemann, E.; Matz, D.; and Pach, J. 1978. *Drug Res.* 28:1274-1277.

229. Judd, L.L.; Janowsky, D.S.: Segal, D.S.; and Huey, L.Y. 1978. In J.M. Van Ree and L. Terenius (eds.), *Characteristics and Functions of Opiods,* pp. 173-174. Amsterdam: Elsevier.

230. Verhoeven, W.M.A.; Van Praag, H.M.; Botter, P.A.; Sunier, A.; Van Ree, J.M.; and de Wied, D. 1978. *Lancet* 1:1076-1077.

231. Weinberger, S.B.; Arnstein, A.; and Segal, D.A. 1979. *Life Sci.* 24:1637-1644.
232. Pert, C.B., and Snyder S.H. 1976. *Biochem. Pharmacol.* 25:847-853.
233. Hollt, V.; Dum, J.; Blasig, J.; Schubert, P.; and Herz, A. 1975. *Life Sci.* 16:1823-1829.
234. Cox, B.M. 1978. In J.M. Van Ree and L. Terenius (eds.), *Characteristics and Functions of Opioids,* pp. 13-23. Amsterdam: Elsevier.
235. North, R.A., and Karras, P.J. 1978. In J.M. Van Ree and L. Terenius (eds.), *Characteristics and Functions of Opioids,* pp. 25-36. Amsterdam: Elsevier.
236. Sharma, S.K.; Klee, W.A.; and Nirenberg, M. 1977. *Proc. Natl. Acad. Sci. U.S.A.* 74:3365-3369.
237. Catlin, D.A.; Hui, K.K.; Loh, H.H.; and Li, C.H. 1978. In E. Cork and M. Trabucchi (eds.), *Endorphins,* pp. 341-350. New York: Raven Press.
238. Redmond, D.E.; Huang, Y.H.; Snyder, S.R.; and Maas, J.W. 1976. *Brain Res.* 116:502-510.
239. Gold, M.S.; Redmond, D.E.; and Kleber, H.D. 1978. *Lancet* 2:599-602.
240. Aghajanian, G.K. 1978. *Nature* 276:196-188.
241. Aghajanian, G.K.; Cedarbaum, J.M.; and Wang, R.Y. 1977. *Brain Res.* 136:570-577.
242. Bird, S.J., and Kuhar, M.J. 1977. *Brain Res.* 122:523-533.
243. Llorens, C.; Martres, M.P.; Baudry, M.; and Schwartz, J.C. 1978. *Nature* 274:603-605.
244. Watson, S.J.; Akil, H.; Sullivan, S.; and Barchas, J.D. 1977. *Life Sci.* 21:733-738.
245. Sastry, B.S.R., and Phillis, J.W. 1977. *Neuropharmacol.* 16:223-225.
246. Stone, T.W., and Taylor, D.A. 1978. *Brit. J. Pharmacol.* 64:369-374.
247. Skolnick, R., and Daly, J.W. 1976. *Europ. J. Pharmacol.* 39:11-21.
248. Kahn, C.R. 1976. *J. Cell Biol.* 70:261-286.
249. Schwartz, J.C.; Costentin, J.; Martres, M.P.; Protais, P.; and Baudry, M. 1978. *Neuropharmacol.* 17:665-686.
250. Nathanson, J.M.; Klein, W.L.; and Nirenberg, M. 1978. *Proc. Natl. Acad. Sci. U.S.A.* 75:1788-1791.
251. Sabol, S.L., and Nirenberg, M. 1977. *Fed. Proc.* 36:736 (Abstr. 2438).
252. Bloom, F.E.; Siggins; G.R.; and Hoffer, B.J. 1972. *Biol. Psychiat.* 4:157-177.
253. Kangawa, K.; Matsuo, H.; and Igarashi, M. 1979. *Biochem. Biohys, Res. Commun.* 86:153-160.

254. Stern, A.S.; Lewis, R.V.; Kimura, S.; Rossier, J.; Gerber, L.D.; Brink, L.; Stein, S.; and Udenfriend, S. 1979. *Proc. Natl. Acad. Sci.* 76:6680-6683.

255. Goldstein, A.; Tachibana, S.; Lowney, L.I.; Hunkapiller, M.; and Hood, L. 1979. *Proc. Natl. Acad. Sci.* 76:6666-6670.

256. Hosobuchi, Y.; Rossier, J.; and Bloom, F.E. 1980. In E. Costa and M. Trabucchi (eds.), *Regulation and Function of Neural Peptides,* pp. 563-570. New York: Raven Press.

257. Oyama, T.; Jin, T.; Yamaya, R.; Ling, N.; and Guillemin, R. 1980. *Lancet* 1:122-124.

258. Hakanson, R.; Ekman, R.; Sundler, F.; and Nilsson, R. 1980. *Nature* 283:789-791.

259. Larsson, L.T.; Childers, S.; and Snyder, S.H. 1979. *Nature* 282:407-410.

260. Clement-Jones, V.; Lowry, P.J.; Rees, L.H.; and Besser, G.M. 1980. *Nature* 283:295-297.

261. Viveros, O.H.; Diliberto, E.J.; Hazum, E.; and Chang, K.J. 1979. *Molec. Pharmacol.* 16:1101-1108.

262. Bayon, A.; Koda, L.; Battenberg, E.; and Bloom, F. 1980. *Brain Res.* 183:103-111.

263. Bayon, A.; Koda, L.; Battenberg, E.; Azad, R.; Bloom, F.E. 1980. *Neurosci. Lett.* 16:75-80.

264. Lange, D.G.; Roerig, S.C.; Fujmoto, J.M.; and Wang, R.I.H. 1980. *Science* 208:72-74.

265. Pasternak, G.W.; Childers, S.R.; and Snyder, S.H. 1980. *Science* 208:514-516.

8

Endogenous Opioids: Brain-Behavior Relations

Donald J. Weisz and
Richard F. Thompson

In this chapter we explore the hypothesis that endogenous opioids may mediate general addictive processes—if general processes exist. The proposal is that many substances of abuse share common physiological mechanisms that give them abuse potential and that the common physiological mechanisms are, at least in part, mediated by endogenous opioids. We certainly do not attempt to prove that substances of abuse have identical acute or chronic effects. That cocaine and alcohol have different acute effects is obvious. Rather, we are searching for a common opioid-mediated physiological element that could underlie addictive behaviors. The common element could be involved in the acquisition of substance-abuse behaviors or in the maintenance of a previously acquired set of behaviors or both.

We have emphasized the brain-behavior literature in our examination of the opioid-mediated commonality hypothesis. First, we surveyed the findings regarding the involvement of endogenous opioids on acquisition and retention of learned responses and on behaviors in general. Learning and performance variables may provide links between various substances of abuse. We then focused on the role of the opiate receptor on one particular behavior, responding for intracranial self-stimulation (ICSS). For over twenty-five years ICSS has been used to study mechanisms of positive and negative reinforcement and of punishment. Certainly there are powerful reinforcers involved in substance abuse. Possibly a common reinforcer is opioid-mediated. We then searched for evidence of opioid mediation in the etiology of abuses of specific substances. We could find evidence for only three substances—morphine, alcohol, and, to a much lesser extent, food. At this time the abuse of no substance has been linked conclusively with opioid mediation; however, with regard to morphine and alcohol, there are suggestive data.

Naloxone, Endogenous Opioids, and Learning

Naloxone Effects

Although the effects of naloxone on behavior are somewhat clearer than are the effects of administered endogenous opioids, they are not as clear or con-

---

This chapter was written during 1980 and publications after 1980 are not included in this review.

sistent as might be hoped. Naloxone, an opiate antagonist, functions as an antagonist to at least some of the endogenous opioids and itself has a variety of biological and behavioral actions. It crosses the blood-brain barrier, and virtually all investigators administer it peripherally. However, it cannot be assumed a priori that its reported actions are necessarily central. The assumption that naloxone acts *only* as a specific blocker of opiate receptors is certainly open to question. Sawynok, Pinsky, and La Bella (1979) cited many instances in which naloxone antagonized antinociceptive effects of what are commonly thought to be nonopiate drugs (twelve in all).

Administration of naloxone has not always produced clear and consistent increase in pain-related reflexes and pain perception in animals and humans. In some studies naloxone has increased nociception (Buchsbaum, Davis, and Bunney 1977; Grevert and Goldstein 1977; Kaplan and Glick 1979) while in others no effect has been found (Akil et al. 1978; Hayes et al 1978). Rats given a session of inescapable shock show significant analgesia (tail-flick test) for a period of time after (Akil et al. 1976; Hayes et al. 1976). During the post stress analgesia period a rise occurs in endogenous brain opioid peptide levels (Madden et al 1977) and a decreased binding of radiolabeled enkephalin (Chance et al. 1978). Earlier studies reported inconsistent effects of naloxone on poststress analgesia (Akil et al. 1978; Hayes et al. 1978). This contradiction appears to have been resolved in a recent study by Liebeskind and associates, (Lewis, Cannon, and Liebeskind 1980). They noted that the positive (naloxone effect) studies used a prolonged intermittent-shock stressor whereas the negative studies used a brief continuous-shock stressor. They replicated both procedures and found that both stressors indeed yield poststress analgesia but that naloxone reversal occurs only with the prolonged intermittent-shock stressor.

The effects of naloxone on learning and memory have been the object of many studies. With regard to aversively reinforced tasks the effects have been consistent. A naloxone-induced increase in retention in both one-trial inhibitory avoidance and active avoidance has been observed. To be effective naloxone had to be administered immediately after training and again thirty minutes later for passive avoidance and both immediately before training and within thirty minutes after training for active avoidance (Messing et al. 1979). A similar enhancement of passive avoidance was reported for direct injections of naloxone into the amygdala (Gallagher and Kapp 1978). Naloxone has been reported to produce facilitation of both avoidance and classical conditioning in shuttle box training and on habituation of orienting to tone in rats (Izquierdo 1979).

An important series of studies by Bolles and Fanselow document a consistent potentiating effect of naloxone on *conditioned* fear. Thus, if a CS previously paired with shock is given prior to a test shock, the test shock produces less defensive behavior (freezing) than if the test shock is presented alone. This effect is blocked by naloxone (Fanselow and Bolles 1979a). In an even simpler situation, the freezing response of rats to a repeated series of shocks was shown to increase with increasing shock intensity or by giving naloxone (Fanselow and Bolles 1979b). Fanselow (1979) trained rats in a signaled-shock situation: given a choice between signaled and unsignaled shock, rats learned to prefer signaled shock. This preference is abolished by naloxone. Ehrman et al. (1979) reported that naloxone increases resistance to extinction of a fear-motivated response and results in unblocking when given during the compound conditioning trails of a block experiment.

One other observation by Fanselow and Bolles (1979b) relates to the naloxone sensitive versus insensitive poststress analgesia studies reviewed before. Naloxone does not increase defensive behavior (freezing) in animals that receive only a single shock, but it does increase freezing substantially to the second of two brief shocks given twenty seconds apart. This provides a possible behavioral component for the two types of poststress analgesia. Prolonged intermittent shock results in conditioned fear to the contextual cues of the apparatus, which results in analgesia in later pain tests via a hypothetical conditioned release of brain opioids. The fact that naloxone blocks intermittent-shock-stress analgesia but not brief-continuous-shock-stress analgesia suggests that different "receptors-opiates-transmitter systems" are involved in the two types of analgesia (see discussion in Lewis, Cannon, and Liebeskind 1980). If conditioned fear is indeed the critical behavioral variable in the two types of stress analgesia, then it follows that the neuronal substrate of conditioned fear involves different receptors-opiates-transmitter systems than does pain itself. Bolles and Fanselow (1980) have developed a model of the functions of endogenous opioids that contrasts fear (conditioned) and pain (unconditioned). If conditioned fear does in fact play an important role in post-shock-stress analgesia, it should be possible to alter the degree of naloxone-sensitive analgesia by varying the similarity of the shock-stress and analgesia-test apparatus. In this context one is reminded of the earlier view that morphine has its major action on anxiety, the conditioned fear associated with pain, rather than on pain itself (Wikler 1973).

A possible negative instance concerning the effect of naloxone on conditioned fear comes from a control group in a careful study of the effect of morphine on potentiated startle by Davis (1979). He used the classic paradigm developed by Brown, Kalish, and Farber (1951). Conditioned fear is first established (in the Davis study) by pairing a light CS with foot-shock. Animals are then tested for habituation of the acoustic startle response where half the tones are paired with the light CS. These pairings yield a potentiated startle response. Davis found a dose-dependent reduction of potentiated startle by morphine that was antagonized by naloxone. Naloxone alone had no effect. This could be due to a ceiling effect—the potentiated startle might be as large as it can be. There are of course other possibilities.

Administration of Endogenous Opioids

Administration of endogenous opioids and their analogs is complicated by several factors. leu- and met-enkephalin are rapidly metabolized. With systemic injection, these substances may not reach the brain. Even when they are injected intracerebrally, it is not clear how long they remain active. B-endorphin is much stabler, but it is not clear to what extent it reaches the brain after peripheral injection (see Rossier and Bloom 1971; chapter 7 of this book). Further, it has been postulated that there are three types of opioid receptor, s, K and μ, morphine being classed as a pure μ-agonist. It might be presumed that the endogenous opioids and their analogs differ in action in terms of these hypothetical receptor types. Several endogenous opioids have been identified, dynorphin being the most recent and potent, and others will no doubt be discovered. Current knowledge is rather incomplete. As yet little is understood of the roles of these substances in the neuronal activity of the brain (see chapter 7). Consequently it is difficult to develop a coherent theory that would permit differentially testable predictions of the effects of these substances on behavioral phenomena. The other side of this coin is of course current limited understanding of brain substrates of most aspects of behavior. This is particularly evident in the case of learning, a process that occupies a central position in many models and theories of the functions of the brain opioids and, more generally, in the theories of substance abuse.

Effects of Administered Endogenous Opioids on Unlearned and Learned Behaviors

The analgesic effects of endogenous opioids have been detailed in several reviews (Olson et al. 1979; Rossier and Bloom 1979; Terenius 1978). In brief, B-endorphin is thirty times more potent than morphine when injected into the brain and two to three times more potent when given intravenously. Effects of leu- and met-enkephalin are much less consistent. The majority of studies indicate analgesia with intracerebral administration but not with intravenous administration. Other central actions of B-endorphin resemble morphine, including both hyperactivity and immobility (see Segal et al. 1977). One effect of central administration of morphine, so-called explosive motor behavior resulting from injection into the periacqueductal gray, may not occur with B-endorphin (Jacquet et al. 1977).

Much recent work has focused on the effects of administered endogenous opioids on learning and memory tasks, stimulated in part by the general notion that these substances may play roles in reward and punishment systems in the brain. The current literature on the effects of administered endogenous opioids and analogs on learning and memory tasks can be described only as complex and inconsistent. As would be expected, task, substance, dose, time of administration, and route of administration are all significant variables. However, they cannot account for the apparent inconsistencies that exist. As a result, it does not seem possible to make any clear generalizations from the diverse results present in this literature. It is not even very easy to summarize them. Nevertheless, we will attempt to summarize the effects substance by substance.

Met-enkephalin. Peripherally or centrally met-enkephalin delays extinction of active avoidance (pole-jumping) (de Wied et al. 1978 a, b). Centrally, large doses posttraining improve retention of passive avoidance (Stein and Belluzzi 1978). Peripherally, it facilitates subsequent maze learning (Kastin et al. 1976), diminishes CO_2 amnesia (Rigter 1978), impairs acquisition of active avoidance learning (Rigter et al. 1980a), and markedly impairs retention of shuttle-box avoidance and habituation of the orienting response (Izquierdo 1979). The effects of M-enkephalin on CO_2-induced amnesia are neither prevented nor reversed by administration of naloxone (Rigter, Greven, and van Riezen 1977).

Leu-enkephalin. Centrally, large doses of leu-enkephalin are ineffective given posttraining in passive avoidance (Stein and Belluzzi 1978). Peripherally, it diminishes CO_2 amnesia but only if given just before the retrieval test (Rigter 1978), impairs active avoidance learning (Rigter et al. 1980a, b), facilitates passive avoidance (Rigter et al. 1980b), and impairs retention of shuttle-box avoidance and habituation of the orienting response (Izquierdo 1979). Naloxone does not prevent or reverse the effect of leu-enkephalin on CO_2 amnesia (Rigter, Greven, and van Riezen 1977).

A-endorphin. Centrally or peripherally, A-endorphin delays extinction of active avoidance (Le Moal, Koob, and Bloom 1979; de Wied et al. 1978a, b). Peripherally, it delays extinction of runway response for water (Le Moal, Koob, and Bloom 1979), facilitates retention of passive avoidance if given immediately after training (de Wied et al. 1978a), has no effect on one-trial inhibitory learning (Martinez and Rigter 1980a), and is without effect on active-avoidance learning (J. Martinez, personal communication).

B-endorphin. Centrally or peripherally, B-endorphin delays extinction of active avoidance (de Wied et al. 1978a, b). Peripherally, it impairs retention of one-trial inhibitory learning but only if given after training (Martinez and Rigter 1980a), and is without effect on active-avoidance learning (J. Martinez, personal communication).

G-endorphin. Centrally or peripherally, G-endorphin enhances extinction of active avoidance (Le Moal, Koob, and Bloom 1979). Peripherally, this effect has been replicated (Le Moal, Koob, and Bloom 1979). In addition, peripheral administration of this opioid delays extinction of a runway response (Le Moal, Koob, and Bloom 1979), improves one-trial inhibitory learning if given before training but not after (Martinez and Rigter 1980a), and is without effect on active-avoidance learning (J. Martinez, personal communication).

ACTH 4-10. Centrally or peripherally, it delays extinction of active avoidance (de Wied et al. 1978a, b). Peripherally, it facilitates retention of passive avoidance if given prior to the retention test (de Wied et al. 1978a) and impairs acquisition of active avoidance (Martinez and Rigter 1980a). This last effect is potentiated by naloxone.

The most consistent effect of endogenous opioids on learned behavior involves resistance to extinction. When administered centrally or peripherally met-enkephalin, A-endorphin, B-endorphin and $ACTH_{4-10}$ all delay extinction of active avoidance behavior (de Wied et al. 1978a, 1978b; Le Moal, Koob, and Bloom 1979). This in itself is of interest in another context: one of the most consistent neurochemical correlates of learning relates to norepinephrine and extinction. Resistance to extinction is inversely related to brain levels of norepinephrine, altered either by locus-coeruleus lesions or pharmacological manipulations. The processes underlying extinction and its relationship to acquisition, learning, are not yet well understood at either behavioral or neural levels. The formal properties of extinction, incidentally, are essentially identical to those of habituation.

One of the puzzling aspects of these studies is the fact that peripheral administration of low doses of leu- and met-enkephalin have behavioral effects. These substances are rapidly inactivated in the blood and probably do not act on the brain (see chapter 7). Martinez and Rigter (1980b) find that prior removal of the adrenal medulla prevents the impairing effects of small doses (10 μ g/kg) of leu- and met-enkephalin on active avoidance learning. It may be, then, that the complex and sometimes contradictory effects of at least the enkephalins on learning and memory performance are due to a variety of peripheral actions. To state it another way, these substances, and perhaps the endorphins as well, might be influencing learning and memory performance by influencing a variety of hormonal and performance factors. In this context we note the powerful effects of vasopressin (facilitates) and oxytocin (inhibitory) on learning and retention reported by de Wied's group. As Rossier and Bloom (1979) note, intravenous B-endorphin causes the release of vasopressin, prolactin, and growth hormone. Levine, Smotherman, and Hennessy (1977) have shown that long-term increased plasma corticosterone levels can become conditioned to the CS in a taste-aversion learning situation and more generally that a wide range of behavioral procedures can influence pituitary-adrenal activity.

A general problem of interpretation in most of the work to date on effects of administered endogenous opioids on learning and memory, then, is the classical problem of learning versus performance. The evidence to date is perhaps more consistent with the view that these substances are not acting directly on central associative processes but rather on performance variables. It might be helpful to utilize behavioral paradigms where learning and performance factors can to some extent be dissociated (see, for example, Thompson et al. 1976b). A simple example of a performance variable would be the freezing response to shock, which Bolles and Fanselow have reported to be increased by naloxone after one prior experience (conditioned fear). Thus if endogenous opioids act to reduce the freezing response, they would increase resistance to extinction in active avoidance and at the same time impair retention of inhibitory or passive avoidance tasks, outcomes that are often found. Such a simple hypothesis cannot of course account for all the results of studies to date, but neither can any other hypothesis. Perhaps the extreme alternative is that there are a number of different types of opiate receptors on neurons in the brain and that the various endogenous opioids act differentially on them in terms of effects on learning. While this hypothesis has the appeal of simplicity, the data do not yet provide very strong support.

There is another line of research that links endogenous opioids with learning processes. It has been postulated (Siegel 1976, 1978; Wikler 1973) that at least some of morphine's effects may be altered by environmental factors. Siegel's familiar compensatory conditioned response (CR) model is focused on the phenomena of opiate tolerance. In brief, Siegel assumes that the context of opiate administration becomes a conditioned stimulus (CS) for a CR that is opposite in direction to the direct effects of the administered substance. The direct evidence is that analgesic tolerance is displayed when rats were tested in that environment in which they previously received morphine but not in a different environment (Siegel 1976), in itself a striking result. It is the other side of the coin from the theory of Bolles and Fanselow that conditioned release of endogenous opioids occurs in conditioned fear. Subsequent tests of this model have given somewhat conflicting results, particularly with the body temperature effects of morphine (Sherman 1979; Eikelboom and Stewart 1979).

In some current and as yet unpublished studies, R. Kesner (personal communication) examined the behavioral properties of morphine tolerance to repeated injections developed by rats in a nondistinctive environment and by rats in a highly distinctive environment. Both groups developed tolerance but the behavioral properties were quite different. Development of tolerance in rats in the nondistinctive environment displayed all nine parametric features of habituation (Thompson and Spencer 1966). In contrast, tolerance in rats in the distinctive environment displayed properties of classical conditioning. As an example, massed trials (administrations) yielded greater tolerance in the nondistinctive environment, as is true for habituation. In the distinctive environment, massed trials led to less tolerance, as is true in classical conditioning. This would seem to support the view that both associative and nonassociative (molecular) processes are involved in tolerance. The close parallel to habituation of tolerance development in the nondistinctive environment is of interest in view of our current understanding of possible synaptic mechanisms of habituation, which at least in certain simplified neural systems are presynaptic (see, for example, Castellucci and Kandel 1976; Thompson and Glanzman 1976).

ICSS

Intracranial self-stimulation (ICSS) has been the object of hundreds of scientific reports since its discovery in 1954 by Olds and Milner. Some areas of the brain were called "reward centers" because animals would acquire and maintain behaviors if the behavior was followed by electrical stimulation of the area. Many hypotheses have been proposed and tested concerning the role of the reward centers and concerning the underlying mechanisms. Of interest is the proposal that substances of abuse possess positively reinforcing properties by virtue of their physiological actions on reward centers. Many drugs with abuse potential have been shown to increase ICSS.

In several chronic studies morphine (in low to moderate doses) has increased response rates during ICSS (Adams, Lorens, and Mitchell 1972; Bush et al. 1976; Lorens and Mitchell 1973) and has lowered current thresholds for positive reinforcement (Esposito and Kornetsky 1977; Marcus and Kornetsky 1974; Maroli, Tsang, and Stutz 1978). However, acute administration of morphine has inhibited ICSS (Olds and Travis 1960; Adams, Lorens, and Mitchell 1972; Lorens and Mitchell 1973). It may be that acute aversive effects of morphine decrease with repeated administration (Lorens and Mitchell 1973; Esposito and Kornetsky 1977). In none of these studies was an attempt made to block morphine's effects with naloxone. In 1979 it was reported that the increased responding for ICSS was blocked by nalaxone but that naloxone by itself had no effect (Lorens 1979). Repeated injections of naloxone over a period of weeks were found to reduce ICSS when stimulation was to the central gray, medial septum, or substantia nigra (Stein and Belluzzi 1978); however naloxone had no effect on ICSS when stimulation was delivered to lateral hypothalamus or to caudate (Holtzman 1976; Lorens and Sainati 1978; Lorens 1979; Wauquier, Niemegeers, and Lal 1974; Kooy, Le Piane, and Phillips 1977). Anatomical specificity and/or magnitude of naloxone pretreatment could be the variables responsible for the opposite findings. An area that supports ICSS, lateral hypothalamus, has been shown in the same preparation to be a site that will support self-administration of morphine. If naloxone was administered along with the morphine to the lateral hypothalamus, morphine self-administration was reduced (Olds 1979).

The evidence suggests that morphine increases ICSS, although immediately after an acute injection there may be an inhibition of ICSS. The involvement of the opiate receptor in ICSS is clouded by the failure of some investigators to find a disruption of ICSS by naloxone.

In addition to morphine, other drugs of abuse have increased ICSS. Ethanol increased responding for ICSS (Carlson and Lydic 1976; Lorens 1979) and the effect was blocked by naloxone in a dose-dependent manner (Lorens 1979). Chlordiazepoxide administration has enhanced markedly ICSS (Olds 1966; Lorens and Sainati 1978; Domino and Olds 1972) and the facilitatory effect of the drug has been blocked completely by naloxone (Lorens and Sainati 1978). Amphetamine and other catecholamine-altering drugs alter ICSS. The literature regarding these effects is enormous (see Wise 1978). There was increased responding for ICSS following d-amphetamine administration (Carey, Goodall, and Lorens 1975; Holtzman 1976; Stein 1964), and naloxone depressed responding in animals injected with d-amphetamine (Holtzman 1976). Given that naloxone may block ICSS when given by itself, the naloxone effect following d-amphetamine administration may be due to a physiological substrate different from the one affected by d-amphetamine.

In summary, at least four drugs of abuse (at the proper doses) have been shown to increase ICSS and that these facilitatory effects can be inhibited by naloxone. We found only one phenomenon, ICSS, in which as many as four drugs of abuse had a similar effect. However, the assumption that reward centers have any behavioral or physiological function for other reinforcers (such as food and water, sex, or drug self-administration) has not been thoroughly tested. With reference to the drug effects on ICSS, we conclude that they suggest a common substrate for the drugs (possibly opioid-mediated) but that more direct methods should be included to determine the role of the opiate-receptor in ICSS. Measurements of turnover rate, levels, and breakdown of the endogenous should be attempted during and following ICSS.

Morphine Addiction and Endogenous Opioids

It is premature to conclude that endogenous opioids are involved in the etiology of morphine and heroin addiction. Certainly the endogenous compounds produce many naloxone-reversible effects that are very similar to those of morphine and heroin. However, if the endogenous opioids play a critical role in the etiology of narcotic addiction, one would expect to find alterations in levels, metabolic activity, receptor availability, turnover rate, or enzymatic degradation of endogenous opioids following or coinciding with the onset of opiate addiction. At present the data addressing this problem are not conclusive.

Levels of endogenous opioids have been found, at times, to be altered following chronic morphine treatment (Przewlocki et al. 1979; Clement-Jones et al. 1979). However, there also have been several studies in which acute or chronic morphine treatment and withdrawal from morphine have failed to alter levels of endogenous opioids (Fratta et al. 1977; Childers, Simantov, and Snyder 1977; Wesche, Hollt, and Herz 1977). One possible variable is the length of narcotic treatment. From the same laboratory there are reports of no changes in endogenous opioids following administration (Wesche, Hollt, and Herz 1979) and of decreases following thirty days of morphine treatment (Przewlocki et al. 1979). Increases in degradation of enkephalin during narcotic addiction are suggested by the finding of increased levels of high-affinity enkephalin degrading enzyme following chronic morphine treatment (Malfroy et al. 1978). This is a potentially important result that needs to be replicated. No studies of turnover rates of endogenous opioids in morphine dependent animals have been done.

As can be seen, few reliable effects on levels or activities of endogenous opioids following morphine treatment have been found. Another, though less direct, approach to the problem is to compare morphine with the endogenous opioids on their addictive properties. Morphine is readily self-administered by animals and there have been reports of self-administration of the enkephalins (Belluzzi and Stein 1977) of an enkephalin analog (Mello and Mendelson 1978), and of B-endorphin (Van Ree, Smyth, and Colpaert 1979). Findings of reliable self-administration of enkephalins and B-endorphin would constitute a major link between the endogenous opioids and the development of narcotic addiction. Such findings would suggest that the reinforcing properties of morphine that lead to acquisition of addiction may be mediated by the opiate receptor. There need to be more investigations of enkephalin and B-endorphin self-administration behavior to determine the reliability of the phenomenon.

The acquisition of an addiction may involve physiological mechanisms different from the maintenance of an addiction during the tolerance or dependence phase (Way and Glasgow 1978). Repeated and frequent administration of exogenous narcotics results in diminution of many acute drug actions (tolerance) and creates a need in the organism to receive the drug repeatedly and generally in increasing amounts (dependence). The endogenous opioids share with morphine and heroin the ability to produce tolerance or dependence. Intraventricularly infused B-endorphin, met-enkephalin, and morphine produced withdrawal symptoms when the animals were challenged by naloxone (commonly used to produce withdrawal in morphine-dependent animals). B-endorphin produced dependence at one-tenth the dose of morphine and met-enkephalin (Wei and Loh 1976). Tolerance to analgesia effects developed after only four to six injections of B-endorphin (Van Ree et al. 1976). The effects of morphine were very similar, but much larger doses of morphine were required (van Loon, de Souza, and Kim 1978). Tolerance to the ACTH-releasing effect of B-endorphin (van Loon and de Souza 1978) and to the hyperthermic effects of met-enkephalin (Scoto et al. 1979) have been observed.

The evidence leads to the following conclusion; that is, after only a few injections tolerance develops to many of the effects of the endogenous opioids, especially those of B-endorphin. Whether the development of tolerance to exogenous administration of the endogenous opioids is due strictly to physiological processes or whether behavioral conditioning plays a role has not yet been examined.

Not only has tolerance been shown with repeated administration of the endogeous opioids but cross tolerance between the endogenous opioids and morphine has been reported. Cross tolerance between morphine and B-endorphin was demonstrated on muscle taken from morphine-pretreated guinea pigs (Puig, Gascon, and Musacchio 1977) and on pain sensitivity in morphine-pretreated rats (Tseng, Loh, and Li 1977; Szekely et al. 1977). Cross tolerance between met-enkephalin and morphine was demonstrated on guinea pig ileum and on mouse vas deferens (Waterfield, Hughes, and Kosterlitz 1976). An enkephalin analog (FK-33-824) prevented withdrawal in morphine-dependent monkeys (Mello and Mendelson, 1978; Roemer et al. 1977). Abstinence reactions during withdrawal in morphine-dependent rats were attenuated by administration of enkephalin analog (Baxter et al. 1977). B-endorphin relieved withdrawal symptoms in morphine-dependent humans (Catlin, George, and Li 1978).

The work leads to a general proposal that some endogenous opioids (probably B-endorphin or met-enkephalin) may be involved with the reinforcing properties of narcotic drugs. There have been some reports of neuropeptide self-administration in animals; there is generalization of cueing properties from one narcotic to at least one endogenous peptide; a synthetic enkephalin served as an excellent substitute for morphine-dependent animals; cross tolerance between some endogenous opioids and exogenous narcotic substances has been demonstrated; tolerance has been observed with repeated administration of endogenous opioids; similar abstinence symptoms have been reported following endogenous opioids or morphine administration.

Ethanol and Endogenous Opioids

Clearly the best evidence for endogenous opioid involvement in the etiology of substance abuse lies in the morphine literature. The next best evidence comes from work on ethanol. Hypotheses regarding a common denominator for ethanol and opiate abuse have evolved from the initial proposal by Davis and Walsh in 1970. (For recent elaborations of opiate models of alcoholism, see Blum et al. 1980a; Myers 1978; Hamilton and Hirst 1980.) Briefly, it has been proposed that at least some of ethanol's reinforcing properties may be mediated by an endogenous opioid system. It is not proposed that all or even most of ethanol's effects are mediated by the endogenous opioids but, rather, that ethanol alters physiological activity of the endogenous opioids in a manner that leads to acquisition of ethanol abuse or maintenance of abuse or both. This is not a survey of the entire literature concerning similarities and differences between ethanol and opiates at the chemical, physiological, and behavioral level. Rather it is a review of findings that directly address the question of an ethanol effect on the endogenous opioids.

One type of research has involved the effects of opiate antagonists on self-administration of ethanol. Pretreatment with naltrexone decreased ethanol self-administration in ethanol-dependent monkeys (Altshuler, Phillips, and Feinhandler 1980). A suppression of ethanol consumption by mice following naloxone pretreatment may have been due to naloxone's anorexic properties since naloxone also decreased consumption of a 5 percent sucrose solution (Gentry, Ho, and Dole 1980). Since naloxone has been shown in some studies to suppress food and water intake, sucrose and water control groups should always be included in future ethanol self-administration studies.

Opiate antagonists have altered other behavioral effects of ethanol. Naloxone administered throughout three days of exposure to ethanol vapor significantly inhibited convulsions in response to withdrawal of ethanol. In the same study naloxone, which had no effect by itself, prevented calcium depletion in animals exposed to the ethanol vapor (Blum et al. 1977). In another report naloxone attenuated an ethanol-induced narcosis (Blum et al. 1975). An ethanol-induced increase in activity was attenuated by naloxone pretreatment, which had no effect of its own (Middaugh, Read, and Boggan 1978). Ethanol was shown to increase responding in rats in a conflict situation (the animal could receive either food or a shock for responding);

naloxone had no effect on the conflict responding patterns but did block ethanol's effects (Koob, Foote, and Bloom 1978). Naloxone inhibited the ethanol-induced depression of electrically-evoked contraction of isolated mouse vas deferens (Blum et al. 1979). In a human study naloxone prevented an ethanol-induced impairment of reaction time (Jeffcoate et al. 1979). In many types of behavioral paradigms opiate antagonists, while usually having no effects by themselves, have blocked effects of ethanol. If the opiate antagonists possess effects only by virtue of their actions on the opiate receptor, then some of ethanol's effects appear to be due to an interaction between ethanol and the endogenous opioids.

Some evidence of a genetic link between opioids and ethanol preference exists. Whole-brain ratios of B-endorphin to enkephalin were two times greater in ethanol-preferring mice than in an ethanol-avoiding strain. Possibly a genetic predisposition to alcoholism is suggested by this finding (K. Blum, personal communication). Further support for a genetic link has come from the finding that two closely related inbred strains of mice highly prefer both ethanol and morphine while mice that avoid ethanol also avoid morphine (Whitney and Horowitz 1978). However, a third closely related strain was found to have a strong preference for morphine but not for ethanol. An investigation of the differences in these strains could uncover commonalities and differences of ethanol and morphine addiction.

Blum's group has provided another possible link between alcohol and the endogenous opioids. Blum et al. (1980b) have reported decreases in endogenous opioid concentrations following ingestion of ETOH by experimental animals. Blum and colleagues found that a 10 percent ETOH solution when chronically administered to Golden Syrian hamsters in a preference test significantly reduced basal ganglia enkephalin. Pinsky and colleagues (1978) reported that chronic alcohol treatment over 15 days led to either an increase in the number of opiate receptors and/or a decrease in the level of bound brain opioids. Their binding study did not permit a more specific conclusion. These findings are highly suggestive. Directly or indirectly ethanol treatment may result in alterations in the endogenous opioid system.

The obvious structural difference between ethanol and the endogenous opioids raises the question of how ethanol could exert influences on the endogenous opioid systems. The most developed hypothesis regarding a possible ethanol-opiate link is the one involving tetrahydroisoquinolines (TIQs). Using in vitro preparations TIQs can be formed by condensing certain ethanol metabolites with endogenous catecholamines (Cohen and Collins 1971; Davis and Walsh 1970). Centrally administered TIQs have been shown to induce ethanol drinking in rats (Myers and Melchior 1977; Myers and Oblinger 1977). Two TIQs, salsolinol and tetrohydropapaveroline (THP) specifically bound opiate receptors in a dose-dependent manner

(Greenwald et al. 1979). A reduction in brain calcium was found following morphine, ethanol, and salsolinol; furthermore the effects were naloxone reversible (Ross, Medina, and Cardenas 1974). Pretreatment with naloxone blocked morphine-induced as well as salsolinol-induced inhibition of guinea pig ileum contractions. While naloxone administered after morphine reversed morphine's effects, naloxone following salsolinol did not reverse the inhibition (Hamilton, Hirst, and Blum 1979). These data strongly argue for some interaction between ethanol and the opioids but probably not at the same peripheral receptor site.

The primary obstacle preventing wider acceptance of the TIQ hypothesis of alcoholism is the failure by several investigators to find ethanol-induced increases in brain levels of TIQs or their metabolites using in vivo preparations (Shier, Koda, and Bloom 1980; Riggin and Kissinger 1977; Collins and Bigdeli 1975; O'Neill and Rahwan 1977). At present there is only one report of ethanol-induced increase in brain levels of a TIQ metabolite when the only drug administered was ethanol. O-methyl-salsolinol, a metabolite of salsolinol, was present in striatal tissue of mice following ethanol administration but not present in control animals (Hamilton, Blum, and Hirst 1978). There is also one report of detection of salsolinol and O-methyl-salsolinol in cerebrospinal fluid and urine of alcoholic patients during and up to eight days after a period of alcohol abuse (Borg et al. 1980). Salsolinol and O-methyl-salsolinol also were found to be elevated in the urine of alcoholics as compared to the urine of nonalcoholic psychiatric in-patients (Collins et al. 1979). If an inhibitor of catecholamine enzymatic breakdown was administered prior to induction of acute alcohol intoxication salsolinol was detected in brain homogenate (Collins and Bigdeli 1975). One further problem for the TIQ hypothesis has come from in vitro attempts to condense TIQs from butanol and catecholamines. Although butanol shares many behavioral and physiological effects with ethanol, TIQs are not condensed when butanol is used instead of ethanol.

Proponents of the TIQ hypothesis of alcoholism believe that only through the use of very sensitive techniques can the TIQs be detected. It is argued that some of the techniques used in attempting to assay TIQs have not been sensitive enough (Hamilton and Hirst 1980). However, the HPLC technique used by Shier, Koda, and Bloom (1980) would have detected the quantities of TIQs found by others if the TIQs had been present (F. Bloom, personal communication). The failures in finding TIQs may also be due to the short half-life of the compounds in vivo. Hirst has estimated the half-life of salsolinol to be approximately twelve minutes (M. Hamilton, personal communiation). Hamilton, Blum, and Hirst (1978) did not find salsolinol but rather a salsolinol metabolite in striatal tissue following ethanol treatment. One further observation regarding the detection of TIQs and their metabolites concerns the nature of the tissue sampled. Given the unequal distributions of catecholamines in the central nervous system, it is suggested that assays be performed on areas rich in catecholamines, for example, caudate nucleus (Hamilton and Hirst 1980). Furthermore if a central action of the TIQs is postulated, it would seem that proposed experiments should be focused on central nervous system tissue or on human cerebrospinal fluid. While the presence of TIQs in plasma or urine would be interesting and suggestive, it would not be very conclusive. At present there is still only one report of an ethanol-induced increase in brain TIQs or their metabolites in which alcohol was the only chemical administered (Hamilton, Blum, and Hirst 1978). The TIQ hypothesis represents the most widely studied potential link between the two classes of drugs. However, there are severe problems with the hypothesis. The first critical question is whether TIQs are produced following ethanol treatment. It would seem that this question must be answered first and that some consensus be formed. One explanation of the ethanol-opiate interactions argues against the common opiate-receptor hypothesis. It has been suggested that ethanol acts on an organism as a nonspecific stress that is sensitive to the actions of naloxone. A role for the endogenous opioids in the mediation of stress has received strong support in the recent publications (see the sections on naloxone and on opioids and learning).

By far the best evidence linking endogenous opioids with a nonnarcotic addictive substance comes from studies on ethanol. Some of ethanol's effects have been blocked by opiate antagonists; possible products of ethanol and catecholamine metabolism possess some opiatelike properties; opiate antagonists have altered ethanol drinking behavior; and brain levels of endogenous opioids may correlate with susceptibility to alcoholism in mice. The present findings do not confirm or reject the hypothesis that the addicting properties of both morphine and ethanol are mediated by a common biochemical mechanism. There appear to be many interactions between ethanol and the opioids. Furthermore, there is evidence of a possible genetic link between alcohol preference and opiate preference. However, it is not clear that the interactions are mediated by a common receptor.

Obesity and Endogenous Opioids

Data suggesting endogenous opioid involvement in obesity are sparse, but models have appeared recently in the literature (Holtzman 1979; Margules et al. 1978; McCloy and McCloy 1979a, b). Opioids have been detected throughout the digestive system (Polak et al. 1977; Smith et al. 1976). In fact the digestive system, the brain, and pituitary contain all or almost all of the endogenous opioids (Smith, et al. 1976; Konturek 1978). For a long time the exogenous opiates have been known to possess potent effects on the gastrointestinal (GI) tract. Morphine decreases intestinal contractions, delays gastric emptying, and decreases gastric contractile activity (Konturek 1978). The endogenous opioids have been shown to possess similar effects (Konturek 1978).

There are also findings that link endogenous opioids with obesity. Significantly higher levels of B-endorphin have been found in the blood plasma of genetically obese rats than in their lean litter mates and in the pituitaries of both obese mice and obese rats than in their lean counterparts; however no differences in brain B-endorphin were found between obese and lean animals (Margules et al. 1978). However, it does not appear that higher levels of pituitary B-endorphin have a causative effect on the development of obesity. There were no differences between genetically obese mice and lean ones in pituitary levels of B-endorphin until the obese mice had gained most of their weight (Rossier et al. 1979). In the same study preobese levels of leu-enkephalin in pars nervosa of pituitary did correlate highly with changes in body weight. Thus, although B-endorphin levels did not predict future weight gain, leu-enkephalin did.

Further evidence regarding obesity and opioids has come from work with naloxone. Naloxone produced a greater decrease in eating in genetically obese animals than in the lean ones (Margules et al. 1978), an effect that has been replicated with mice (Shimomura et al. 1980). In rats made obese by lesions of the ventromedial hypothalamus (VMH), naloxone suppressed food intake more in the obese group than in lean controls (King 1979). However, other data are contradictory. Naloxone did not affect food intake in several obesity syndromes (VMH lesions, ovariectomized rats, and hypothalamic knife cuts) (Gunion and Peters 1978). All experimental animals were tested at normal body weights in this study. It is possible that naloxone is effective only when animals are overweight. Another possibility is that the opioids are primarily involved when eating is induced by stress. Naloxone decreased food intake in normal animals when the animals were stressed by tail pinch, twenty-four-hour food deprivation, and 2-deoxy-glucose (Lowy, Maickel, and Yim 1980). However, naloxone had no effect when food intake was stimulated by an insulin injection. In the same vein, food deprivation has been shown to produce analgesia in rats. This analgesic response was reduced significantly by either naloxone or feeding (McGivern and Berntson 1980). Eating can be induced in rats by the tail-pinch method. This type of stress-induced eating was depressed by naloxone (Morley and Levine 1980).

Central effects of endogenous opioids have also been found. Intraventricular but not peripheral, B-endorphin increased intake of a liquid diet (Kenney et al. 1978). Centrally administered B-endorphin also increased food intake, an effect blocked by the opiate antagonist naltrexone (Grandison and Guidotti 1977) and blocked by naloxone (Tseng and Cheng 1980).

Depression of water intake following naloxone administration has also been reported (Holtzman 1974, 1975, 1979). Water intake was decreased by naloxone or naltrexone in water-deprived rats (Maickel et al. 1977).

The effects of endogenous opioids on gastrointestinal functioning are robust and are the subject of continued investigation. Apparently centrally administered B-endorphin and enkephalins alter food and water intake. The nature of the interactions between endogenous opioids in the gastrointestinal tract and those in the brain have been hypothesized (Holtzman 1979; Margules et al. 1978), but no data yet elucidate the effects of peripheral opiates on the brain areas that control feeding and drinking. Until these effects are discovered, we only can speculate as to the possible role of endogenous opioids on obesity.

Conclusions

Data reviewed suggest the following oversimplified generalizations. Some endogenous opioids are analgesic; however, conditioned fear is more effective in the presumed release or action of the opioids than is pain itself. Although the terms vary slightly, various reviewers have reached similar tentative conclusions: endogenous opioids act to reduce stress, modulate the aversiveness of a stressor, or modulate conditioned fear. Resistance to extinction of learned responses is increased by administration, central or peripheral, of all endogenous opioids tested except G-endorphin. The increased resistance to extinction effect following opioid administration may be due to interactions with the catecholamines, because low levels of catecholamine (especially norepinephrine) are correlated with increased resistance to extinction. Further support comes from neurochemical studies in which many interactions between opioids and catecholamines have been shown. Another catecholamine-sensitive behavior, intracranial self-stimulation, also appears sensitive to changes in the endogenous opioids. The effects of endogenous opioids on retention tasks are not clear although improvement of memory following endogenous opioids administration is seldom observed. Many of the actions of endogenous opioids on retention may be peripheral. Because of the scarcity of studies utilizing central opioid administration, no conclusions can be made regarding the role of the endogenous opioid system in learning and memory processes.

With regard to involvement of the endogenous opioids in the abuse of specific substances, the best evidence comes from studies on morphine and heroin. Aspects of morphine addiction are probably mediated by endogenous opioids. While it is clear that alcohol has robust interactions with the endogenous opioid system, the direct link between the two has not been found. The link may be an opioid receptor, but probably it is not. One hypothesis is that alcohol metabolites act on an as yet unknown receptor to alter the activity of the endogenous opioid system. The TIQ (tetrahydro-isoaninoline) hypothesis of alcoholism is exciting, but, first, concensus needs to be reached regarding the presence or absence of TIQs during and following alcohol intoxication. Most probably endogenous opioids alter feeding processes, but it is not known whether the actions are pharmacological or physiological.

At this time there is not sufficient evidence to conclude that endogenous opioids mediate the addictive processes of even one substance of abuse. On the other hand, the null hypothesis of no endogenous opioid involvement in the etiology addictive processes also has not been proved. The question now becomes to make the best guess. The endogenous opioid system is probably involved with morphine dependence or tolerance processes and possibly in the acquisition of morphine abuse behaviors. Endogenous opioids may be involved in the etiology of alcoholism, but there is as yet no convincing evidence for a link between opiates and alcohol. No evidence, very fragmentary evidence, and negative evidence have been found regarding interactions of the endogenous opioid system with a host of other substances including benzodiazepines (such as Valium), barbiturates, marijuana, and PCP. There are some positive findings regarding benzodiazepines and opioids, but the evidence of GABA-benzodiazepines interactions and of naloxone's effects on GABA makes judgment on the question of a direct benzodiazepine-opioid interaction impossible.

It would seem that a hypothesis of a general involvement of one brain system with several substances of abuse is premature. The endogenous opioids seem to have complex interactions with many other neurochemical systems and therefore apparently would affect many diverse behaviors. It may be that one role of the endogenous opioids is critical for addictive processes. But more likely the system has roles for many behaviors. Certainly possible relationships with substances of abuse should be explored. The endogenous opioid hypothesis of substance abuse should not be the sole line of investigation in the field. Other possible hypotheses should be pursued as well.

One excellent candidate for a more generalized role of the endogenous opioid system in addictive processes lies with the hypothetical function of the endogenous opioids in adaptive behaviors, including learning, responsiveness to stress, conditioned fear, and defensive behavior. Perhaps for substances that act to reduce the effects of stress or reduce the aversiveness of stimuli, the endogenous opioid system is a common link. Perhaps some of the environmental factors are mediated by endogenous opioids. At present most of the evidence for a role of endogenous opioids in stress reduction comes from whole body manipulations of endogenous opioids and a central role is not clear. It is very important that emphasis be placed on central manipulations and on central measures of endogenous opioids since few studies can be found on relationships of behaviors to central levels, turnover rates, or activities of endogenous opioid systems. Certainly peripheral administration of chemical agents can provide useful information, but the information cannot be used to form definite conclusions regarding central processes without additional research.

Research on potential endogenous opioid involvement in substance abuse should continue. Barbiturates, marijuana, benzodiazepines, and PCP should be examined with regard to possible effects on levels or activities of endogenous opioids. Bloom's criteria (chapter 7) provide an excellent conceptual framework for directing research regarding the evidence needed to link a brain system such as might be formed by the opioids with the etiology of substance abuse. Bloom's criteria are conceptually very similar to the criteria that have been proposed to identify neuronal circuits and systems in the brian that are critically involved in learning and memory (see Thompson et al. 1976).

A word of caution is in order against the steering of resources into one line of drug research. The physiological functions of the opioid peptides are only beginning to be understood. Most likely many interactions with other peptides and with putative neurotransmitters will be discovered, and almost certainly newfound endogenous opioids will be shown to be involved in a wide range of behaviors. Thus it could be a great mistake to decide prematurely that one behavior, namely substance abuse, should be researched to the exclusion of everything else. Because the presence in the central nervous system of many opioids have only recently been discovered, relatively little is known. Many questions have been raised in the literature and only a few have been answered. To limit the research options on the basis of a few findings is not good scientific practice. Much potential good can be lost by such an approach.

References

Adams, W.J.; Lorens, S.A.; and Mitchell, C.L. 1972. *Fed. Proc.* 140: 770-771.

Akil, H.; Madden, J.; and Patrick, R.L. 1976. In H.W. Kosterlitz (ed.), *Opiates and Endogenous Opioid Peptides*, pp. 63-70. Amsterdam: Elsevier.

Akil, H.; Watson, S.J.; Berger, P.A.; and Barchas, J.D. 1978. In E. Costa and M. Trabucchi (eds.), *The Endorphins*, pp. 125-139. New York: Raven Press.

Altshuler, H.L.; Phillips, P.E.; and Feinhandler, D.A. 1980. *Life Sci.* 26: 679-688.

Baxter, M.G.; Follenfant, R.L.; Miller, A.A.; and Sethna, D.M. 1977. *Brit. J. Pharmacol.* 59:523.

Belluzzi, J.D., and Stein, L. 1977. *Nature* 266:556-558.

Blum, K.; Briggs, A.H.; De Lallo, L.; and Elston, S.F.A. 1979. *Fed. Proc.* 38:1028.

Blum, K.; Briggs, A.H.; Elston, S.F.A.; Hirst, M.; Hamilton, M.; and Vereby, K. 1980a. In H. Rigter and J.C. Crabbe (eds.), *Alcohol Tolerance and Dependence*, pp. 371-391. Amsterdam: Elsevier.

Blum, K.; Futterman, S.; Wallace, J.E.; and Schwertner, H.A. 1977. *Nature* 265:49-51.

Blum, K.; Sar, M.; Sheridan, P.J.; Briggs, A.H.; Elston, S.F.A.; and De Lallo, L. 1980b. *Fed. Proc.* 39:606.

Blum, K.; Wallace, J.E.; Eubanks, J.D.; and Schwertner, H.A. 1975. *Pharmacologist* 124:197.

Bolles, R.C., and Fanselow, M.S. 1980. *Behav. and Brain Sci.* 3:291-301.

Borg, S.; Krande, H.; Magnuson, E.; and Sjoquist, B. 1980. Unpublished manuscript. Department of Clinical Alcohol and Drug Research, Karolinska Institute and Department of Alcohol and Drug Addiction Research, Karolinska Institute, S-104, Stockholm, Sweden.

Brown, J.S.; Kalish, H.I.; and Farber, I.E. 1951. *J. Exp. Psychol.* 41:317.

Buchsbaum, M.S.; Davis, G.C.; and Bunney, W.E., Jr. 1977. *Nature* 270:620-622.

Bush, H.D.; Bush, M.F.; Miller, A.; and Reid, L.D. 1976. *Physiol. Psychol.* 4:78-85.

Carey, R.J.; Goodall, E.; and Lorens, S.A. 1975. *J. Comp. Physiol. Psychol.* 88:224-230.

Carlson, R.H., and Lydic, R. 1976. *Psychopharmacology*, 50:61-64.

Castellucci, V., and Kandel, E. 1976. In T.J. Tighe and R.N. Leaton (eds.), *Habituation: Perspectives from Child Development, Animal Behavior, and Neurophysiology*, pp. 1-47. Hillsdale, N.J.: Lawrence Erlbaum.

Catlin, D.H.; George, R.; and Li, C.H. 1978. *Life Sci.* 23:2147-2154.

Chance, W.T.; White, A.C.; Krynock, G.M.; and Rosecrans, J.A. 1978. *Brain Res.* 141:371-374.

Childers, S.; Simantov, R.; and Snyder, S.H. 1977. *Europ. J. Pharm.* 46:289-293.

Clement-Jones, V.; McLaughlin, L.; Lowry, P.J.; Besser, G.M.; and Rees, L.H. 1979. *Lancet* 2:380-382.

Cohen, G., and Collins, M.A. 1971. *Science* 167:1749-1751.

Collins, M.A., and Bigdeli, M.G. 1975. *Life Sci.* 16:585-602.

Collins, M.A.; Nym, W.P.; Borge, G.F.; Teas, G.; and Goldfarb, C. 1979. *Science* 206:1184-1186.

Davis, M. 1979. *Europ. J. Pharmacol.* 54:341-347.

Davis, V.E., and Walsh, M.J. 1970. *Science* 167:1005-1007.

de Wied, D.; Bohus, B.; van Ree, J.M.; and Urban, J. 1978a. *J. Pharm. Exp. Therapeutics* 204:570-580.

de Wied, D.; Kovacs, G.L.; Bohus, B.; van Ree, J.M.; and Greven, H.M. 1978b. *Eur. J. Pharm.* 49:427-436.

Domino, E.F., and Olds, M.E. 1972. *Psychopharmacologia* 23:1-16.

Ehrman, R.N.; Josephson, P.J.; Schull, J.; and Sparich, C. 1979. Paper presented at meeting of Eastern Psychological Association, New York.

Eikelboom, R., and Stewart, J. 1979. *Psychopharmacology* 61:31-38.

Esposito, R., and Kornetsky, C. 1977. *Science* 195:189-191.

Fanselow, M.S. 1979. *Physiol. Psychol.* 7:70-74.

Fanselow, M.S., and Bolles, R.C. 1979a. *Bull. Psychon. Soc.* 14:88-90.

Fanselow, M.S., and Bolles, R.C. 1979b. *J. Comp. Physiol. Psychol.* 93: 736-744.

Fratta, W.; Yany, H.Y.; Hong, J.; and Costa, E. 1977. *Nature* 268:452-453.

Gallagher, M., and Kapp, B.S. 1978. *Life Sci.* 23:1973-1978.

Gentry, R.T.; Ho, A.; and Dole, V.P. 1980. *Alcohol: Clin. Expert. Res.* 4:215.

Grandison, L., and Guidotti, A. 1977. *Neuropharmacol.* 16:533-536.

Greenwald, J.E.; Fertel, R.H.; Wong, L.K.; Schwarz, R.D.; and Bianchine, J.R. 1979. *Fed. Proc.* 38:379.

Grevert, P., and Goldstein, A. 1977. *Psychopharmacology* 53:111-113.

Gunion, N.W., and Peters, R. 1978. *Soc. Neurosci. Abstr.* 6:527.

Hamilton, M.G., and Hirst, M. 1980. *Substance and Alcohol Actions/ Misuse* 1:121-144.

Hamilton, M.G.; Blum, K.; and Hirst, M. 1978. *Alcohol: Clin. Exp. Res.* 2:133-137.

Hamilton, M.G.; Hirst, M.; and Blum, K. 1979. *Life Sci.* 25:2205-2210.

Hayes, R.L.; Bennett, G.J.; Newlon, P.G.; and Mayer, D.L. 1976. *Soc. Neurosci. Abstr.* 2:939.

Hayes, R.L.; Bennett, G.J.; Newlon, P.G.; and Mayer, D.L. 1978. *Brain Res.* 155:69-90.

Holtzman, S.G. 1974. *J. Pharmacol. Exp. Therapeutics* 189:51-60.

Holtzman, S.G. 1975. *Life Sci.* 16:1465-1470.

Holtzman, S.G. 1976. *Psychopharmacology* 46:223-227.

Holtzman, S.G. 1979. *Life Sci.* 24:219-226.

Izquierdo, I. 1979. *Psychopharmacology* 60:199-203.

Izquierdo, I.; Dias, R.D.; Souza, D.O.; Carrasco, M.A.; Elisabetsky, E.; and Perry, M.L. 1980a. *Behav. Brain Res.* 1:451-468.

Izquierdo, I.; Souza, D.O.; Carrasco, M.A.; Dias, R.D.; Perry, M.L.; Eisinger, E.; Elisabetsky, E.; and Vendite, D. 1980b. *Psychopharmacology* 70:173-177.

Jacquet, Y.F.; Klee, W.A.; Rice, K.C.; Ilizima, I.; and Minamikawa, J. 1977. *Science* 198:842-845.

Jeffcoate, W.J.; Cujllen, M.H.; Herbert, M.; Hastings, A.G.; and Walder, C.P. 1979. *Lancet* 2:1157-1159.

Kaplan, R., and Glick, S.D. 1979. *Life Sci.* 24:2309-2312.

Kastin, A.J.; Scollan, E.L.; King, M.G.; Schally, A.V.; and Coy, D.H. 1976. *Pharmacol. Biochem. Behav.* 5:691-695.

Kenney, N.J.; McKay, L.D.; Woods, S.C.; and Williams, R. 1978. *Soc. Neurosci. Abstr.* 4:1976.

King, B.M.; Castellanos, F.X.; Kastin, A.J.; Berzas, M.C.; Mauk, M.D.; Olson, G.A.; and Olson, R.D. 1979. *Pharmacol. Biochem. Behav.* 11:729-732.

Konturek, S.J. 1978. *Scand. J. Gastroent.* 13:257-261.

Koob, G.F.; Foote, S.L.; and Bloom, F.E. 1978. *Soc. Neurosci. Abstr.* 4:495.

Kooy, van der, D.; Le Piane, F.G.; and Phillips, A.G. 1977. *Life Sci.* 20:981-986.

Le Moal, M.; Koob, G.F.; and Bloom, F.E. 1979. *Life Sci.* 24:1631-1636.

Levine, S.; Smotherman, W.P.; and Hennessy, J.W. 1977. In L.H. Miller, C.A. Sandman, and A.J. Kastin (eds.), *Neuropeptide Influences on the Brain and Behavior*, pp. 163-177. New York: Raven Press.

Lewis, J.W.; Cannon, J.T.; and Liebeskind, J.C. 1980. *Science* 208:623-625.

Lorens, S.A. 1979. *Alcohol: Clin. Exper. Res.* 3:185.

Lorens, S.A., and Mitchell, C.L. 1973. *Psychopharmacologia* 32:271-277.

Lorens, S.A., and Sainati, S.M. 1978. *Life Sci.* 23:1359-1364.

Lowy, M.T.; Maickel, R.P.; and Yim, G.K.W. 1980. *Life Sci.* 26:2113-2118.

Madden, J.; Akil, H.; Patrick, R.L.; and Barchas, J.D. 1977. *Nature* 265:358-360.

Maickel, R.P.; Braude, M.C.; and Zabik, J.E. 1977. *Neuropharmacol.* 16:863-866.

Malfroy, B.; Swertz, J.P.; Guyon, A.; Roques, B.P.; and Schwartz, J.C. 1978. *Nature* 276:523-526.

Marcus, R., and Kornetsky, C. 1974. *Psychopharmacologia* 38:1-13.

Margules, D.L.; Moisset, B.; Lewis, M.J.; Shibuya, H.; and Pert, C. 1978. *Science* 202:988-991.

Maroli, A.N.; Tsang, W-K; and Stutz, R.M. 1978. *Pharmacol. Biochem. Beh.* 8:988-991.

Martinez, J.L., and Rigter, H. 1980a. *Neurosci. Lett.* 19:197-201.

Martinez, J.L., and Rigter, H. 1980b. *Soc. Neurosci. Abstr.* 6:319.

McCloy, J., and McCloy, R.F. 1979a. *Lancet* 2:156.

McCloy, J., and McCloy, R.F. 1979b. *Lancet* 2:753.

McGivern, R.F., and Berntson, G.C. 1980 *Science* 210:210-211.

Mello, N.K., and Mendelson, J.H. 1978. *Pharmac. Biochem. Behav.* 9:579-586.

Messing, R.B.; Jensen, R.A.; Martinez, J.L.; Spiehler, V.R.; Vasquez, B.J.; Soumireu-Mourat, B.; Liang, K.C.; and McGaugh, J.L. 1979. *Behav. Neural Biol.* 27:266-275.

Middaugh, L.D.; Read, E.; and Boggan, W.O. 1978. *Pharmacol. Biochem. Behav.* 9:157-160.

Morley, J.E., and Levine, A.S. 1980. *Science* 209:1259-1261.

Myers, R.D. 1978. *Alcohol: Clin. Exp. Res.* 2:145-154.

Myers, R.D., and Melchior, C.L. 1977. *Pharmacol. Biochem. Behav.* 7: 381-392.

Myers, R.D., and Oblinger, M. 1977. *Drug Alcohol Dependence* 2:469-484.

Olds, J., and Milner, P. 1954. *J. Comp. Physiol. Psychol.* 47:419-427.

Olds, J., and Travis, R.P. 1960. *J. Pharmacol. Exp. Therapeutics* 128: 397-404.

Olds, M.E. 1966. *J. Comp. Physiol. Psychol.* 62:136-140.

Olds, M.E. 1979. *Brain Res.* 168:351-360.

Olson, G.A.; Olson, R.D.; Kastin, A.J.; Castellanos, F.X.; Kneale, M.T.; Coy, D.H.; and Wolf, R.H. 1979. *Neurosci. Biobehav. Rev.* 3:285-299.

O'Neill, P.J., and Rahwan, R.G. 1977. *J. Pharmacol. Exp. Therapeutics* 200:306-313.

Pinsky, C.; La Bella, F.S.; and Leybin, L.C. 1978. In D.E. Smith, S.M. Anderson, M. Buxton, M. Gottlieb, W. Harvey, and T. Chung (eds.), *A Multicultural View of Drug Abuse.* Boston: G.K. Hall.

Polak, J.M.; Bloom, S.R.; Sullivan, S.N.; Facer, P.; and Pearse, A.G.E. 1977. *Lancet* 1:972-974.

Przewlocki, R.; Holt, V.; Duka, T.H.; Lkeber, G.; Gramsch, C.H.; Haarmann, I.; and Herz, A. 1979. *Brain Res.* 174:357.

Puig, M.M.; Gascon, P.; and Musacchio, J.M. 1977. *Eur. J. Pharmacol.* 45:205-206.

Riggin, R.M., and Kissinger, P.T. 1977. *Anal. Chem.* 49:530-533.

Rigter, H. 1978. *Science* 200:83-85.

Rigter, H.; Greven, H.; and van Riezen, H. 1977. *Neuropharmacol.* 16: 545-547.

Rigter, H.; Hannan, T.J.; Messing, R.B.; Martinez, J.L.; Vasquez, B.J.; Jensen, R.A.; Veliquette, J.; and McGaugh, J.L. 1980a. *Life Sci.* 26:337-345.

Rigter, H.; Jensen, R.A.; Martinez, J.L.; Messing, R.B.; Vasquez, B.J.; Liang, K.C.; and McGauuh, J.L. 1980b. *Proc. Nat. Acad. Sci.* 77: 3729-3732.

Roemer, D.; Buescher, H.H.; Hill, R.C.; Pless, J.; Bauer, W.; Cardinaux, F.; Closse, A.; Hauser, D.; and Huguenin, R. 1977. *Nature* 268:547-549.

Ross, D.H.; Medina, M.A.; and Cardenas, H.L. 1974. *Science* 186:63-65.

Rossier, J., and Bloom, F.E. 1979. In H.H. Loh and D.H. Ross (eds.), *Neurochemical Mechanisms of Opiates and Endorphins*, pp. 187-225. New York: Raven Press.

Rossier, J.; Rogers, J.; Shibasaki, R.; Guillemin, R.; and Bloom, F.E. 1979. *Proc. Nat. Acad. Sci.* 76:2077-2080.

Sawynok, J.; Pinsky, C.; and La Bella, F.S. 1979. *Life Sci.* 25:1621-1632.

Scoto, G.M.; Spadero, C.; Spampinato, S.; Arrigo-Reina, R.; and Ferri, S. 1979. *Psychopharmacology* 60:217-219.

Segal, D.S.; Browne, R.G.; Bloom, F.E.; Ling, N.; and Guillemin, R. 1977. *Science* 198:411-413.

Sherman, J.E. 1979. *Learn. Motivation* 10:383-418.

Shier, W.T.; Koda, L.Y.; and Bloom, F.E. 1980. *Alcohol: Clin. Exp. Res.* 4:228.

Shimomura, J.; Oku, J.; Glick, Z.; and Bray, G.A. 1980. *Fed. proc.* 39: 761.

Siegel, S. 1976. *Science* 193:323-325.

Siegel, S. 1978. *J. Comp. Physiol. Psych.* 92:1137-1149.

Smith, T.W.; Hughes, J.; Kosterlitz, H.W.; and Sosa, R.P. 1976. In H.W. Kosterlitz (ed.), *Opiates and Endogenous Opioid Peptides*, pp. 57-62. Amsterdam: Elsevier/North-Holland Biomedical Press.

Stein, L. 1964. *Fed Prc.* 23:836-841.

Stein, L., and Belluzzi, J.D. 1978. *Adv. Biochem. Psychopharmacol.* 18: 299-311.

Szekely, J.I.; Ronai, A.Z.; Dunai-Kovacs, Z.; Graf, L.; and Bajusz, S. 1977. *Experientia* 33:54-55.

Terenius, L. 1978. *Ann. Rev. Pharmacol. Toxicol.* 18:189-204.

Thompson, R.F.; Berger, T.W.; Cegavske, C.F.; Patterson, M.M.; Roemer, R.A.; Teyler, T.J.; and Young, R.A. 1976. *Am. Psychologist* 31:209-227.

Thompson, R.F., and Glanzman, D.G. 1976. In T.J. Tighe and R.N. Leaton (eds.), *Habituation: Perspectives from Child Development, Animal Behavior, and Neurophysiology*. Hillsdale, N.J.: Lawrence Erlbaum.

Thompson, R.F., and Spencer, W.A. 1966. *Psychol. Rev.* 173:16-43.

Tseng, L., and Cheng, D.S. 1980. *Fed. Proc.* 39:606.

Tseng, L.; Loh, H.H.; and Li, C.H. 1977. *Biochem. Biophys. Res. Comm.* 74:390-396.

van Loon, G.R., and de Souza, E.B. 1978. *Res. Comm. Chem. Path. Pharmacol.* 22:203-204.

van Loon, G.R.; de Souza, E.B.; and Kim, C. 1978. *Can. J. Physiol. Pharmacol.* 56:1067-1071.

van Ree, J.M.; de Wied, D.; Bradbury, A.F.; Hulme, E.C.; Smyth, D.G.; and Snell, C.R. 1976. *Nature* 264:792-794.

van Ree, J.M.; Smyth, D.G.; and Colpaert, F.C. 1979. *Life Sci.* 24:495-502.

Waterfield, A.A.; Hughes, J.; and Kosterlitz, H.W. 1976. *Nature* 260: 624-625.

Wauquier, A.; Niemegeers, C.J.; and Lal, H. 1974. *Psychopharmacologia* 37:303-310.

Way, E.L., and Glasgow, C. 1978. In M.A. Lipton, A. Di Mascio, and K.F. Killam (eds.), *Psychopharmacology: A Generation of Progress*, pp. 1535-1555. New York: Raven Press.

Wei, E., and Loh, H. 1976. *Science* 193:1262-1263.

Wesche, D.; Hollt, V.; and Herz, A. 1977. *Arch. Pharm.* 301:79.

Whitney, G., and Horowitz, G.P. 1978. *Behav. Genetics* 8:177-182.

Wikler, A. 1973. *Cond. Reflex* 8:193-210.

Wise, R.A. 1978. *Brain Res.* 152:215-247.

9 Commonalities in Substance Use: A Genetic Perspective

Gerald E. McClearn

For a geneticist, commonality can be translated into the basic genetic concept of pleiotropy, which may be briefly defined as the influence by one gene on two or more phenotypes (Schaie et al. 1975:233). Phenotype, in turn, may be defined as any observable structural or functional property of an individual (ibid.). Thus, to study the genetics of commonalities of drug use and abuse phenotypes is to address oneself to those features that can be traced to shared genetic influence.

The primary function of a gene is to produce a specific polypeptide, which may be a protein or a subunit of a protein. Of particular importance to this discussion are those proteins that are enzymes. Pleiotropic effects arise because the causal pathway from the enzyme to the measured phenotype may be complexly branched. A hypothetical example is provided in figure 9-1, where a gene is represented by paired circles because all genes except sex-linked ones occur in pairs with one from each parent. This gene pair is shown as giving rise to a partiuclar enzyme that then influences a network of anatomic, biochemical and physiological processes (shown as squares) that ultimately lead to the two phenotypes, the large circles on the right labeled I and II.

Different alternative forms of a given gene, called *alleles*, may exist. Therefore, the *genotypes* of individuals may vary. For example, if two alleles, A_1 and A_2, exist for the gene pair, three different pairings are possible: A_1A_1, A_1A_2, A_2A_2. The A_1A_1 and A_2A_2 combinations (or genotypes) are said to be homozygous and the A_1A_2 genotype is said to be heterozygous. These different genotypes can give rise to differences in the enzyme that is influenced by that gene pair and therefore in all structures and functions that are downstream toward the phenotypes I and II.

It is easy to see how two drug-use phenotypes might covary if they share some basic biochemical process in which the enzyme is involved. However, it is not only at the level of primary gene products or their immediate sequelae that genetically influenced commonalities can be sought. The protein might influence downstream variables of hormones and neurotransmitters that ultimately contribute to the development of a personality attribute of susceptibility to peer group pressure. Then if peer pressure is exerted for multiple drug use in a population of individuals varying with respect to this susceptibility, a commonality that is genetically based but many steps removed

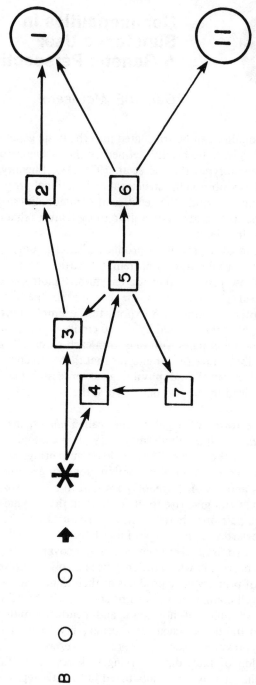

Source: Gerald E. McClearn and Sally M. Anderson 1979. Genetics and ethanol tolerance. *Drug and Alcohol Dependence* 4:61-76. Reprinted by permission.

Figure 9-1. Schema Showing Pathways of Influence of a Particular Gene Pair on Two Hypothetical Phenotypes

from primary gene action could result. The point is that the perspective of genetic commonalities is pertinent not only to so-called biological determinants but also to more behavioral and social factors.

Most issues in substance abuse will be vastly more complex than implied by the single-gene model of figure 9-1. Presumably, substance use and abuse involve many processes that may be interrelated to different degrees. The concepts of avidity, uptake, distribution, disposition, sensitivity, tolerance, and dependence all come readily to mind as possible components in the total behavioral pattern of substance use and abuse. It is reasonable to expect that these components will have different genetic determinants so that a picture more like that of figure 9-2, undoubtedly still grossly over simplified, may be more representative of the real world. This figure portrays polygenic inheritance, which is a logical counterpoint to pleiotropy. In

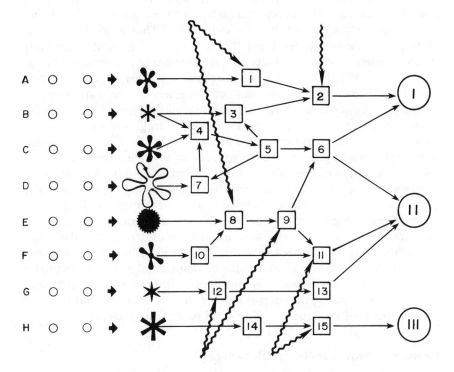

Source: Adapted from Gerald E. McClearn and Sally M. Anderson. 1979. Genetics and ethanol tolerance. *Drug and Alcohol Dependence* 4:61-76.

Figure 9-2. Schema Illustrating Pathways of Influence of Several Gene Pairs on Two Hypothetical Phenotypes

pleiotropy, one gene influences many phenotypes; in polygenic inheritance one phenotype is influenced by several genes.

It can be seen from this representation that what we call a phenotype is an arbitrary matter. Any of the boxes in the causal nexus leading from the gene pairs on the left to phenotypes I and II on the right could be a phenotype in its own right if we chose to measure it. If I and II are indices of consumption of two different substances, genetic commonality might be expressed in terms of covarying of consumption as a function of different genotypes. It might also be possible to regard commonalities involving the upstream attributes, however; [7] might be correlated with [4] or either of these might be correlated with one or both of the ultimate phenotypes I and II. Some of the intermediate processes may covary while others may not. Thus, [2] and [6] may be correlated with each other and with both I and II. The same pattern will be observed for [6] and [11]. However, [2] and [11] will not covary.

From this complexity of the causal nexus we may then expect to encounter commonalities that are partial. Phenotypes I and II may share some part of the determinant network, but each may have some causal factors impinging upon it that are not shared with the other. Thus we expect less than perfect correlations between I and II. Furthermore, we might conceivably find a correlation or commonality between the level of consumption of one substance and the ability to acquire tolerance to another, without any correlation between the two consumption measures or the two tolerance measures. This possibility forces examination of the issue of commonality among the component aspects of use of a single drug. Not only is it of intrinsic interest to learn of the relation between avidity for a drug, its disposition parameters, target organ sensitivity, ability to acquire various kinds of tolerance and dependence liability; it may be *necessary* to understand these interrelations in order to deal with issues concerning which particular aspects of drug I use are related to which particular aspects of drug II use.

With this rather theoretical prelude, we may now turn to some empirical evidence. First, it will be useful to examine a few examples from the rather substantial body of evidence that shows that genetic differences can indeed influence drug related variables considered singly. Next a very few examples will be noted that are pertinent to the issue of within-substance commonality of process. Finally, the sparse evidence that relates to the most central issue—cross-substance commonality—will be briefly reviewed.

Genetics of Substance-Related Behavior

Animal Models

The literature demonstrating genetic influence on differences in drug self-administration and drug sensitivity in animals has been growing at an accelerating rate. The scope of this research effort may be examined in a 1978 review monograph by Broadhurst.

The simplest sort of evidence available involves the comparison of inbred strains. The logic of these strain comparisons is quite straightforward; inbreeding continued for a sufficient number of generations gives rise to genetic uniformity within a strain. That is to say, all animals within an inbred strain are genetically alike and homozygous for all gene pairs. (The idealized state of complete genetic homogeneity is perhaps not attained in the real world, but it is a useful working approximation.) Strains of different origin have a dismissably small probability of having the same genotype. Two strains may thus be assumed to differ in genotype, even though the number and identity of the genes for which they differ are unknown. If two or more such strains are treated as similarly as possible, then differences between them in a phenotype are prima facie evidence for genetic influence on that phenotype. Strain differences are thus very strong evidence that genes influence the phenotype, but the evidence is not very detailed.

The laboratory mouse is particularly convenient for this sort of research by virtue of the large number of inbred strains available, and strain differences have been shown in this species for a variety of processes for many drugs. Perhaps the most studied substance to date has been ethanol, and examples from mouse research with this drug will be used here to illustrate the principal points. An early study in this area (McClearn and Rodgers 1959) examined preference for a 10 percent solution of alcohol over water in a free-choice situation. Of several strains investigated, the A and DBA were very low in consumption of the solution. The DBA in particular were total abstainers within the limits of resolution of the techniques employed. The C57BL mice, on the other hand, consumed on the average about two-thirds of their total daily fluid intake from the 10 percent ethanol solution.

By manipulating genotype through appropriate matings, it was possible to provide the persuasive demonstration of the influence of genes on alcohol consumption displayed in figure 9-3 (McClearn 1982). The two strains with which the matings were begun were the low-preference A strain and the high-preference C57BL strain. Mating of C57BL with A animals produced a hybrid F1 generation, which, with respect to those gene pairs relevant to alcohol preference and for which the parent strains differ, have 50 percent of their alleles from the C57BL parent and, of course, 50 percent from the A strain parent. Because of the uniformity within each parent strain, the F1 animals are all genetically alike although they are heterozygous for each gene pair for which the parent strains differed in allelic constitution. Thus *each* F1 animal has 50 percent C57BL and 50 percent A alleles. The F2 generation is obtained by intermating F1 animals. In the F2 generation there is an opportunity for genetic segregation, and each

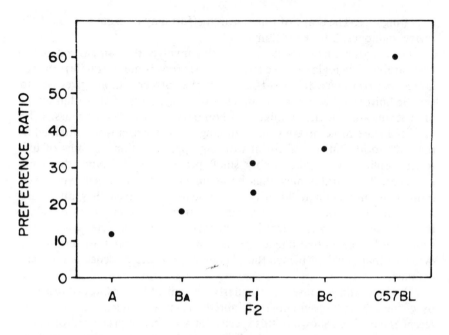

Source: Gerald E. McClearn. 1981. Animal models of genetic factors in alcoholism. *Advances in Substance Abuse*, vol. 2, pp. 185-217. Greenwich, Conn.: JAI Press. Reprinted by permission.

Figure 9-3. Relationship of Alcohol Preference Ratio to Percentage of C57BL Alleles

F2 animal differs genetically from each other one; on average, however, they have 50 percent C57BL alleles and 50 percent A alleles. The backcrosses are produced by mating F1 animals to C57BL and to A animals, respectively. The backcrosses to C57BL have 75 percent C57BL alleles, on average; the backcross to A have 25 percent C57BL alleles, on average. Figure 9-3 shows the systematic gene dose-response relationship of C57BL alleles and alcohol preference.

Either because of observed differences in some phenotype or by virtue of reproductive isolation, different substrains may come to be identified within a strain. For simplicity these substrain specifications will be omitted in this chapter, but for the next example it is necessary to distinguish between the C57BL/10 and C57BL/Uae strains. In general, a moderate to high alcohol preference has been described for numerous substrains of C57BL. Poley (1972), however, found the C57BL/Uae animals to have very low alcohol preference. Whitney and Horowitz (1978) replicated the basic result. Although this nonpreferring substrain had been separated from an original C57BL/6 stock for approximately forty generations, it had been maintained by strict sibling mating during that interval. The genetic drift that might have occurred presumably could have involved only one or a very small number of gene pairs. This outcome, therefore, shows the potential of one or a few gene pairs in causing a major change in voluntary alcohol ingestion. This does not in any way infirm a general model of polygenic influence on alcohol preference, however. The particular allele involved may serve a necessary but insufficient role in the total genetic causal system. That is to say, the allelic configuration of the normal C57BL/6 or C57BL/10 animals for that particular gene pair may be necessary for the influence of the alleles of other alcohol preference influencing gene pairs to be expressed. The further exploration of possibly quite limited genetic differences among substrains could constitute a very useful tool in studying the mechanisms underlying single phenotypes. As we shall see later, substrains may also be extremely useful in addressing issues of commonality.

Yet another type of evidence on genetic influence on drug use behavior is provided by the study of the resemblance of relatives. Reed (1977), for example, studied a variety of responses to an administered dose of alcohol in parents and offspring of a genetically heterogeneous (HS) mouse stock. The regression of offspring score on parent score or the intraclass correlation of siblings permits the estimation of the heritability of the phenotype, which is the proportion of the total phenotypic variance that is attributable to additive genetic variance. The heritability estimates for open-field activity change, heart-rate change and duration of loss of righting response were 0.12, 0.18, and 0.17, respectively. No significant estimate of heritability was obtained for ataxia, change in emotionality, change in rectal temperature, or time to lose righting response after the injection.

A further type of evidence can be derived from selective breeding experiments. In selective breeding, animals of similar extreme phenotypes within a genetically heterogeneous population are mated together to produce the next generation. An example is provided by McClearn and Kakihana (1973) who measured sensitivity to administered alcohol by observing the duration of loss of righting response in a population of HS animals subsequent to an intraperitoneal dose of alcohol. Those animals who had the shortest sleep time were mated together and those animals who had the longest sleep time were mated together. This procedure was followed in subsequent generations with the ultimate result that two lines of greatly differing sensitivity to ethanol were generated. It is possible to calculate heritability retrospectively from such a study. In the present instance, this realized heritability was estimated to be 0.18. The success of a selective breeding program provides incontrovertible evidence of a nonzero heritability in the base population. Perhaps of greater importance is the fact that the animals of the two lines constitute tools of great utility in further research on the mechanisms through which the genes influence the selected phenotype.

Human Research

Information on genetic influence on substance use and abuse in human beings has been generated mostly from the study of identical (monozygous or MZ) and fraternal (dizygous or DZ) twins. The logic of twin studies is simple: members of MZ twin pairs are identical in genetic constitution whereas fraternal, or DZ, twins are only as similar genetically as are ordinary siblings. Therefore, to the extent that MZ twin pairs resemble each other more than DZ twin pairs do, one might infer a genetic influence on the phenotype being assessed. A difficulty is that such an inference would be valid only if the pertinent environmental factors are no more or less similar in the case of MZ than of DZ twins. If MZ twins share environmental influences more than DZ twins do, then a greater similarity of MZ twins can be due to their greater genetic similarity, the greater similarity of their environments, or both. This fundamental problem of the classic twin method has been subject to considerable scrutiny in recent years, particularly in respect to behavioral phenotypes. It is easily demonstrable that with respect to numerous environments, MZ twins, on the average, are exposed to or seek out more similar circumstances than do DZ twins. Of course, these demonstrations are significant only if the particular environments have an influence on the phenotype being investigated. Results from several recent studies that have addressed the issue specifically suggest that the magnitude of the problem had been exaggerated in respect to many cognitive factors. There has been no direct examination of the importance of this environmental confound in twin studies on substance use and abuse. Results must therefore be interpreted with appropriate caution.

A landmark study by Partanen, Bruun, and Markkanen (1966) examined by questionnaire the alcohol consumption of a large number of Finnish twins. Both for frequency of drinking occasions and for amount consumed per occasion, MZ twins were more alike than DZ twins.

Loehlin (1972) analyzed questionnaire data from young American twins in the National Merit Scholarship and Kaprio et al. (1978) examined responses of twins in the Finnish twin register with generally similar results. Failure to find greater similarity of MZ than of DZ Italian twins in alcohol consumption measures was reported by Conterio and Chiarelli (1962), however.

Dealing with an index of alcohol abuse or alcoholism, Kaij (1960) produced evidence from Swedish twins that alcoholism was influenced by heredity. These data from twins are complemented by data on the risk of alcoholism in family members of alcoholic probands (Åmark 1951; Winokur et al. 1970). Family evidence of this sort, of course, is susceptible to the same difficulties of interpretation as are twin data. Family resemblance may be due to shared genes, shared environments, or both. Stronger evidence, disentangling to a substantial extent the genetic and environmental sources of variance, has been produced from studies of alcoholism in half-siblings (Schuckit, Goodwin, and Winokur 1972) and in adopted children of alcoholic and nonalcoholic parents (Goodwin et al. 1973).

Consumption measures of other drugs have also been obtained in twin studies. Evidence of heritable influence has been shown for tobacco use (Fisher 1958a,b; Todd and Mason 1959; Friberg et al. 1959; Rassachou-Nielsen 1960; Conterio and Chiarelli 1962, Dies et al. 1969, Crumpacker et al. 1979; Medlund et al. 1976; Kaprio et al. 1978, Partanen, Bruun, and Markkanen 1966; Perry 1973) and for consumption of coffee and tea (Conterio and Chiarelli 1962; Medlund et al. 1976; Perry 1973). A study by Pedersen (1980) explored alcohol, tobacco, coffee and tea, sleeping pill, and tranquilizer use in a powerful extension of the twin method that utilized observations on MZ and DZ twin pairs, their spouses, and children. Evidence of "familiality," a term that acknowledges the possible confounding of shared genotypes and environments, was obtained for use of spirits, coffee and tea, tranquilizers, and cigarettes.

To conclude this brief review, evidence both from animal models and from human research suggests that individual differences in a broad variety of drug use variables are subject to hereditary influence. It is thus defensible to consider that commonalities of drug use might arise from shared genetic factors.

Within-Substance Commonality

From theoretical considerations, the possibility was earlier raised that certain features of use of one substance might covary with certain features (not necessarily homologous ones) of another substance. If indeed the correlations among avidity, sensitivity, tolerance, and dependence within a single substance are less than perfect and also differ substantially in magnitude one from the other, it would seem to be the case that a program of search for commonalities should involve the assessment of multiple variables concerning each substance under investigation. This point does not require detailed elaboration, so only a few illustrative examples will be mentioned.

Inbred strains have been convenient for addressing this issue in animal research. For example, one study sought to determine if the differences among inbred strains in alcohol preference were related to differences in sensitivity to alcohol (McClearn 1962). The activity of mice exposed to ethanol vapor was compared to that of control animals from six different strains. Strain differences in response to the ethanol were large, with some strains (C57BL and DBA) showing a reduction in activity, some appearing to be unaffected (RIII and BALB/c), and some (C3H and A) showing an increase in activity. For present purposes the principal outcome is that C57BL and DBA animals, respectively the highest and lowest in preference, are affected similarly by this measure. One might conclude, therefore, that preference and sensitivity are not necessarily related.

However, using a different measure of sensitivity, Kakihana et al. (1966) found C57BL mice to have shorter sleep time than the low-alcohol-preferring BABL/c strain. Similarly Schneider et al. (1973) showed that C57BL required more infused alcohol to depress jaw-jerk reflex than did DBA animals. Thus, by these measures, there seems to be an inverse relation between preference and sensitivity.

Goldstein and Kakihana (1974) found that C57BL mice exhibited less severe withdrawal symptoms as measured by convulsions elicited by handling than did DBA, BALB/c, or Swiss Webster mice upon withdrawal from alcohol administered via inhalation for three days. Grieve, Griffiths, and Littleton (1979) replicated the strain difference in withdrawal severity between C57BL and DBA, with TO Swiss mice being intermediate. Furthermore, C57BL were rapid, TO Swiss were slower, and DBA were slowest in development of cellular tolerance to ethanol.

A picture emerges of a relation among preference, sensitivity, tolerance and withdrawal as follows:

	Preference	*Sensitivity*	*Tolerance*	*Withdrawal*
C57BL	High	Low	Fast	Mild
DBA	Low	High	Slow	Severe

Regrettably, this evidence of association among phenotypes from strain differences is limited. The process of inbreeding forces genetic uniformity within a strain for all genes. Thus insofar as genes influence any phenotype, it will tend to be more or less stabilized at some value. Even if several phenotypes are completely unrelated, in the sense that their causal nexuses are nonoverlapping, an apparent but fortuitous association can be generated by luck of the draw. Absence of an association is more compelling than its presence because absence clearly indicates that an association is at least not obligate. (See McClearn 1982a,b for more detailed discussions of this issue.)

The suggestive evidence of an association provided by strain comparisons needs to be supported by other types of evidence. Particularly appropriate for such purposes are selectively bred lines or genetically heterogeneous stocks, in which correlations between the allegedly related phenotypes can be examined.

Erwin, McClearn, and Kuse (1980), for example, studied the relation among voluntary alcohol consumption, acute tolerance, and central nervous system sensitivity in the HS stock of mice. Consumption and acquisition of acute tolerance were positively associated ($r = 0.47$), but neither of these variables was associated with sensitivity.

In conclusion, it is clear that the theoretical concern expressed earlier is justified. The outcome of commonalities research may be very dependent upon which components of substance-related behavior or response are examined and upon the particular operational definitions of those components.

Cross-Substance Commonality

The issue of cross-substance commonalities is more central. The basic question of genetic influence is whether and to what extent genes have pleiotropic effects on attributes relating to two or more substances. That is, we are concerned with the extent to which covariance in respect to these attributes is due to genetic factors. Unsurprisingly, inbred strain research provides much of the information. Given the demonstrated strain differences in alcohol preference, an attractive approach has been to inquire as to their responses to other substances. Schneider et al. (1973), for example, offered C57BL and DBA mice a choice of water and the 3-carbon alcohol propylene glycol. The strain differences in voluntary intake of propylene glycol were very similar to those of ethanol. A subsequent study (Hillman and Schneider 1975) replicated the high and low preference of C57BL and DBA animals for propylene glycol and also demonstrated the low preference of BALB/c and CBA mice, which are also low consumers of ethanol. In addition, it was shown that the activity of C57BL animals was less affected by injected proplylene glycol than that of the other strains. This result contrasts with that in which C57BL and DBA sensitivities to ethanol measured by activity change were similar (McClearn 1963). Thus perhaps the preference commonality for these two CNS depressants is not paralleled by a sensitivity commonality, at least as measured in these studies.

In further study Strange, Schneider, and Goldbort (1976) assessed preference of C57BL and DBA strains for several 3-carbon alcohols including propylene glycol. Briefly, C57BL preference exceeded that of DBAs for 1,2-propanediol (propylene glycol) and for 1-propanol. Both strains consumed only small amounts of 2-propanol and of 1,3-propanediol. The results of assessment of sensitivity to these alcohols are complex. Three dose levels were used for each substance. At the lowest dose employed of 1,2-propanediol, the strains did not differ in effect on activity; at the middle and high dose C57BL mice were still unaffected, but the DBAs became more active. At the two lowest doses of 1,3-propanediol, neither strain was affected, but at the highest dose both showed substantial reduction of activity.

For 1-propanol neither strain was affected by the lowest dose, and the intermediate and high doses were lethal to all animals of both strains.

In the case of 2-propanol, the DBA mice showed increased activity at the low dose, while C57BL mice were unaffected. At the intermediate dose, C57BL were depressed and DBA were unaffected. The high dose was hypnotic, with the DBAs displaying a longer sleep time.

These results show a limited preference commonality including ethanol, 1,2-propanediol, and 1-propanol but excluding 1,3-propanediol and 2-propanol. In sensitivity, the C57BL mice appear to be less sensitive whenever there is a strain difference. However, at several doses, neither strain was affected, and at one dose of one substance, C57BL animals were most affected. Clearly, the discovery or failure to discover a sensitivity commonality depends upon dose.

Griek (1974) compared C57BL and DBA strains on sensitivity to ethanol, morphine sulfate, and sodium amobarbital, using three doses and two measures for each drug. In the case of each drug, the strains were found to differ when one test was used and not to differ when the other was used. When differences were shown, DBA animals were more sensitive. They showed greater analgesic response to morphine (in a hot-plate test) and longer sleep times in response to ethanol and to sodium amobarbital. A sensitivity commonality is suggested, although the issue of situational specificity is highlighted by the fact that in half the measures (a tail-clip test of analgesia and measures of loss of righting reflex), no strain differences were found.

Of more direct relevance to commonality, Griek also studied the production of cross tolerance to these substances. In general, ethanol pretreatment altered subsequent response to both morphine and sodium amobarbital. With one exception, when cross tolerance was found in one strain, it was also found in the other. The exception was the case of ethanol pretreatment effect on tail-clip measures of analgesia to morphine sulfate: cross tolerance was shown by DBA mice but not by C57BL mice. An analysis of blood levels of the drugs at time of recovery of righting reflex suggested that tolerance and cross tolerance in C57BL mice are principally functional, related to central nervous system sensitivity changes, whereas the DBA tolerance and cross-tolerance are primarily dispositional, related to changes in drug metabolism. Pretreatment with morphine produced cross tolerance with ethanol but not with sodium amobarbital.

Randall and Lester (1974) sought to investigate the generality of the difference in sensitivity of C57BL and BALB/c strains to ethanol. Finding that C57BL are *more* sensitive to pentobarbital than are BALB/c animals, the authors concluded that there was no commonality with respect to brain sites involved in the hypnotic effect of the two drugs.

Inbred strains have also been featured in several studies on amphetamine, scopolamine, and other drugs. Scott et al. (1971), for example, found that C57BL aggression was reduced more than that of BALB/c mice subsequent to amphetamine administration. Similarly, Oliverio et al. (1966) found DBA to show a greater increase than C3H in escape-avoidance conditioning after scopolamine. For other examples, the review by Broadhurst (1978) should be consulted. All of these studies share the interpretational limitations cited earlier. The association between traits suggested by a relation between two strains on each of two substances *might* be completely fortuitous.

Single-gene manipulations on an inbred strain background offer an elegantly persuasive approach to the study of commonalities but one that has not yet been extensively used. Mutations provide one source of material for this method. Mutations occur within inbred strains just as they occur in any breeding population. When such a mutational event is recognized it is possible by appropriate matings to provide two groups—the original genetically homogeneous inbred strain and another strain, like the original in all respects except for the single newly mutated allele. Thus any differences between the two groups in respect to two substances could be persuasive evidence that that gene has pleiotropic, commonality-generating influence with respect to the two substances.

An approximation to this situation has been utilized to examine the possibility of commonality between alcohol preference and morphine addictability. The identification of an alcohol-avoiding C57BL substrain (C57BL/Uae) (Poley 1972; Whitney and Horowitz 1978) was described earlier, and the point was made that these animals probably differ from other C57BL substrains by only one or a few genes.

Horowitz (1976) showed that the C57BL/6J substrain displayed a high consumption of saccharin-adulterated morphine solution in a two-bottle-choice situation in contrast to several other inbred strains. Indeed these animals were sometimes observed to self-administer lethal doses. Whitney and Horowitz (1978) compared the alcohol-nonpreferring C57BL/Uae to the alcohol-preferring C57BL/6J and C57BL/10J substrains in this situation and found no differences in the consumption of morphine. Quite clearly, there is no necessary and obligate commonality between avidity for alcohol and avidity for morphine in these animals.

Another approach that provides stronger evidence than conventional inbred strain studies is the comparison of selectively bred lines. In the selective breeding paradigm, animals from a genetically heterogeneous stock are measured on the attribute of interest under investigation; animals displaying large amounts of it are mated together and animals displaying small amounts are mated together. This process repeated over generations will, if the attribute in question is influenced by genes at all, result in a divergence of the two lines. Successful selective breeding not only provides irrefutable evidence of a genetic component in the variance of the base population but also provides research animals of very high potential value in the study of commonalities. One example is provided by the Colorado Selection Study for sensitivity to ethanol. Gradual and systematic separation was obtained between lines displaying, respectively, long duration of loss of righting response and short duration of loss of righting response subsequent to an intraperitioneal injection of a dose of ethanol shown to be hypnotic for all animals of the base population (McClearn and Kakihana 1973).

The reason that comparisons of selected lines provide more substantial evidence of association of phenotypes is that selection pressure should result in alteration of allelic frequencies only for those genes that influence the phenotype under selection. Then any other correlated phenotypes must be part of the causal nexus of the selected phenotype. These considerations apply only to the ideal situation, however, and various difficulties and problems can render selected line comparisons less clear-cut. For example, in the long sleep (LS) and short sleep (SS) lines, fertility problems at one point reduced each line to a very few reproducing individuals. This resulted in inbreeding, which may have forced some apparent but fortuitous associations such as those that may occur in inbred strain comparisons.

The LS and SS lines were studied by Siemens and Chan (1975) with respect to sensitivity to sodium pentobarbital. Although sleep times differed, the brain concentrations at the time of regaining the righting response were practically identical. This result suggests a lack of commonality of alcohol and barbiturate sensitivity. This conclusion was supported and extended by the work of Erwin et al. 1976) who found that the median effective dose (ED_{50}) values for sodium pentobarbital or ether were very similar in LS and SS animals. In addition, sleep times following hypnotic doses of pentobarbital, chloral hydrate, trichloroethanol, or paraldehyde did not differ between these two lines. On the other hand, the ED_{50}s for loss of righting response following injection of several other alcohols (methanol, butanol, and t-butanol) were approximately twice as high in SS than in LS mice. These results demonstrate both an area of hypnotic sensitivity commonality among several alcohols and noncommonality with various other hypnotic substances.

The area of commonality was further illuminated by Church, Fuller, and Dudek (1976) who showed that LS animals were more sensitive than SS animals to salsolinol. Salsolinol is a substance formed from a reaction of dopamine with acetaldehyde that is a metabolic product of ethanol. These results provide a realistic exemplar of the theoretical picture of shared causal pathways presented earlier. The limits of the commonality are emphasized by Sanders's (1976) observations that SS mice are *more* sensitive to *subhypnotic* doses of ethanol (confirmed by Church (1977)) and of pentobarbital.

Human research directly pertinent to the genetics of substance use commonality is very rare. A study of Pedersen published in 1980, however, provides some pertinent data and demonstrates the potential of utilizing biological relatives in respect to polysubstance use. The research involved a family-of-twins design, in which MZ twins and DZ twins as well as their spouses and their children were studied. Included in the assessment were numerous indices of use of beer, wine, spirits (with a separate index of heavy drinking on single occasions), coffee or tea, tobacco, tranquilizers, and sleeping medications. Because of considerations of distributions, the latter two measures were excluded from the multivariate analyses that sought to establish the commonalities among these substances. Table 9-1 gives the phenotypic correlations that were obtained. Only a modest commonality is revealed among the alcoholic beverage use indices, with the relation between beer and spirits use being the largest. Heavy drinking is related about equally to these measures. Heavy drinking appears unrelated to coffee or tea use but does show a small covariation with smoking status (smoker versus nonsmoker). Smoking status is most closely related to consumption of spirits.

Of greater interest is that the number of comparisons possible between persons in this design permits the decomposition of this correlation matrix into two matrices, one in which the covariation is due to shared genes plus shared (family-common) environmental factors and one in which the covariation is influenced by environmental factors operating outside the family. These results are shown in table 9-2, where the standardized familial covariances are shown above the diagonal and standardized nonfamilial covariances are shown below the diagonal. Several interesting relationships emerge from this analysis. The covariation of beer and wine with spirits use seems to be derived principally from nonfamilial environmental sources. Indeed familial factors exert almost no influence on any commonalities in alcoholic beverage consumption. However, the relation of wine use to the heavy-drinking index is largely familial, with the associations of beer and

Table 9-1

Phenotypic Correlations of Drug-Use Measures of Intact Family Sample

Variables	Beer	Wine	Spirits	Coffee/Tea	Heavy Drinking	Smoking Status
Beer	. . .	.16	.34	− .01	.34	.16
Wine	.16	. . .	.21	.02	.34	.18
Spirits	.34	.21	. . .	.14	.47	.26
Coffee or tea	− .01	.02	.14	. . .	.09	.20
Heavy drinking	.34	.34	.47	.09	. . .	.18
Smoking status	.16	.18	.26	.20	.18	. . .

Source: Nancy L. Pedersen. 1980. Genetic and Environmental Factors for Usage of Common Drugs. Unpublished PhD dissertation, University of Colorado, Boulder. Reprinted by permission.

Table 9-2
Phenotypically Standardized Familial Covariances (above Diagonal)
and Phenotypically Standardized Nonfamilial Covariances (below Diagonal)
of Drug-Use Measures of Intact Family Sample

Variables	Beer	Wine	Spirits	Coffee/Tea	Heavy Drinking	Smoking Status
Beer	. . .	.08	.09	−.04	.10	.04
Wine	.08	. . .	.02	.10	.24	.10
Spirits	.25	.18	. . .	.04	.15	.12
Coffee or tea	.03	−.08	.10	. . .	.03	.20
Heavy drinking	.24	.10	.32	.05	. . .	−.05
Smoking status	.12	.08	.14	.00	.22	. . .

Source: Nancy L. Pedersen. 1980. Genetic and Environmental Factors for Usage of Common Drugs. Unpublished PhD dissertation, University of Colorado, Boulder. Reprinted by permission.

spirits to this index largely influenced by nonfamilial factors. Smoking status relates appreciably to two variables. The association with coffee or tea use is derived from familial influences; the association with heavy drinking has its origin in nonfamilial influences.

Conclusion

The data base on genetic factors in substance use commonalities is regrettably small. It is adequate, however, to illustrate the merits of a differential approach to the commonalities issue: an approach that examines differences in magnitude, composition, and source of the covariation that exists. Furthermore, the available evidence demonstrates the utility for further research in the area of genetically based animal models and the usefulness of incorporating biological relatives in human studies. Explication of the genetic and environmental sources of variance and covariance through shared causal pathways should be of great value in addressing the societal problems of substance use and abuse.

References

Broadhurst, P.L. 1978. *Drugs and the Inheritance of Behavior: A Survey of Comparative Psychopharmacogenetics*. New York: Plenum.

Church, A.C. 1977. Motor responses to acute alcohol administration in mice selected for differential alcohol-induced sleep time. *Behav. Genetics* 7:49 (abstract).

Church, A.C., Fuller, J.L. and Dudek, B.C. 1976. Salsolinol differentially affects mice selected for sensitivity to alcohol. *Psychopharmacol.* 47:49-52.

Conterio, F., and Chiarelli, B. 1962. Study of the inheritance of some daily life habits. *Heredity* 17:347-359.

Crumpacker, D.W., Cederlof, F.L., Kimberling, W.J., Sorensen, S., Vandenberg, S.G., Williams, J.S., McClearn, G.E., Grever, B., Iyer, H., Krier, M.J., Pedersen, N.L., Price, R.A., and Roulette, I. 1979. A twin methodology for the study of genetic and environmental control of variation in human smoking behavior. *Acta Genet. Med. Gemellol.* 28:174-195.

Dies, R., Honeyman, M., Reznikoff, M., and White, C. 1969. Personality and smoking patterns in a twin population. *J. Proj. Tech. Pers. Assess.* 33:457-463.

Erwin, V.G.; Heston, W.D.W.; McClearn, G.E.; and Deitrich, R.A. 1976. Effects of hypnotics on mice genetically selected for sensitivity to ethanol. *Pharmacol. Biochem. Behav.* 4:679-683.

Erwin, V.G., McClearn, G.E., and Kuse, A.R. 1980. Interrelationships of alcohol consumption, actions of alcohol, and biochemical traits. *Pharmacol. Biochem. Behav.* 13:297-302.

Fisher, R.A. 1958a. Lung cancer and cigarettes? *Nature* 182:180.

Fisher, R.A. 1958b. Cancer and smoking. *Nature* 182:596.

Friberg, L., Kaij, L., Dencka, S.J., and Jonsson, E. 1959. Smoking habits of monozygotic and dizygotic twins. *Brit. Med. J.* 1:1090-1092.

Goldstein, D.B., and Kakihana, R. 1975. Alcohol withdrawal reactions in "long-sleep" and "short-sleep" mice. *Pharacologist* 17:197.

Goodwin, D.W., Schulsinger, F., Hermansen, L., Guze, S.B., and Winokur, G. 1973. Alcohol problems in adoptees raised apart from alcoholic biological parents. *Arch. Gen. Psychiatry* 28:238-243.

Griek, B.J. Cross Tolerance between Morphine and Alcohol. 1974. Unpublished doctoral dissertation, University of Colorado, Boulder.

Grieve, S.J., Griffiths, P.J., and Littleton, J.M. 1979. Genetic influence on the rate of development of ethanol tolerance and the ethanol physical withdrawal syndrome in mice. *Drug Alcohol Depend.* 4:77-86.

Hillman, M.G., and Schneider, C.W. 1975. Voluntary selection of and tolerance to 1, 2 propanediol (propylene glycol) by high and low ethanol-selecting mouse strains. *J. Comp. Physiol. Psychol.* 88:773-777.

Horowitz, G.P. 1976. Morphine self-administration by inbred mice: A preliminary report. *Behav. Genet.* 6:109-110 (abstract).

Kaij, L. 1960. *Alcoholism in Twins.* Stockholm: Almquist and Wiksel.

Kakihana, R., Brown, D.R., McClearn, G.E., and Tabershaw, I.R. 1966. Brain sensitivity to alcohol in inbred mouse strains. *Science* 154:1574-1575.

Kaprio, J., Sarna, S., Koskenvuo, M., and Rantasalo, I. 1978. *The Finnish Twin Registry: Baseline characteristics, Section II*. Helsinki: University of Helsinki Press, 1978.

Loehlin, J.C. 1972. An analysis of alcohol-related questionnaire items from the National Merit Twin Study. *Ann. New York Acad. Sci.* 197:117-120.

McClearn, G.E. 1962. Genetic differences in the effect of alcohol upon behavior of mice. In J. D. J. Havard (ed.), *Proceedings of the Third International Conference on Alcohol and Road Traffic*, pp. 153-155. London: British Medical Association.

McClearn, G.E. 1982a (in press). Genetic factors in alcohol abuse—animal models. In B. Kissin and H. Begleiter (eds.), *The Biology of Alcoholism*, vol. 6. New York: Plenum.

McClearn, G.E. 1982b. Animal models of genetic factors in alcoholism. In N.K. Mello (ed.), *Advances in Substance Abuse*, vol. 2. Greenwich, Conn.: JAI Press.

McClearn, G.E., and Kakihana, R. 1973. Selective breeding for ethanol sensitivity in mice. *Behav. Genetics* 3:409-410.

McClearn, G.E., and Rodgers, D.A. 1959. Differences in alcohol preference among inbred strains of mice. *Quart. J. Stud. Alcohol* 20:691-695.

Medlund, P., Cederlöf, R., Floderus-Myrhed, R., Friberg, L., and Sörensen, S. 1976. A new Swedish twin registry. *Acta Med. Scand.* Suppl. 600.

Oliverio, A.; Bovet-Nitte, F.; and Bovet, D. 1966. Action de la scopolamine et de quelqué médicaments parasympatholoytiques surle conditionnement d'évitement chez la fourif. *C.R. Acad. Sci.* 262:1796-1801.

Partanen, J., Bruun, K., and Markkanen, T. 1966. *Inheritance of Drinking Behavior: A Study of Intelligence, Personality, and Use of Alcohol in Adult Twins*. Helsinki: The Finnish Foundation for Alcohol Studies, 1966.

Pedersen, N.L. 1980. Genetic and Environmental Factors for Usage of Common Drugs. Unpublished doctoral dissertation, University of Colorado, Boulder.

Perry, A. 1973. Heredity, personality traits, product attitude, and product consumption—an exploratory study. *J. Marketing Res.* 10:376-379.

Poley, W. 1972. Alcohol-preferring and alcohol-avoiding C57BL mice. *Behav. Genetics* 2:245-248.

Raaschou-Nielsen, E. 1960. Smoking habits in twins. *Danish Med. Bull.* 7:82.

Randall, C.L., and Lester, D. 1974. Differential effects of ethanol and pentobarbital on sleep time in C57BL and BALB mice. *J. Pharmacol. Exp. Therap.* 188:27-33.

Reed, E.T. 1977. Three heritable responses to alcohol in heterogeneous randomly mated mouse strain. *J. Stud. Alcohol* 38(3):618-632.

Sanders, B. 1976. Sensitivity to low doses of ethanol and pentobarbital in mice selected for sensitivity to hypnotic doses of ethanol. *J. Comp. Physiol. Psychol.* 90:394-398.

Schaie, K.W., Anderson, V.E., McClearn, G.E., and Money, J. (eds.). 1975. *Developmental Human Behavior Genetics.* Lexington, Mass.: D.C. Heath.

Schneider, C.W.; Evans, S.K.; Chenoweth, M.B.; and Beman, F.L. 1973. Ethanol preference and behavioral tolerance in mice. *J. Comp. Physiol. Psychol.* 82(3):466-474.

Scott, J.P.; Lee, C.T.; and Ho, J.E. 1971. Effects of fighting, genotype and amphetamine sulfate on body temperature of mice. *J. Comp. Physiol. Psychol.* 76:349-352.

Schuckit, M.A., Goodwin, D.W., and Winokur, G. 1972. A study of alcoholism in half siblings. *A. J. Psychiatry* 128:1132-1136.

Siemens, A.J., and Chan, A.W.K. 1975. Effects of pentobarbital in mice selectively bred for different sensitivities to ethanol. *Pharmacologist* 17:197 (abstract).

Strange, A.W., Schneider, C.W., and Goldbort, R. 1959. Selection of C_3 alcohols by high and low ethanol selecting mouse strains and the effects on open field activity. *Pharmacol. Biochem. Behav.* 4:527-530.

Todd, G.F., and Mason, J.I. 1959. Concordance of smoking habits in monozygotic and dizygotic twins. *Heredity* 13:417-444.

Whitney, G., and Horowitz, G.P. 1978. Morphine preference of alcohol-avoiding and alcohol-preferring C57BL mice. *Behav. Genet.* 8:177.

Winokur, G., Reich, T., Rimmer, J., et al. 1970. Alcoholism: III. Diagnosis and familial psychiatric illness of 259 alcoholic probands. *Arch. Gen. Psychiatry* 23:104-111.

Åmark, C. 1951. A study in alcoholism: Clinical, social-psychiatric and genetic investigations. *Acta Psychiatrica Neurologica Scandinavica* Suppl. 70.

Index